Bring Learning Alive!

THE TCI APPROACH FOR MIDDLE AND HIGH SCHOOL SOCIAL STUDIES

Bert Bower   Jim Lobdell   Sherry Owens

TCi

Teachers' Curriculum Institute

Special thanks to Dawn Lavond, teacher at S.C. Rogers Middle School, Moreland School District, San Jose, California, and to Cheryl Cook-Kallio, Social Studies Department Chair at Irvington High School, Fremont Unified School District, Fremont, California, for the use of their classrooms for photography.

Managing Editor: Laura Alavosus
Content Editor: Anne Maloney
Project Editor: Bev Cory
Production Manager: Lynn Sanchez
Production Designer: Jeff Kelly
Photographer: Tim Stephenson
Photo Editor: Katy Haun
Cover Design: Tim Stephenson
Illustrations: DJ Simison
Operations Manager: Ellen Mapstone

Teachers' Curriculum Institute
P.O. Box 50996
Palo Alto, CA 94303

ISBN 1-58371-011-6
2 3 4 5 6 7 8 9 10 07 06 05 04

Contents

Introduction

Social studies teachers across the nation are facing the daunting challenge of teaching a standards-based curriculum, the efficacy of which is often measured by high-stakes tests. Typically, middle and high school teachers are accountable for dozens upon dozens of content and skill standards for any given course. The pressure to teach to the standards is clearly affecting the state of social studies education. On the positive side, holding schools responsible for measuring student progress on social studies concepts is focusing welcome attention on social studies in the overall school curriculum. On the other hand, the renewed emphasis on standards and testing is starting to reverse progress that has been made toward a more dynamic approach to teaching social studies. In their effort to address standards and boost test scores, many teachers concentrate on "covering" all the material and often revert to more traditional drill-and-kill teaching methods. This, in turn, has made social studies an unpopular subject for too many students.

Has the standards movement brought an end to engaging, dynamic instruction? At Teachers' Curriculum Institute (TCI), we don't believe this is an either-or proposition. Our years of classroom experience have shown that when social studies is taught through an active, student-centered approach, students *do* learn and remember important content. We have created a teaching approach that is mindful of the challenges of standards-based instruction, yet also promotes innovative, effective instruction that excites students about social studies.

How did this approach come about? It started in the 1980s when, as a small group of middle and high school history teachers, we began experimenting with innovative instructional methods that generated unprecedented excitement among our students. Weaving educational research and theory with the realities of classroom teaching, we developed the series of instructional practices that has come to be known as the TCI Approach. Through TCI, founded in 1989, we have shared our ideas in workshops and summer institutes, helping teachers nationwide revitalize their social studies programs at the grassroots level. We have also published our own curricular materials, both core and supplemental programs, in a line that continues to expand each year.

We are continually refining and improving our teaching methodology to create a better experience for the diverse students in our social studies classrooms. *Social Studies Alive! Engaging Diverse Learners in the Elementary Classroom* (2003) introduced our methods to K–5 teachers. This book, *Bring Learning Alive! The TCI Approach for Middle and High School Social Studies,* is a parallel introduction to our methods for social studies teachers at grades 6–12. Our purpose is to convey a clear picture of the instructional practices that characterize the TCI Approach and to provide some practical tools for implementing those practices. As you study this approach, you will be reminded that outstanding teaching truly supports standards-based instruction, and, even more important, excites students and fosters their love of *learning*.

Teachers revitalize their social studies programs with ideas they learn in TCI workshops and summer institutes.

The TCi Approach

 Theory-Based Active Instruction

 Standards-Based Content

 Preview Assignment

 Multiple Intelligence Teaching Strategies

 Considerate Text

 Graphically Organized Reading Notes

 Processing Assignment

 Multiple Intelligence Assessments

What Is the TCI Approach?

The TCI Approach provides a powerful structure for rich classroom instruction—an approach that differs dramatically from lectures, recitation, and seatwork. It is characterized by eight features:

Theory-Based Active Instruction Lessons and activities are based on three well-established educational theories:
- Multiple intelligences (Howard Gardner)
- Cooperative interaction (Elizabeth Cohen)
- Spiral curriculum (Jerome Bruner)

Standards-Based Content Dynamic lessons build mastery of state and national social studies standards.

Preview Assignment A short, engaging assignment at the start of each lesson helps you preview key concepts and tap students' prior knowledge and personal experience.

Multiple Intelligence Teaching Strategies Lessons incorporate six types of multiple intelligence activities that ignite all students' passion for learning:
- Visual Discovery
- Social Studies Skill Builder
- Experiential Exercise
- Writing for Understanding
- Response Group
- Problem Solving Groupwork

Considerate Text Carefully structured reading materials enable students at all levels to understand what they read.

Graphically Organized Reading Notes Comprehensive graphic organizers, used to record key ideas, further help students obtain meaning from what they read.

Processing Assignment An end-of-lesson processing assignment, involving multiple intelligences and higher-order thinking skills, challenges students to apply what they learned.

Multiple Intelligence Assessments Carefully designed tests encourage students to use their various intelligences to demonstrate their understanding of key concepts while preparing them for standardized tests.

The TCI Approach is most effective when all eight features are used in concert, but it is not a formulaic prescription. At times you will need to adapt or tailor some elements of the TCI Approach to match your teaching style and meet the needs of your students.

"This approach revolutionized my attitude about teaching because it showed me how to incorporate the multiple intelligences into my daily teaching repertoire."
—High School Teacher

Why Use the TCI Approach?

Some of the teaching methods inherent in the TCI Approach will require that you make some or even many changes in the way you teach. Why should you risk change? Here are some of the reasons given by teachers who use the TCI Approach.

Teachers need innovative, practical alternatives to conventional social studies teaching. Most teachers have discovered that conventional teaching reaches fewer and fewer students each year. They report that changes among their students—increased ethnic and linguistic diversity, shortened attention spans, lack of parental involvement, time-consuming jobs, teen pregnancy, substance abuse, and negative peer pressure—are making it increasingly difficult to teach. They need ways to reach their students that are dynamic yet practical. The TCI Approach provides an effective alternative to the traditional, teacher-centered classroom.

Teachers need ways to help students see how the past is connected to the present. Students forget much of what they learn in social studies classes because they have no way to apply that knowledge. Teachers need to teach that social studies concepts affect not only the past, but students' lives today—ideas like the use and abuse of power, discrimination, democratic involvement, immigration, and human settlement of the land. A study of the power of the federal government to alleviate poverty during the Roosevelt administration is brought up to date by a look at the government's efforts to help the homeless today. The importance of music in West African culture comes to life as students create their own music to communicate with other class members. An important goal is to help students become lifelong learners by constantly challenging them to apply their social studies knowledge to the world around them.

Students are encouraged to become lifelong learners as teachers challenge them to apply their historical knowledge to the world around them.

Teachers need guidance on how to create a supportive learning environment. Urging students to take risks, praising them for their attempts, and treating mistakes and "failures" as learning opportunities can create a supportive learning environment. The result is more cooperative, tolerant behavior.

To use their critical thinking skills, students need to become active learners. Students should learn social studies by involvement: leading, facilitating, acting, singing, discussing, drawing, making decisions, presenting, and critiquing. Active tasks require students to apply new knowledge as they solve a problem, analyze a situation, understand a perspective, or evaluate alternatives. This type of thinking involves higher-order intellectual skills.

Students must be responsible for their own learning. Challenging students to create a product (a graphic organizer for their reading notes, a matrix, a poem, a written dialogue, a visual metaphor, an illustrated spectrum) or a presentation (a PowerPoint display, a panel discussion, a dramatization, an oral report) allows them to take ownership of the learning process. This results in a high level of involvement and follow-through on class activities.

"I love this approach. It not only has helped to motivate my students' learning, but also has made me more reflective as a teacher."
—Middle School Teacher

Students need more time to work together. Rather than just having students work individually or sit collectively during a lecture, using strategies that depend on student interaction with peers teaches vital social skills and leads to learning gains.

Teachers who are sensitive to issues of multiculturalism need realistic ways to teach social studies from a variety of perspectives. Teaching from a multicultural perspective, and stressing that the differences among races, nations, and ethnic cultures are at least as profound and as durable as the similarities, helps students learn to appreciate and navigate those differences in their increasingly globalized world.

Teachers need to nurture their zest for teaching. Most teachers enter the profession with a sense of purpose: to reach the unreachable student, to create a better future by educating the leaders of tomorrow, to prepare students for participation in a democratic society. The stressful reality of school life, however, dims many a teacher's initial optimism. Teachers using the TCI Approach often report a renewed sense of idealism as they rediscover the mission and the enjoyment they first associated with teaching. They find they are reaching all their students, not just the "best," and they report that this is the way they always wanted to teach—with a sense of purpose, passion, and fun.

What You Can Expect from This Book

This book is an instructional methods text that will give you a thorough understanding of how to implement the TCI Approach in your middle or high school social studies classroom. Part 1 further explores the eight features of the approach and describes the steps for using each of the six multiple intelligence teaching strategies. Part 2 explains the process for creating a cooperative, tolerant environment in your classroom—a key to your success with all other parts of the TCI Approach. Part 3 gives you tips on using the Interactive Student Notebook as an engaging way for students to organize information and ponder historical questions. Part 4 helps you hone your skills in using the TCI Approach, whether you have purchased TCI curricular materials or are designing your own units. Part 5 may be the most practical section of the book, with sample lessons that you can actually try in your classroom or that you can use as models for developing rich interactive and collaborative lessons of your own. The lessons in this section include examples of all six multiple intelligence teaching strategies.

Each part of the book takes into account the needs and perspectives of two groups of potential users: (1) those of you who are completely new to the TCI Approach and would like to learn more, either about using TCI's published programs or about adapting the general approach to design powerful, multiple-intelligence lessons that support any curriculum, and (2) those of you who are already using TCI's programs and want to strengthen your lesson presentations with creative ideas that get immediate classroom results. For both groups, the book is chock-full of practical instructional tips and strategies, supported by examples from published TCI activities. Whether you teach history, geography, civics, economics, or some combination of these, the TCI Approach will help you offer more active, meaningful instruction in an energized, revitalized classroom.

The Elements of the TCI Approach

Theory-Based Active Instruction

Yes! They are highly diverse, but according to the theory of multiple intelligences, every student is intelligent—just not in the same way.

The TCI Approach was developed by teachers who carefully combined the realities of classroom experience with educational research and theory. From years of working with students, these teachers knew for a fact that when kids are active, they stay focused, are more motivated, and learn better. Thus, "active learning" was an essential ingredient of their emerging approach. To this foundation, they added ideas drawn from Howard Gardner's theory of multiple intelligences, Elizabeth Cohen's research on cooperative groupwork, and Jerome Bruner's idea of the spiral curriculum. Educational theory, then, contributed the three key premises behind the TCI Approach: (1) students learn best through multiple intelligences, (2) cooperative interaction increases learning gains, and (3) all students can learn via the spiral curriculum.

Redefining Intelligence: The Theory of Multiple Intelligences

One of the greatest professional challenges facing teachers today is the wide range of ability levels found in the typical classroom. In an eighth-grade U. S. history class, Stephen reads at the eleventh-grade level, while Stacy struggles with a fifth-grade book; Tricia turns out essays acceptable to a high school teacher, while Shirley still writes at a sixth-grade level; Juan is a skilled orator, while Dominga hardly says a word. Many middle and high schools have confronted this challenge by placing students in academic tracks—college preparatory, general, special education, or vocational—as early as seventh grade. But tracking poses a fundamental dilemma. A crucial goal of social studies education is to prepare students for effective participation in a pluralistic society, yet policies that separate students from one another according to academic ability also tend to separate them by social class, race, and language.

Academic segregation sends students at every level a clear message: equal participation and cooperation by diverse groups in society is possible in theory only. Learning theorists and psychologists, however, have proposed an alternative conception of intelligence that promises to move us beyond the outdated practice of placing students in academic tracks.

Howard Gardner, a neuropsychologist at Harvard University, argues that we must develop a new way of looking at human intelligence:

> "In my view, if we are to encompass adequately the realm of human cognition, it is necessary to include a far wider and more universal set of competencies than has ordinarily been considered. And it is necessary to remain open to the possibility that many—if not most—of the competencies do not lend themselves to measurement by standard verbal methods, which rely heavily on a blend of logical-mathematical and linguistic abilities. With such considerations in mind, I have formulated a definition of what I call an 'intelligence'; an intelligence is the ability to solve problems, or to create products, that are valued within one or more cultural settings." (Gardner 1993, p. x)

"With the three premises built into all the lessons and activities, what was once a dusty, dry area of learning for most teachers and students is now fresh, exciting, and engaging."
— Middle School Teacher

Actively involved students are motivated students. Here, they step into history as they study Manifest Destiny though a painting.

Students use an array of intelligences to create a human monument commemorating life in the Byzantine Empire after the fall of Rome.

Gardner relies on neurological research to argue that the human mind has at least seven relatively autonomous human intellectual competencies, each with its own distinctive mode of thinking, to approach problems and create products. (Gardner has more recently identified an eighth intelligence, and is investigating at least one other.) The TCI Approach taps into the following seven intelligences as described by Gardner:

- **Linguistic intelligence** is responsible for the production of language and all the complex possibilities that follow, including poetry, humor, storytelling, grammar, metaphors, similes, abstract reasoning, symbolic thinking, impromptu speaking, oral debate, conceptual patterning, and all genres of the written word. Linguistic intelligence is awakened by the spoken word; by reading someone's ideas or poetry; by writing one's own ideas, thoughts, or poetry; and by listening to a speech, lecture, or group discussion.

- **Logical-mathematical intelligence** is most often associated with what is called scientific thinking or deductive reasoning: the ability to observe and understand details as part of a general pattern. Inductive thought processes are also involved, such as the ability to make objective observations, and, from the observed data, to draw conclusions, to make judgments, and to formulate hypotheses. Logical-mathematical intelligence involves the capacity to recognize patterns, to work with abstract symbols, and to discern relationships and see connections.

- **Visual-spatial intelligence** deals with such things as the visual arts (including painting, drawing, and sculpting), navigation, mapmaking, and architecture, all of which involve the use of space and knowing how to get around. Games such as chess and marbles, which require the ability to visualize objects from different perspectives and angles, are also included. The key sensory base of this intelligence is the sense of sight, but the ability to form images and pictures in the mind is also involved.

- **Body-kinesthetic intelligence** is the ability to use the body to express emotion (as in dance and body language), to play a game (as in sports), or to create a new product (as in devising an invention). Learning by doing has long been recognized as an important part of education. Our bodies know things our minds don't and can't know in any other way. People such as actors, clowns, and mimes demonstrate the endless possibilities for using the body to know, understand, and communicate in ways that touch the human spirit.

Let Your Students "Feel" Concepts

Few techniques are more powerful for connecting students with important concepts than creating opportunities for them to step into the shoes of relevant figures and react to the issues, passions, and events affecting them.

Musical and intrapersonal intelligences come into play as these students learn about four forms of government— monarchy, oligarchy, tyranny, and democracy—by trying different ways of choosing music to play for the class. Here, a monarch makes the decision. Students note their feelings, and later link this experience to the rise of democracy in ancient Greece.

- **Musical-rhythmic intelligence** includes the recognition and use of rhythmic and tonal patterns, as well as sensitivity to sounds in the environment, the human voice, and musical instruments. Of all forms of intelligence identified thus far, musical-rhythmic intelligence has the greatest "consciousness altering" effect on the brain. Music calms you when you are stressed, stimulates you when you are bored, and helps you attain a steady rhythm during such acts as typing and exercising. It has been used to inspire religious beliefs, to intensify national loyalties, and to express great loss or profound joy.

- **Interpersonal intelligence** involves the ability to work cooperatively in a group and the ability to communicate, verbally and nonverbally, with other people. It builds on the capacity to notice contrasts in moods, temperament, motivations, and intentions among other people. Those with highly developed interpersonal intelligence can have genuine empathy for another's feelings, fears, anticipations, and beliefs. Counselors, teachers, therapists, politicians, salespeople, and religious leaders usually have strong interpersonal intelligence.

- **Intrapersonal intelligence** involves knowledge of internal aspects of the self such as feelings, the range of emotional responses, thinking processes, self-reflection, and a sense of (or intuition about) spiritual realities. Intrapersonal intelligence allows you to be conscious of your consciousness. Self-image and the ability to transcend the self are part of the functioning of intrapersonal intelligence.

Cooperative Interaction: A Vital Key to Learning

The second theoretical premise behind the TCI Approach is easily stated: Cooperative interaction leads to learning gains. Researchers report that cooperative groupwork promotes higher student achievement and productivity than either competitive or individualist teaching methods; the more students have the opportunity to interact with each other—by discussing a controversial topic, preparing one another for a quiz, interviewing each other—the more they will learn and remember.

However, sociologists have discovered when students perform a collective task, some are more influential than others. Elizabeth Cohen (1986) has found that students expect certain performances from one another. Students prejudge what their peers will be able to contribute on the basis of perceived academic ability and peer status. As a group, they believe some students are "low status" and others are "high status." When high-status and low-status students work together, a self-fulfilling prophecy results: perceived high-status students tend to interpret most of the questions, talk more, and have their opinions accepted more than perceived low-status students. This unequal pattern of interaction results in unequal learning gains: high-status students, because they interact more, learn more; low-status students, because their interaction is severely limited, learn less.

Virtually every teacher faces the problem of unequal status interaction. Researchers have shown that an unequal status order exists in every classroom, no matter how homogeneous a classroom may appear (Berger, Rosenholtz, and Zelditch 1980). Unless we acknowledge this problem and deal with it frankly, our efforts at increasing student interaction may ultimately make things worse if high-status students reap all the benefits.

Fortunately, research has uncovered practical ways to combat the problem. Cohen has found that when teachers use heterogeneous groups and learn how to change expectations for competence, the low-status students participate more and high-status students no longer dominate. Cohen's work has focused exclusively on students working in groups of four or five; the classroom implications of her studies are explored in greater detail in the later discussion of the strategy "Problem Solving Groupwork" (p. 76).

Many of the techniques that Cohen has found effective with small groups can be used with larger groups and paired instruction as well. Using these ideas in combination with Howard Gardner's theory of multiple intelligences, you can create effective cooperative interaction. All students in the heterogeneous classroom become convinced they have a valued skill to contribute. With the TCI Approach, your activities combat the problem of unequal status interaction by tapping into the multiple intelligences, enabling you to create cooperative interaction that leads to learning gains for all students.

"Groupwork is an effective technique for achieving certain kinds of intellectual and social learning goals. It is a superior technique for conceptual learning, for creative problem solving, and for increasing oral language proficiency."
— Elizabeth Cohen
Professor of Education,
Stanford University

"Theory. Theory. Theory. Teachers always hear theories. But the beauty of this approach is that finally theory is put into practice. This changes what happens in the classroom."
— High School Teacher

Through a spiral curriculum, students learn basic concepts and progressively apply them to higher-level questions.

All Students Can Learn: The Spiral Curriculum in Action

The third theoretical premise behind the TCI Approach is the idea of the spiral curriculum, championed by educational theorist Jerome Bruner in his landmark book *The Process of Education* (1960). Underlying this theory is the belief that all students can learn if a teacher shows them how to think and discover knowledge for themselves. "The quest," according to Bruner, "is to devise materials that will challenge the superior student while not destroying the confidence and will-to-learn of those who are less fortunate." The concept of the spiral curriculum can be applied to individual activities as well as to entire lessons and units.

The idea is to carefully structure lessons to lead students through a step-by-step process of discovery. Students should first explore an event, idea, or personality by using elemental cognitive skills—observation, description, identification, recall—and then spiral to ever-higher levels of cognition such as synthesis, application, and interpretation. This enables students from a variety of academic levels to learn together effectively and gives all students the cognitive building blocks they need to reach higher-order thinking.

Defined broadly, higher-order thinking is the challenged and expanded use of the mind; lower-order thinking is the routine, mechanistic application of the mind (Newmann, Onosko, and Stevenson 1990). Lower-order and higher-order thinking skills can be carefully dovetailed into one another to form a seamless series of steps that challenges students to learn more by progressing from the fundamental to the sophisticated.

By carefully spiraling your questions from the basic to the complex, you can give your students the building blocks they need to use higher-order thinking skills to derive meaning from political cartoons.

- What do you see here?
- Who is the man on the gangplank?
- Who are the men on the dock?
- What are they trying to tell the immigrant? Why?
- Why might Americans have negative feelings toward foreigners?
- What do the shadows represent?
- What irony does the cartoon depict?

By leading students through this process of discovery, you ensure that students from a variety of academic levels will have the conceptual information they need to answer complex questions. In the TCI Approach, each lesson is designed with the spiral curriculum in mind, carefully orchestrating activities that allow students to move from the simple to the complex and challenge them to use higher-order thinking skills. This approach is highly effective in the heterogeneous classroom and leads all students to a greater understanding and appreciation of social studies.

Standards-Based Content

Teachers report consistent positive results on standardized test scores after implementing the TCI Approach.

Introduction

The advent of the standards-based curriculum in social studies has been a mixed blessing. Too often, the emphasis is on coverage over depth, expedience over exploration, memorization over real understanding. Ultimately, this is proving shortsighted. Students are increasingly turned off to social studies, and many develop an active dislike for these subjects. In such an environment, student performance on standards-based tests is sure to plummet. That's why educators need to find an approach that is mindful of standards but still supports hands-on, active learning, to keep students excited about social studies. This is the goal of the TCI Approach.

How Does the TCI Approach Address State and National Standards?

Given that standards-based reform has been driving efforts to improve student achievement across the curriculum, any instructional approach must revolve around the content standards and curriculum frameworks that are being formulated at the district, state, and national levels. All of TCI's published programs are designed to meet the standards of the National Council for the Social Studies, as well as most state standards for history and the social sciences. On the TCI Web site (www.historyalive.com), you will find state correlations linked to each individual program. Whether you use TCI's published curricular programs or create your own lessons based on the TCI Approach, addressing the standards is fundamental; any use of this methodology falls short unless it also targets the essential content for which students are accountable.

Aligning instruction with academic content standards is working. Texas, for example, is a state with high-stakes testing of social studies standards. Thousands of teachers throughout Texas have been trained in the TCI Approach, and they have achieved impressive learning gains, as documented in TAKS (Texas Assessment of Knowledge and Skills) scores at five sites (TCI 2002; note that the name was TAAS, Texas Assessment of Academic Skills, when the data was collected).

But there's another piece here that cannot be overlooked: Even with increased emphasis on accountability, you don't have to abandon sound instructional practices to "teach to the test." Those Texas teachers were not doing drill-and kill; they were helping students recreate 18th century debates, write journals from a mid-19th century slave's perspective, and reenact the grueling working conditions that resulted from early 20th century industrialization. As a result, interviews of the social studies supervisors and key teachers involved in the study noted a renewed enthusiasm and professionalism among their colleagues, and an increase in student engagement and enjoyment of history. And these findings are key to the success of the TCI Approach.

"[This TCI program] has completely energized my teachers. The revolutionary approach to teaching encouraged them to work in concert with each other as opposed to the traditional isolation that teachers experience."

— Middle School Principal

Enthusiastic teachers plus engaged students equals classroom success.

In an environment of high-stakes testing, turning standards into quality instruction is crucial.

Aligning content to state and national standards is only one part of boosting test scores. TCI has discovered another factor that contributes to the mastery of important standards: a consistent pattern of high-quality social studies instruction that is implemented at every grade level.

TCI's published curriculums achieve this, offering school districts the nation's first fully articulated, methodological scope and sequence. That is to say, teachers using TCI materials employ the same teaching strategies, adapted to be developmentally appropriate at each grade level, from students' first experience with social studies in kindergarten through their high school courses.

Districts that have implemented TCI programs across all grade levels are seeing great results. Their students enjoy the experience of learning social studies in ways that are both engaging and memorable. They are getting, even before middle school, foundational concepts in the four main strands of social studies: history, geography, civics, and economics, so that they are well prepared for more in-depth studies in middle and high school.

The benefits of this comprehensive approach are many: better coordination between lower-elementary, upper-elementary, middle school, and high school programs; less pointless reteaching of the same content, yet positive redundancy of key concepts, which leads to increased retention and application of ideas; and more efficient use of time, as students move from grade to grade both better prepared and already organized to learn.

The ultimate goal of the TCI Approach, then, goes far beyond raising standardized test scores. Our mission is to engage all learners in the diverse classroom so that social studies becomes one of their favorite subjects. In this way, students will not only perform better academically, but will also become lifelong learners. In the world our students will soon inherit, no outcome could be more vital.

In the coming sections, you'll learn precisely how the elements of this dynamic approach work in concert to create learning experiences for students that are relevant, engaging, and memorable.

"I love what [TCI] has done for my students' achievements. Specifically, our Hispanic sub-group raised its score an incredible 30% with the use of the TCI program. That is a major WOW!"

— Middle School Teacher

Preview Assignment

Preview activities are quick and simple. Students record responses to short, engaging assignments in their Interactive Student Notebooks.

Introduction

With the TCI Approach, lessons begin with a Preview assignment, a short, engaging task that foreshadows upcoming content. Some Preview assignments challenge students to predict what a lesson will be about; others draw a parallel between key social studies concepts and students' lives. The goal is to spark interest, activate prior knowledge, tap a wide range of intelligences, and prepare students to tackle new concepts.

Students generally complete Preview assignments in their Interactive Student Notebooks, which you will continue to learn about in other sections of this book. In brief, the Interactive Student Notebook is a powerful classroom tool for organizing student learning. Students use it throughout a lesson, from the Preview assignment, to the graphically organized Reading Notes, to the final Processing assignment. Turning to the Preview assignment at the beginning of each lesson serves as a reminder to students that for this work, they will be using their multiple intelligences and critical thinking skills to organize information in new and engaging ways.

Examples of Preview Assignments

There is no single formula for a good Preview assignment. The TCI Approach encourages a wide variety of paths into a lesson. Following is a sampling of the variety of ways you might have students preview their lessons.

Analogies Students can respond to prompts that encourage them to explore a situation in their lives that is analogous to a circumstance or event they will be studying.

Examples

• Before students learn about ancient Egypt's social pyramid, have them draw a "social pyramid" for their school, arranging several individuals and groups on their pyramid, including the principal, teachers, and student council. Ask several students to share their drawings. Afterward, explain to students that just as their school has a specific hierarchy, so did the society of ancient Egypt.

• Before a lesson on issues that led to the Civil War, students write responses to this prompt: *In what ways were the conflicts between the North and the South like a rivalry between siblings?* Conduct a class discussion as several students share their responses. Afterward, explain to students that the tensions between the North and South were in many ways like the tensions in a rocky relationship, and that they will be learning about the differences between the North and the South that created these tensions.

Reviewing for Previewing Students recall the key points of a previous unit or lesson to make predictions about or connections to the topic they will be studying.

Examples

• Before students learn about the form and function of a mosque, project images of the architecture of a Gothic cathedral (from a previously studied unit). Have students recall the names and functions of the parts of a cathedral. After reviewing the images, explain that students will now be studying the form and function of a mosque, another place of worship, and that they will look for similarities and differences between the two types of buildings.

• Before students read excerpts from Thomas Paine's pamphlet *Common Sense,* have them write a one-paragraph response to this prompt: *Given what you know about the American Revolution so far, predict what arguments for independence might be presented in a pamphlet entitled "Common Sense."* Have several students share their paragraphs. Afterward, explain that students will be studying a revolutionary pamphlet that had a tremendous impact on American colonists and helped convert many of them to the cause of independence.

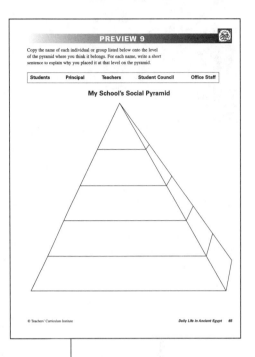

Students preview the social hierarchy of Egypt by completing a social pyramid of their school.

By reviewing the architectural components of a Gothic cathedral, students prepare to learn about the form and function of a mosque.

Students use the Interactive Student Notebook throughout a lesson, from the Preview assignment, to the graphically organized Reading Notes, to the final Processing assignment.

Comparing Personal Experience with Key Concepts Students answer questions relevant to their life or relate a personal experience that foreshadows key themes of the upcoming lesson.

Examples

• Before students learn about the achievements of India's Gupta Empire, have them write a paragraph about a "golden age" in their own life. You might have to define the term *golden age* as a time of special accomplishment. Have several students share their writing. Afterward, explain that students will be learning about the golden age of the Gupta Empire and the achievements that earned this age that title.

• Before students learn about the vital role music played in West African culture, have them respond to this prompt: *Describe the differences among the types of music played at birthday parties, marriage ceremonies, and funerals.* Have several students share their responses. Afterward, explain to students that differences in rhythm, tempo, and tone of music help people—whether American or West African—to communicate the distinct emotions and feelings associated with certain events.

• Before students learn about the travels of Marco Polo, have them respond to this prompt: *Describe a situation in which someone you know was accused of lying, even though the person was telling the truth.* Have three or four students share their answers. Afterward, explain that they will learn about and then try to defend Marco Polo, a man accused of exaggerating what he saw and experienced in China during the 13th century.

• Before students study the different approaches taken by Martin Luther King Jr. and Malcolm X during the civil rights movement, ask them to respond to the following question: *What is the best way to make sure your opinion is heard when someone does not agree with your ideas?* Have students share their answers and lead a discussion based on their ideas. Afterward, point out to students that they did not all suggest the same way to make sure their opinions are heard, just as Martin Luther King Jr. and Malcolm X suggested very different courses of action during the civil rights movement.

Creating Simple Prototypes Students create a product that has some personal relevance and is similar to—but smaller or simpler than—the product they will be creating in an upcoming activity.

Examples

• Before students study the original American colonies and create travel brochures to attract people to a specific colony, have them do this Preview assignment: *Create a simple advertisement, using both words and visuals, that city officials might use to encourage people to settle in your community.* Ask several students to share their responses. Afterward, explain that advertisements often reflect only the ideal view of a subject. Tell students to keep this in mind when creating their travel brochures in the upcoming activity.

- Before students study the use of propaganda in World War I, have them respond to the following prompt: *Describe your favorite advertisement from TV, radio, magazines, or a billboard. Explain which aspects of the advertisement make it memorable to you.* Ask several students to share their answers. Afterward, discuss the purpose of advertising and the devices used to sell products and shape opinion. Tell students that they will learn about the tools and purpose of propaganda posters during World War I and apply what they discover to create a propaganda poster for an issue they feel strongly about.

Predicting To foreshadow an upcoming lesson, students predict what, why, how, or when certain events might have occurred.

Examples

- Before students chronicle the development of the Muslim Empire, have them respond to this prompt: *List the challenges you think the Muslim community might have faced after the death of Muhammad.* Have three or four students share their lists. Afterward, explain that in this lesson they will learn how Muslims struggled to remain united and to spread Islam beyond the Arabian Peninsula after Muhammad's death.

In this Preview, students recall compelling advertisements they have seen. This helps them link their prior experience to a lesson on the use of propaganda in World War I.

- Before students explore how the Aztec and Incan Empires fell, have them write a paragraph in response to this prompt: *What factors enabled Spanish leaders like Cortés and Pizarro, with armies of only a few hundred soldiers, to conquer the enormous empires of the Aztecs and Inca?* Have several students share their responses. Expect many students to suggest that guns gave the Spanish an advantage. Afterward, explain that students will explore the role that guns, as well as a variety of other factors, played in the conquest of the Aztecs and the Inca.

Before a lesson on Alexander the Great, students express their personal views on what makes a good leader.

Provocative Propositions Have students respond to a provocative proposition. The proposition should introduce a key theme or concept that will be explored in the upcoming lesson.

Examples

- Before students learn about Alexander the Great, have them draw a figure of a "good leader" and define the qualities they believe make a good leader. After students share their ideas, explain that they will now learn about a figure who is considered one of the great leaders of all time.

- Before students learn about the gold-for-salt trade in West Africa, have them write a paragraph that supports or refutes this proposition: *Salt is worth its weight in gold.* Have three or four students share their arguments. Expect that most students will refute the proposition. Point out that the value of most goods is based on how much of the good is available (supply) and how many people want it (demand). Afterward, explain that students will learn that salt was as valuable to people living in West Africa as gold is to Americans today.

Responding to Visual Images Students respond to an image that will be used later in the lesson. They might quickly sketch the image, record impressions of it, or predict what they believe is happening.

Examples

- Before introducing students to colonial society, have them create a spoke or web diagram with "Colonial Settlers" at the center. As they view images of paintings of colonial life, have them write on the spokes particular words or phrases that describe the Europeans who first settled in America. Have two or three students share their diagrams. Afterward, explain that students will learn about the origins and development of the British colonies in America.

Preview manifest destiny by inviting students to analyze *American Progress* (1872), an allegorical painting by John Gast that depicts westward expansion.

- Before students learn about the exploration and settlement of America's vast inland empire in the 1800s, have them view an image of an allegorical painting of Manifest Destiny, sketch the image, and respond to this prompt: *Label at least three details in the image that you think represent important historical ideas that might be part of this unit. What topics do you think we will explore? Based on the details in this image, what do you think the title of the unit might be?* You might allow students to discuss the prompt in pairs before writing their answers. Lead a brief discussion. Afterward, explain that they will be studying the concept of manifest destiny and how it affected westward expansion.

Responding to Music Students record their initial responses to music related to the activity or lesson. They might describe the tone, connect the lyrics to content themes, or record their sensory responses.

Examples

- Before students learn about resistance to apartheid oppression, have them listen to a South African resistance song and respond to these questions: *What is the tone of the song? What examples of oppression does the song refer to? What form of resistance does the song urge?* Afterward, explain to students that they will learn about apartheid and various forms of resistance to it.

- Before students learn about the reform movements in America in the 1800s, have them listen to a song from the women's suffrage movement and respond to these questions: *What emotions are expressed in the lyrics? Do the melody and lyrics seem to go together? Why or why not? Why do you think women would write and sing a song like this? Do you think this song's message still has meaning today? Why or why not?* Allow students to share their observations. Afterward, explain that students will learn about the reform movements and the important role women played.

"What If" Sketch Given a particular situation, students draw a sketch showing what might happen next, or what would happen if some key event did not happen, or if some fundamental idea did not exist.

Examples

• Before students learn about industrialization during the second half of the 19th century, show them an image of an industrial city. Have them sketch that same city as it might look like if steel and oil did not exist. Have several students share their ideas. Afterward, explain that students will see how improved techniques in steel processing and oil refining dramatically changed life in the United States during the second half of the 19th century.

• After they study Marxist theory but before they begin a study of the Russian Revolution, show students an image of Tsar Nicholas II being chased by wolves. Have them sketch what would happen next in this scene if there were a successful Marxist revolution in Russia. Afterward, explain that students will learn about what did happen next: the Russian Revolution.

Students sketch what they predict will happen next in Russia based on their interpretation of this 1905 cartoon of Tsar Nicholas.

"You Are There" Scenarios Students record their responses to a "You Are There" scenario that introduces a key theme of the upcoming content.

Examples

• Before a lesson in which students recreate a press conference on the eve of the Civil War, ask them to pretend they are advisors to President Lincoln and to write a one-paragraph response to this prompt: *In response to the bombing of Fort Sumter, President Lincoln should (1) send in Union reinforcements, (2) evacuate Union troops, or (3) do nothing.* Ask students to justify their recommendation. Call on three or four students to share their responses with the class. Then explain that this lesson will enable them to better understand the various perspectives that surrounded the issues of secession and civil war in 1861.

• Before a lesson on the Bill of Rights, show students an image of British soldiers ransacking the belongings of a colonial home with family members present. Ask individuals to assume the role of one of the characters in the image and share what is happening, why they think it is happening, and how they feel. Allow several students to share their responses. Afterward, explain that they will learn about illegal search and seizure, one of the issues that would be addressed in the Bill of Rights.

Visual Discovery

Steps at a Glance

1 Use powerful images to teach social studies concepts.

2 Arrange your classroom so projected images will be large and clear.

3 Ask carefully sequenced questions that lead to discovery.

4 Challenge students to read about the image and apply what they learn.

5 Have students interact with the images to demonstrate what they have learned.

Introduction

Today's students are bombarded daily with images. Constant exposure to television, videos, computer games, the Internet, magazines, and advertisements has created a visual generation. Many teachers are beginning to notice, however, that while students certainly "consume" many images daily, they are not necessarily critical viewers who understand what they see. In fact, far from being visually literate, many of our students are so numbed by the sheer quantity and rapidity of media images that they are left visually illiterate.

As one of the multiple intelligence strategies used in the TCI Approach, Visual Discovery turns what is usually a passive, teacher-centered activity—lecturing—into a dynamic, participative experience. Students view, touch, interpret, and bring to life compelling visuals as they discover key social studies concepts. The strategy sharpens visual-literacy skills, encourages students to construct their own knowledge through higher-level thinking, develops deductive reasoning, and taps visual, intrapersonal, and body-kinesthetic intelligences. Seeing and interacting with an image, in combination with reading and recording notes related to the content, helps students learn and remember salient ideas that are typically soon forgotten after the traditional lecture.

STEP 1

Use powerful images to teach social studies concepts.

The key to a successful Visual Discovery activity is using just a few powerful images that represent the key concepts of the lesson. The right image will stay in students' minds for months or even years and will serve as a powerful visual referent to help them recall key information.

A few well-selected images that students carefully "read" with their visual-literacy skills will have a far greater impact than a profusion of images viewed passively. Since images are not shown as fast-paced videos or computer animations, it is essential that each has a strong visual impact and tells a rich story. The best images

- are clearly tied to your content standards and teaching objectives.
- illustrate key events or concepts.
- graphically show human emotion, drama, suspense, or interaction.
- have the potential for students to step into the scene and bring it to life.
- are interesting or unusual.

"Pictures show the story; notes only tell it."

— High School Student

For example, the first image at right, which shows U.S. troops landing in Khe Sanh, South Vietnam, illustrates the massive deployment of U.S. troops for the Vietnam War. It is a strong visual reminder of the concept of deployment. The heavily laden troops seem to be rushing into an uncertain future. This sets up an excellent opportunity for the teacher to assume the role of on-scene reporter and ask students who step into the image what they expect to confront in the jungles of Vietnam.

For the same lesson, the second photograph at right, showing U.S. troops patrolling a river, captures the danger and hardship of jungle warfare. Ask students to place themselves in the shoes of these young men and then tell them two simple facts: most soldiers served a 13-month tour of duty, and their average age was 19. Read from the diary of an American marine who wonders whether he'd gotten himself "out in the bushes for nothing," and students will be left with a lasting impression.

STEP 2 — Arrange your classroom so projected images will be large and clear.

Careful attention to your classroom's geography is essential for a successful Visual Discovery activity. Most classroom arrangements actually inhibit interaction; students often sit in long rows where the "lucky ones" get the last seats and occasional naps. The front of the classroom is often a clutter of desks, tables, and file cabinets that make it difficult to see and touch projected images. To arrange your classroom for maximum success during Visual Discovery activities, consider the following:

Identify the best wall on which to project images. The wall should be located in an area of the room that you can make fairly dark. With too much light, the image will be difficult to see, and students will have trouble locating fine details. If your room is too dark with the lights off, use a table lamp to add soft, unobtrusive lighting. When you project a transparency on the wall, make the image as large as possible. The larger the image, the more interaction and excitement it will generate. You can easily create a large screen by covering the wall with butcher paper.

Set up your classroom for an interactive presentation. Typically, the best classroom configuration for a Visual Discovery activity is parliamentary style, with two groups of desks facing each other. Leave approximately 10 feet between the groups—enough space to discourage casual conversation, but close enough to allow students on one side to hear students on the other. The center aisle allows students to walk quickly and safely to the front of the classroom to participate actively in each lesson. You now have not one but four front rows. This room arrangement gives you more space to move around the classroom and quickly reach any student needing individual attention.

This is the most common classroom arrangement for Visual Discovery, with a wide center aisle and front staging area.

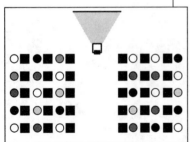

Ask carefully sequenced questions that lead to discovery.

STEP 3

For each projected image, ask a series of questions that spiral from the basic *(What do you see?)* to the critical thinking level *(What do you suppose these people are expecting to happen?)*. Students often rush to interpret images before carefully inspecting all the visual details. While these interpretations may carry some truth, students will come to sounder conclusions if you slow things down and encourage them to look for the details in the image.

As students offer facts and details about what they are seeing, move to the next level of questioning only when most of your students can "see" the answers to your questions. In this way, you will give students the building blocks they need to understand the most important concepts in each image. Be sure to link each successive question to the questions preceding it.

Your final questions may be at such a high level that only a portion of the class can answer them, but this is okay. This powerful questioning strategy enables all students to learn and challenges students at every level. Do be aware, however, of flagging interest. To keep student engagement high, you will probably want to project a new image every 5 to 15 minutes.

Using the Detective Analogy to Develop Effective Spiral Questions

As students learn how to analyze and interpret images, a helpful analogy is to compare their tasks to those of a detective. This detective analogy suggests three levels of investigation: gathering evidence, interpreting evidence, and making hypotheses from the evidence. Whether you are using spiral questions in a published Visual Discovery activity or are developing and sequencing your own questions to help students explore an image, keep in mind these three levels of investigation:

Level I: Gathering Evidence Start by telling students to think of themselves as detectives, and to regard the projected image as a scene from a time or a place that they need to investigate. At this level, the detective's task is to look for evidence—details that may reveal something about the scene. Explain that the evidence should be things they could actually touch if they were able to step into the scene.

Level II: Interpreting Evidence At this level, your student detectives begin to interpret the details or evidence they gathered at the scene. Have them formulate ideas or make inferences based on the existing evidence, such as the time period, place, or people in the scene. As your detectives share their ideas, encourage

In this image from the Great Depression, we see townspeople lined up to receive free food. This sequence of questions will allow students to discover a wealth of information about the image:

- What do you see in this photograph?
- What does the sign on the truck indicate?
- What are the people doing here?
- What feelings might these people be experiencing?
- Why aren't these people talking with one another?
- Would people in need act the same way today? Why or why not?

them to state their interpretation, then follow up with a "because" statement that cites their supporting evidence. Typically, questions at this level are *what, when, where,* and *who* questions.

Level III: Making Hypotheses from Evidence At this level, the student detectives must use the evidence and their own critical thinking skills to determine the "motives" behind the scene they are investigating. Have them make hypotheses about what is happening and why. Typically, questions at this level are *why* and *how* questions that require higher-order thinking skills such as justifying, synthesizing, predicting, and evaluating.

The detective analogy helps students grasp the concept of discovering or uncovering the stories images have to tell. For example, the following series of spiral questions demonstrates how the three-level "detective" structure helps students interact with a painting related to the immigration experience.

In the image pictured below, we see a group of emigrants leaving Hamburg, Germany, for the United States around the turn of the century.

Level I: Gathering Evidence
- What do you see in this image?
- What are some key details, or pieces of evidence, you see?
- How would you describe the scene and the people?
- What do you hear or smell in this scene?

Level II: Interpreting Evidence
- What do you think is the approximate date of this scene? Give one piece of evidence to support your answer.
- Where might this scene have taken place? Give two pieces of evidence to support your answer.
- What do you think is happening in this scene? Be prepared to support your opinion with two pieces of evidence.

Level III: Making Hypotheses from Evidence
- How do you think these people were feeling at this time and place?
- Why do you think these people are immigrating to America?

STEP 4

Challenge students to read about the image and apply what they learn.

Once students have used their visual-literacy skills to analyze an image, they are ready to read something about the image in order to answer questions, fill in content gaps, further their knowledge, and enrich their understanding. This simple technique helps reluctant students to become more skilled and inspired readers. For an example of this approach in action, consider the following segment of a lesson about the growth of democracy during the Jacksonian Era. Here students are viewing one of several lesson-related images, a painting that reflects Jackson's Indian Policy.

1. **Students analyze the image.** Students "read" the painting of the Trail of Tears as the teacher guides them with spiral questions. They reach these conclusions: *Native Americans are going somewhere—traveling by foot, on horseback, and in wagons. They carry their belongings with them. They are accompanied by soldiers and appear to be unhappy about where they are going.* Having discovered much from the image on their own, students are eager to continue the learning process.

2. **Students read their text to gather more information and record notes.** With their interest piqued, students now open their books to find out more about the topic—information that either reinforces or corrects assumptions they made when they analyzed the image. Students gather a wealth of details: *The Cherokee had developed what many considered an advanced civilization. Wealthy planters and poor settlers were determined to force them out and seize their lands. Thousands of Native Americans who refused to leave were rounded up and marched west in handcuffs. Many died on the terrible journey west.* Then, they write a summary paragraph in their Interactive Student Notebook.

3. **Students process what they have learned.** After completing the reading and their notes, students have more information and a better understanding of the Trail of Tears. At this point the teacher projects the image again and asks students to compare the reality of history with the images portrayed in the painting. Students then return to their Interactive Student Notebook, where they add facial expressions and speech bubbles to two outlined heads, representing a Native American and one of the common people, to reflect how each group felt and thought about Jackson's Indian policy.

Using images to motivate and set the context for reading will help increase students' literacy. When students, especially those without strong linguistic skills, experience success at interpreting visuals, they are more motivated to read. They also have a better context for understanding what they read. As a result, most will bring greater effort and more patience to that reading. Ultimately, this approach helps both individual students and the entire class become better critical viewers and thinkers.

Students use their visual literacy skills to "read" the projected image of the Trail of Tears. The textbook provides them with historical details about the forced relocation of the Cherokee.

Act as the "on-scene reporter" to ask probing questions that challenge students to think deeply about social studies.

STEP 5 — Have students interact with the images to demonstrate what they have learned.

One way to assess what students have learned during a Visual Discovery activity is to ask them to "step into" the visuals and bring them to life. Your students will now use their visual, body-kinesthetic, intrapersonal, interpersonal, and logical-mathematical intelligences to demonstrate what they have learned.

Some images are so rich with drama, detail, and emotions that they simply invite students to step in and recreate the moment. This is the time for act-it-outs, the term used in the TCI Approach for mini-dramatizations of an image. Following are five ways to structure successful, dynamic act-it-outs. Your students' level of experience with this type of activity, as well as the nature of the image projected, will determine which form of act-it-out would be most effective. To ensure in-depth participation, you (or a student) will sometimes assume the role of an on-scene reporter and interview each of the characters about his or her role.

Scripted Act-It-Out For each significant character in the scene, prepare a simple script that the actor can read to bring the image to life. This is particularly effective for images that have two figures engaged in conversation. In some cases, you might include blank spaces or lines in the scripts, where actors must insert appropriate information from their notes.

Use this approach early in the year or semester to introduce act-it-outs. With a script in hand, your student actors will experience success while they hone their presentation skills, such as speaking in a loud, clear voice and facing the audience. The first few times, you may want to choose the actors, selecting students who you know will feel comfortable in front of the class and do a good job. Later you can either ask for volunteers or continue to select students yourself.

A scripted act-it-out for an image of Martin Luther King Jr. and Malcolm X discussing affirmative action might look like this:

Students might participate in a scripted act-it-out to bring to life this image of two figures from the civil rights movement.

Martin Luther King Jr.: I think affirmative action is a positive step for women and people of color.

Malcolm X: Once again I have to disagree with you. What do you find so positive about it?

Martin Luther King Jr.: Well, for one thing, it helps to even the playing field for groups in American society who have traditionally been discriminated against in employment, job contracts, and admission to higher levels of education.

Malcolm X: I won't argue that African Americans and others haven't been discriminated against, but I'm not convinced that affirmative action is the way to correct the issue. Let's say a black man gets picked for a job over some white people. The whites will say he got the job just because he is a minority, not because he is qualified.

Martin Luther King Jr.: That may or may not be true, but once people have the opportunity, they can prove that they are qualified. Typically in the past, we haven't even had the opportunity.

Malcolm X: Precisely my point! Why should we wait around for a government program to give us a chance? Let's create our own opportunities for our own people. Let's support minority-owned businesses that will provide opportunities for our people without the government telling people what they have to do.

Act-It-Out with Role Cards Rather than using complete scripts, you might sometimes provide each student actor with a role card that simply tells his or her name (when it is unknown, use an appropriate fictional name) and a brief explanation of who this character is. The cards should provide actors with some cues—ideas, key phrases, or questions—to help them prepare for their roles and accurately represent their characters. Give actors their role cards before you begin asking spiral questions about an image. This way, they can be thinking in terms of their character as their understanding of the image grows. During the act-it-out, assume the role of on-scene reporter and interview the characters.

This type of act-it-out is best used after students have experienced success on stage in a couple of scripted act-it-outs. Again, you may want to choose the actors

An act-it-out can bring to life this Depression-era image of unemployed steelworkers huddled around a shanty-town fire. Role cards help students identify with these impoverished figures.

the first few times, selecting students who will feel comfortable in front of the class and do a good job. After students have some experience with this form of act-it-out, you can ask for volunteers. Later in the year, you can have students prepare the role cards themselves.

Here is a role card that might be used with an image of unemployed men during the Depression:

> Your name is Joe. You used to work in a factory, but you haven't had a job for two months. You have a wife and three children. When your character is asked how he feels, include the words *ashamed, worried,* and *discouraged* in your answer.

In the next example, the role card describes a figure in an image of Europeans boarding a ship to immigrate to the United States in the late 1800s.

> Your name is Antonio. You are from southern Italy. You are the second oldest son in your large family. Be prepared to answer these questions:
> * What is your name, and where are you from?
> * Why are you leaving your homeland?
> * What do you hope to find in America?
> * How do you feel about what is happening?
> * Do you think you will ever see your family again? Why or why not?

Talking Statues Act-It-Out For images that include a large number of characters or that represent especially poignant moments in time, such as the sit-in at the Woolworth's lunch counter during the civil rights movement, ask everyone to pretend to be one of the figures or objects in the image. Tell students to imagine what their character is thinking or feeling at that precise moment. Then ask a group of volunteers to come forward, and have them "freeze" into the precise body positions of the different figures. One by one, touch each character on the shoulder. That figure "comes to life" long enough to state what he or she is thinking or feeling, then freezes back into position. Each "talking statue" statement should be brief—ideally no more than one sentence.

You would typically use this form of act-it-out toward the beginning of the year or semester when you want to give many students the experience of being on stage, but in a limited and highly structured way.

Group Presentation Act-It-Out For images with several figures, you can put students into groups of four or five and assign one character to each group. On an overhead transparency or a handout, give each group some questions to discuss and to answer from the perspective of their character. Once groups have prepared their responses, ask a volunteer from each group to step into the image and take on the assigned role. During the act-it-out, you will assume the role of the on-scene reporter and interview the characters, asking questions similar to those discussed in the groups.

This type of act-it-out works better later in the year when students are familiar with the act-it-out format and are ready to take on more responsibility.

Impromptu Act-It-Out Besides the various forms of planned act-it-outs, you can call for impromptu act-it-outs whenever you encounter an image that involves clearly dramatic interaction. After the class has analyzed an image, completed any related reading, and recorded their notes, have volunteers step into the image— with their notes, if needed—and assume the roles of some of the figures. Either you or students in the audience can then act as on-scene reporters to interview the figures. For images that are "read" easily, consider using the impromptu act-it-out before students turn to the related reading, to further pique their interest in the text.

Impromptu act-it-outs are most successfully used later in the year or semester, when students are confident about dramatizing images and need less structure, or when they are already familiar with the historical content of the image and can react to it spontaneously.

Impromptu act-it-outs are often tense and emotionally charged as students feel and appreciate the passions reflected in the image. Using this image of a Vietnam War protest, you might have students step into the roles of protesters and police.

Social Studies Skill Builder

Steps at a Glance

1 Use engaging tasks to teach social studies skills.

2 Teach the skill through modeling and guided practice.

3 Prepare students to work in pairs.

4 Set clear expectations, allow students to practice the skill repeatedly, and give immediate feedback.

5 Debrief the lesson to help students make connections to key social studies concepts.

Introduction

Skills such as mapping, categorizing, analyzing primary sources, graphing and interpreting graphs, and reading a timeline are a vital part of any middle and high school social studies course. Without these skills, students will not fully grasp many concepts. Why teach about the Proclamation of 1763, for example, if students cannot locate the Appalachian Mountains on a map? Why compare and contrast ancient Greece and imperial Rome without first teaching students how to use a simple matrix or Venn diagram?

Despite the importance of teaching these basic social studies skills, many instructors reserve little time for—and apply even less creativity to—this task. In the words of one high school history teacher, "I don't have time to cover social studies *and* teach skills. Students should come prepared from the lower grades. Besides, when I do teach skills, my students say it's boring."

The Social Studies Skill Builder strategy in the TCI Approach turns the traditional, rote tasks usually associated with skill-based worksheets into more dynamic, interactive activities. Students work in pairs on fast-paced, skill-oriented tasks such as mapping, graphing, identifying perspective, and interpreting political cartoons. The teacher begins an activity by quickly modeling the skill and then challenging students to practice the skill repeatedly. Students receive immediate feedback as they work. The activity ends with a debriefing session that allows students to use their new skill to gain greater insights into key social studies concepts.

STEP 1 Use engaging tasks to teach social studies skills.

Teaching the basic skills that students need to be successful for social studies may seem daunting, especially if you and your class perceive such work as boring. With Social Studies Skill Builders, the skills are imparted through lessons that both you and your students will enjoy. Here are some tips to conducting skill-driven activities that are inherently engaging:

Use stimulating resources that lend themselves to multiple-ability tasks. Good primary source documents are intriguing and offer students a real piece of history to analyze. For an activity on the use of propaganda in World War I, a colorful collection of posters from that era, depicting the points of view of both the Central Powers and the Allies, invites students to look for bias. A collection of labor songs from the Great Depression, drawings of key inventions during the Chang Dynasty, or political posters from a presidential campaign all can be the basis for exciting lessons.

Challenge students to use multiple intelligences during the activity. For example, during the World War I propaganda activity, students view a reproduction of a wartime poster. Pairs quickly sketch the poster, search for symbols, discuss the poster's meaning, and record their answers. In this process, they are using linguistic, visual, interpersonal, and logical-mathematical intelligences.

Encourage student pairs to work as a team, but require them to record information individually. Even though students work with partners, they are individually accountable for all content and have their own work to complete. In the World War I propaganda activity, after jointly discussing the poster, each student fills in a matrix that has columns for noting the caption, describing the symbols, and recording interpretations. Each student thus creates a personal record of what the pair discussed. Recording what they talked about helps students be specific and remember their ideas—and enables you to assess individual progress.

Give your students the opportunity for repeated hands-on practice. Start with an assortment of similar resources (photographs, drawings, quotations, songs) to give students lots of different pieces to analyze in the same way. Then provide handouts—maps, matrices, lists of questions, pieces of graphing paper—with space for students to practice the same skill many times. For example, for an activity about America's rapid industrialization, you provide a series of placards,

"I thought I was incapable of learning history. Before it was just a textbook, lectures, and a bunch of jumbled facts. But the way this class was organized made sense. It really made history clear."

— High School Student

For a Social Studies Skill Builder, students sit in pairs and work as a team to solve skill-oriented problems.

each containing an image and a line graph that together illustrate some aspect of industrialism in the early 1900s—such as the amount of raw steel produced, or the miles of railroad track in operation. Pairs examine a placard and, using the information in the image and graph, answer questions from a matrix on their handout. When they finish, they select a new placard and repeat the process. In this way, students have several opportunities to practice interpreting a line graph and relating the data to industrial growth.

Spiral from the basic to the complex to give students deep historical insights. The structure of a Social Studies Skill Builder should spiral from the simple to the more complex, challenging students to answer progressively higher-level questions. For example, consider an activity that focuses on disagreements over slavery before the Civil War. A series of placards provides pictures and information about key historical figures. Students start by identifying each figure by name and by state of residence. Second, they describe that person's views on slavery. Third, they describe actions taken by the figure that exemplify his or her views. This spiraling allows students to discover increasingly complex information, preparing them for a final discussion of such questions as these: *Was owning a slave ever justified? Which groups in the South benefited most from slavery? How did slavery affect the moral climate of our nation?* Most students participate enthusiastically in this high-level discussion because they now have the knowledge base from which to expound about perspectives. The spiraling allows each student to understand and articulate complex issues.

Teach the skill through modeling and guided practice.

Introduce each Social Studies Skill Builder by quickly modeling and leading your students through guided practice of the skill. Modeling consists of demonstrating and explaining the steps your students are to follow as they develop the skill on their own. Here, for example, is the way you could model a Social Studies Skill Builder activity on mapping physiographic features of the United States:

1. **Give students an outline map of the United States.** Have them point to north, east, south, and west on their maps, draw a compass rose in the southeast corner, and label the cardinal and intermediate points. Project a transparency of the same map and model drawing the compass rose on the transparency.

2. **Write the term *physiographic feature* on the map transparency.** Explain that *physio* means "physical," *graphic* means "written down or recorded," and *feature* means "a particular characteristic of something." Thus, a physiographic feature is a physical characteristic of the land—such as a lake, mountain, or river—that is recorded on a map.

3. **Tell students that they will now use their geographic knowledge to answer a set of map-hunt clues.** They will record on their outline map the location that is indicated by each clue, labeling a specific location or drawing in a physical feature such as a principal river, mountain range, or flatlands.

4. **Show students how to create a key in one corner of their map.** Demonstrate possible symbols for open water, rivers, mountains, and flatlands.

5. **Read a map-hunt clue, such as *This is the largest bay along the California coastline.*** Ask students to use their atlases to find the answer. When they do, label the San Francisco Bay on the map transparency, including the symbol for water, and ask students to do the same on their maps.

6. **Tell students they will now use the skill they just learned, labeling a physiographic map, to answer a full set of map-hunt clues.**

This kind of modeling and guided practice ensures that students are ready to practice the skill on their own.

"This strategy has changed how my students react to geography lessons. Instead of saying, 'Oh, we have to do another map,' they say, 'Great, we get to do something interesting.' Having them work in pairs creates social interaction that adds spice and allows them to share the burden on tough assignments."

— High School Teacher

One key to success is careful and thorough modeling of the task to be completed by students.

Prepare students to work in pairs.

STEP 3

After you have modeled the skill, place students in pairs. Because students will be discussing skill-oriented questions with discrete, defined answers, a group of two is ideal. Pairs have more opportunity for interaction and will stay on task more easily than they would in a larger group. Here are some tips for preparing for paired skills work:

Carefully establish mixed-ability pairs. Since these skill tasks require the use of multiple intelligences, it makes sense to pair students with complementary abilities. This will help ensure that each partner has something of value to contribute and that interaction is more equitable. If an activity requires linguistic and visual skills, for example, try to put a strong linguistic student with one who excels visually. You shouldn't need to spend more than 15 minutes of prep time on this pairing process, and it is time well spent, as it will result in students' working together much more effectively.

Before class, prepare a transparency that shows who will sit where. On a transparency, draw a permanent classroom map showing the arrangement of desk pairs. Make sure your map shows desks placed evenly around the classroom, both to limit distractions and to allow you to move freely among the pairs. Use an erasable marker to write students' names next to the desks at which you want them to work. This will help students move efficiently into pairs.

Instruct students in each pair to sit side by side with the edges of their desks touching. Project the map for students to use as a guide for arranging their desks. Tell them they are not officially a team until the right edge of one desk is touching the left edge of the other desk and both students are seated facing forward.

When students have found their partners, have them introduce themselves.

Encourage students to greet each other. Once students have found their partners and are sitting correctly, tell them to introduce themselves and shake hands. Model this behavior with one of your students. If appropriate, use humor to ease the tension; it will help pairs work together more effectively.

Conduct a quick team-builder to warm up students for working together. This might be as simple as having students repeat this statement "Partner, if you need a helping hand, I'm here to help. And if I need a helping hand, I'm counting on you." Or, you might ask them to discuss a question related to the skill they will be learning.

4 Set clear expectations, allow students to practice the skill repeatedly, and give immediate feedback.

After you have modeled the skill and placed students in mixed-ability pairs, clearly state what you expect from them so you can evaluate their work fairly. You can do this easily and efficiently with a transparency that lists exactly what is expected. You may want to award points for each part of an assignment your students successfully complete.

Checking work and awarding points as students progress through an activity will motivate them to work quickly and conscientiously in a game-like atmosphere. It will also assure that students create high-quality products, as they know you are scrutinizing each answer. And it gives you a break from taking papers home at night.

The greatest challenge facing teachers who give their students immediate feedback is managing the constant, and possibly overwhelming, flow of students waiting to have their work evaluated. Here are some tips to avoid the logjam of too many pairs waiting for feedback:

- Familiarize yourself with the relevant handout, and perhaps create a key, so you can quickly check students' work for essential points.
- Give pairs more than one artifact or question to work on at a time so they take longer to finish.
- Ask students who have accurately completed the activity to assist in correcting their peers' work.
- Circulate around the classroom to correct handouts rather than having students come to you.

"My students like Social Studies Skill Builders because they learn without pain. The game-like atmosphere gets them so involved in analyzing placards and writing answers that they hardly realize how much they are learning."

— Middle School Teacher

Checking work as students proceed through the activity keeps them on task.

Students explore the values behind Kennedy-era programs by analyzing a series of posters and placing them along a values spectrum. This helps students connect the past to the present.

Debrief the lesson to help students make connections to key social studies concepts.

Most teachers find that there comes a point during each Social Studies Skill Builder when most students, but not all, have finished working. It may be more effective to debrief the activity at this point than to wait for everyone to finish. To ensure that all your students have access to the same content, consider asking pairs to take turns reporting to the class what they discovered. A pair might interpret an artifact, explain a primary source, or answer a geography question for the entire class while the other students take notes to make the information their own.

After everyone in class has been exposed to all the content, challenge students to think holistically about the fragmented bits of content they have learned. During this debriefing, your students should consider as a whole all the questions, artifacts, or primary sources they have explored and arrange them in some type of significant order—perhaps along a continuum, in categories, or according to geographic relationships. Following are some ways of organizing content during this important debriefing step:

Political Spectrum Draw a line on the board or place masking tape on the floor to represent a spectrum. Label the two ends of the spectrum with opposing terms, such as *Conservative* and *Liberal,* or *Totalitarian* and *Democrat.* Students then stand along this spectrum to show where particular figures or ideas best fit.

For example, consider a Social Studies Skill Builder for which pairs of students review scenarios of foreign policy actions by different countries and decide whether they represent isolationism or imperialism. For the debriefing, students position themselves physically on the spectrum where a particular scenario would fall, and the class discusses the appropriateness of each placement. This procedure allows the class to thoroughly analyze each scenario and clarifies for everyone the assessment of the most difficult scenarios.

Values-Orientation Spectrum You can create a similar spectrum for students to stand along that represents value judgments between poles such as *Community Interest* and *Individual Interest.* Challenge students to place various ideas or opinions along the spectrum. For example, suppose that students have been exploring Kennedy-era programs (such as the Peace Corps and VISTA) by analyzing a series of promotional posters. During the debriefing session, you would ask students to place the posters along a spectrum between *Values Our Government Emphasizes Today* and *Values Our Government Does Not Emphasize Today.* This activity challenges students to connect the past to the present in a powerful, memorable way.

Moral Continuum Another variation on the spectrum is to challenge students to place the actions of individuals, groups, or nations along a moral continuum between such poles as *Ethical* and *Unethical,* or *Expedient* and *Principled.* For example, suppose an activity asks student pairs to analyze a series of placards with a photograph and written information that indicates how some group in America responded to the Holocaust: the Roosevelt administration, the general public, Congress, youth, Jews, the media, the military, the State Department. During the debriefing, you would ask students to physically stand with their placards between two poles labeled *Just* and *Unjust.* This not only reviews the history of the U.S. response to the Holocaust, but also leads students to a much deeper understanding of different American responses to Nazism.

Chronology For some Social Studies Skill Builders, students might place a series of events or trends in chronological order. For example, after analyzing placards that show paintings from the Middle Ages and the Renaissance, students could try placing the placards in chronological order. As they trace the evolution of artistic style from the Middle Ages to the Renaissance, they discover how a common theme, such as the Madonna or the crucifixion of Christ, changes as it is interpreted over time by different artists.

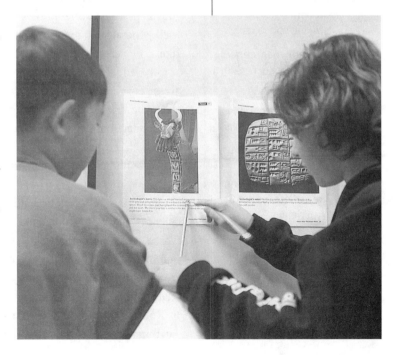

These students are analyzing a series of Sumerian artifacts. During the debriefing, they will categorize their findings to determine if ancient Sumer was a civilization.

Logical Categorization You can debrief some skills activities by having students use their logical intelligence to sort placards by category: attributing a series of quotes to their correct authors, classifying art by its historical period, or assigning a group of governmental programs to their correct administrations. For example, an activity might have student pairs matching Cold War terms—*socialism, totalitarianism, democracy, freedom, communism,* and *equality*—with placards of political cartoons. For the debriefing, students could first categorize the placards into two groups, American or Soviet, and then match the Soviet terms with the American terms, grouping *socialism* with *capitalism* and *freedom* with *equality.* Categorizing the terms gives students a fundamental understanding of these difficult historical concepts.

Experiential Exercise

Steps at a Glance

1 Use short, memorable experiences to help students grasp social studies concepts.

2 Prepare your students for a safe, successful experience.

3 Make the experiences as authentic as possible.

4 Allow students to express their feelings immediately after the experience.

5 Ask carefully sequenced questions to help students make connections between their experience and key concepts or events.

Introduction

Too often in the conventional classroom, students don't learn social studies, they memorize it. History, geography, economics, and civics are often presented—by teacher and textbook alike—as a series of names, dates, and facts. Some students are adept at memorizing these; most are not. But even students who memorize well generally do not retain the information longer that it takes to regurgitate it on a test. Fewer still are able to demonstrate real understanding of, or appreciation for, the effect that various concepts and events have—or have had—on their own lives. Lost are the rich human dramas, the compelling experiences of the individuals who have shaped our history and our political and economic realities, and the connections between concepts and events. As a key strategy in the TCI Approach, Experiential Exercises ensure that your students grasp and remember even the highest-level concepts.

Experiential Exercises tap into students' intrapersonal and body-kinesthetic intelligences, allowing students to "experience" key social studies concepts firsthand. These short, memorable activities make abstract ideas or remote events accessible and meaningful. To help students understand the strengths and weakness of the Roman Empire, for example, you might distribute students in a large donut-like shape (the empire surrounding the Mediterranean), variously assigning them roles as Romans, Provincials, or Barbarians. "Roman" armies gather wealth from the far-flung provinces, but also encounter the difficulty of defending the empire from Barbarian invasions. Or, to understand the lifestyle of medieval monks, students might take "vows" of poverty, obedience, and silence—and proceed through the entire activity while trying to honor those vows. And to understand the factors that drive modern-day Mexicans to migrate to the United States, students might take on the roles of central Mexican villagers, sharing their views about emigration during a typical evening stroll in the village plaza. Students react to each experience as if it were real life, gaining an appreciation of key concepts that they will remember for a long time.

STEP 1
Use short, memorable experiences to help students grasp social studies concepts.

Experiential Exercises awaken students to the richness, drama, and reality of key concepts and events. However, not every lesson lends itself to this strategy. As you plan lessons, know that there are certain times when Experiential Exercises work especially well:

Dare to Risk

It is better to take a risk and fail than to pass out another worksheet.

Students re-create life in a trench during World War I as they view images of the battlefields and listen to excerpts from *All Quiet on the Western Front.*

Use them when you can easily re-create a key concept or event. Standards-based social studies content demands that you cover a lot of territory in a relatively short time, so it makes sense to conduct Experiential Exercises only when they are easy to implement. Re-creating World War I trench warfare may seem daunting, but it takes just 10 minutes to transform your room into a simulated battlefield. Move desks into two sets of two rows on opposite sides of the room, and have students crouch in these opposing "trenches." Project transparency images from Europe's western front, and play or create sounds of the battlefield. Read passages from E. M. Remarque's *All Quiet on the Western Front,* and ask students to react to situations in the novel as if they were soldiers. The result will be rich, experiential learning with economy of time and energy.

Use them when your topic is best taught through body-kinesthetic or intrapersonal intelligence. Some lessons are best absorbed through physical or emotional experience. The tedium, physical strain, and dehumanizing nature of assembly-line work, for example, cannot be communicated adequately through readings or images; students must feel its physical and emotional effects. In an activity designed to allow students to experience the assembly line (shown in the photo on page 46), muscles ache and minds wander as students spend a class period mass-producing a drawing, each student specializing in one tiny part. By performing a

repetitive and mind-numbing task, students gain a wealth of knowledge—through body-kinesthetic and intrapersonal learning—on the merits and weaknesses of mass production. They will literally have a "muscle memory" of some of the advantages and disadvantages of assembly-line work.

Use them when you want to evoke an emotional response so that students react empathetically to concepts they might otherwise find remote or unimportant. Experiential Exercises can be used to increase students' empathy for the experiences of individuals or groups of people by tapping into their intrapersonal intelligence. For example, today's students have a difficult time understanding the devastation of people who lost their savings when the banks failed during the Great Depression. They become much more empathetic after an activity in which they experience something like the pain of a failing economy themselves. To set up the experience, you would first give a quiz on which students earn points important for their grade. The next day, you tell them regretfully that half of their quizzes were "lost"—misplaced, inadvertently thrown away, or stolen. Explain that students whose quizzes were lost simply will not receive any points. After allowing students to react and voice their incredulity, debrief the activity. Draw parallels between the students' feelings of helplessness and anger and those of the victims of the bank collapse. In both cases, a trusted institution (the teacher or the bank) loses something of extreme value (points or money). This intrapersonal experience gives students insights that otherwise would have gone untapped.

Use them when you want to emphasize how a historical occurrence affects the way people felt or reacted. For students to understand the behavior of people in history, for example, they must appreciate the conditions that shape people's responses. Experiential Exercises can replicate the conditions of a time or place so that students respond in ways similar to those of individuals in the real-life situation. To help students understand McCarthyism, for example, you can give them an appreciation for the fear of communism and paranoia of the time. In an Experiential Exercise, you create a situation analogous to the dread of being labeled a communist. Give each student a slip of paper, either blank (good) or containing a dot (bad). Students keep their designation secret as they move about the room, trying to form a large "dot-free" group while relying only on questioning and suspicion. Afterward, carefully sequence questions to help students draw parallels between the "fear of dots" and the resulting classroom behavior, and the fear of communism and the rise of McCarthyism.

Use them when you need to capture a moment or feeling that is central to understanding a particular concept. Some concepts are so central to economics or to history that, unless students truly grasp them, they gain little from your instruction. In teaching about the American Revolution, for example, you must continually refer to the concept of *taxation without representation* because it affected nearly all aspects of the period. Students need a powerful, indelible understanding of the concept to fully comprehend the motivation behind the revolutionary movement and the formation of the new government.

In an Experiential Exercise, you tell students that budget constraints have made it necessary for them to pay 10 cents per page for photocopied handouts, including that day's two-page quiz. As you attempt to collect this "tax," students will voice outrage and injustice—not unlike the feelings experienced by colonists prior to the Revolution. As students learn about the Sons and Daughters of Liberty and the Continental Congress, they can draw on how they felt about "unfair taxation" in the classroom to better appreciate colonial motivations for forming protest organizations. And as students study the formation of the new government, they can be reminded of this experience to help them appreciate the colonists' desire for a representative government.

Prepare your students for a safe, successful experience.

STEP 2

Experiential Exercises can be risky because you cannot always control students' responses. The fundamental goal is usually to provoke an emotional reaction to a situation. Strong emotions—frustration, joy, anger, fatigue, apprehension, empowerment, passion, fear, and camaraderie—sometimes surface during these activities. It is wise to take a few precautionary steps to ensure all goes well.

Make sure the activity is appropriate for your students. Consider the makeup and maturity level of your students before using an Experiential Exercise. Some teachers, for example, have chosen not to use an activity on World War I trench warfare during a time of war because students may have friends and relatives fighting overseas.

Address safety concerns ahead of time. If the Experiential Exercise requires students to move around the classroom in unusual ways, begin by clearly explaining which behaviors are acceptable and unacceptable or potentially unsafe. For

"I used to have no feeling about social studies at all. After doing these activities, I really feel something. That helps me understand more."

— High School Student

"When former students return for a visit, they ask 'Are you still using Capture the Flag to teach the American Revolution?' What they remember most about my class are the dramatic Experiential Exercises we did. They leave a lasting impression."

— Middle School Teacher

Consider Alternate Venues

If an Experiential Exercise requires a significant rearrangement of your classroom and you teach multiple classes or float, consider setting up the activity in the school library or multipurpose room.

In the Experiential Exercise shown below, students explore the population density of several places—such as Australia, the United States, and Japan. To ensure this is a safe experience, address any potential concerns before the activity begins.

example, in an activity where groups compete to "claim" the most classroom furniture to experience the way European powers scrambled for African territory in the late 1800s, you might tell students that they may not run or touch any other student as they scramble to claim furniture.

Prepare administrators and families when appropriate. Both administrators and the parents of your students need to know that you have a sound rationale for using what might appear to be an unconventional teaching strategy. Before doing any Experiential Exercise that may evoke strong student reaction, notify your administrators and, if appropriate, send a letter home to parents explaining the intent of the lesson and how it works. This proactive communication gives you the chance to address anyone's concerns ahead of time. Also, consider inviting administrators and parents to attend class; the experience can help them understand the power of these exercises. Besides, having another adult on hand can help you manage the activity.

Arrange the classroom appropriately. Many Experiential Exercises require unusual room arrangements. Set up the classroom before students arrive. If students must move desks, time is lost and students are distracted from the mission of the activity. For example, an activity to introduce manifest destiny from the Native American perspective might require 10 students to move away from their usual "home" in the class to a small, undesirable area partitioned by desks. Having these desks in place before students enter class is imperative. Not only does it save instructional time, but also the strange classroom arrangement piques interest and readies students for the activity.

Communicate clear behavioral and learning expectations. While students often find Experiential Exercises unusual and fun, it is critical that you set clear behavioral and learning expectations. Students must know that each activity has a specific academic purpose. This is especially true in activities such as one in which students spend an entire class period as medieval monks performing various monastic tasks in complete silence. Without expectations for absolute silence clearly communicated, students are apt to giggle and talk, undermining the activity. However, if you unequivocally outline the behavioral expectations and the objective, students assume their roles and remain silent and purposeful throughout the activity.

Give students clear directions. Most Experiential Exercises require students to participate in activities that are far different from those they encounter in the conventional classroom. As a result, students need precise directions to feel comfortable—and an activity might fail if you give unclear directions. In the "dot" activity mentioned earlier, in which students experience the fear of the McCarthy era, directions are initially confusing to students. Skilled teachers handle it this way: At the beginning of class, they tell students that the procedures are complicated. They carefully explain the directions and encourage students to ask clarifying questions, explaining that they will *not* answer any procedural questions after the exercise starts. When the burden of clarification is placed on the students, most questions are answered before the activity begins, and the exercise can unfold without interruption.

Anticipate student reactions. Because Experiential Exercises are designed to elicit emotional responses, you must be prepared for student reactions. When students sit in World War I "trenches" for 45 minutes, know that they will feel tired and cramped; when students assume the roles of colonists to debate independence, expect passionate, forceful arguing; when quizzes are "lost" to convey the impact of Depression-era bank failures, expect students to feel angry and frustrated. Although most responses are predictable, don't be surprised when the occasional frustration boils over into heartfelt anger. Always be prepared to diffuse intense feelings.

Recognize teachable moments. Experiential Exercises often turn on teachable moments—that particular instance when an activity has led students to the brink of insight. This can happen at nearly any time. Recognizing and taking advantage of these moments is paramount to helping students grasp key concepts. Keep your learning objectives clearly in mind as each activity unfolds.

STEP 3 Make the experiences as authentic as possible.

Experiential Exercises require your students' trust and a bit of risk taking on your part. You need to bring considerable creativity to the task; a key ingredient for success is tapping into the performer within you. Think of these activities as interactive theater, and have fun acting, preparing your classroom, readying props, and adding special effects. Following are five ways you can make Experiential Exercises so authentic that your students will not forget what they learned.

Keep a straight face when appropriate. When you tell students you have lost some of their quizzes from the previous day (to emulate the losses of bank depositors during the Depression), or tell students they must purchase needed quiz handouts at 10 cents per page (to drive home the concept of taxation without representation), you must maintain a serious demeanor. If you show amusement, students will catch on to the activity, and the impact of the lesson will be lost.

Assume an appropriate persona. Some Experiential Exercises require you to assume a certain persona, and most include a bit of dramatic presentation on your part. For example, during an activity in which students analyze Stalinist propaganda posters to discover the benefits of socialist rule, you play the part of a Communist party leader enthusiastically challenging students to learn about life under Stalin's rule. At the same time, you punish any student caught expressing dissident opinions. So whether the activity calls for a dramatic reading to set the tone or a feigned emotion to elicit student responses, let out the actor in you to create a memorable moment for your students.

Whether the activity calls for a dramatic reading to set the tone, a straight face to conceal a rigged game, or a feigned emotion to elicit student responses, let out the actor in you.

Students will appreciate your willingness to "ham it up," resulting in a more authentic experience for all.

Students find Experiential Exercises unusual and fun. Simple togas add to the authenticity of an activity related to ancient Greece.

Ham it up. You may be surprised at how catching your enthusiasm can be. During the dot activity (re-creating the fears of the McCarthy era), you need to fuel the feelings of suspicion and paranoia by your own exaggerated behavior as you warn students to be very careful whom they trust. Students will revel in your example, resulting in a more authentic experience for all.

Use simple props and costumes. Most classes are filled with potential props. Desks can become mountains; butcher paper can turn into transportation routes; pieces of cloth can become costumes, national flags, or blankets aboard an immigrant ship. Some teachers even ask students to bring appropriate props from home. Props can add creativity, authenticity, and a sense of playfulness that helps engage and center students' attention.

Use music and sound effects. Students who have strong musical intelligence will appreciate any attempt you make to reinforce content through music and other sounds. Sounds of loud manufacturing machines inside a factory make students' experience on the "assembly line" more real; sounds of gunfire heighten students experience in the "trenches" of World War I; protest songs sung by women help capture the spirit of their calls for reform. "Music memory" will help students remember concepts and events long after you turn off the CD player or stop singing.

Allow students to express their feelings immediately after the experience.

Experiential Exercises create rich, memorable experiences. If meaningful learning is to occur, these activities must be skillfully debriefed so that students can talk about their feelings and relate their experiences to the relevant concepts. Before you try to make connections between the activity and the concept, however, allow students to focus on the *affect* of their experience. Prompt their discussion with this single question: *What feelings did you experience during this activity?* This question serves three purposes:

1. **Students are encouraged to identify and articulate their feelings.** Some students, particularly those with weak intrapersonal intelligence, have difficulty identifying, describing, and sometimes dealing with their feelings. Focusing the initial portion of the class discussion on the affect of an Experiential Exercise helps all students better understand how they reacted.

2. **Students are able to share their feelings in the proper environment.** In a cooperative, tolerant classroom (discussed further in Part 2), students feel comfortable sharing freely and honestly how they felt and reacted. If you neglect to encourage this sharing during class time, students' emotions may spill out in other classes or even at home, where the "teachable moment" is lost.

3. **Students know that their reactions are acceptable.** Letting students discuss their feelings without judgment sends them a powerful message: it is okay to have and share powerful emotions. This validation will set the foundation for the rest of the debriefing.

Help students identify, articulate, and share their feelings in the proper environment.

Ask carefully sequenced questions to help students make connections between their experience and key concepts or events.

Once students have discussed their feelings, they are ready to find the connections between the Experiential Exercise and the corresponding social studies concepts. This is best done with a series of carefully sequenced questions, spiraling from basic to higher-order thinking skills.

The questions should be carefully crafted to help students discover concepts and reach conclusions on their own; resist the temptation to offer your own analysis until students have been encouraged to draw their own conclusions. Answering the questions yourself robs students of the opportunity.

The following series of questions shows how you might debrief an assembly-line activity that simulated the physical, mental, and emotional stress of assembly-line work:

- What feelings did you experience during this activity?
- Describe the kind of work you did on the assembly line.
- What made assembly-line work difficult? What made it desirable?
- How did you cope with the repetitiveness?
- How do you feel about the product you were making?
- How do you think turn-of-the-century assembly-line workers felt about their jobs?
- Why do you think factory owners used the assembly line as a method of production?
- What are the positive aspects of mass production? What are the negative aspects?
- In what ways do you think this activity was similar to real assembly lines?
- In what ways do you think this activity was different from real assembly lines?

Be intentional about helping students grasp the differences between the classroom activity and the social studies concept or event it parallels. This student is completing a T-chart comparing the classroom activity to historical reality.

A skillfully facilitated discussion centering on these questions has powerful results. Students can intelligently discuss the substantive issues surrounding the rise of industrialism—the drudgery of assembly-line work, the alienation of workers from the final product, the expediency and efficiency of mass production, the benefits of standardized products—for an entire period. And this all occurs as an introduction, before they have ever read about, heard a lecture on, or viewed a movie about the Industrial Revolution.

Notice that the last two questions ask students to compare how the experience was both like and unlike reality. As students explore how Experiential Exercises compare to real life, they begin to see the differences in magnitude, scope, and seriousness between the classroom activity and historical reality. Failing to confront these differences after the assembly-line activity would trivialize the experience of workers during the Industrial Revolution. Additionally, neglecting to make comparisons to real life after an Experiential Exercises runs the risk that students will underestimate the complexities of the concept or event they are exploring.

"The most important part of an Experiential Exercise is what happens after the experience. That is when I have to skillfully help my students make connections between the activity and the concept we are learning. Without this, much of the learning can be lost."
— Middle School Teacher

Writing for Understanding

Steps at a Glance

1 Use writing to help your students learn key social studies concepts.

2 Give students rich experiences to write about.

3 Have students record their ideas, thoughts, and feelings in prewriting activities.

4 Provide students with authentic writing assignments.

5 Guide students through the writing process.

Introduction

Have you ever given your students what you thought was an engaging writing assignment, only to find they responded with shallow, poorly organized, incoherent prose? Take, for example, the history teacher who asked his students to write a short essay comparing various methods African Americans used to achieve equal rights in the United States. He believed that after listening to some lectures and discussions, reading the textbook, and completing several worksheets, students would have plenty to write about. Their essays, however, lacked substance, creativity, and detail. What had gone wrong?

In truth, this writing assignment and its predictable, disappointing outcomes might be found in any classroom. A new approach to writing is vital. To write forcefully and in detail about social studies topics, students need interactive experiences about which to write. In the TCI Approach, the Writing for Understanding strategy taps into students' multiple abilities so that *all* learners—even those with lesser linguistic skills—have something memorable to write about. Purposeful writing assignments motivate students to write with style and meaning.

Before asking students to write about the methods used by African Americans to achieve equality in the United States, for example, the history teacher mentioned above could have asked them to become "experts" on Martin Luther King Jr. and Malcolm X. First, his students might have read primary and secondary source accounts of both men's views and analyzed images about key events in their lives. Then, his students could have assumed the roles of the two figures and debated the effectiveness of different methods for achieving equality. Finally, he could have had students write a dialogue between the two men that reflected their differing viewpoints. With time to record their thoughts, reactions, and feelings along the way, and with clear expectations for writing the dialogue, his students would have written more forcefully and with greater depth.

Use writing to help your students learn key social studies concepts.

STEP 1

Writing for Understanding activities will improve both your students' understanding of key social studies concepts and their writing ability. In the conventional social studies classroom, writing is used almost exclusively for assessment. While it is valuable to have students demonstrate what they learn through essays, test questions, or position papers, writing assignments should also be used to facilitate learning. The TCI Approach considers writing not as an end itself, but an access to learning. In addition to helping students learn content, Writing for Understanding activities help build strong expository writing skills that will serve students throughout their lives. This is why:

Writing challenges students to clarify, organize, and express what they have learned. When asked to verbalize their understanding of a social studies issue, students often respond with vague, unorganized thoughts. Requiring students to put their thoughts in writing challenges them to form their thoughts into explicit, detailed, and tangible ideas. After a study of the aftermath of the Civil War and Reconstruction, for example, students might have a general opinion about the effect on the present-day condition of African Americans. But an assignment to write a letter to Frederick Douglass about the issue—citing historical and contemporary evidence—forces students to clarify their ideas, organize what they have learned, and express their ideas coherently.

When students strive to shape their thoughts into a coherent piece of writing, they are led to a greater understanding of the content.

Writing requires students to analyze and synthesize. Writing leads students into higher-level thinking skills, where they draw conclusions, make connections between events or concepts, and develop informed opinions. Through written work, students are better able to analyze specific events or concepts and to synthesize a large body of information. At the conclusion of a unit on the Great Depression, for example, students might look at poverty in the United States today. They could analyze pictures of individuals living in poverty, examine data on current economic trends, and synthesize their knowledge of the Depression, the New Deal, and contemporary conditions by writing a coherent plan, suggesting a course of action to alleviate poverty in America.

Writing enables students to reach deeper understanding as they draw on previous learning for supporting details. Too often, students make generalizations or express opinions without having any supporting details or facts. Having students write about the content they are learning is an excellent way to teach them the value of supporting arguments with solid evidence and precise details. Writing a position paper on whether European colonization benefited or hurt Africa, for example, forces students to analyze what they have learned and to formulate an argument, supported with historical detail.

Ownership of written products motivates students to excel. Students will invest more time and energy in learning social studies when they are challenged to write creatively about the content. If you encourage your students to develop their individual voices, their writing will become a form of self-expression rather than just a chronicle of facts or a regurgitation of textbook content. While learning about the plight of Chinese immigrants who were detained on Angel Island, students may view slides, listen to primary source accounts of life in the detention center, and read some of the actual poetry Chinese immigrants wrote on the walls of the processing center. Students could then go on to write and illustrate their own poems describing the experiences and feelings of detainees on Angel Island.

The writing process compels students to refine their ideas. Navigating the steps of the writing process—brainstorming, writing rough drafts, revising, and editing—requires students to practice focused thinking and precise expression. Whereas the spoken word is transitory, a written idea can be reviewed, revised, and embellished. The process of writing a polished, well-supported piece leads to greater understanding of a topic. When students reflect on the Lewis and Clark journey, they assume the role of William Clark and write a journal entry in first person present tense, as if they were there. Prompted by a word bank of key terms that Clark himself used, students write a first draft, share and critique their drafts in small groups, and then refine their work, finally comparing it with Clark's own journal. In the process, they become immersed in the day-to-day experiences of that time.

Students "experience" the Lewis and Clark expedition as they examine primary source materials—maps, illustrations, and Clark's own journal entries—to create their own account of life on the new frontier.

STEP 2

Give students rich experiences to write about.

In the conventional classroom, students generally do not have much to say about the social studies content they are taught. Essays, position papers, and test answers often lack detail, and they rarely exhibit any original style or creative expression. At best, student writing efforts tend to be a simple summation of memorized vocabulary and facts.

To facilitate powerful writing in your classroom, you need to give students a variety of memorable, interactive experiences on which to base their writing. These activities must tap into the multiple intelligences to give all learners, even those with lesser linguistic skills, something to say. As students participate in these activities—whether viewing powerful images, role playing, discussing complex issues, or acting out key events—they develop ideas and form opinions *before* they begin writing. Here are two examples of activities that prepare and inspire students to write:

In Ancient Athens Students take a "walking tour" of Athens during its Golden Age. During their tour, they visit and read about six sites in the city as they explore various features of ancient Greek culture. At the temple in Delphi, students discover how Greek mythology influenced modern-day language. At the Parthenon, they design a new temple for the acropolis and discover the influence of Greek architecture in today's western culture. In the marble shop, they reconstruct Greek sculptures. At the Theater of Dionysus, students practice and write parts for Greek drama. They converse with Socrates at the agora. They also "participate" in the pentathlon at the Panathenaic Games. Afterward, students create an illustrated scrapbook describing what they have learned.

Students are anxious to write after they assume the roles of labor and management to argue about working conditions in a factory during the Industrial Revolution. From their experience, they have a wealth of ideas to draw from.

Visiting sites on a walking tour of Athens during the Golden Age provides students with rich experiences to inspire their writing. Here, students prepare a Greek drama at the Theater of Dionysus.

Get It While It's Fresh

Ask students to begin writing during or immediately after an Experiential Exercise or other multiple-intelligence task. When they write in the midst of a classroom experience, their writing takes on the emotions of the moment and will be filled with richer detail.

America in the 1960s Students explore the cultural rift between the American mainstream and the counterculture during the 1960s. First, working in pairs, students read about these two groups. Then, as a class, they discuss the historical influences and values of the mainstream and counterculture, and students complete a T-chart to highlight the contrasts. Next, students assume the roles of representatives from the mainstream or the counterculture and respond to a series of prompts as they "talk out" six topics: fashion, communal living, political activism, sexuality, music, and drugs. After a class discussion about the rift between the two groups, students write an editorial stating whether they believe the effects of the counterculture on American society were positive or negative.

STEP 3 — Have students record their ideas, thoughts, and feelings in prewriting activities.

Prewriting activities are essential if students are to write effectively. No matter what the topic, they need to start by gathering a wealth of concrete details. With the TCI Approach, you can easily combine prewriting activities with interactive experiences, allowing students to generate the specific ideas they need. For example, suppose students have just completed a role play that simulates discrimination. Immediately after the experience, give students time to write down all their reactions, feelings, and reflections. In no time, they will have the specific ideas they need for their writing. Other engaging ways to help students generate ideas are to have them role-play dialogues between figures; participate in panel discussions to explore different viewpoints on controversial issues; examine historical photos, illustrations, or art; or listen to music that represents a particular concept, period, or event.

Once students have the ideas, they must organize and plan their writing. Here are examples of several effective methods for organizing social studies ideas:

Structured Matrices and Charts Arranging their thoughts in a simple matrix or chart helps students see the relationships among ideas. In a lesson on how the Communist Revolution affected village life, for example, students examine seven sets of artifacts and written information about Liu Ling, a village in Shaanxi province. They record notes in a matrix, organized by aspects of life—standard of living, work, health and hygiene, and marriage—before and after the revolution. This prewriting enables students to organize their thoughts before they assume the role of a villager and write a journal about their post-revolutionary life in Liu Ling in 1962.

Students record a variety of rich details—information, ideas, feelings, and impressions—as they prepare to create autobiographic sketches written from the perspective of people affected by the Depression.

Venn Diagrams Another prewriting tool for organizing ideas is the Venn diagram. It is useful for recording ideas for purposes of comparison, such as in a lesson about the differing viewpoints of Martin Luther King Jr. and Malcolm X, and the methods African Americans used to achieve equal rights in the United States. Students complete the diagram by writing unique characteristics of each leader in the appropriate section and characteristics common to both leaders in the center section. The completed diagram provides a wealth of information for students as they write a dialogue between King and Malcolm X.

Postcards Having students record on "postcards" their initial impressions of what they are learning is an effective way to prepare them for writing a more substantive letter. For example, as students "tour" Mexico City by viewing images and visiting sites, they record information, observations, and impressions on postcards of each site. Their postcards detail their discoveries about the history, culture, neighborhoods, and environment of Mexico City. This becomes the basis for a letter in which they summarize what they learned on the tour.

^{STEP}
4

Provide students with authentic writing assignments.

While traditional essays and position papers are appropriate for some topics, asking students to write in other genres promotes experimentation and makes their writing more exciting and novel. There is often more authenticity in their work, and more of a sense of purpose, when students write dialogues, poetry, stories, newspaper eulogies, speeches, or letters. When a writing assignment is compelling enough for students to care about, inspired writing almost always follows. The following forms of writing will challenge your students to write creatively while still reflecting on the concepts being taught.

Dialogues Have students write a dialogue that highlights the opposing viewpoints of two figures. Dialogues should be written in a conversational tone and include the salient points for each speaker. For example, students might write a dialogue between a turn-of-the-century worker and her boss that focuses not only on typical worker's grievances (long hours, low pay, unsafe working conditions), but also on management's concerns (competition, low productivity, worker absenteeism). Other suitable pairs for a dialogue would be a Loyalist and a Patriot in 1776, a Japanese courtier and a samurai warrior, Thomas Hobbes and John Locke, Harriet Tubman and John C. Calhoun, a present-day democrat and republican, or a property developer and a conservationist.

In this Writing for Understanding activity, student pairs recreate an argument between a Loyalist and a Patriot and then write a dialogue based on their discussion.

Eulogies Students can broaden their understanding of the past by writing eulogies that extol the virtues of a prominent historical figure or civilization. Eulogies should be written in formal language; they include a brief summary of the person (or civilization), an elaboration of that person's legacy, and a conclusion about how the achievements of that person still affect the world today. A eulogy to the Roman Empire, for example, would include a summary of the accomplishments of the Roman Empire and a list of how those accomplishments are seen in the world today. Other people and civilizations students could write eulogies about include Kublai Khan, Hiawatha, Abraham Lincoln, Susan B. Anthony, Socrates, the Soviet Union, and the Mayan civilization.

Hero/Wanted Poster To focus on controversial figures, have students create a Hero/Wanted poster that both praises and criticizes a figure. Each poster should have an illustration, background information, and lists of the person's accomplishments and "crimes." Students will use critical thinking skills as they explore dual perspectives. For example, a poster of Hernán Cortés would list his accomplishments in one place (expanded the Spanish empire, brought Christianity to new peoples, behaved courageously in battle) and his alleged crimes in another (he was a traitor and marauder; he killed many Aztecs and destroyed most Aztec cultural traditions). Other poster candidates include Ghengis Khan, Martin Luther, Alexander the Great, Joseph Stalin, Mao Tse Tung, Huey Long, and Indira Gandhi.

Journal Entries Show students how to write journal entries that bring events to life. Encourage students to adopt a narrative format that uses (insofar as is possible) the colloquial language of the time or place. Each entry should include the correct date and a detailed account of the figure's feelings and experiences. Use visual or musical prompts to give students ideas. For example, for their journal entries about the Lewis and Clark expedition, students might start with illustrations from William Clark's own journal and a map detailing the journey's route. Before writing a slave journal, they examine a story quilt stitched by a slave in the 1880s and listen to a spiritual. Other ideas for journal writing include reflections from a 17th century British journalist on social life in the American colonies, a journal from a participant in the French Revolution, and excerpts from the diary of a civil rights activist who participated in the Freedom March.

Students write letters home from the trenches, describing the living conditions, the rigorous lifestyle, and the physical and emotional trauma of trench warfare.

Letters Challenge students to write letters that convey the feelings of a key figure to a particular audience. Encourage them to use descriptive narrative and to integrate as much detailed, accurate information about the event as possible. You can motivate students with prewriting activities that make them feel as though they have witnessed the event. During a unit on World War I, for example, place students on the floor between rows of desks representing trenches, and show the a series of images depicting the horrors of warfare on Europe's western front. As they are in the trenches, have them write two letters home, one to their family and one to a trusted friend. Other personas they might adopt include an Arab traveler writing home about a visit to Timbuktu, Dorothea Lange writing to President Roosevelt about victims of the Depression, or a bomber pilot writing home about dropping an atomic bomb on Hiroshima.

Newspaper Editorial Help students understand bias by assigning them to write an editorial about an event. Editorials should clearly state their position on the issue, use language that reflects the bias of the newspaper, and contain supporting evidence. For example, students might assume the role of an Islamic editorial writer commenting on the Crusades—seen not as a Holy War, but as a military invasion of Islamic territory and as a calculated war of genocide against the Muslims. Other opinion pieces might include an editorial for a South Carolina newspaper on the eve of the Civil War, an editorial on the Boston Tea Party for a colonial newspaper, and an editorial on the Reformation for a Catholic newspaper.

Interviews Encourage students to interview real individuals and to write oral histories. Prepare students by conducting a mock interview in class, asking well-conceived, thoughtful questions. Then have students make a list of 20–30 questions to ask their interviewee. After the interview, their write-ups should include an introduction to the interviewee, direct quotes and paraphrasing from the interview, and an analysis of the interviewee's perspective. One powerful oral history topic for today's students is the Vietnam War. Require them to identify someone who was affected by the war—such as a protestor, a conscientious objector, a soldier, a parent of a soldier, a local politician—and then ask questions like these: *What do you remember about the war? How did it affect you personally? How did the war change our nation?* Other topics for oral histories include World War II, the civil rights movement, the Cold War, recent immigrants, the Gulf War, and presidential elections.

Poetry and Song Lyrics These genres encourage students to write about topics, events, or specific groups with empathy and emotion. It is best to assign a specific style of poetry or song lyric, and ask students to use descriptive, evocative language while still making direct references to the topic. For example, after viewing images about the internment of Japanese Americans during World War II, challenge students to write haiku from the perspective of those interned. Other possibilities include illuminated poems about medieval Europe, an acrostic poem about Montezuma, lyrics to a *corrido* (folk song) about the Mexicano heritage in the Southwest, or a biographical poem to celebrate the accomplishments of an important Renaissance figure.

Position Papers Teach students how to write position papers, taking a definitive stand on controversial issues. Position papers should include an introduction framing a controversial issue, a clear statement of the student's position, supporting evidence, compelling arguments against the opposing viewpoint, and a persuasive conclusion. For example, students might write that the grievances aired in the late 19th century by women reformers at Seneca Falls have not been redressed today. As evidence, they might include the fact that women earn less than men do, do more housework, and still hold only a small percentage of management positions. Other position papers might address whether the United States should be praised or condemned for its actions in the Cold War, whether Africa benefited from European colonialism, or whether Russians were better off under communism.

"Oral histories have been a tremendous success with my students. Initially, students are reluctant and a little scared to take the risk to interview someone. But after they talk to someone and record original historical findings, they produce fabulous writing and have a real sense of accomplishment."
— High School Teacher

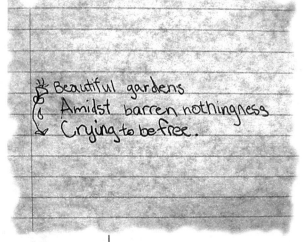

A high school student wrote this haiku in response to images of desert internment camps for Japanese Americans during World War II.

Guide students through the writing process.

Once students have completed a prewriting activity in which they gathered several ideas and details, they are ready to move through the rest of the writing process. They start with your precise guidelines, write a first draft, receive peer feedback, revise and edit their rough draft, and finally write their final drafts. This investment in time yields powerful writing and increased learning. Here are the steps to follow:

1. **Give clear expectations and precise guidelines for writing assignments.** Confusion is a major obstacle to coherent writing. Give your students a handout that clearly states guidelines and deadlines for all parts of the assignment. Nothing will help them more to translate their fragmented thoughts into a coherent piece of writing than this vital step.

2. **Have students write a first draft.** Once students finish collecting and listing their ideas, have them experiment with an organizational structure in a rough draft. Stress that while this draft does not have to be polished, it must be well organized and complete. Quickly review their drafts and note any suggestions.

3. **Use peer-feedback groups.** Divide students into heterogeneous groups of three or four. Before students move into groups, emphasize that feedback should be honest, constructive, and specific. Each student in a group should use a pen or pencil of a different color. Students exchange papers with someone else in the group. When a student receives another's paper, she writes her name in the upper-right corner, marks any problems, makes any comments, and passes the paper to another group member. When the author gets his paper back, he will know who made which suggestions, enabling him to seek further clarification as he writes his final draft.

In peer-feedback groups, students react to one another's papers. Writers use this feedback as they revise their rough drafts.

4. **Require students to make revisions.** Students should use the feedback they received from you and their peers to revise and improve their original drafts.

5. **Have students edit their final drafts.** Before they turn in their final drafts, require students to have their papers edited by someone else: a classmate, a parent, or another teacher. Remind students that if their editor finds many errors, they must rewrite the paper. Minor changes can be made directly on the final draft.

Precise directions for writing double as a simple, ready-made rubric for the basic requirements of a writing assignment.

Guidelines for Writing a Slave Journal Entry

Imagine you are a slave who helped create a story quilt about slavery that is similar to the one your class created. Write an entry in your journal that explains how the quilt represents your experience as a slave. Your journal entry must include these things:

- A date and location, such as November 4, 1853, Johnson Plantation, South Carolina.

- An introduction explaining how you and other slaves created the story quilt, including details about yourself and the slaves who assisted you. Include the names of the other slaves.

- An explanation of at least four quilt squares. Explain how the symbols and words on the quilt represent aspects of slave life.

- At least eight of these words: *hope, music, dance, religion, hot, cotton, running away, family, cabin, banjo, fear, pride, encourage, resist, pain, whip, master, food, clothing, togetherness.*

- Two statements to future generations that explain what you think is most important to remember about slavery.

Response Group

Steps at a Glance

1. Challenge students to discuss controversial and complex issues in small groups.

2. Create heterogeneous groups and a suitable classroom arrangement.

3. Prepare students to answer provocative critical thinking questions.

4. Allow groups time to prepare their responses.

5. Facilitate a lively class discussion.

Introduction

Imagine being a history teacher, intent on conducting a class discussion about whether equality exists for women today in politics, employment, and education. Is the discussion dominated by one or two confident students, while the rest listen passively? When you call on other students to draw them in, do you get just a few words in response? Social studies teachers know that being able to share and understand different points of view is essential. Dynamic class discussion cultivates different points of view and inspires critical thinking. In many classrooms, however, in-depth, lively, and high-quality class discussions are rare. Many students simply lack the knowledge or the confidence to participate.

Response Group activities, another strategy of the TCI Approach, are a way to sidestep the problems inherent in class discussion. Students first work in small groups with thought-provoking resources—perhaps viewing compelling images, reading primary sources, or listening to music—and then discuss related critical thinking questions among themselves. After the small-group discussion, a single presenter shares the group's findings with the entire class. Because students have the time to examine the resources closely and the comfort of trying out their ideas in a small group, everyone is prepared to articulate answers, and their responses are longer and more detailed than during conventional class discussions.

Challenge students to discuss controversial and complex issues in small groups.

Working in Response Groups helps students grapple with the ambiguities of issues in social studies, recognize the complexity of historical events, and discuss the consequences of public policies. Response Group activities are most effective when you want to challenge students to do the following:

Discuss controversial issues. Many social studies issues are provocative and controversial, motivating students to argue and debate. Response Groups help students prepare for such debate. During a lesson on the impact of the civil rights movement on current issues, for example, you might provide images and secondary source materials that prompt students to debate such controversial civil rights issues as busing and affirmative action. Similarly, images of medieval serfs and photographs depicting homelesss people today could inspire students to debate which group had better living conditions and what implications that might have for government policies regarding homelessness.

Analyze primary source readings to make discoveries. A key social studies objective is teaching students to draw conclusions about issues or events from reading primary source documents. These readings are often difficult. In Response Groups, students work together to decipher their meaning. For example, students might compare Justinian's Code of Law from Byzantium to parts of the Penal Code, discussing the relative merits of each and discovering the influence of Justinian's Code on America's current legal structure. Or, group members might read about Alexander Hamilton and Thomas Jefferson, and be challenged to use their knowledge to attribute quotes to one of the two statesmen.

Solve a historical problem. Students are motivated to learn when they are allowed to develop their own solutions to real problems. When you give students the context of a historical dilemma—events leading to the issue, the basis of the problem, possible courses of action—and allow them to determine a solution, they feel a sense of ownership. By becoming involved in the history this way, students want to know what really happened. To learn about the Cuban missile crisis, for example, Response Groups could undertake a simulation of the tense situation President Kennedy faced in October 1962. Groups analyze an aerial photo of the missile sites in Cuba and receive information about Cuba's proximity to the United States, the existence of American medium-range missiles in Turkey, and Kennedy's desire to keep missiles out of Cuba. They consider five possible courses of action that Kennedy might take, and rank the relative merits of each. After debating what Kennedy should have done, the class learns what

"The discussion was immediate and animated. Students could hardly wait to share their ideas."

— Middle School Teacher

The ambiguity of political cartoons such as this one makes for intense Response Group discussions.

actually happened. After this experience, students are eager to analyze Kennedy's actions.

Use musical-rhythmic intelligence to better understand a historical period.
Music can foster a deeper understanding of the attitudes, values, and issues of an era. This often-overlooked resource could be featured, for instance, in a lesson on changing attitudes toward the Civil War. Response Groups listen to four songs that offer strikingly different views. The first three ("Johnny Is My Darling," "Bonnie Blue Flag," and "Marching Song of the First of Arkansas") show the

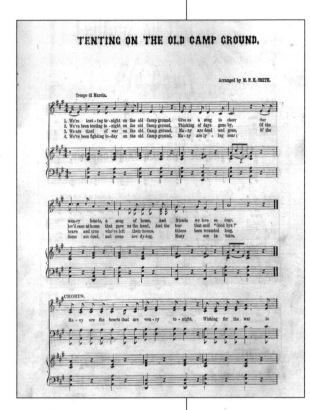

similarities and differences in how Northerners, Southerners, and African Americans perceived the war at its outset; the final song ("Tenting Tonight") provides a soldier's point of view on the brutality and inhumanity of the war. Students go into the class discussion prepared to talk about how perspective and time changed people's attitudes toward the war, and how the songs reflect these changes.

Understand multiple perspectives on an issue or event.
To enable students to understand several perspectives, have groups assume the roles of different figures commenting on events or situations. As students discuss issues from different points of view, they begin to appreciate the complexity of social studies. For example, to examine various perspectives on colonial rebellion, each Response Group assumes the role of a historical figure—Samuel Adams, Crispus Attucks, John Dickenson, Abigail Adams, King George III, Thomas Hutchinson. Groups respond in character to events pictured in paintings: the Boston Massacre, the Boston Tea Party, and the tar and feathering of a tax collector. As they voice and hear a wide array of perspectives, students are awakened to the complexity of colonial rebellion.

Tap into students' musical-rhythmic intelligence by encouraging them to respond to appropriate period pieces that capture the attitudes, values, and issues of a historical era.

Use visual-literacy skills to make discoveries. Working in Response Groups, students can make important discoveries through their visual-spatial intelligence. Pictures, paintings, illustrations, and maps are sometimes the best documents to convey concepts. For example, to teach about the family values of middle-class America in the 1950s and early 1960s, you might provide pictures from three popular television shows from the era, such as "Hazel," "I Love Lucy," and "Father Knows Best." By examining the images, groups determine what family values were reflected in the shows. This prompts rich class discussion on the values of the era and leads students to examine the impact of the media in shaping social values today.

STEP 2

Create heterogeneous groups and a suitable classroom arrangement.

Suitable groupings and classroom setup are both important to successful Response Group activities. You need to spend some upfront time creating mixed-ability teams of students and teaching them how to arrange themselves quickly and efficiently for groupwork. Follow these guidelines to prepare for and to kick off a Response Group activity:

1. **Carefully form groups before the activity begins.** Try to put students with a variety of abilities and characteristics in each group. Also consider the subject matter. For example, if the topic is an exploration of cultural or gender issues, you would want to consider ethnic or gender diversity when you form groups. Be intentional about your group selection.

2. **Make an overhead transparency of the seating arrangement.** Make a diagram showing the classroom arrangement for Response Groups, similar to the diagram shown below. List group members' names by each cluster of desks so that students know where to sit and who is in their group.

3. **Explain the importance of the seating arrangement.** Students need to understand the importance of desk arrangement for these activities. Make explicit the goal of the arrangement: to allow all students to see the overhead and to interact with group members and fellow classmates at the same time.

Classroom Arrangement: Have Patience

Recognize that an effective classroom arrangement for Response Groups—where students can easily talk to one another and see the projected images—is difficult for students to set up quickly. Be patient, but expect your students to get it right.

Have students arrange their desks so they can see the overhead and interact with their group and the entire class. Create heterogeneous groups of three or four to enliven discussion.

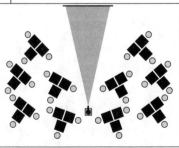

4. **Have students practice moving into Response Groups.** Students—even high school students—must be taught how to move into groups, especially into a unique arrangement like this. You might conduct a "Desk Olympics" to teach them to move desks quickly and safely (see page 143). Consider asking three volunteers to model moving first inefficiently and then efficiently into a group. Challenge students to discover ways they can move more quickly, such as putting the desks around them in the correct formation before they move into their groups, gesturing appropriately to indicate who should go where, and being considerate as they race around the room to get into position.

5. **Wait until all groups are precisely arranged to begin the activity.** Waiting for groups to be in proper formation sends a clear message: Exact group configuration is important for facilitating a effective discussion.

STEP 3
Prepare students to answer provocative critical thinking questions.

Everyone can remember taking part in a heated discussion over an unusual news event, controversial song lyrics, or a distressing human dilemma. The passion you feel during such moments is what every social studies teacher hopes to create during class discussions. Fostering such lively discussion among your students requires two kinds of preparation. First, you need to give them something exciting to discuss and enough background information to discuss it with intelligence. Then, you need to pose subjective questions that create intellectual tension, invite controversy, and require students to analyze, synthesize, compare, discover, and hypothesize.

Compelling primary source images challenge students to evaluate the decision to place Japanese in internment camps during World War II.

How to Provide Students with Inspiring Resources and Needed Information To engage in meaningful, high-level discussions, students must have either sufficient background knowledge or exceptionally rich resources that prompt their critical thinking. To ensure success in Response Group activities, you must provide any needed background information quickly so that students can spend the bulk of their time grappling with critical thinking questions. Following are several ways to do this.

Give a mini-lecture. Often the most expedient way to prepare students for high-level discussion is through a brief lecture, especially for a relatively simple concept or event. In an activity about the relocation of Japanese Americans during World War II, for example, you might lecture about the government's rationale for the internment of Japanese Americans before students, in Response Groups, examine visual images and discuss related questions. Mini-lectures must be succinct—no more than 5 minutes per question—and focus solely on information students need in order to answer the high-level questions.

Provide students with appropriate readings. Interesting readings can prepare students for discussion and provide them with a reference throughout the activity. This is most effective when students are discussing complex issues and need more substantive resources than class notes. In a lesson about the compromises made during the Constitutional Convention, for example, you might give students historical readings that summarize the major conflicts that delegates faced. Students could read and refer to these summaries as their groups discuss possible compromises.

Use compelling images to create understanding. Powerful images are sometimes more effective than lectures or readings at providing background information. With spiral questioning, you can help students discover the key information in such images. For example, for the simulation activity on the Cuban missile crisis, students start by examining an image taken from a U-2 spy plane, showing Soviet missile sites in Cuba. After responding to questions about details in the image, the purpose of the missile sites, and President Kennedy's reaction to them, most students will have the requisite knowledge to discuss critical thinking questions about the president's choices.

Allow students to discover information on their own. Some Response Group activities can be set up to allow students to make discoveries for themselves. These types of activities do not require in-depth background knowledge. You will divulge as little information as possible before the discussion begins. Instead, you provide students with resources, give brief instructions, and allow them to discuss the insights they gain from the materials. For example, in an activity on sub-Saharan Africa, students analyze images and descriptive paragraphs that depict four climate zones—tropical, savanna, semiarid, and desert—to discover how inhabitants in each climate zone adapt to their environment to secure such necessities as food, shelter, and transportation.

"I like to sit back and watch groups make discoveries on their own. Even though they don't always come up with the right answer, it's exciting to watch them develop their deductive thinking skills. And afterward they really want to know the answer."
— Middle School Teacher

Allow students to use their discovery skills to interpret images without extensive background information. For example, students discuss what this photo of a market on the Niger River reveals about how people adapt to their environment.

How to Provide Provocative Critical Thinking Questions Posing meaningful questions that will lead to high-level thinking is esential to good Response Group discussion. The following methods will prompt critical thinking and energetic discussion.

Ask a single, direct question. To compare two political cartoons on the New Deal, for example, students might discuss this question: *What is the cartoonist's message in each of these political cartoons?* To help students discover how New England colonists adapted to their environment, you might show them a detailed drawing of life in a Massachusetts coastal town and have them discuss this question: *Judging from this picture, in what ways did colonists in New England adapt to their environment?*

Ask a series of related questions. To have students speculate on the type of dwellings that housed various African tribes during the 10th century, for example, you might show images of different climatic regions and ask: *What resources could Africans use for shelter? Of the resources available, which would make the most durable shelter? What environmental elements—heat, rain, wind, predators—should be considered in building the shelter? What do you think this shelter might look like?*

Ask students to quantify their answer on a spectrum. After studying the Cold War, for example, students might consider whether certain actions of the United States should be praised or condemned. Students could discuss where to place visual icons of Cold War events—the Vietnam War, the arms race, the Bay of Pigs invasion, and the Berlin blockade—on a spectrum between *Totally Praised* and *Totally Condemned.* They would have to support their opinions with historical facts.

Working in a small group, students discover how exciting and frustrating multiple perspectives can be as they attempt to place visual icons that represent U.S. involvement in Cold War events along a spectrum ranging from *Totally Praised* to *Totally Condemned.*

Ask students to evaluate possible solutions to problems. To resolve the conflict at the Constitutional Convention between large states and small states over representation in Congress, students might read a summary of the controversy, examine a map of the United States, and discuss:

> If you were delegates to the Constitutional Convention, what do you think would be the best way to resolve the problem of representation in Congress? Rank the following choices from 1 (best choice) to 4 (worst choice) and be prepared to defend your rankings.
> a. Have representation in Congress based on population.
> b. Have an equal number of members of Congress from each state.
> c. Create a Congress with two parts. Have representation for one part based on a state's population and representation for the other part based on an equal number of representatives per state.
> d. Redraw the boundaries of the states so that the population is equal in all states. Then base representation in Congress on an equal number of representatives per state.

STEP 4

Allow groups time to prepare their responses.

In Response Groups, students have sufficient time to discuss, refine, and record their responses to the critical thinking questions. During this step, you should see high levels of interaction in the small groups— leading to increased gains in learning. With this type of activity, every student has the opportunity to comment on and share ideas—something that is virtually impossible in conventional class discussions. Follow these guidelines to inspire animated, purposeful small-group discussions:

1. Assign and rotate the role of presenter. At the beginning of a Response Group activity, assign the role of presenter to one member of each group. Explain that this student will act as the group's leader while the group is working on the first question, making sure all members share their ideas, and will act as spokesperson for the group in the whole-class discussion. Rotate the role of presenter for each critical thinking question.

2. Have each student record answers during group discussion. Provide a handout that lists all the critical thinking questions, and have students record answers for each one. Although the presenter will share the group's key ideas during the whole-class discussion, using the handouts allows students to refine their ideas through writing, and also keeps everyone accountable for the group's work.

3. Give groups adequate time to discuss critical thinking questions. Groups generally need 3 to 7 minutes to discuss each critical thinking question and record their answers. Circulate to monitor group discussion, but without interrupting to interject your own opinions.

"I like it when we get to pretend we are government leaders and have to come up with ways to deal with some historical event. Groups argue with each other and before you know it the period's over."

— High School Student

Small-group discussion gives students the opportunity to develop their ideas in a supportive environment before sharing them with the class.

Less Is More

Set a time limit for small-group discussion to encourage purposeful, focused discussion. This creates a sense of urgency and helps keep students on task.

S TEP
5

Facilitate a lively class discussion.

After Response Groups have had adequate time to contemplate and discuss a critical thinking question or group of questions, they will be ready for whole-class discussion. Your students should have plenty of ideas they are eager to share. The challenge is to facilitate the discussion so that the different points of view are brought forth in a lively, engaging, and civil fashion.

To begin class discussion, ask presenters from two or three groups to share their answers. This will likely offer the class a range of views on the question. You can foster intellectual debate if, rather than allowing presenters to simply give prepared responses, you try one or more of these approaches:

- Ask whether any presenters have ideas that are dramatically different from those already stated.
- Allow two presenters with very different opinions to argue their points.
- Ask a presenter who has not yet spoken to consider the ideas already mentioned and explain which point he or she most agrees or disagrees with.
- If the discussion brings forth only one point of view, promote deeper discussion by acting incredulous and arguing the unheard perspective.
- Challenge students to support their ideas with examples and facts.

To add a gracious note to controversial debates, you might suggest that presenters use phrases like, "(Name of previous speaker), my group respectfully agrees/disagrees with your group because…."

Lively discussion ensues after students have had time to prepare responses with their group members.

As the activity unfolds, expect more thoughtful and longer responses from pre-senters than you have experienced during more traditional class discussions. If a few presenters seem to dominate the discussion, be sure to call on a different group's presenter for the next critical thinking question.

During this whole-class discussion you will witness one of the benefits of Response Group activities: Discussions focus on students' ideas, not on the teacher's. During conventional discussions, teachers usually have to coax students into sharing ideas and often end up talking more than the students. With presen-ters prepared to articulate their groups' ideas, discussion is often so animated that there is scarcely time to hear from all presenters. You are simply the facilitator, and will rarely have to interject your own ideas into the discussion.

"I came in here thinking my views were pretty much planted in cement. Now I see that there is another side. The things we discuss actually confuse my views and make me think."

— High School Student

Problem Solving Groupwork

Steps at a Glance

1. Challenge students with engaging, multiple-ability projects.

2. Prepare all students for successful groupwork.

3. Give group members clearly defined roles and requirements.

4. Give groups autonomy and time to prepare high-quality products.

5. Have groups present their work.

Introduction

Most educators know the value of successful groupwork. When students work effectively in small groups, the benefits are bountiful: increased tolerance for others, collaborative problem solving, effective negotiation, more equitable interaction. But when groupwork *doesn't* go smoothly, hurt feelings, unequal interaction, bickering, and worse are likely to be just as plentiful.

As another key strategy of the TCI Approach, Problem Solving Groupwork activities teach students the skills necessary to work together successfully in small groups, both in the classroom and later in life. During Problem Solving Groupwork tasks, students sit in heterogeneously mixed groups to work on challenging projects, such as preparing a dramatization of some aspect of history. The projects are carefully designed to require the use of multiple abilities, with the idea that every student will be able to contribute. Within a group, each student takes a well-defined role—such as researcher, stage manager, director, or script writer. As students work on the task, the teacher serves as a resource and checks on group progress. After completing their task, groups present their products to the class.

STEP 1

Challenge students with engaging, multiple-ability projects.

Successful groupwork tasks challenge students to use their problem solving skills to find innovative answers to complex problems as they complete engaging, multiple-ability projects. Groups might be asked to create a dramatic presentation about the content, to bring the ideas of an important figure to life, or to devise a visual metaphor that represents a key concept.

Nothing kills the enthusiasm and meaningful interaction of a small group faster than a simple task with discrete answers, such as labeling physiographic landmarks on a map or plotting the points of a line graph. You simply do not need four or five brains to figure out answers to factual questions. If you assign menial tasks, be prepared for limited engagement, discipline issues, and complaints about "boring" group projects. However, you *do* need four or five people to tackle open-ended questions—tasks that are challenging and engaging enough to warrant the collective genius of several students and inspire them to use their best critical thinking skills.

"Too often we give students answers to remember rather than problems to solve."

—Roger Lewin

Challenging projects that require a range of abilities— such as these minidramas where students incorporate visuals, sound effects, simple props, and audience involvement to learn about various groups of westerners—help ensure that every student is engaged.

The most successful tasks for Problem Solving Groupwork not only require higher-order thinking skills, but also require the input of multiple abilities. Too many times, groupwork collapses as some students dominate the process while others sit back and leave the driving to their domineering peers. Elizabeth Cohen and her research associates at the Stanford School of Education discovered that the problem of unbalanced student interaction stems from status differences, or differences in how students rank each other on scales of academic ability and social popularity.

Students who are perceived to have higher status among their peers usually dominate group interaction, completely ignoring the contributions of their lower-status peers, who often revert to bad behavior or silent sulking as a result of being cut out of group interaction. To remedy this, Cohen (1986) suggests groupwork tasks that require a wide range of abilities, so that *all* students are necessary if the group is to generate the highest quality product. When all students have something to contribute, no one is left out; furthermore, studies show that more equal interaction leads to higher learning gains for all students.

Before giving your students a Problem Solving Groupwork task, quickly analyze it by asking these five questions (adapted from Shulman, Lotan, and Whitcomb 1998):

1. Does the task require multiple abilities?
2. Does the task have more than one answer, or is there more than one way to solve the problem?
3. Does the task challenge students to use their problem solving skills?
4. Does the task allow for multiple perspectives?
5. Will the task be challenging enough to create initial frustration, yet give students a sense of accomplishment once they complete it?

If you answer yes to all these questions, chances are that the task will offer engaging and challenging groupwork for your students. Consider how this Problem Solving Groupwork task meets the requirements: While examining the growth of U.S. imperialism at the turn of the century, students are challenged to think metaphorically about the motives behind expansionism and the reactions of those being influenced by the Americans. Each group explores and completes a project on the involvement of the United States in one of the following territories: Cuba, the Philippines, Hawaii, Panama, China, the Dominican Republic, and Puerto Rico. The task is to create two illustrated metaphors, one from the U.S. perspective, and the other showing how people in the territory saw the U.S. role. Students draw or paint the metaphors on a sheet of poster board divided in half. A title for each half identifies the perspective and the metaphor. Underneath each title, students create a bold, artistic image of the metaphor. Near the image, they write the word "because" followed by three reasons the metaphor accurately describes U.S. foreign policy.

This open-ended task successfully engages students' problem solving skills. Students create a wonderful variety of metaphors, such as Uncle Sam as the police officer of the world, the United States as a bloodthirsty octopus strangling its territories, and the United States as a wise and patient father, overseeing the democratic development of its unruly territories. The activity leads students to consider U.S. imperialism from multiple perspectives, challenges them to create an interesting visual product, gives students with many different skills something to contribute, and leaves them with a sense of accomplishment.

"To do the work right, you have to have the ideas of everyone, not just one person. It takes everyone to make it work."

— Middle School Student

From the perspective of the Phillippines, U.S. foreign policy was like an octopus.

BECAUSE
1. the U.S. took over the government and wouldn't let Filipinos govern themselves.
2. the U.S. took Filipino land for their military bases.
3. the U.S. crushed a Filipino revolt for independence.

From the perspective of the United States, U.S. foreign policy in the Phillippines was like a protective father.

BECAUSE
1. the U.S. helped the Filipinos to defeat Spain.
2. the U.S. saw the Filipinos as unfit for self-government.
3. the U.S. planned to educate and "civilize" the Filipinos.

STEP 2 — Prepare all students for successful group-work.

To succeed at cooperative tasks, students must know how to behave in groups without direct supervision. It is essential, therefore, that you set aside class time to create and model a new set of cooperative norms, such as those suggested in the list below. (How to set up and model these cooperative norms is discussed in detail in "Creating a Cooperative, Tolerant Classroom," page 145.)

Groups function best when they have clear guidelines for cooperation, both individual and group accountability, and a range of abilities represented.

How to Work Cooperatively in Groups

1. Smile, be friendly, and introduce yourself.
2. Arrange desks properly.
3. Use positive body language.
4. Use eye contact.
5. Listen to others.
6. Take turns giving ideas.
7. Use positive comments.
8. Be helpful.
9. Disagree in an agreeable way.
10. Follow directions and stay on task.

While these skills apply to any activity, they are imperative for Problem Solving Groupwork. Students will learn to depend on each other. They will learn to ask for and receive help. They will learn to respect the ideas and values of everyone in the classroom, including the teacher. And, the concrete behaviors they learn will not only help them succeed during groupwork tasks, but also as they interact with friends, family members, and, in the future, employers.

Once students have learned and practiced the guidelines for cooperation that you expect them to follow, they are ready to join a group and complete a Problem Solving Groupwork task. You will need to carefully group your students for maximum success. Plan to spend about 15–20 minutes prep time with your class list, dividing students into heterogeneous groups. Balancing groups in terms of gender and ethnicity is relatively easy. A few weeks into school, you will have an idea of the social circles that exist and can use groupwork to manage cliques. The most challenging variable is determining predominant intelligences. The best way to do this is to carefully observe your students as they work on multiple-ability projects. To get a rough idea of your students' multiple intelligences, you can administer a simple diagnostic test, such as the two Multiple Intelligence Surveys included on pages 149–152. Use the results, coupled with your observations, to balance groups by cognitive ability.

STEP 3 — Give group members clearly defined roles and requirements.

After dividing students into heterogeneous groups and ensuring that the Problem Solving Groupwork assignment requires multiple abilities, one of the most effective techniques to create smooth-functioning and productive groups is giving each student a specific role to perform. This will help ensure that each student contributes and will help prevent one member from dominating the group process.

Student Handout 16

Preparing a Minidrama

Your group will create a three-scene minidrama that brings alive the images in your transparency and tells the story of your group's journey to the West. Your audience will learn why you moved west, the hardships you faced, and the legacies you left.

____**Step 1:** Review the roles. After your teacher assigns your role, read the information below. Make sure everyone understands his or her responsibilities.

Director: You will lead the group during Step 3. Make sure your sceneboards contain all of the required elements.

Script Manager: You will lead the group through Step 4 as it prepares the script for the minidrama. Make sure everyone writes his or her own dialog and is equally involved in developing the script.

Props Manager: You will lead the group through Step 5 as it prepares materials for the minidrama. Make sure that the drama is as realistic as possible.

Stage Manager: You will lead the group through Step 6 as it rehearses. Then, during the minidrama, you will direct the audience to make sound effects.

____**Step 2:** Learn about your group. Carefully examine the transparency to see what it reveals about your western group. Then take turns reading aloud the section in *History Alive! The United States* that corresponds to that western group. As you read, take notes in the appropriate section of the Reading Notes and answer these questions:
- Why did this group move to the West?
- What hardships did they face?
- What legacies did they leave to the West?

____**Step 3:** Brainstorm ideas and create three sceneboards. The first scene must show the reasons the group moved to the West; the second scene, the hardships they faced; and the third scene, the legacies they left. The Director should use the boxes on the next page to create sceneboards that outline your story. Make sure your sceneboards include
- simple sketches showing characters' positions during each scene, and the costumes and props they will use.
- captions describing the characters' most important actions.
- speech bubbles containing key dialog.
- points at which the audience will participate.

Student Handout 16

Preparing a Minidrama

____**Step 4:** Write the script. Work together to develop the script. Each person must write his or her own dialog. As you develop your script, the Script Manager should make sure it
- describes reasons the group moved to the West.
- describes the hardships they faced.
- presents the legacies they left.
- allows everyone to participate equally.

____**Step 5:** Prepare materials. Your minidrama must include costumes, props, and a 30-second introductory statement. As you prepare materials, the Props Manager should make sure
- everyone has an appropriate costume or prop.
- the introductory statement gives a brief overview of the content of your minidrama and sets the location and time period of the first scene.

____**Step 6:** Rehearse. You must be able to present your minidrama in five minutes or less. As you rehearse, the Stage Manager should make sure
- the Script Manager can deliver the introductory statement smoothly.
- the presentation flows smoothly.
- costumes and props are used effectively.
- lines are spoken clearly, at an appropriate volume, and with dramatic emphasis.
- the audience participates by providing at least two sound effects.

____After rehearsing your minidrama several times, ask the teacher to watch your presentation. Make notes of your teacher's feedback in the space below.

The key to creating these individual roles is to find an efficient division of labor so that each student is doing part of the groupwork task, yet all parts of the task are interdependent. When the roles are properly set up, each student will have a personal sense of accomplishment, and the group cannot make a successful presentation without the cooperation of all members. Once you have assigned roles, make sure students know exactly what they are to do to complete their project. Then, as they work, carefully monitor each step of their progress.

Student Handout 16 (shown opposite) illustrates a Problem Solving Groupwork activity with specific roles and discrete steps. In this activity, students are assigned to groups of four to create a minidrama about one group of western settlers—either explorers, Californios, mountain men, missionaries, pioneer women, Mormons, forty-niners, or Chinese. The handout defines four student roles for each group and gives clear directions for each stage of the groupwork process.

In this project, there is a clear division of labor: Each role has a name and a list of expected behaviors. Because group members must work together to complete their jobs, the roles also provide for positive interdependence. Also note that, to assist with planning and time management, students are given clear steps on how to proceed. The teacher initials each step after it is completed, thus keeping groups on task.

When students take on well-defined, essential roles, each group member is guaranteed the chance to participate in the group's work.

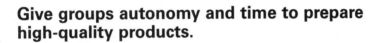

Step 4 Give groups autonomy and time to prepare high-quality products.

Assigning students to work in small groups changes your role. No longer are you the direct supervisor of students, responsible for ensuring that they complete their tasks exactly as instructed. No longer is it your responsibility to make sure that everything said is accurate by correcting it on the spot. Instead, you delegate authority to groups of students. They are empowered to make mistakes, to assess their errors, and to discover ways of correcting them.

This does not mean that you relinquish your authority. It is your job to set the multiple-ability tasks, form the heterogeneous groups, assign the roles, and monitor progress, even as you hold groups responsible for creating high-quality products. There are several ways to facilitate the groupwork process in your new role of "supportive supervisor."

Challenge groups to figure out procedures on their own. At the beginning stages of a groupwork project, it is common for students to have questions about procedures. Most will be answered by the handout. Tell students to study the directions and see if they can discover the answers to their questions. Many teachers allow only the group facilitator to approach the instructor with questions, and further indicate that this is not allowed until the group is certain that they cannot figure out the answer themselves. Some teachers accept only whole-team questions, indicated by all group members having their hands in the air.

Create a Sense of Urgency

Some Problem Solving Groupwork tasks may take only a single period; others may require several periods. To make sure your students manage their time wisely, you might initially tell them that they will have a shorter time to complete the project than you think they actually need. You can always tell them later that they will have an additional class period to complete the task if "they make an extra effort to create a really quality product."

Your role during the group-work process is to monitor, let go, and allow students to work.

Observe students carefully from a discreet distance. Show that you are interested in the groupwork process by moving about the classroom and discreetly listening in on groups. If you sit behind your desk, busy with another project, students may infer that you do not value their efforts. As a result, they may tend to socialize or tune out during groupwork tasks. Carefully monitoring the groups will also help you identify potential problems and provide you with the information you might need to help a group that becomes stuck.

Ask key questions of groups that are not making progress. If a group gets stuck, you might ask a few open-ended questions to redirect their focus or discussion. Suggest that the group deal with your questions on their own, but tell them that you will return shortly to find out how they resolved a particular problem.

Challenge students to practice cooperative norms. If a group appears not to be meeting a particular expectation for cooperation—such as sharing materials—you might stop for a moment and ask group members which behavior expectation they are forgetting to practice. If necessary, post a list of cooperative norms as a reminder. Challenge students to identify the missing skill and determine how they might incorporate it to help their group run more smoothly.

Provide additional resources. Plan ahead. Try to have quality Web sites, books, magazines, newspapers, art supplies, musical selections, or other resources available to maximize students' use of class time. If students will be requesting additional resources, prepare the school librarian to assist in handling their needs.

Encourage students to plan for the possibility of absent group members. Tell students that, at any time, they may need to take on an additional role. Have group members leave all materials (scripts, visuals, notes, costumes, masks) in the classroom so that one absence does not bring the group process to a halt. Encourage students to exchange phone numbers so they can keep each other informed of absences. Also make sure students are fully aware of the consequences of being absent—that part of their grade depends on their participation in groupwork projects. You can give an alternative assignment to those students who are absent for the majority of an activity.

Praise groups for solving difficult questions. If you observe that a group, after considerable trial and error, has solved a difficult problem, take a moment to specifically recognize their achievement. Nothing encourages students more than recognizing and praising true accomplishment.

Have groups present their work.

At the end of each Problem Solving Groupwork project, groups share their products. For a history class, this product might be a colonial brochure advertising the features of a particular English colony in America, a minidrama bringing to life a scene from medieval life in China, or a newscast about the effects of World War II on some segment of the American population. Here are some strategies to ensure that you enjoy high-quality presentations.

Set high expectations for presentations. Tell your students that you have heard (you heard it right here!) about other students who made a similar product or presentation that was truly outstanding. Give detailed descriptions of elaborate props, colorful artwork, quotes from key personalities, great costumes, and anything else you would like to see your students include in their presentation.

Arrange your classroom for dramatic, intimate presentations. Clear a stage area in front of the classroom and ask students to arrange their desks into a crescent shape around "the stage." Use the overhead projector to provide dramatic lighting. This theater-in-the-round focuses student attention on the presentations.

Have plenty of props on hand to enhance presentations. Think of ways students can use props—masks, posters, costumes, backdrops, physical objects—not only to make their presentations more dramatic, but also to put them more at ease. Consider keeping a box of props in your room for use at a moment's notice. You will marvel at how creative your students can be when presented with the simplest items—towels, sheets, hats, colorful cloth remnants, and old clothes. Let them have fun.

Have students record what they see and hear on a handout. To help students in the audience remember the salient points of each presentation, provide a handout on which to take notes. You might set up a matrix that allows students to record similar information about each presentation for later comparison. For example, as each group presents a minidrama on medieval life in Europe, the rest of the class takes notes on a matrix with four labeled columns: *What is the topic of this minidrama? What happened in the minidrama? What did it teach about feudal life? Compare the minidrama to life today.*

Debrief each presentation for deeper meaning and historical accuracy. After each presentation, ask the group some probing questions to reveal further historical information. This is also an appropriate time to point out any inaccuracies students introduced. For example, during a panel discussion on the Progressive period, one actor portrayed Teddy Roosevelt as a quiet, unassuming person. The teacher explained that while the actor's words reflected historic reality, his demeanor did not.

Lessening Performance Anxiety

Acknowledge that students may be feeling anxious about performing in front of their peers, and ask the rest of the students to be particularly attentive and supportive. As the first group assembles for their presentation, give a warm introduction and lead the class in a round of applause.

Encourage students to use simple props and costumes to enhance their presentation to the class.

Students work in groups of four and prepare a music video to interpret "The Heart of the Appaloosa," a song that describes the displacement of the Nez Percé by settlers.

As another example, during a minidrama on life in the Depression, students portrayed people waiting in a bread line as indignant and aggressive. The teacher pointed out that during the Depression, Americans instead felt great shame at taking government "handouts." Students are eager to know how accurately they portrayed history and appreciate your comments.

Prepare a list of critical thinking questions for a class discussion after the last presentation. After the final group presents, hold a class discussion that ties together everything students saw and heard. A few well-chosen questions will challenge your students to use critical thinking skills. Here, for example, are questions you might ask after groups have tried to "sell" to the world some ideology from the United States or the former Soviet Union (capitalism, socialism, freedom, equality, individualism, collectivism, democracy, or totalitarianism):

- What are the advantages and disadvantages of both systems?
- Which American value do you most cherish? Which Soviet value do you wish American society would adopt?
- What are the connections between Soviet values of equality, collectivism, socialism, and totalitarianism?
- What are the connections between the American values of freedom, individualism, capitalism, and democracy?
- What problems were created when these contrasting systems represented the ideologies of the two greatest superpowers?

Showcase students' products. When the product of groupwork is something you can post, conduct a gallery walk in your classroom, having students view the projects and read accompanying explanations. Display student work on bulletin boards, in trophy cases, or in the library. Consider inviting other classes to attend your group presentations. Or display photographs of student work on your school's Web site.

"Allowing my students to work in groups on projects changed my role in the classroom. No longer was I the sage on the stage; rather, I became the guide on the side. Everyone benefited."

— Middle School Teacher

These students represent John Locke and Louis XIV (and their press agents) in a panel discussion on the question, *Should people be trusted to govern themselves?* A follow-up class discussion will tie together what students have learned about various perspectives on the ideal form of government.

Considerate Text

Learning to read expository text is essential for academic success. You can support students by providing considerate text—reader-friendly text, structured with the audience in mind. Additional reading supports include brief prereading activities, focus questions that give a purpose for reading, and the use of graphic organizers for taking notes on the reading

Introduction

Many a social studies teacher is familiar with the chorus of moans and groans heard when students are asked to take out their textbooks. If we relegate social studies instruction to the mind-numbing task of reading a lifeless textbook, we risk dampening students' enthusiasm not only for social studies, but also for reading.

For students of every age, one enduring challenge is motivating them to *want* to read. The TCI Approach meets this challenge head-on by engaging students in "real-life experiences" in class—experiences that cultivate their interest in social studies, with the result that students eagerly turn to the textbook to learn more.

Additionally, the TCI Approach emphasizes the importance of using textbooks that adhere to the principles of "considerate text"—expository text that is structured to maximize comprehension by its target audience. Teachers know that learning to read expository text is a lifelong skill, critical for students' future success. With reader-friendly text, we can capture students' interest while developing a host of expository reading skills.

The TCI Approach recognizes that a successful reading of expository text involves four stages: (1) previewing the content, (2) reading, (3) taking notes, and (4) processing the content, or reviewing and applying what has been learned. And even if your textbook is not "considerate" of readers' needs, the TCI Approach helps you structure lessons and activities to support readers at each of these four stages.

What Is Considerate Text?

In recent years, conventional social studies textbooks have become increasingly longer, cluttered with gratuitous visuals and excessive sidebar content. At the same time, more and more secondary students struggle with reading skills. Clearly, it is time to recognize the importance of "considerate text," a phrase coined by reading researchers to describe textbook content that facilitates comprehension (Armbruster 1984).

Research identifies three characteristics of considerate text: clear structure, coherent writing, and audience awareness. These often overlapping features are recognizable in the following aspects of a TCI textbook:

A Clear Organizational Structure Chapters are organized in a straightforward yet elegant manner. Clear and comprehensive chapter introductions and summaries help students see the big picture during prereading and review activities. Headings and subheadings are signals that help the reader mentally outline the content.

Comprehensible Text A single-column format, clear prose, and visual aids make expository text easy to follow and understand. Content is grade-level appropriate. Main ideas are explicitly stated, and the follow-up text includes clear supporting details, in logical order, linked by familiar transition words.

"[Considerate text] enables the teacher to work with the textbook rather than around it."

— Kate Kinsella
Reading Specialist

Readers of all abilities can be successful when considerate text supports the powerful multiple-intelligence activities used for social studies instruction.

"Chunking" of Concepts Each new topic is presented in a single, focused section, and each section is usually presented on a single page or two facing pages. Research shows that "chunking" new information in this way makes it easier for students to identify the main concepts.

Manageable Chapter Length Each chapter is dedicated to the exploration of a few key social studies concepts and refrains from veering off course with unnecessary features. Consequently, chapters are relatively short, compared to traditional textbooks. This helps students stay focused on the main ideas.

Careful Vocabulary Development Vocabulary is grade-level appropriate, carefully geared to students' prior knowledge. Important new terms are identified with bold type and are defined immediately, either in the text or the margin. Such conscientious vocabulary support, supported by a comprehensive glossary, helps students learn new terms.

Clear, Helpful Images and Graphic Organizers Illustrations and photographs have a specific purpose: to lend deeper meaning to the text. When images are clear and large, and pages are uncluttered, readers are able to use their visual-literacy skills to preread each section. In addition, text is supported by "graphic organizers," or images that contain visual referents for the main concepts being presented. These graphic organizers help readers focus on key content and make connections.

How You Can Support Reading in Social Studies

Ask any group of middle and high school teachers how many of them have students who are below-level readers, and you will see an almost unanimous show of hands. Many students struggle with reading, and most social studies textbooks are difficult to read. While you may not consider yourself a reading teacher, it is essential to attend to this issue and develop classroom strategies to help students with their reading.

According to Dr. Kate Kinsella (2001), reading specialist at San Francisco State University, whose studies have informed the TCI Approach, "Learning to read in social studies should not be a 'sink or swim' challenge…. All students need specific coaching in a manageable repertoire of reading and thinking strategies for every subject area."

The good news is that you need not become a reading specialist to help students develop powerful skills for "reading to learn" in social studies. Your first step is to create an invigorating classroom experience that will draw reluctant readers into potentially daunting texts. Beyond that, many of the reading skills they need can be seamlessly woven into your social studies instruction. You can give students effective strategies for accessing and evaluating information, analyzing and categorizing data from the textbook, and constructing meaning from what they read.

"Developing readers in social studies need a balance of expository and narrative texts at their actual instructional level rather than their frustration level."

— Kate Kinsella
Reading Specialist

In your social studies classes, instruction needs to support students at each of the four stages of the expository reading process, as follows:

- **Previewing** Include in-class preview activities and meaningful prereading assignments that allow students to preview key concepts and that motivate them to read.
- **Reading** Give students well-written and engaging material at the appropriate instructional level, and offer graphic organizers that provide a focus for their reading.
- **Taking notes** Insist that students take notes on their reading and that they use graphic organizers to structure the content they are recording.
- **Processing** Wrap up every lesson with a powerful processing assignment that helps students review and apply what they have learned.

The TCI Approach helps you support students' reading at each stage through one of these parallel elements: Preview assignments, considerate text, graphically organized Reading Notes, and Processing assignments. Included in the following sections are a number of tools and models you can use to help students with these four stages of the expository reading process.

Use Short Prereading Activities to Build Schema

As you read in the section "Theory-Based Active Instruction" (page 10), the TCI Approach adheres to the principle that instruction should be a carefully structured, spiraled experience, in the tradition of Jerome Bruner. Students begin by discovering how key social studies concepts relate to their own lives. Ultimately, they then learn how those same concepts apply, in ever more complex ways, to the world around them. Preview activities are the starting point for this spiral curriculum and are essential for building the students' schema.

By *schema,* we mean the students' ability to activate relevant prior knowledge or personal experience as a foundation for understanding progressively more complex concepts (Keene and Zimmermann 1997). In *Teaching Reading in the Content Area: If Not Me, Then Who?* Rachel Billmeyer (1996) explains, "A schema provides a structure or guide for understanding. New information must be matched with existing schema so that it can be understood." Schemabuilding Preview assignments are an essential element of the TCI Approach. A broad sampling of good ideas for these can be found on pages 22–27. Following are some additional ways to prepare students for reading expository text.

Good news! You don't have to be a reading specialist to have successful readers in your class. Effective strategies and an invigorating classroom experience will engage and assist even reluctant readers.

Prereading Prereading is a relatively quick, preliminary scanning of expository text in preparation for a more thorough reading. Conducting a prereading helps readers in a number of ways:

- They become familiar with the overall content and organization of the material before they begin serious reading.
- They establish a clear purpose for reading and a sense of direction while they read.
- They determine the difficulty level, length, and importance of the material so that they can allot a realistic amount of time for reading.
- They remember more of what they read because of the built-in repetition of key points.

One tool that helps you train students in the prereading process is a handout that guides them through this process. The handout illustrated below was designed for prereading a TCI textbook, but it can be easily adapted for use with any other text.

Prereading Handout

1. What is the **title** of the chapter?

2. Read the **introduction**. List the two topics you are most excited to learn about in this chapter.

3. Sketch the **graphic organizer** in the space below.

4. List the **headings** for each section in the chapter.

5. Look at the **pictures** in the chapter. Select the one you find most interesting. Write one sentence that explains how you think the picture relates to the chapter.

6. Read the chapter **summary**. Write one sentence that explains what you think is the main idea of the chapter.

Anticipation Guides Another tool that can help build schema, the anticipation guide, requires a bit of teacher preparation. This is a prereading tool that also has value during the reading and the post-reading phase.

To create an anticipation guide, collect a series of statements about major concepts in the reading. The format is generally true-false, agree-disagree, or likely-unlikely. Students respond individually to each question both before and after the reading. This tool helps activate students' thoughts and opinions about content before reading, and then allows them to use the knowledge gained from reading to validate or reformulate their earlier predictions (Tierney, Readance, and Dishner 1995). Follow these steps to prepare an anticipation guide:

1. Identify major concepts and supporting details in the reading selection. Keep in mind what students probably already know or believe about that content.
2. Create short, clear declarative statements about the content, some true and some not. Five to eight statements are usually adequate.
3. Place the statements in a format that encourages anticipation and prediction.
4. Have students respond individually to each statement.
5. Lead a prereading discussion, taking a hand count to tally responses to the statements. Ask students to share justifications for their responses.
6. Help the class formulate a series of questions about points of uncertainty or disagreement. This list will help students read with a clearer purpose and greater motivation.
7. Return to the guide after students have read the assigned text. Ask whether the reading led students to change their minds about any of the statements.

Anticipation Guide for Chapter 15
Manifest Destiny and the Growing Nation

T or **F**   1. In the mid 1800s, many people in the United States believed they had the right and duty to expand across the North American continent.

T or **F**   2. President Thomas Jefferson's purchase of Louisiana was opposed by western farmers.

T or **F**   3. Florida was acquired by Secretary of State John Quincy Adams by trickery.

T or **F**   4. To deal with the dispute between the U.S. and Great Britain over Oregon Country, President James Polk agreed to continue "joint occupancy" of Oregon.

T or **F**   5. The annexation of Texas was opposed by many Americans because Spain still claimed Texas.

T or **F**   6. The War with Mexico began with a border dispute in Texas.

T or **F**   7. In the Treaty of Guadalupe Hidalgo that ended the Mexican War, Mexico ceded about half of its territory to the U.S.

T or **F**   8. The Gadsden Purchase of 1853 was made mainly to provide a good railroad route to California.

Prereading exercises allow students to anticipate what they will learn and prepare them to understand the assigned reading.

The KWL Strategy Another widely used reading strategy for approaching a new chapter, especially with upper elementary and middle school students, is the KWL graphic organizer (Ogle 1986). The three letters stand for the three responses students make before and after their reading: recalling what they *know* (K), determining what they *want* to learn (W), and identifying what they *learned* from reading (L). Again, the main purposes are to motivate readers and to allow them to elaborate on or amend their prior knowledge.

Here are the steps for employing the KWL strategy:

1. Set up a simple three-column chart on the board or overhead. Lead students in a brainstorming session of what they already know about the key content in the reading.
2. List what the students think they know in the first (K) column. Have students individually record in their own charts those items from the list they already know.
3. Elicit what information students anticipate they will learn from the reading selection. List these in the second (W) column. Have students list this information on their own charts for reference as they read.
4. Have students read the material, recording notes as they read.
5. Hold a follow-up class discussion, listing in the third (L) column what was learned from the reading, what questions were answered, and (in an optional fourth column) what new questions emerged.

K what we KNOW	**W** what we WANT to know	**L** what we LEARNED	**?** new questions we have

Guide Questions Guide questions are an easy way to help establish a purpose for reading expository text. To write them, you simply change the chapter title and each subsequent section heading into specific questions. Then, as students read, you have them look for answers to the guide questions.

Well-constructed guide questions help students focus their attention while reading, and they make the assignment easier to understand and finish. Guide questions that begin with *What, Why,* and *How* work especially well because they require a long, more detailed answer. *Who, Where,* and *When* questions are less useful because they can be answered with a simple fact or one-word answer.

With all expository text, establish a purpose for reading by giving students guide questions. Well-constructed questions help students focus their attention.

Guide Questions for Chapter 15
Manifest Destiny and the Growing Nation

1. Section 15.1 **Introduction**
   Guide question: *Was O'Sullivan right that expansion was a matter of destiny?*

2. Section 15.2 **The Louisiana Purchase**
   Guide question: *What impact did the acquisition of Louisiana have on the United States?*

3. Section 15.3 **Florida**
   Guide question: *How did the United States acquire Florida?*

4. Section 15.4 **Texas**
   Guide question: *Why did many Americans feel Texas was so valuable?*

5. Section 15.5 **Oregon Country**
   Guide question: *How was the United States able to acquire the Oregon Country?*

6. Section 15.6 **War with Mexico**
   Guide question: *Why did the United States go to war with Mexico?*

Use the Built-in Supports for Reading

Elements of the TCI Approach that are detailed elsewhere in this book enable you to support the reading process without veering from your instructional plan. These elements include multiple intelligence activities, graphically organized Reading Notes, and Processing assignments.

Multiple intelligence activities motivate students to read for understanding. The greatest strength of the TCI Approach is the activities that allow students to "experience" social studies concepts as they use their multiple intelligences during hands-on activities. When motivated, students dive into their reading with unusual gusto. They learn that the reading will help them understand the "real-life" experiences they are having in class. This gives all students—especially those with lesser linguistic skills—a genuine purpose for reading. And with purpose comes the motivation to read for deeper understanding. Use of a considerate text complements this process.

As students complete Reading Notes, they construct meaning from text. Even motivated, purposeful readers need strategies to help them comprehend and remember what they have read. In the words of a teacher and consultant on literacy and reading in middle and upper grades, "All readers, those who struggle and those who don't, need to be taught strategies that proficient readers naturally use to construct meaning from text" (Harvey 1998).

Mutiple intelligence activities are great motivators for reading. These students are using a floor map that represents territorial acquisitions by the United States in the first half of the 19th century. Afterward, they will be eager to read about how Americans justified their westward expansion.

Use a Processing assignment that challenges students to apply what they have learned through their reading. Such an assignment is more fun and more effective than answering end-of-chapter questions.

The TCI Approach helps students construct meaning from the text they read in each chapter by challenging them to complete innovative Reading Notes. As they read, they use graphic organizers—flowcharts, Venn diagrams, visual metaphors, spoke diagrams, sensory figures, matrices—to record key social studies concepts. In the process, they answer important questions, identify main ideas, make connections to prior learning, and synthesize new information. Ultimately, the completed Reading Notes serve as a visual referent that helps jog students' memories when they want to recall key social studies concepts.

Processing assignments challenge students to actively demonstrate their understanding of what they read. The final support for reading comprehension is having students demonstrate what they have learned. You won't need end-of-chapter questions because, as many reading specialists will attest, such questions seldom help either the teacher or the student effectively assess what was learned. Instead, the TCI Approach asks that you challenge students to use their multiple intelligences to process and apply what they have learned while creating a personal product that reflects the depth of their understanding. The section "Processing Assignment" (p. 102) contains many examples of such products.

Graphically Organized Reading Notes _____

Recording key ideas in graphically organized notes will help students remember content long after the lesson is over. Graphic organizers help students create a lasting "mental snapshot" of the most important information.

Introduction

One of the most powerful ways to improve students' comprehension and retention in any subject area is to have them complete innovative, graphically organized notes on the reading they do for each lesson. Unlike traditional, outline-style notes, graphically organized notes inspire students to think carefully about what they have read as they record main ideas in a form that engages both their visual and linguistic intelligences. Graphic organizers help students see the underlying logic and interconnections among concepts. When students record information in engaging, visual ways, they are better able to recall key social studies concepts months—even years—later. Graphically organized Reading Notes, like Preview assignments, are recorded in the Interactive Student Notebook (further discussed in "Using the Interactive Student Notebook," page 162).

Illustrated in this section are some of the inventive graphic organizers that have been suggested for lessons following the TCI Approach. Each will help students record notes on their reading in a meaningful and memorable way.

Venn Diagrams Students can use a Venn diagram as a graphic organizer to compare and contrast key figures, groups, concepts, or places.

Example

In a lesson about the Constitution, students play a game in which they learn how one branch of government can check the power of the other. In a Venn diagram in their Reading Notes, they capture key features of a system in which the national and state governments share power.

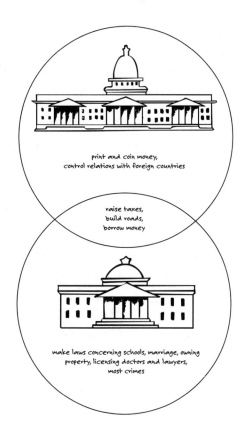

print and coin money, control relations with foreign countries

raise taxes, build roads, borrow money

make laws concerning schools, marriage, owning property, licensing doctors and lawyers, most crimes

Spoke Diagrams As a visual alternative to outlining, spoke diagrams or webs are a powerful way for students to organize related pieces of information.

Example

In a lesson on Africa, students are introduced to the major features of Kilwa, the Kongo Kingdom, and the Zimbabwe state. As they view, analyze, and discuss visual images as a class, each student creates an illustrated spoke diagram to record the class findings.

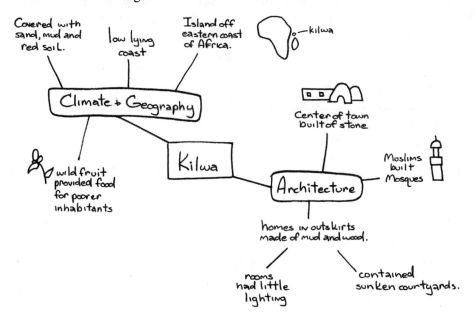

Covered with sand, mud and red soil.

low lying coast

Island off eastern coast of Africa.

kilwa

Climate & Geography

wild fruit provided food for poorer inhabitants

Kilwa

Center of town built of stone

Architecture

Moslims built Mosques

homes in outskirts made of mud and wood.

rooms had little lighting

contained sunken courtyards.

Illustrated Outlines Students can use a more traditional outline form but add simple drawings and symbols to graphically highlight and organize their notes.

Example

In a lesson on the first people who settled North America, students discover the relationship between Native Americans and the land. Simple sketches for each main topic help students create meaningful notes.

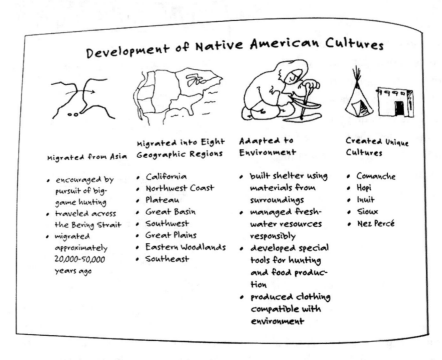

Development of Native American Cultures

Migrated from Asia
- encouraged by pursuit of big-game hunting
- traveled across the Bering Strait
- migrated approximately 20,000-50,000 years ago

Migrated into Eight Geographic Regions
- California
- Northwest Coast
- Plateau
- Great Basin
- Southwest
- Great Plains
- Eastern Woodlands
- Southeast

Adapted to Environment
- built shelter using materials from surroundings
- managed fresh-water resources responsibly
- developed special tools for hunting and food production
- produced clothing compatible with environment

Created Unique Cultures
- Comanche
- Hopi
- Inuit
- Sioux
- Nez Percé

Matrices Setting up a matrix is a good way for students to organize large bodies of information in their notes.

Example

For a lesson about important and controversial issues facing the United States during the Progressive Era, students participate in a panel debate in which several historical figures discuss the question, *Is something wrong with America?* Students record their findings in an illustrated matrix.

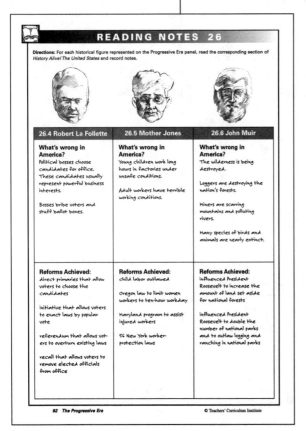

READING NOTES 26

Directions: For each historical figure represented on the Progressive Era panel, read the corresponding section of *History Alive! The United States* and record notes.

26.4 Robert La Follette	26.5 Mother Jones	26.6 John Muir
What's wrong in America? Political bosses choose candidates for office. These candidates usually represent powerful business interests. Bosses bribe voters and stuff ballot boxes.	**What's wrong in America?** Young children work long hours in factories under unsafe conditions. Adult workers have terrible working conditions.	**What's wrong in America?** The wilderness is being destroyed. Loggers are destroying the nation's forests. Miners are scarring mountains and polluting rivers. Many species of birds and animals are nearly extinct.
Reforms Achieved: direct primaries that allow voters to choose the candidates initiative that allows voters to enact laws by popular vote referendum that allows voters to overturn existing laws recall that allows voters to remove elected officials from office	**Reforms Achieved:** child labor outlawed Oregon law to limit women workers to ten-hour workday Maryland program to assist injured workers 56 New York worker-protection laws	**Reforms Achieved:** influenced President Roosevelt to increase the amount of land set aside for national forests influenced President Roosevelt to double the number of national parks and to outlaw logging and ranching in national parks

Annotated Images Simple sketches of powerful images, which students annotate with information they have read in their textbook, can help them understand difficult content.

Example
In a lesson about reform movements of the mid-19th century and the role of women in those movements, students annotate images of reformers carrying protest signs to record facts and ideas they have gleaned from their reading.

Illustrated Timelines A timeline is an important organizing tool that helps students to sequence a series of events in chronological order. Adding illustrations makes the sequence more memorable.

Example
As students review the major steps in the evolution of democracy, they create a timeline with a symbol, illustration, or picture for each of the steps.

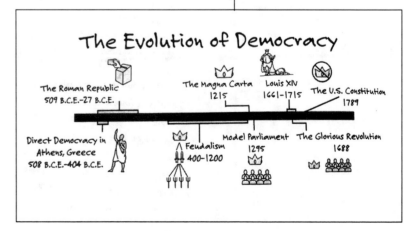

Mind Maps To better understand the beliefs of important figures, students can fill in outlined heads with quotations and paraphrased thoughts that represent the person they are learning about.

Example
Students read about and discuss critical thinking questions related to the ideas of Thomas Jefferson and George Washington. They draw and label a simple outline of the heads of Jefferson and Washington and record important quotations and paraphrased beliefs for each figure inside the appropriate outline.

- Our country is too large to have all affairs directed by a single government.
- The small landowners are the most precious part of the state.
- ...powers not delegated to the United States...are reserved to the states, or to the people....
- I am not among those who fear the people.

Jefferson

T-Charts Students can use T-charts to compare classroom experiences with key social studies concepts or events, to contrast advantages and disadvantages of a topic, or to compare and contrast two different ideas.

Example
Students participate in an activity to simulate the struggle to maintain unity in the Mauryan Empire and then read about that period in history. Completing a T-chart helps them connect specific experiences from the activity with historical details from the period.

In-class Experience	History of India 184 B.C.E. to 320 C.E.
• Blue, Green, Orange, and Red groups earned tokens by crossing chairs blindfolded	• Regional kingdoms produced goods that could be traded for profit
• Purple group earned tokens by assisting other groups across chairs	• Mauryan leaders collected taxes from regional kingdoms in exchange for protection
• Purple group assisted all groups across chairs in round 1 of the activity	• Early Mauryan leadership effectively governed regional kingdoms
• Purple group earned lots of tokens in round 1 of the activity	• Mauryan leaders profited from their control of regional kingdoms
• Some groups earned more tokens by crossing chairs without assistance	• Kingdoms that traded independently with foreign nations became wealthy
• Some groups chose to cross the chairs without assistance from the Purple group	• Regional kingdoms eventually broke away from the Mauryan Empire

Sensory Figures Students can annotate simple drawings of prominent figures to show the thoughts, feelings, and experiences identified with certain content or concepts.

Example

In a lesson about Egypt's rival, Kush, students analyze images depicting important events and leaders from four periods. As they read about each period, they complete a sensory figure of a Kush leader to show what he might have seen, heard, touched, or felt at the time.

"The Reading Notes are very useful. They help me organize my thoughts, which is usually very difficult for me."

— Middle School Student

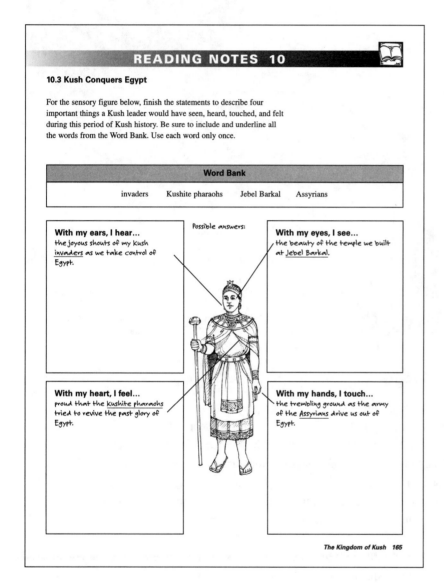

READING NOTES 10

10.3 Kush Conquers Egypt

For the sensory figure below, finish the statements to describe four important things a Kush leader would have seen, heard, touched, and felt during this period of Kush history. Be sure to include and underline all the words from the Word Bank. Use each word only once.

Word Bank
invaders   Kushite pharaohs   Jebel Barkal   Assyrians

Possible answers:

With my ears, I hear...
the joyous shouts of my kush <u>invaders</u> as we take control of Egypt.

With my eyes, I see...
the beauty of the temple we built at <u>Jebel Barkal</u>.

With my heart, I feel...
proud that the <u>kushite pharaohs</u> tried to revive the past glory of Egypt.

With my hands, I touch...
the trembling ground as the army of the <u>Assyrians</u> drive us out of Egypt.

The Kingdom of Kush **165**

Processing Assignment

Processing assignments challenge students to show their understanding of new ideas in a variety of creative ways. For example, the photo above shows how a student represented her understanding of the five main beliefs of Hinduism by creating a mandala. Students say assignments like these make the most important information "stick" in their memory

Introduction

Processing assignments are lesson wrap-up activities that challenge students to synthesize and apply the information they have learned. Simply recording notes on a lesson does not mean students have learned information. They must actively do something with the information if they are to internalize it. In the TCI Approach, Processing assignments take students beyond low-level regurgitation of facts and details, instead challenging them to complete tasks that incorporate multiple intelligences and higher-order thinking skills.

There are many different and engaging ways to help students process new ideas. They might transform written concepts into an illustration or flow chart, summarize the main point of a political cartoon, or organize historical events into a topical net. They might state their position on a controversial issue, wonder about hypothetical "what if" situations, and pose questions about new ideas presented in the lesson. For each Processing assignment, the intent is to have students *actively apply* what they learned in a lesson so that you—and they—can assess their understanding. Processing assignments, like Preview assignments and graphically organized Reading Notes, are recorded in the Interactive Student Notebook (further discussed in "Using the Interactive Student Notebook," page 162).

Examples of Processing Assignments

Following are a wide variety of types of Processing assignments, with representative examples linked to specific content. You will notice that some of the formats are similar to those suggested for graphic organizers in Reading Notes (as discussed on pages 96–101). Others replicate the form of writing assignments that are described for Writing for Understanding (pages 56–65), although Processing assignments are typically less complex than the pieces that students do in Writing for Understanding lessons.

Advertisements Students can design advertisements that represent migration, settlement, or the significance of a specific site.

Examples

- Create a classified advertisement that would appeal to 19th century immigrants looking for job opportunities in the United States. Include a title written in bold letters and at least three job listings. For each job listing, include a catchy heading, a two-sentence description of the job, and an appropriate visual.
- Create a page from a travel book that travelers might use to find information about unfamiliar customs of India. The page should contain a title, brief descriptions of three customs, colorful visuals, and other creative touches.
- Design a real estate advertisement that would encourage people to move to Constantinople in the sixth century.

Address Multiple Intelligences

Processing assignments can tap into visual-spatial intelligence by including graphs, maps, illustrations, pictowords, and visual metaphors; musical intelligence by asking students to compose a song or react to a piece of music in writing; intrapersonal intelligence by allowing students to reflect on how concepts and events affect them; interpersonal strengths by serving as a place to record group discussions and project notes; and logical-mathematical intelligence through the use of sequences, graphs, and charts.

FANTASTIC JOB OPPORTUNITIES FOR IMMIGRANTS

No skill necessary! We will train you.

Steel mill ower needs hundreds of workers for all shifts. Carnegie steel is willing to provide lodging in company town for those willing to operate Bessemer furnaces.

Come to Constantinople!

"I'm not just a citizen of Constantinople – I'm also the emperor!" – Constantine

Only Constantinople has:
- 13 miles of walls for protection!
- water on 3 sides of the city!
- control of the Bos Porus Straight!
- stable sucessions of emperors!
- control of the eastern Roman empire!

LOCATION
LOCATION
LOCATION

Custom of India

Pilgrimages: If you are traveling near rivers, especially the Ganga River, you might notice people bathing in the water. These are pilgrims, people who have journeyed to a holy place. Hindus make pilgrimages to experience God and to make up for their sins.

Annotated Illustrations Students could make annotated illustrations to recount a story of travel or migration, to represent a moment in time, or to label architectural features.

Examples
- Create a simple illustration of an Inca village. Below your illustration, write a description of a day in the life of a commoner from sunup to sundown.
- Draw a mosque and label its parts.
- Make an annotated illustration of an immigrant's journey from Europe to settlement in the United States.

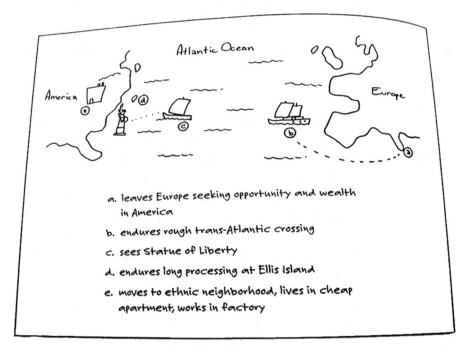

a. leaves Europe seeking opportunity and wealth in America

b. endures rough trans-Atlantic crossing

c. sees Statue of Liberty

d. endures long processing at Ellis Island

e. moves to ethnic neighborhood, lives in cheap apartment, works in factory

Book or Compact Disk Covers Students might design covers for books or compact disks to highlight and illustrate important concepts.

Examples
- Create a compact disc cover for the song "La Discriminación." The cover should include a title and visuals that illustrate important themes and issues in the song.
- Using both words and graphics, create a cover for an issue of *National Geographic* that highlights archaeological discoveries made at Mohenjo-Daro. The cover must include an imaginative subtitle, visuals of three artifacts, and brief captions that explain what each artifact reveals about daily life in Mohenjo-Daro.
- Design a cover for *Common Sense.* Include on the front cover a two-sentence summary of the life and experiences of Thomas Paine, a quotation from *Common Sense* with a one-sentence explanation of what the quotation means, and three comments from other revolutionary leaders.

Caricatures Students could draw a caricature to represent the main characteristics of a group, or to convey how an individual or group is or was perceived by another group.

Examples

- Draw a caricature of a European immigrant at the turn of the century. Label the immigrant's clothes, possessions, and body parts to show what a typical immigrant might have felt or been prepared for upon arrival in America.
- Draw a caricature of Christian armies during the Crusades from a Muslim perspective.
- Draw a caricature of Alexander Hamilton. Label aspects of the caricature to show his views on these topics: the nature of human beings, best type of government, political parties, ideal economy, and the Constitution.

Commemorative Markers Students can design and create plaques or markers to commemorate and summarize the significance of important places and events.

Examples

- Create a historical marker for the Alamo. The marker should include a drawing of the Alamo, a succinct summary of the events that transpired there in 1836, and a brief explanation of the Alamo's significance in the history of the Southwest.
- Create a historical marker to commemorate the birthplace of Siddhartha Gautama, the Buddha. The marker should include a picture of Siddhartha from some stage in his life, a brief summary of his life, and an explanation of the importance of his life in the history of Asia.

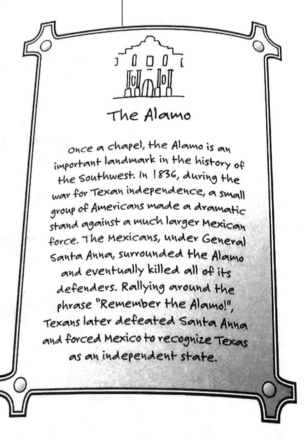

Eulogies Students can write eulogies to extol the virtues of prominent historical figures or civilizations.

Examples
- Write a eulogy for the Roman Empire that summarizes the accomplishments of the empire and describes how those accomplishments—in law, architecture, art, and government—are seen in the world today.
- Write a eulogy for Susan B. Anthony, including an appropriate inscription for her tombstone.
- Write a eulogy for the Ottoman Empire that contains the following words: *millet system, Muslim, sultan, diversity, peace.*

The Glory of the Ottoman Empire Is Not Forgotten

Oh Sultan, what diversity your majesty governed!
Muslim, Christian, Jew,
So many languages, so many cultures,
All working in harmony because of your brilliant
millet system.
Each faith governed by a leader
overseen by you,
practicing ancient cultures in peace.
Who but the mighty Ottomans could have devised
such a plan of tolerance and cooperation?
The glory of Allah
and the magnificence of the
Mediterranean World
were showcased in cosmopolitan Constantinople,
Your brilliant capital and crossroads of the world.
But the West could not be sated simply by trade;
The sweet wealth of Ottoman lands
was too tempting.
Arabia's oils, Turkey's ports, the fruits of Palestine
and the wheat of the Nile were too much.
They came, the French and the British
and the Russians,
but they did not understand your
legacy of tolerance.
They sowed division, separation,
and the Ottoman Empire shrunk.

Facial Expressions By drawing heads with pertinent facial expressions and related thought bubbles, students can summarize the feelings of groups who have different perspectives on a single topic.

Examples
- Draw heads and show the facial expressions of the negotiators from each country represented at the Paris Peace Conference at the end of World War I. Make thought bubbles revealing each leader's goals for the peace treaty.
- Draw heads and show facial expressions to represent the feelings that hawks, doves, military leaders, and war protesters had about the Vietnam War in 1969. Make thought bubbles above the heads to show what each group might be thinking.
- Draw heads and show facial expressions to represent the feelings of the Mongols, the Chinese government, and the Chinese peasants after the Mongol invasion. Make thought bubbles above the heads to show what each group might be thinking.

"Processing new content draws kids into social studies because these assignments are crafted with special attention to all intelligences."
— High School Teacher

Flow Charts Students can draw flow charts to represent causal relationships or to show steps in a sequence.

Examples
- Create a flow chart with simple drawings showing how the textile industry grew.
- Create a flow chart that shows the cause of the Russian Revolution.
- Create a flow chart that chronicles how the Cold War intensified from 1945 to 1949.

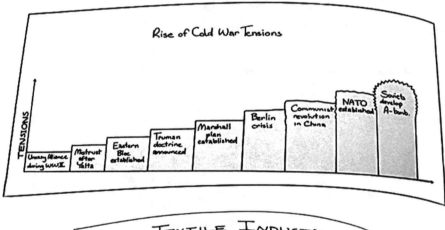

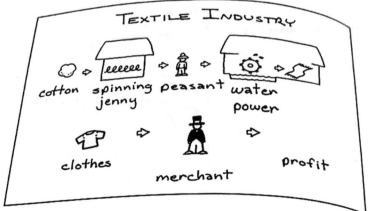

Forms of Poetry Students might write a poem, perhaps in a specified style or format, to describe a person, place, event, or the feeling of a moment.

Examples
- Using the word *depression,* write an acrostic that describes the impact of the Great Depression.
- Write a biographical poem on Buddha that follows this format:
  Line 1: First and last name
  Line 2: Four adjectives describing the Buddha
  Line 3: Relative (son, daughter, husband, wife) of…
  Line 4: Resident of (city, and/or country)…
  Line 5: Who lived from (year to year)
  Line 6: Who searched for…
  Line 7: Who taught…
  Line 8: Who is remembered for…
  Line 9: First and last name

The Buddha
Siddhartha Gautama
Pious, experienced, wise, holy
Son of King Suddhodana and Queen Maya
Resident of India near the Himalayas
Who lived during the fifth century B.C.E.
Who searched for enlightenment
Who taught moderation through the Eightfold Path
Who is remembered for developing a belief system
still important today
Final name of Buddha means Enlightened One

D evastating
E conomic collapse
P overty strikes
R eality grim
E verywhere
S avings lost
S adness grows
I nsecurity mounts
O minous
N owhere to turn.

Illustrated Dictionary Entries Students can explain key terms in a lesson by making their own illustrated dictionary entries. They define the term in their own words, provide a synonym and an antonym, and draw an illustration that represents the term.

Examples
- Create an illustrated dictionary entry for the term *samsara* (enlightenment).
- Create an illustrated dictionary entry for the term *monopoly*.

Illustrated Proverbs Students can choose a familiar proverb that helps explain complex concepts, and then illustrate the proverb to show how it pertains to the situation they are studying.

Example
- Complete this statement: "The Loyalist arguments against colonial independence are best represented by this proverb...." Choose one of the following proverbs or another one familiar to you:

Don't bite the hand that feeds you.
Children should respect their elders.
Don't cut off your nose to spite your face.

Below the proverb, make a simple drawing of the proverb and label the historical comparisons.

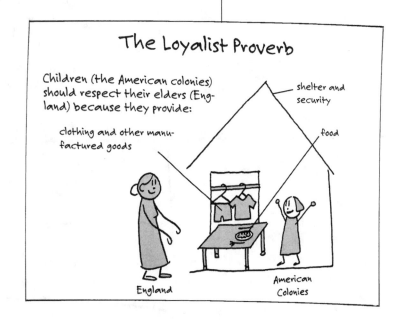

Invitations Students can design invitations that highlight the main goals and salient facts of important events.

Examples

- Design an invitation that might be sent to prospective participants in a conference held to debate how the resources of the Brazilian rainforest should be used. The invitation should include information about when the convention will begin and end, who will be participating, where it will be held, and what will be accomplished. Invitations should include a bold title, an eye-catching visual, and other creative touches common in formal invitations.

- Design an invitation that might be sent to prospective delegates to the Constitutional Convention. The invitation should include information about when the convention will begin and end, where it will take place, who has been invited, and what will be accomplished at the meeting. Invitations must include a bold title, a catchy statement to entice delegates to attend, and other creative touches common in formal invitations.

A Convention to Revise the Articles of Confederation

You are cordially invited to participate in the most important political meeting since the signing of the Declaration of Independence

Beginning May 14, 1787, and lasting until the completion of our work

Pennsylvania State House, Philadelphia, Pennsylvania

Attendees will include George Washington and Benjamin Franklin

It is our express purpose to revise the Articles of Confederation so that our government is better able to maintain order and promote prosperity

Journals Assuming the role of a key figure, students write journal entries that recount that person's feelings and experiences, using the language of the era.

Examples
- Pretend you are a Confederate soldier at the beginning of the Civil War who has relatives living in the North. Explain why you are fighting for the Confederacy and what you will do if you encounter a relative on the battlefield.
- Pretend you are an Arab traveler on the Silk Road to China. Write a log that describes the highlights of your trip.
- Pretend you are a peasant, an aristocrat, or a member of the clergy during the radical stage of the French Revolution. Keep a journal of how the events of this stage affect you.

Metaphorical Representations Students might illustrate analogies that metaphorically explain difficult or abstract concepts.

Examples
- Complete this statement: "The scramble for African territory among European powers was like…." Use one of the following analogies or one of your own: *prospectors racing to stake a claim in the gold country; concertgoers clamoring for the best seats; sharks in a feeding frenzy.* Make a simple drawing of your analogy and label the historical comparisons.
- Complete this statement: "The three branches of government under the Constitution are like…." Use one of the following analogies or one of your own: *a three-ring circus, a football team, a musical band, a three-part machine.* Make a simple drawing of your analogy and label the historical comparisons.
- Complete this statement: "The many changes in communist policies in China were like…." Use one of the following analogies or one of your own: *shifting winds, a seesaw, a tennis game.* Make a simple drawing of the analogy and label the historical comparisons.

"When I have to write as somebody living in another place and time, it really helps me figure out what people were dealing with back then."
— High School Student

Mosaics Students might create mosaics to synthesize information from a broad content area. Within the overall design, they can combine visuals and words on individual "tiles" to represent similarities, differences, and important concepts.

Examples
- Create a mosaic on Latin American demography. The mosaic should include an appropriate title, at least five colors, "tiles" whose sizes and shapes match the importance of the various topics, key words or phrases and a symbol on each tile, and graphics that show imagination and creativity.
- Create a mosaic to summarize key details on how Native Americans adapted to their environment. The mosaic should include an appropriate title, at least five colors, "tiles" containing visuals of various environmental adaptations, key words or phrases that describe each visual, and graphics that show imagination and creativity.

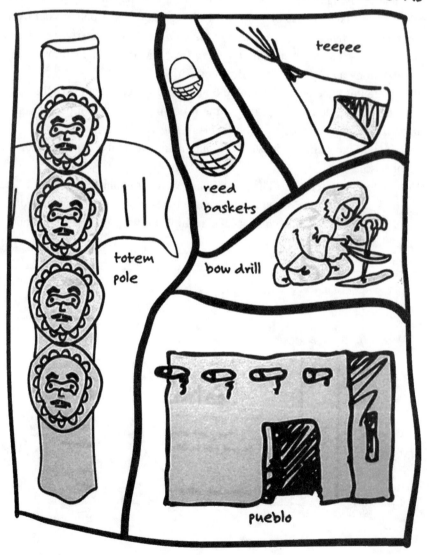

Mosaic of Adaptations Made by Native Americans

Perspective Pieces Students can make drawings or write newspaper articles to represent different perspectives on controversial figures, events, and concepts.

Examples

- Create a Janus figure—a drawing based on the Roman god portrayed with two opposite faces—to represent the English and French perspectives on Joan of Arc. Label each part of the figure and explain its symbolism.
- Design a commemorative plaque for Hernán Cortés from the Spanish perspective. Then, design a Wanted poster for him from the Aztec perspective.
- Write two newspaper articles summarizing the bombardment of Fort Sumter. The first article should represent the perspective of a Union journalist, and the second should represent the opposing Confederate viewpoint.
- Draw a simple representation of a pioneer and a Native American and list their different perspectives on the advantages and disadvantages of westward expansion by white settlers.

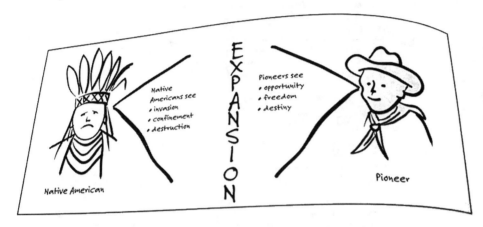

Pictowords To help define difficult concepts and themes, students can create pictowords, or symbolic representations of words or phrases that show their meaning.

Examples

- Create a pictoword for *imperialism.*
- Create a pictoword for *escalation.*
- Create a pictoword for *appeasement.*
- Create a pictoword for *fascism.*

Political Cartoons and Comic Strips Students might create political cartoons and comic strips that provide social or political commentary on important events.

Examples

- Create a political cartoon that comments on the relationship between the North and the South on the eve of the Civil War. As symbols for the North and South, you may use siblings, a wife and husband, neighbors, or images of your own.
- Create a comic strip that depicts the steps involved in the silent trading of gold and salt in 10th-century West Africa. Captions or voice bubbles for the comic strip should contain these terms: *North African, Wangaran, Soninke, gold, salt, Sahara Desert, Niger River, Ghana.*

Postcards After studying specific content, students could design and write messages on postcards to summarize information about places or events.

Examples

- Assume the role of a colonist who has settled in one of the thirteen colonies in the early 18th century. Write a postcard to a friend in Europe describing the colony in which you have settled. Describe the key features of the colony and the colonists' reasons for settling there. Create an image for the reverse side of the postcard that includes drawings, maps, or other visuals that highlight interesting aspects of the colony.
- After taking a "bus tour" that explores four aspects of life in Mexico City—its history, culture, neighborhoods, and environment—students can design and write a postcard summarizing what they learned.

Posters Students can draw posters to emphasize key points about political ideas, a key figure's point of view, or the reason behind important events.

Examples

- Create a campaign poster that might have been used in the election of 1828. The poster should list Andrew Jackson's qualifications for the presidency, include a memorable campaign slogan, and employ colorful visuals. At the bottom of the poster, include graffiti that opponents of Jackson might have scrawled on such a poster.
- Have students design a Wanted poster for King John. The poster should list grievances the English have against John and the benefit of forcing him to sign the Magna Carta.

Report Cards Graded evaluations are a way for students to assess the policies of leaders or governments.

Examples

- Evaluate the Allies' response during World War II. Give a letter grade (A+, A, A−, B+, and so on) and a corresponding written explanation on each of these topics: policy toward Germany before 1939, effectiveness of military actions, response to the Holocaust, and concern for enemy civilians given wartime conditions.
- Evaluate Hatshepsut's performance as a pharaoh. Give a letter grade (A+, A, A−, B+, and so on) and a corresponding written explanation on each of these topics: expanding the empire, fostering trade with other peoples, and balancing the power among different groups in Egypt.

Sensory Figures Students make a simple drawing of a prominent figure and label it with descriptions of what that person might be seeing, hearing, saying, feeling, or doing—to convey significant thoughts, feelings, and experiences.

Examples
- Create a sensory figure for Mansa Musa's pilgrimage to Makkah.
- Create a sensory figure for Lady Murasaki Shikibu that represents daily life in Japan's Imperial Court during the 11th century.
- Create sensory figures for Malcolm X and Martin Luther King Jr. that show how their different backgrounds and experiences shaped their respective philosophies.
- Create a sensory figure for Elizabeth Cady Stanton after the Seneca Falls Convention.

I have heard rumors that some of the people living in the countryside are envious of our comfortable lifestyle here at Heian.

I am careful never to laugh with my mouth open because it is considered quite rude.

I saw two courtiers using black and white tiles to play Go, a chinese board game.

Since we nobles often make our own perfume, it is possible for me to identify my friends by their fragrance alone.

It warmed my heart to learn that one of my closest friends is engaged to a member of the royal family.

I love the feel of my beautiful silk robes.

My feet long to venture beyond the halls of the court at Heian someday.

Spectrums By placing information along a spectrum, students can show their understanding of multiple perspectives on a topic or express an opinion about an issue.

Examples
- Draw a spectrum ranging from *Favors Capitalism* to *Favors Socialism*. Place along this spectrum the major political and industrial figures from 1890 to 1940 that we have studied: Eugene Debs, Henry Ford, Emma Goldman, Herbert Hoover, John L. Lewis, Huey Long, John D. Rockefeller, Franklin Roosevelt, Teddy Roosevelt, and Booker T. Washington. Then write a one-sentence response to support your opinions.

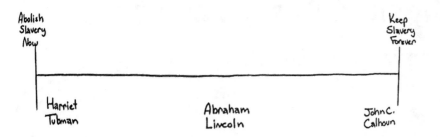

- Draw a spectrum ranging from *Abolish Slavery Now* to *Keep Slavery Forever.* Use information from the class discussion and your textbook to place John C. Calhoun, Abraham Lincoln, and Harriet Tubman on the spectrum. Then write a one-sentence justification for your placement of each figure.

- Draw a spectrum ranging from *Praiseworthy Motive* to *Condemnable Motive.* Place along this spectrum each of the five motives for European imperialism: economic, political, religious, ideological, and exploratory. Then write a one-sentence justification for your placement of each motive.

Multiple Intelligence Assessments

Challenge students to tap more than just their linguistic intelligence in your assessments. Here a teacher explains an assessment task in which students will be asked to analyze political cartoons.

Introduction

An effective assessment process in social studies emphasizes activities in which students use their various intelligences to both demonstrate and further their understanding of key concepts in authentic ways. Because learning is reinforced through such assessment, students reach a deeper and longer-term understanding of new material. They also perform better on standardized tests because the assessment focus is on cultivating richer understanding of key information and concepts, not on test preparation in and of itself. The TCI Approach supports the belief that effective assessment

- **measures what matters most.** Evaluative activities and tests should focus on key concepts and higher-level thinking, not on what is easiest to assess.
- **taps into multiple intelligences.** An array of assessments allows all students the opportunity to show what they know.
- **involves activities that are indistinguishable from good learning activities.** Assessment activities should be both educational and engaging, involving challenging, real-life problems and tasks.
- **fosters the habit of self-reflection.** Assessment activities should encourage students to evaluate their own work and to reflect on their own progress.
- **prepares students for standardized tests.** Assessment should include some questions and tasks similar to those students will encounter on standardized tests.

Assessing Students' Performance During Daily Activities

Effective assessment begins with the assessment of day-to-day activities, which benefits both teachers and students. Regular on-going assessment provides timely feedback on the effectiveness of your instruction. If you can identify what is working for students and what is not, you can adjust your instructional plans accordingly. For students, you are sending the message that every activity is important—not just busywork—and therefore worth assessing. This regular feedback encourages students to apply high standards to all of their work. It also helps students identify their strengths and weaknesses in a safe, low-stakes setting, and encourages them to reflect on ways to improve their future efforts.

You can build assessment into almost any activity in two ways. First, when you begin an activity, take time to make your expectations for students clear and explicit. You can do this orally or in writing—or, when possible, by providing models of finished products. Second, at the end of an activity, allow time for students to reflect on how well they met your expectations, either by asking them to do a self-assessment of their work or by conducting a debriefing with the entire class.

Following are suggestions for assessing four of the specific activity types in the TCI Approach: Visual Discovery, Social Studies Skill Builders, Experiential Exercises, and Response Groups. Ways to assess activities based on Problem Solving Groupwork and Writing for Understanding will be addressed later in this section.

Visual Discovery You can assess students' visual-literacy skills and understanding of key concepts presented in a Visual Discovery activity based on
- their answers to your questions during the visual analysis.
- their participation in act-it-outs that bring the images to life.
- the thoroughness of their notes in the Interactive Student Notebook.

"Standard pencil-and-paper short-answer tests sample only a small portion of intellectual abilities.... The means of assessment we favor should ultimately search for genuine problem-solving or product-fashioning skills in individuals across a range of materials."

— Howard Gardner

Giving students regular feedback makes the assessment process a natural part of the classroom experience.

Part of your assessment for Social Studies Skill Builders might focus on each student's ability to work effectively with a partner.

Social Studies Skill Builders As pairs present their work to you for feedback during Social Studies Skill Builders, you can assess
- the quality and accuracy of their written answers.
- each student's ability to work effectively and cooperatively with a partner.
- how well the pair manages their time and stays on task.

Experiential Exercises After you have debriefed Experiential Exercises, you may want to assess your students on
- how well they met your behavior standards and learning expectations.
- their responses to questions during the debriefing.
- follow-up activities in which they connect what they learned in the activity to broader social studies concepts.

Response Groups During Response Group activities, you may want to assess your students on
- participation in group discussions.
- the presenter's ability to clearly express the group's ideas.
- the quality of their written responses.

How to Assess Groupwork Equitably

Assessing groupwork raises many questions: Should group evaluations be determined by the quality of the final product or the process used to create it? Should each student in a group receive the same grade? How do you create individual accountability within a group? What do you do about the student who does very little but whose group does excellent work, or the outstanding student whose group does mediocre work? How do you keep track of the goings-on in all groups so that you can evaluate the groups fairly? What role, if any, should students have in the evaluation process?

Following are five steps for evaluating groupwork activities that address these questions. They give students a clear understanding of how they will be assessed, enable you to hold both individuals and groups accountable, and make the grading process equitable. One tool for group assessment, the Brag Sheet, is shown opposite.

1. **Set clear criteria for evaluation.** Tell students they will be assessed not only on the quality of the final product, but also on how effectively they work as a team. This underscores the value of using cooperative skills.

2. **Make both individuals and groups accountable.** Weigh half of a student's grade on individual contribution and half on the group's performance. Every member gets the same group grade; individual grades differ. In this way, students who do outstanding work in a weak group will be rewarded for their efforts, and students who do little but benefit from being in a productive group will not receive a high overall grade. Importantly, students find this system fair and equitable.

Groupwork Brag Sheet

Name: _____ My role in the group was: _____

Please list all the ways you helped your group complete this task.

Please list all the ways you helped your group work effectively and cooperatively.

Using this scale, evaluate yourself and the members of your group on the criteria listed.

1 (*never*) **2** (*rarely*) **3** (*sometimes*) **4** (*usually*) **5** (*always*)

Name _____ _____ Was your work of high quality?
Comments _____ Was your work completed on time?
 _____ Did you contribute ideas during group discussions?
 _____ Did you offer assistance to other group members?
 _____ Did you maintain a positive attitude during groupwork?
 _____ **Total**

Name _____ _____ Was their work of high quality?
Comments _____ Was their work completed on time?
 _____ Did they contribute ideas during group discussions?
 _____ Did they offer assistance to other group members?
 _____ Did they maintain a positive attitude during groupwork?
 _____ **Total**

Name _____ _____ Was their work of high quality?
Comments _____ Was their work completed on time?
 _____ Did they contribute ideas during group discussions?
 _____ Did they offer assistance to other group members?
 _____ Did they maintain a positive attitude during groupwork?
 _____ **Total**

Name _____ _____ Was their work of high quality?
Comments _____ Was their work completed on time?
 _____ Did they contribute ideas during group discussions?
 _____ Did they offer assistance to other group members?
 _____ Did they maintain a positive attitude during groupwork?
 _____ **Total**

Name _____ _____ Was their work of high quality?
Comments _____ Was their work completed on time?
 _____ Did they contribute ideas during group discussions?
 _____ Did they offer assistance to other group members?
 _____ Did they maintain a positive attitude during groupwork?
 _____ **Total**

---

3. **Record notes as groups work and when they present their final products.** Observe groups as they work, and take notes on how well they exhibit cooperative skills and how each group member is (or is not) contributing to the group's success. Then record notes on the quality of their final product when they share it with the class. In this way, you can quickly formulate a group grade that is based on both how students worked and what they produced.

4. **Have students complete self-assessments.** At the end of groupwork activities, have each student complete a Brag Sheet (see page 121), a self-assessment in which they evaluate their contribution to the group as well as the group's performance. This allows students to reflect on the group's effort and gives you additional information on which to base your assessment. It also gives students the opportunity to "brag" about their contributions—such as extra work done outside of class—so that their work gets evaluated fairly. Make it clear that Brag Sheets are confidential.

5. **Determine group and individual grades.** Use the notes you recorded during the activity plus students' Brag Sheets to formulate group and individual grades. Base the group grade on how well the group worked together (process) and the quality of what they produced (product). Record the group and individual grades on each Brag Sheet, total them, write comments, and return the Brag Sheets to your students.

How to Assess Writing Assignments Efficiently

Assessing written work can be taxing and time-consuming, especially if you expect to thoroughly review and grade every piece of writing your students produce. Here are some alternatives that will give your students substantive feedback on their writing while saving you from an overwhelming paper load:

Use peer-feedback groups. When students exchange and review one another's papers during the writing process, this will minimize the time it takes you to review rough drafts. Consider providing an Editing Checklist to guide students (see page 123). Reading one another's work gives students the chance to see a variety of individual writing styles. See page 64 for a complete description of the peer-feedback process.

Grade only final drafts. When students write both a rough draft and a final draft, you might give them some feedback on the rough draft, but actually grade only the final draft.

Use focused grading. Grade for only one or two specific parts of the assignment other than content. For example, you might look for an introduction that grabs the reader's attention, the quality of supporting details, a good thesis statement, a conclusion that summarizes the main points, rich vocabulary, strong writer's voice, or organization. Clearly define the criteria for assessment. Or, at the beginning of each assignment, consider *not* telling students which portion you will grade; this will encourage high quality in all areas of their writing.

Use a portfolio system. Develop a portfolio system in which students keep selected samples of their work through the semester. After students complete several writing assignments, have them choose two or three to revise further. Thoroughly grade these "best" writing products. This is an excellent way to monitor individual student progress.

Stagger due dates. To manage your paper load, stagger the due dates you set for major writing assignments among your classes. Allot ample time between due dates, and don't set a due date immediately before the end of a grading period.

Use a rubric. Create a basic rubric to allow students to assess their own work during the writing process. Tailor the form to reflect the criteria of particular assignments. Include space for both student and teacher comments. Communication and feedback is key to improving future writing assignments. See the example rubric in the Writing Evaluation Form on page 124.

"Self-evaluation is new to most students. They think once they turn a paper in, it is out of their lives forever. Asking them to take the time to evaluate their work forces them to reconsider some of their efforts, answers, and choices."
— High School Teacher

Editing Checklist

1. Describe the appearance of the paper. Is it typed? Well-formatted? Clean?

2. List any spelling errors.

3. List punctuation or capitalization suggestions.

4. Give examples of sentences that are hard to read, and offer alternatives.

5. Give examples of arguments that were not supported with details or examples, and suggest alternatives.

6. Comment on the paper's organization.

Editor's signature _____

Writing Evaluation Form

Name _____

Assignment _____ Date _____

	Student Assessment	Teacher Assessment	Points
1. First draft completed on time			
2. Helpful suggestions given in peer-feedback group to other writers			
3. Revision notes made on first draft			
4. Revisions incorporated into final draft			
5. Careful editing of final draft for spelling, grammar, and punctuation errors			
6. Final draft completed on time			
7. Historical information used correctly			
8. Ideas supported with detail			
9. Sentences clear and understandable			
10. Appropriate format and organization			

Student comments

Total

Teacher comments

How to Make Assessment of Student Notebooks Manageable

As part of the TCI Approach, the Interactive Student Notebook is a powerful tool for organizing student thoughts and notes. However, you must develop an effective system for assessing notebooks to keep the task from becoming burdensome and time-consuming, or both you and your students will become discouraged. The following suggestions will help you manage the load of assessing notebooks while still giving students regular, helpful feedback.

Informal Assessment Here are some ways to assess notebooks informally on a regular basis, thus giving students immediate feedback as well as saving you time during more formal evaluations of notebooks:

Monitor notebooks aggressively in the first few weeks of the course. Glance at notebooks each time they are used for the first two weeks of the semester. Walk around the classroom while students are working, giving positive comments and helpful suggestions. This is especially important early in the year as you establish expectations for notebook quality.

Check homework while students are working. While students work on another assignment, walk around the classroom and conduct a quick check for the previous night's homework. Give each student a special stamp or a mark, such as 0 = not done; ✔− = needs work; ✔ = average work; ✔+ = excellent. This helps ensure that students complete their work on time and allows you to give them immediate feedback.

Set a clear, high standard. Provide a model of outstanding work for a particular assignment or set of class notes. Have students, in pairs, assess their own notebooks according to the model.

Allow students to use their notebooks on a quiz or test. This reward comes as a pleasant surprise to students who have thorough, accurate content information in a well-organized notebook. If they have done a good job with their notebooks, their quiz or test grade should reflect this.

A bit of personal encouragement and guidance early on will help get your students off to a good start.

Formal Assessment Some teachers collect and formally assess notebooks every three to four weeks; others do so less frequently. Regardless of how often you decide to assess, here are some suggestions for making the process easy for you and meaningful for students.

Explain the criteria used to grade notebooks. At the beginning of the year, clearly explain the criteria on which notebooks will be assessed. This may include the quality and completeness of assignments, visual appearance, neatness, and organization. Consider creating a simple rubric that identifies the criteria and how they will be assessed.

Stagger notebook collection and grading. If you use Interactive Student Notebooks in all your classes, do not collect them all at once—stagger their collection so that you have only one class set to evaluate at a time.

Grade selectively. Don't feel compelled to grade every notebook entry. Carefully assess the most important entries, and consider spot-checking the others.

Notebook evaluation sheets are most effective when tailored to meet the specific needs and expectations you have for your students. Use these sample sheets for ideas as you design your own.

Name _____

Notebook Evaluation Sheet

Directions: Before turning in your notebook, grade yourself on each of the assignments below as well as on Visual Appearance and Extra Credit. Grade yourself fairly and honestly; I will grade you as well. I will clearly tell you what I am looking for. Keep in mind that my grade is binding, but if there is a discrepancy, you may politely arrange a time to meet with me to discuss the difference in assessment. After we meet, I reserve the right to change the grade if I made an error in judgment; however, I also reserve the right to stick by my original grade.

Notebook Assignment	Due Date	Possible Points	Student Assessment	Teacher Assessment
Character Collages on Chinese Beliefs	9/8	15	13	14
Class Notes on Chinese Beliefs	9/9	10	10	9
Compare Dynastic/Communist China	9/10	8	6	7
Class Notes on Rise of Communism	9/10	5	5	5
Illustrated Timeline of Communist China	9/12	15	13	12
Feelings on China Debate	9/13	10	9	9
Notes on Textbook Reading pp. 123–8	9/14	8	7	6
Extra Credit		20	15	18
Visual Appearance		15	13	12
Totals		106	91	92

Student Comments: I don't know how well I did. This notebook was kind of a pain at times. I think I included everything you asked for, but they were some weird assignments. I think this notebook will help me remember things for a long time.

Teacher Comments: You did a good, solid job on this notebook. Keep in mind that you can use more of your excellent visuals for extra credit. You really used the left side of the notebook well to make sense of what you were learning in class.

Create a notebook evaluation form. To aid in assessing the notebooks, create a notebook evaluation sheet and distribute it to students to fill out before they turn in their notebooks. Examples of notebook evaluation forms are shown below and opposite. Use them as a basis for creating your own evaluation sheet. The form on page 126 allows you to designate which assignments will be graded. Before using such a form, make sure students know the assessment criteria for the assignments—such as completeness, neatness, aesthetic appearance, organization, and effective use of color. The form shown below allows for a more holistic assessment of the notebook. Tailor the forms to suit your needs.

Have students do a self-assessment of their work. When students self-assess their notebooks, it enables them to reflect on their learning and to critically review their progress. Explain that if your assessment differs markedly from theirs—better or worse—they will have the opportunity to discuss with you the reasons for your assessment. Make it clear that ultimately your grade is binding.

Name _____

Notebook Evaluation Sheet

	Student Evaluation	Teacher Evaluation

Quality and Completeness
- All class notes and right-side work are completed and of high quality, even for days when you are absent
- All left-side work is completed and of high quality

20   25   30   40   44
Needs Improvement   Fair   Good   Excellent

Student: 40	Teacher: 41

Visual Appearance and Organization
- Left- and right-side work is organized and neat
- Effective highlighting and use of color

20   25   30   40   44
Needs Improvement   Fair   Good   Excellent

Student: 42	Teacher: 35

Extra Credit
- Newspaper cutouts, drawings, graphics, or unassigned personal responses
- Other items

0   2   4   6   8   10   12
Needs Improvement   Fair   Good   Excellent

Student: 6	Teacher: 8

Student Comments
I liked doing this notebook. It really helped me think about China. But I don't know how good my drawings were.

Total | Student: 88 | Teacher: 84 |

Teacher Comments
Great job. Next time, think about your visuals a little more. You don't need to be a great artist, but try to make your visuals include more historical details.

How to Create Tests That Honor Multiple Intelligences

At the end of a topic of study and as the final part of the assessment process, students should be given a comprehensive test that allows them to demonstrate, in a variety of ways, what they have learned. The test should not, however, follow the form of traditional tests in which students respond to questions that demand only simple recall of basic facts. Instead, end-of-lesson tests should

- blend closed and open-ended questions.
- require students to do some form of writing.
- measure reading comprehension in the content area.
- contain elements found on standardized tests—such as multiple-choice questions—so that students are confident when they encounter them.
- tap more than just linguistic intelligence. Since traditional tests in social studies are usually purely linguistic, an effective test should also tap other intelligences, such as visual-spatial, logical-mathematical, intrapersonal, and musical-rhythmic.

Following are several types of questions (drawn from existing end-of-unit assessments in various TCI products) that you might consider using.

Standard Multiple Choice

- The Declaration of Independence was written to explain
  A. why the colonists thought "taxation without representation" was unfair.
  B. what Britain needed to do to win back the loyalty of the colonies.
  C. why it was time for the colonies to separate from Great Britain.
  D. what other nations could do to help the colonies win their freedom.

- What is an example of a cultural effect that trade had on the peoples that used the Silk Road?
  A. China became wealthy trading silk.
  B. Rome became powerful trading jade.
  C. Buddhism spread from India to China.
  D. Daoism spread from China to Rome.

Justified Multiple Choice

- Which of the following is the best definition of *capitalism?* Justify your answer in a paragraph. Explain why you chose that answer and did not choose the others.
  A. an economic system based on governmental control of the economy
  B. an economic system based on free competition between businesses, an open market, private ownership, and private businesses competing for business
  C. an economic system based on little private ownership, people working mainly for themselves, and subsistence farming

- Which of the following is the best description of the Freedom Charter? Justify your answer in a paragraph. That is, explain why you chose this answer and did not choose the others.
  - A. proclaimed that South Africa belonged to black Africans only and called for a violent overthrow of the white government
  - B. proclaimed that South Africa belonged to all who live in it and called for wealth to be redistributed equally among blacks
  - C. proclaimed that South Africa belonged to black Africans only and called for wealth to be redistributed equally among blacks and whites

Visual Prompts

- This picture illustrates the writing of
  - A. the Olive Branch Petition.
  - B. *Common Sense.*
  - C. the Mayflower Compact.
  - D. the Declaration of Independence.

- The picture suggests that the first draft was
  - A. difficult to understand.
  - B. the length of a book.
  - C. revised several times.
  - D. perfect as first written.

Visual Analysis

Look at this allegorical print by William Balfour Ker, *From the Depths* (1906). Who do the people at the top of the image represent? Who do the people in the lower part of the image represent? What does the image depict? What does this image reveal about the Industrial Revolution?

Music Analysis

- Listen to this piece of music, "Cafalleria Rusticana." Which style or period of art does it reflect: classical, romantic, or verismo? Explain your choice by referring to at least two qualities of the music.

- Listen to this piece of music, "Hail, Columbia!" Does the sound and spirit of this song best reflect the ideals of Thomas Jefferson or Alexander Hamilton? Justify your answer by drawing connections to two ideas of either Jefferson or Hamilton.

Graphic Questions

- Create a Venn diagram that shows three unique powers of the Senate, three unique powers of the House of Representatives, and three powers that both houses share.

- Create a flow chart to explain how England changed from a traditional to an industrial society. Use the following vocabulary terms and create a visual to represent each: *subsistence farming, factory system, cottage industry, capitalism, mercantilism, revolution.*

- Create a real estate advertisement that would encourage people to move to Constantinople in the 6th century. Include an appropriate title, five reasons to come to Constantinople, a quote from a person living in Constantinople, and appropriate creative touches.

Multiple Intelligence Tasks

- Pretend you are a publisher who is about to publish a book about the writing of the Declaration of Independence. Design a cover for the book. Make sure your book cover includes the following:
  — a short, catchy title for the book that will make people want to read it.
  — at least three visuals that represent either (A) the Declaration of Independence or (B) key events that led to writing the Declaration.
  — a one-sentence recommendation of the book. The recommendation should be from an important historical figure whose opinion on the topic would influence people to read the book. (Example: "Best thing I've read since *Common Sense*"—Thomas Paine)

- Create a political cartoon that represents whether you think the actions of the United States during the period of manifest destiny should be praised or condemned. Your cartoon should include the following:
  — at least one figure or symbol to represent the United States.
  — at least two figures or symbols to represent the other countries or groups affected by manifest destiny.
  — at least one figure or symbol to represent one of the key events from the period of manifest destiny.
  — thought or speech bubbles that tell what figures in the cartoon are feeling and why, or a one-sentence caption that summarizes the message of the cartoon.

Use Culminating Projects as an Alternative Method of Assessment

The Culminating Project is an effective alternative assessment tool because it allows all learners to use their various intelligences to create products that demonstrate their mastery of the content. In a well-conceived Culminating Project, the requirements and standards for each project are known in advance, and the teacher—often the students' adversary during a traditional test—coaches students to complete their work thoughtfully and to the best of their abilities. The essential questions and concepts central to the project are introduced in the beginning of a unit, guide the unit, and are reinforced during each lesson.

As they develop Culminating Projects, students apply their various intelligences to demonstrate an understanding of content in meaningful ways. For example, a Culminating Project might challenge students to design a museum celebrating the rise of Islam which addresses the question, *How were people's lives affected by the spread of the message of Islam?* Another might ask students to perform a griot's tale to demonstrate their knowledge of the empires and kingdoms of sub-Saharan Africa.

Culminating Projects share many or all of the following characteristics:

The project is central to the unit. It focuses on the key questions, difficult issues, essential understandings, and important concepts of the unit.

The project is known to students in advance. This kind of assessment is not a last-minute creation hidden until test day. Students know at the beginning of a unit how they will be assessed and have time to prepare accordingly.

The project requires students to think deeply about important course content. Unlike traditional tests with a greater emphasis on recall, Culminating Projects challenge students to exercise higher-level thinking skills—comprehension, application, analysis, synthesis, and evaluation—as they complete complex problem solving tasks.

Students create a meaningful product or performance. Rather than simply memorizing content for an exam, students make use of what they have learned to create a unique product or performance that demonstrates their knowledge.

The project demands that students use a variety of intelligences. Well-designed projects tap into more than one intelligence. Many projects combine group and individual activities.

Students know the standards by which their work will be judged. Standards of excellence are communicated to students when they begin their projects. As they work, students are encouraged to assess their own efforts and to seek feedback from their peers or their teacher to use in revising and improving their final products or performances.

"Culminating Projects allow the students to articulate what they learned through learning styles they are comfortable with. I've seen students produce work I didn't know they were capable of. These projects also lowered students' test anxiety because they don't have to show everything they know in 50 minutes."

— High School Teacher

The project fosters the habit of self-assessment. Students are encouraged to critically evaluate their own work and to reflect on their own growth and progress over time.

The teacher acts as a coach. When teachers use Culminating Projects rather than traditional assessments, their role shifts from that of proctor to coach. Just as a basketball coach does everything within reason to help players perform at their peak on the court, the teacher does everything possible to help students reach the highest level of performance they are capable of on their projects.

The following examples demonstrate the breadth and depth of Culminating Projects:

Creating an Annotated Mural of Modern Latin America Students work in groups to create a mural that pictures modern Latin America and answers this question: *What are the most important ideas you learned about modern Latin America?* The mural must include four sections: Overview of Latin America, Modern Mexico, the Brazilian Rainforest, and Latin American Cultural Connections to the United States. The mural also must incorporate a variety of elements—maps, timelines, symbols, illustrations, quotes—to demonstrate what students have learned. In the center of the mural, students list five conclusions that can be drawn about modern Latin America. Students then write a two-page artist's statement in which they explain the meaning of their group mural.

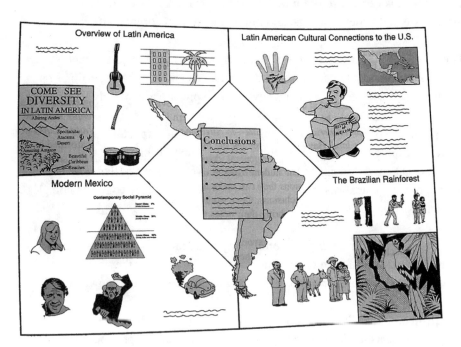

An Illustrated Storybook About the Roaring Twenties and the Great Depression Students work in pairs to create an illustrated storybook that answers this question: *What are the key lessons of the Roaring Twenties and the Great Depression?* The storybook must have five sections: Post-World War I Tensions, Good Times of the 1920s, Causes of the Great Depression, The Human Impact of the Great Depression, and The New Deal. After outlining their ideas, students write the text, draw illustrations, and add other artistic adornments in booklets that describe the major events of the Roaring Twenties and the Great Depression and the key lessons people can learn from them. The storybook is to be written for a fifth-grade audience and should demonstrate a clear understanding of the major historical issues and legacies.

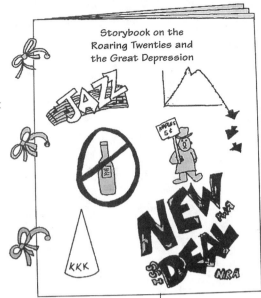

Publishing a News Magazine on Change in Europe Students work in groups of four to "publish" a news magazine on Europe's transition to the modern world. Their final product should answer this question: *How did innovation and reform during the Renaissance, Reformation, and Age of Exploration change life in Europe?* The news magazine must feature at least three of these topics: religion, art and architecture, science and technology, business, education, urban life, and exploration. Other elements of the news magazine include an introductory letter from the editors, a table of contents with a timeline of key events, profiles on the top three newsmakers of the era, and a concluding article on the legacy of this period. Groups use materials they accumulated throughout the unit—original writing, visuals, and historical notes—and resources that they collect through additional research.

> *"Culminating Projects help me to pull everything together in the end. I get to see how much I've learned."*
>
> — High School Student

Europe's Changing Times
The Transition to the Modern World

Exploration

Revival

Reform

Discovery

Part 2

Creating a Cooperative, Tolerant Classroom

Creating a Cooperative, Tolerant Classroom

"I like the other kids in this class. They're friendly and we help each other out."

— Middle School Student

Introduction

In social studies classrooms across the nation, the same scene plays out on the first day of school: students cautiously and self-consciously enter their new classrooms, feeling excited but also guarded, apprehensive, and sometimes scared. The interactive, experiential, stimulating learning that is at the heart of the TCI Approach cannot take place until students feel comfortable with sharing ideas, taking risks, working cooperatively, tolerating differences, and disagreeing honestly with the teacher and their classmates. Thus every year, with each new class, you need to take purposeful steps to develop a "safe" community in your classroom.

Using a systematic process to create a cooperative, tolerant classroom environment will yield powerful results:

- Students interact more freely and learn more because they are safe from ridicule, put-downs, and bullying.
- The class develops a sense of community and trust.
- All students feel valued and respected.
- Classroom management is proactive and consistent, rather than reactive and punitive.

- Students learn to tolerate differences, respect ideas, and appreciate diversity.
- You and your students develop a collaborative, rather than an adversarial, relationship.
- You and your students feel comfortable taking risks.
- Cooperative interaction is an integral part of whole-class instruction, group-work activities, and paired work.
- Ethnic and cultural diversity is perceived as an opportunity, not a problem.

"My teacher takes time to greet us each day, it really makes us feel welcome. I like it."

— Middle School Student

Ten steps for creating a cooperative, tolerant classroom follow. For each step, you are told the rationale, what to do, and when to do it. Use the steps as they appear, or adapt them to your own teaching style and the age and social-skill levels of your students.

STEP 1 — Greet your students at the door every day as they enter your classroom.

Rationale Students like to be recognized for who they are: young people with a wide range of needs, interests, and feelings. Making time to say hello, smile, and talk with them demonstrates respect for them as people, conveys a warmth students quickly recognize and respond to, and models important social skills.

Greeting students as they enter your room makes them feel immediately welcome and sets the tone for a cooperative, tolerant classroom.

What to Do Explain to your students that you will greet them at the door each day so that you can make a personal connection with them. Stand by your classroom door between classes. As your students enter your classroom, greet them with a friendly *Hello, Good morning, or How's it going?* As the year progresses and you know your students better, your banter with them will become more informed and less superficial. If you are unable to be at the door on a given day, assign a student to the job of "greeter" to welcome the rest of the class on your behalf.

When Start the first day of class, and do it every day.

Establish the classroom expectation that students will be tolerant and respectful of one another.

Explain your expectations for classroom behavior.

Rationale The key to creating a cooperative, tolerant classroom is to involve students in regulating their own behavior. They will need guidance, but you can grant students control over their actions by establishing a simple set of classroom rules. These make your expectations clear, but also show that you trust students to know which behaviors will uphold the rules and which ones won't. You need not make a rule for every conceivable misbehavior; that only sends the message that you do not trust your students to know how to behave properly.

What to Do Tell students that their behavior in your classroom will be guided by a few rules, or guidelines. Explain that these guidelines will help them build a cooperative, tolerant classroom community. Here are three suggested rules; modify them to meet your needs. You may also want to involve your students in shaping the class rules.

1. Treat everyone, including the teacher, with respect.
2. Use kind words and actions toward others.
3. Do everything you can to help yourself and others learn.

Give your students specific examples of respectful conduct, appropriate words and actions, and behaviors that facilitate learning. As an example of respectful behavior, you might explain how to disagree with someone in a positive way by using their name, restating their argument, and then giving your own position. State explicitly that racist, sexist, and homophobic comments will not be tolerated.

Post the guidelines in the classroom, have students place them inside their notebooks, and frequently review them. Most importantly, model these behaviors throughout the year. If you do not set a convincing example, or if your behavior contradicts the guidelines, your students will quickly ignore them.

When Introduce these guidelines the first day of class and review them every day the first several times the class meets, especially as new students join the class. Then review them as necessary, especially as they relate to working cooperatively in groups. (Specific behaviors for groupwork are discussed further in Step 6, page 145.)

Stage an icebreaker to make students more comfortable with their new classmates.

Rationale Students are often nervous and anxious as they try to adapt to a new setting, a new group of classmates, and a new teacher. Until they feel more at ease, students may not interact appropriately or be willing to take risks with one another. Many students, in fact, will not participate in class discussions until they are confident that their comments will not be belittled or quickly categorized as "wrong." Consequently, it is crucial that you invest time to break the ice and start building classroom rapport. The sooner students feel comfortable, the sooner meaningful learning can take place.

What to Do Give each student a copy of one of these icebreakers: "Get the Autograph of Someone Who…" or "Multiple Intelligences Bingo" (pages 140–141). Explain that students will need to obtain signatures from classmates who fit each of the characteristics mentioned on the sheet. In so doing, they must talk to at least 18 different people. Before asking for a signature, students must introduce themselves *(Hello, my name is…)*. After obtaining someone's signature for a given characteristic, students must ask that person a related question. *(Where outside of the state did you go last summer? What type of musical instrument do you play?)* This helps students learn the names of their classmates and find out a little about them, instead of simply shoving the paper at one another without any real interaction. Tell students that you, too, are available for signatures. You may even want to complete this activity with them.

After most students have completed the activity, go through the categories to find out which students in the class fit each characteristic. Students begin to make connections with each other as they acknowledge the talents, interests, and experiences represented in the class. By the end of the class period, you and the students will feel far more comfortable with one another.

When Conduct an icebreaker during the first week of class. You may want to use similar activities periodically to build and maintain the sense of community in the class, or when new students arrive.

Icebreakers—such as having students pair up to talk about their favorite book or game— give students an opportunity to become comfortable with one another in an informal setting.

Get the Autograph of Someone Who...

For each of the 35 categories below, find someone in the class who fits the description. Before you get his or her autograph, you must shake the person's hand and introduce yourself ("Hello, my name is . . . ") and ask one question about the item the person is signing. For example, for the first category about leaving the state, you might ask, "Where did you go?" You are allowed only two signatures from the same person. You will have to circulate throughout the classroom.

1. Has left the state over the summer _____
2. Has the same shoe size as you _____
3. Likes to watch football _____
4. Likes to draw _____
5. Plays a musical instrument _____
6. Has been to a play _____
7. Has had braces _____
8. Is wearing jeans _____
9. Is in another class with you _____
10. Is new to this school _____
11. Is from a different ethnic group than you _____
12. Has traveled to another country _____
13. Has the same color eyes as you _____
14. Likes to read in bed _____
15. Was born outside the United States _____
16. Likes to dance _____
17. Has a hair style different from yours _____
18. Is much taller than you _____
19. You have never spoken to before _____
20. Loves history _____
21. Dislikes history _____
22. Has been surfing or ice skating _____
23. Likes the outdoors _____
24. Has more than two brothers and sisters _____
25. Is an only child _____
26. Likes to sing _____
27. Speaks another language _____
28. Likes the same TV show as you _____
29. Likes to swim _____
30. Was born in the same month as you _____
31. Has ridden a bike over 25 miles in one day _____
32. Knows how to sew _____
33. Chews gum _____
34. Likes broccoli _____
35. Plays on a sports team _____

Multiple Intelligences Bingo

Circulate through the room to find people who have the characteristics listed below. When you find someone who meets the description, write his or her name in the box below the description. You may put each person's name in a box only once. When you have a line of five names horizontally, vertically, or diagonally, call out "Bingo" loudly.

meets with friends to do homework or study for tests	is a good storyteller	doodles on lecture notes	loves the outdoors	plays on a sports team
likes to play chess	keeps a personal journal	loves to play computer games	is a good speller	reads a lot
plays a musical instrument	can tap out a song on the piano after hearing it once	often has people ask him or her for advice	prefers working alone	likes doing puzzles
loves puns and word games	is a good artist	has a hard time sitting still	likes to take things apart and put them back together again	hums while working
can tell when someone is singing off-key	belongs to a club	likes science class	wants to know how things work	is independent, does not like to conform

"The future of America... will rest with people who can think and act with informed grace across ethnic, cultural and linguistic lines."

— Robert Hughes
Culture of Complaint: The Fraying of America

Convince students that learning how to work effectively with others will benefit them throughout their lives.

Rationale Students sometimes need to be convinced that what they are learning is worthwhile, so take the time to explain the short-term and long-term benefits of cooperation. Cooperative learning is not only a sound pedagogical approach supported by research, but also a means to teach students valuable "people skills" that will serve them away from school, especially given our increasingly diverse population.

What to Do Make a transparency of "Survey of Employers" (see below). Ask students this question: *Other than being able to do the job, what do you think most employers look for in an employee?* Allow them a few moments for discussion and then project the survey.

Point out that these top-rated characteristics—including communication skills, teamwork skills, and interpersonal skills—are not directly addressed in most schools' curricula. Explain that throughout your class, students will have an opportunity to develop those attributes as they work with others on a variety of activities. In this way, they will not only be learning social studies, but also effective ways to work with others.

This step will take only about 20 minutes. Make it clear to students that you will be teaching not only subject-matter content, but also cooperative skills that will serve them outside of class also.

When Do this sometime during the first week or two of class, before holding any formal small-group activities. You may also want to send a copy of "Survey of Employers" home to families to let them know why working effectively with others will be emphasized in your class.

Survey of Employers

Employers were asked to rank the qualities or skills they consider most important in their employees. Employers said they look for these characteristics (listed in order of importance):
1. communication skills—verbal and written
2. honesty and integrity
3. teamwork skills—works well with others
4. interpersonal skills—relates well to others
5. strong work ethic
6. motivation and initiative

Source: "Job Outlook 2002 Survey of Employers," conducted by the National Association of Colleges and Employers

STEP 5

Teach students how to move efficiently and properly into groups of various sizes.

Rationale While it may seen unnecessary to teach students—particularly high school students—how to move their desks into groups, a 15- to 20-minute investment will pay dividends in time saved throughout the year. Part of the success of groupwork activities depends on groups sitting in precise configurations. Without clearly stated expectations about how to move into groups quickly, students will waste valuable time. Students must be able to move into groups and be ready to start work in no more than one minute. This is particularly vital for teachers who teach more than one subject or float from room to room. You can accomplish this with just a brief training.

What to Do Tell students they will be working in several different types of small groups throughout the year and must know how to move into each type of group quickly and efficiently. Explain that before they move into groups, you will tell them (1) the materials they need to take with them, (2) whom they will be working with, and (3) where they will be working. Advise the class that you consider groups to be ready to go only when everyone is seated quietly and properly, with materials at hand.

Emphasize that their desk arrangement is important to group success. When working in pairs, students should place their desks either side by side, with the sides touching, or facing one another, with the front edges touching. (The type of activity will determine which placement to use.) For most other larger groups, the front corners of the desks must touch. This allows each student to face all group members.

With these expectations clear, allow students to practice moving into groups. Randomly assign students to various-sized groups and indicate where they should meet. Instruct them to take all of their class materials. When the directions are clear, say, "Go!" Time them, and watch that their movement meets your expectations. If necessary, allow them to discuss what went wrong. They may discover it is best to use the desks that are already in the vicinity of their assigned spot rather than dragging their own desks across the room. Have them repeat the process until they can do it in "record time."

It may seem silly at first to teach students how to move into exact arrangements. But soon your students will be able to move into different-size groups quickly and begin working without disruption or delay.

Be prepared for students to think this exercise is silly at best and condescending at worst. Understand their feelings, but explain that it really will make a difference in how well the activity goes, and consequently in how much they will learn. Some teachers treat this like a game, called the Desk Olympics (page 144). They create various events, such as Side-by-Side Pairs and Groups of Four, and post "Olympic records" for best times. If you play Olympic theme music before each event, students will get caught up in the fun and competition, while at the same time they are internalizing your expectations for moving into groups.

When Do this during the first few weeks of class, before assigning any formal groupwork activities that require room rearrangement.

"After I took time to teach Desk Olympics, my students can now enter the room, read the map posted on the board, efficiently move all the desks into the new arrangement and find their designated spots in minutes."

— High School Teacher

Desk Olympics

You will be working in groups of different sizes throughout this course and must practice moving into groups efficiently. When your teacher says "Go!" you must move into whatever configuration is shown below and bring everything—backpacks, notebooks, pens, jackets—with you. You will be timed on how fast you get into perfect formation.

Event 1
Side-by-Side Pairs

Time

Event 2
Face-to-Face Pairs

Time

Event 3
Groups of Three

Time

Event 4
Groups of Four

Time

Event 5
Groups of Five

Time

Use role-playing activities to teach your students cooperative skills.

STEP 6

"Students have more need of models than of critics."
— Joseph Joubert
18th century French moralist

Rationale For groups to function cooperatively, students must know what it means to work in a cooperative fashion. Too often teachers put students into groups and simply say, *Cooperate*. But many students lack the necessary social skills or have little prior experience working as a team. Therefore you must teach these skills, or you will find yourself continually reacting to inappropriate behavior. Role-playing activities allow students to identify what both cooperative and noncooperative behaviors sound, look, and feel like.

What to Do There are two ways to teach and reinforce cooperative skills: You can use a five-step process to separately teach any of ten specific skills, or use a scripted role play that more generally models appropriate and inappropriate behaviors for groupwork.

For the five-step process, make and display a transparency of "Cooperative Skills" (page 147). Tell students that you are going to ask for some volunteers to demonstrate some of the specific do's and don'ts of groupwork. For example, here is how you might approach one of the ten listed behaviors (Cooperative Skill 7):

A teacher joins in this role play to demonstrate how inappropriate behavior can disrupt the groupwork process.

1. **Name the behavior.** On the board, on a transparency, or on large paper, start a T-chart with the skill as the heading: *Use positive comments, encourage, and express appreciation.*

2. **Demonstrate the behavior.** Have three volunteers join you in the middle of the room. As a group task, ask them to quickly generate a list of the ten greatest concerns in the United States today. Encourage everyone to participate, and praise group members who come up with good ideas.

3. **Define the behavior.** Label the two columns of the T-chart "Looks Like" and "Sounds Like." Ask students to identify actions you took and words you said that were positive, encouraging, and appreciative, and list them on the chart. Here are possible entries:

Looks Like	Sounds Like
Made eye contact	Great idea!
Smiled and leaned forward	Please repeat that so everyone can hear.
Nodded head	Right!
Gave "thumbs-up" sign	Thanks.
Gave high-five to group member	Do you have any other good ideas?

Cooperative skills must be taught. Insisting that students shake hands and introduce themselves each time they work in a new group will reinforce appropriate behavior.

4. Practice the behavior. Once students have clearly defined the behavior, give them a simple discussion task and allow them to practice in groups. Circulate around the room to observe their interactions.

5. Process the students' experience. This is where the most long-term learning occurs. Allow students to share their experiences before you comment on what you observed. Ask, *How did you feel when the people in your group used positive comments toward you? How did it feel to express your positive ideas? How did using this skill affect your group's ability to work together? Why do you think this is an important cooperative skill?*

This process can be used for any cooperative skill. To decide which cooperative skills you need to teach or hone, observe your students' behavior. Depending on the time you have and your students' social skills, you might use this process for only the more difficult skills.

An alternative way to teach and reinforce cooperative skills is to have students role-play a scenario in which they model both appropriate and inappropriate behaviors. This works especially well with older students and when you want to focus on specific situations, such as observing presentations by classmates, dealing with a reluctant group member, or staying on task. Simply establish a scenario, give a small group of students role cards describing the behaviors you want them to model during the scene, and sit back while they conduct the role play. Afterward, ask the class what they saw, heard, and felt.

For example, here are some role cards you might distribute for a role play of noncooperative behaviors that contribute to ineffective groupwork:

Student 1: Your desk is not touching the other desks in your group. You may even turn your desk so it is facing away from the group. Do not attempt to be a part of the group.

"I really know what's expected of me in this class and it helps!"

— Middle School Student

Student 2: You take out makeup or something else to distract you. Make no effort to be a part of the group and make no eye contact or conversation with group members.

Student 3: You become the "commander." Tell everyone which role they will have (such as director, actor, graphics person, or researcher), and act authoritatively. Do not let anyone else have a say in getting the group on task. Do not use group members' names when speaking to them.

Student 4: Your words and attitude are negative. Say things like, *"I hate this class"* and *"I don't want to work with these people."*

After talking about what was inappropriate and counterproductive in this unhappy group, you might have the same students (or four others) role-play behaviors that contribute to effective, supportive groups:

Student 1: You help arrange all the desks properly. You politely remind others to remove everything from their desks except for materials they will need for the assignment. Introduce yourself to other group members and look them in the eye when you do so.

Student 2: You are helpful and offer to collect materials for the group.

Student 3: Ask, *"Does everybody know each other?"* If not, make sure everyone is introduced. You remind the group of the time allotted and suggest that everyone start by choosing a role for this activity.

Student 4: You act as timekeeper, volunteering to watch the clock to make sure the group is on target. Offer to take the group's work to the teacher to be checked before the group proceeds to the next step of the assignment.

When Teach cooperative skills before assigning any activities that involve working in groups. You can teach these skills over several sessions.

Cooperative Skills

1. Break tension and be friendly.
2. Learn and use names.
3. Arrange desks properly.
4. Use positive body language.
5. Be aware of eye contact.
6. Listen to others and take turns giving ideas.
7. Use positive comments, encourage, and express appreciation.
8. Be helpful and assist each other.
9. Disagree in an agreeable way.
10. Stay on task.

Be Patient!

Forming heterogeneous groups is an imperfect science. Expect that some groups may not work as well together as others.

Working in mixed-ability groups will help your students take responsibility for their own learning.

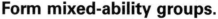

Form mixed-ability groups.

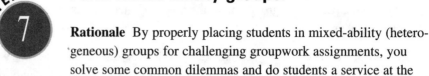

Rationale By properly placing students in mixed-ability (heterogeneous) groups for challenging groupwork assignments, you solve some common dilemmas and do students a service at the same time. First, you expose all students to high-level content because they benefit from the collective talent of the group; no one gets left behind. Second, you break social cliques and foster intercultural understanding. Third, you give students the skills they need to be able to work with different kinds of people in school, in community groups, and on teams.

What to Do No matter what size the group—pairs, or groups of three or four—you need to make each one as balanced as possible in terms of gender, ethnicity, intelligences (as defined by Howard Gardner), and social group. It may take a while to find suitable groupings, but your ability to create smooth-functioning groups will improve with each groupwork activity.

Set aside about 15 minutes of planning time, with class lists, to think through the assignment of students to mixed-ability groups. Balancing groups in terms of gender and ethnicity is relatively easy. Even after a short while, you will already have an idea of the cliques that exist and of students you prefer not to have working together.

The greatest challenge is determining students' predominant intelligences. The best way to do so is by carefully observing them throughout the school year. A quicker way to get a rough idea of your students' cognitive strengths, however, is to give one of the diagnostic surveys that follow. Do not reveal the answer key until students have completed their surveys. Use the results, coupled with your observations, to balance groups according to Gardner's seven intelligences.

Emphasize to students that diagnostic tools like these are rough and are not meant to suggest that people are capable only in their predominant intelligences. Everyone has a mix of intelligences, and in addition, our intelligences evolve and change over time.

Depending on the success of your mixed-ability groups, you might have students remain in the same group for several activities. Or you could switch groups to give students a change of pace, or to try for more effective groupings.

When Assign students to groups before their first groupwork activity and after you have completed Steps 1 through 6 of "Creating a Cooperative, Tolerant Classroom."

Identifying Your Multiple Intelligences: Survey 1

This survey will help you identify your areas of strongest intelligence. Read each statement.
If it expresses some characteristic of yours and sounds true for the most part, write T.
If it doesn't, write F. If the statement is sometimes true and sometimes false, leave it blank.
Everyone will have different answers. Think about what is true for *you*.

1. _____ I'd rather draw a map than give someone verbal directions.
2. _____ If I am angry or happy, I usually know why.
3. _____ I can play (or used to play) a musical instrument.
4. _____ I compose songs or raps and perform them.
5. _____ I can add or multiply quickly in my head.
6. _____ I help friends deal with feelings because I deal with my own feelings well.
7. _____ I like to work with calculators and computers.
8. _____ I pick up new dance steps quickly.
9. _____ It's easy for me to say what I think in an argument or debate.
10. _____ I enjoy a good lecture, speech, or sermon.
11. _____ I always know north from south no matter where I am.
12. _____ I like to gather together groups of people for parties or special events.
13. _____ I listen to music for much of the day, on the radio, CDs, or other media.
14. _____ I always understand the drawings that come with new gadgets or appliances.
15. _____ I like to work puzzles and play games.
16. _____ Learning to ride a bike (or to skate) was easy.
17. _____ I am irritated when I hear an argument or statement that sounds illogical.
18. _____ I can convince other people to follow my plans.
19. _____ My sense of balance and coordination is good.
20. _____ I often see patterns and relationships between numbers faster than other people.
21. _____ I enjoy building models (or sculpting).
22. _____ I like word games and puns.
23. _____ I can look at an object one way and see it turned backward just as easily.
24. _____ I can identify when there is a key change in a song.
25. _____ I like to work with numbers and figures.
26. _____ I like to sit quietly and reflect on my feelings.
27. _____ Just looking at the shapes of buildings and structures is pleasurable to me.
28. _____ I like to hum, whistle, and sing in the shower or when I'm alone.
29. _____ I'm good at athletics.
30. _____ I enjoy writing detailed letters to friends.
31. _____ I'm usually aware of the expression on my face.
32. _____ I'm sensitive to the expressions on other people's faces.
33. _____ I stay in touch with my moods. I have no trouble identifying them.
34. _____ I am sensitive to the moods of others.
35. _____ I have a good sense of what others think of me.

Scoring Your Multiple Intellegences: Survey 1

The numbers in the boxes below correspond to the numbered statements in the survey. Put an X in the box for each item you marked T. For example: The first box in row A is for statement 9. If you marked 9 with a T, put an X in that box. If you marked it F, leave the box empty. When you have finished, add up the Xs in each row. A total of four Xs in any row indicates strong ability. (Your teacher will tell you which intelligence to write for each row.)

A 9 10 17 22 30 = ⬜ _____ intelligence

B 5 7 15 20 25 = ⬜ _____ intelligence

C 1 11 14 23 27 = ⬜ _____ intelligence

D 8 16 19 21 29 = ⬜ _____ intelligence

E 3 4 13 24 28 = ⬜ _____ intelligence

F 2 6 26 31 33 = ⬜ _____ intelligence

G 12 18 32 34 35 = ⬜ _____ intelligence

Teacher Answer Key: Do not reveal to students until after they have scored their tests.
A = interpersonal
B = body-kinesthetic
C = intrapersonal
D = logical-mathematical
E = musical-rhythmic
F = verbal-linguistic
G = visual-spatial

Identifying Your Multiple Intelligences: Survey 2

For each scenario, rank the seven options by putting a 1 next to the option you like the most, a 2 by the your next choice, and so forth. Everyone will have different answers.

1. As you plan a summer trip with your friends, you are asked to be responsible for one of the following:
   A. _____ Calling all your friends to tell them of the group's plans.
   B. _____ Running the errands needed to prepare for the trip.
   C. _____ Keeping a trip diary recording your thoughts and feelings.
   D. _____ Figuring out the distance to your destination.
   E. _____ Preparing songs to sing on the trip.
   F. _____ Writing a story about your trip for the newspaper.
   G. _____ Mapping the group's journey.

2. What would your friends say is true about you?
   A. _____ You are happiest when you are talking to other people.
   B _____ You like to dance or play sports.
   C. _____ You are in touch with your thoughts and feelings.
   D. _____ You have fun working on computers or with numbers.
   E. _____ You like to sing, rap, or tap out rhythms.
   F. _____ You enjoy writing notes or letters.
   G. _____ You draw, sketch, or paint well.

3. Which of the following electives would you most prefer?
   A. _____ Peer Counseling
   B. _____ Drama
   C. _____ Psychology or Comparative Religions
   D. _____ Architectural Design, Auto Shop, or Computer Literacy
   E. _____ Band or Chorus
   F. _____ Creative Writing or Journalism
   G. _____ Art

4. Rank your preferences for the following extracurricular activities:
   A. _____ Working as a tutor or joining a team.
   B. _____ Taking part in the school play, a dance production, or a martial arts class.
   C. _____ Dealing with feelings or personal issues with a group of peers.
   D. _____ Designing the set for a play, joining the chess team, or joining the math club.
   E. _____ Joining a musical group such as a jazz band, a chorus, or a rap group.
   F. _____ Working as a writer for the school newspaper or joining the debate team.
   G. _____ Painting murals on the school's walls.

5. What would you most like to be when you get older?
   A. _____ A counselor, social worker, or teacher
   B. _____ A dancer, actor, builder, or athlete
   C. _____ A psychologist or poet
   D. _____ A scientist, computer programmer, or banker
   E. _____ A singer, songwriter, or musician
   F. _____ A lawyer, writer, or journalist
   G. _____ A cartoonist, painter, or graphic artist

Scoring Your Multiple Intellegences: Survey 2

Each column below corresponds to a numbered item in the survey. Look for the number ranking you gave to each lettered choice under item 1, and copy those numbers into the boxes in column 1. Then do the same for the remaining columns. When you have finished, add the numbers in each row and write the total in the last box. The *lower* your score, the *stronger* your ability in that intelligence. Thus, a score of 1 indicates strong ability; a score of 7 indicates weaker ability. (Your teacher will tell you which intelligence to write for each row.)

	1	2	3	4	5			
A	☐	☐	☐	☐	☐	=	☐	_____ intelligence
B	☐	☐	☐	☐	☐	=	☐	_____ intelligence
C	☐	☐	☐	☐	☐	=	☐	_____ intelligence
D	☐	☐	☐	☐	☐	=	☐	_____ intelligence
E	☐	☐	☐	☐	☐	=	☐	_____ intelligence
F	☐	☐	☐	☐	☐	=	☐	_____ intelligence
G	☐	☐	☐	☐	☐	=	☐	_____ intelligence

Teacher Answer Key: Do not reveal to students until after they have scored their tests.

A = interpersonal   E = musical-rhythmic
B = body-kinesthetic   F = verbal-linguistic
C = intrapersonal   G = visual-spatial
D = logical-mathematical

Allow newly formed groups to engage in team-building activities to build group cohesion.

STEP 8

Team-building activities help students feel at ease in their group and strengthen their ability to work as a team.

Rationale Before students can effectively engage in groupwork activities, they must feel comfortable with their group members and believe in the value of teamwork. It is imperative that team-building activities—exercises designed to create a more comfortable, cohesive group environment—precede groupwork tasks. The investment in time (5 to 30 minutes) pays off in opportunities for students to interact safely, to get a feel for the interpersonal dynamics within the group, to break social tension, to value teamwork, and to feel at ease working together.

What to Do Once you have created mixed-ability groups and have taught students how to move into groups, they are ready for a team-building activity. With students in their groups, follow this procedure:

1. **Tell students that they will be doing a team-building activity.** Explain that the activity is designed to help them see the importance of teamwork and feel more comfortable with their group members.

2. **Give each student a copy of "Lost on the Moon."** (See page 156.) Read the scenario and the directions aloud, answering any questions students have. Emphasize that students are to complete Phase 1 entirely on their own and that there should be no talking until everyone has completed the individual rankings. This should take 4 to 6 minutes.

3. **Have groups complete Phase 2, their team rankings.** Encourage students to use their cooperative skills while working on a group solution. You may want to display a copy of the "Cooperative Skills" list (page 147) as a reminder. As students exchange probable solutions, there may be heated discussion. That is okay. If students within a group cannot agree, remind them of the directions: They are to decide on the rankings that "best satisfy" all members. Expect that some groups will finish within 10 minutes while others will take significantly longer.

4. **After all groups have completed Phase 2, reveal the answers.** Hand out "Answers to Lost on the Moon" (page 157). Talk about NASA's rationale for each ranking. Have students compute the error points for both individual and group rankings by finding the absolute difference between each pair of numbers. In most cases, the total number of error points will be significantly lower for the group rankings, supporting the notion that teamwork is valuable.

5. **Hold a class discussion on the value of teamwork.** Center the discussion on these questions: *Were your answers more accurate when you worked individually or as a group? What do you attribute this to? In what ways can working together be beneficial? When working in your group, which of the cooperative skills did you use?*

In most cases, this exercise will allow students to experience the value of teamwork and to feel more comfortable within their groups. If, based on your observations and the discussion following the activity, you feel that students are relatively comfortable with their groups and are ready to take on a curricular task, your team building is complete. Following are some signal behaviors that tell you when students are ready to begin curricular groupwork:

- relaxed body language
- friendly facial expressions
- laughter
- interaction that includes all group members
- prolonged discussion

As you create new groups throughout the year, a quick (5- to 10-minute) team-building activity can increase the comfort level and enhance the quality of groupwork. The following ideas are all quick, simple, and engaging team-builders.

- **Finish That Thought** Ask students to discuss a simple, nonacademic topic—something that everyone will find interesting to talk about—to ease the tension of working together. Remind students to give other group members their full attention as each student responds to the prompt.

   If I had a million dollars I would…
   I am most proud that I can…
   The funniest thing that ever happened to me was…
   Next year, I will be able to…
   If I were the teacher of this class, I would…
   My very favorite meal is…
   If you walked into my room at home, you'd see…
   The best pet in the world would be…
   My favorite movie is…

- **Team Handshake** Have groups develop a team handshake—a special way for people to shake hands that shows they belong to a particular group. This quick, kinesthetic task will help bring students together and ease tension. Teams might share their handshake with the class.

- **Team Logo** Pass out pieces of butcher paper and have each group design a logo using words, symbols, drawings, and color. The logos should reflect the interests and personalities of the group members. Have groups share their logos with the class.

- **Human Statues** Assign each group something different that they must work together to mimic with their bodies, such as a tree, a computer, a car, a table, a bicycle, a slide, an octopus, an elephant, or an airplane. You may want to award bonus points (or another reward) to groups who can physically represent their object or animal so well that the class can immediately identify it.

Team-builders—like creating human statues—help students quickly establish themselves as a team.

• **Famous Person** Have groups choose a famous person they would like to "join their group." They must explain why that person would be a helpful group member for the activity.

• **Team Sport** Have students choose a sport to represent their group and tell three ways their group is similar to that sport. *(Our group is like volleyball because…)*

• **Group Commonalities** Give groups 2 minutes to discover and list as many things as they can that all group members have in common.

• **Line Up** Have group members line up quickly according to their birth dates, the first letter of their middle names, their number of siblings, who lives closest to school, or some other criterion. Groups might compete in several fast-paced lineups.

When Use "Lost on the Moon" when students are embarking on their first formal groupwork activity, usually during the third, fourth, or fifth week of classes. Use the simpler team-builders whenever you form new groups for subsequent activities.

Lost on the Moon

Your spaceship has just crash-landed on the lighted side of the moon. You were scheduled to rendezvous with a mother ship 200 miles away on the surface of the moon, but the rough landing has ruined your ship and destroyed all the equipment on board, except for the 15 items listed below.

Your crew's survival depends on reaching the mother ship, so you must choose the most critical items available for the 200-mile trip. Your task is to rank the 15 items in terms of their importance for survival. Place a 1 by the most important item, a 2 by the second-most important, and so on through 15, the least important.

First you will do the ranking individually. Then you will be allowed to consult with your group members to do a team ranking. Share your individual solutions and reach a consensus ranking for each of the 15 items that best satisfies all group members. NASA experts have determined the best solution. Their answers will be revealed later.

Item	Phase 1 Your Individual Ranking	Phase 2 Your Team's Ranking
Box of matches		
Food concentrate		
50 feet of nylon rope		
Parachute silk		
Solar-powered portable heating unit		
Two .45-caliber pistols		
Case of dehydrated milk		
Two 100-pound tanks of oxygen		
Stellar map of moon's constellation		
Self-inflating life raft		
Magnetic compass		
5 gallons of water		
Signal flares		
First-aid kit with injection needles		
Solar-powered FM receiver-transmitter		

Answers to Lost on the Moon

When you and your group have completed ranking the 15 items from the "Lost on the Moon" list, record your ranks and your team's ranks in the appropriate spaces below. Then subtract your ranks and NASA's ranks to compute your error points. Do the same to compute your team's error points. Error points are the absolute difference between your ranks and NASA's—disregard plus or minus signs. Finally, add up the total error points to compare your individual error points to those of your team's. The lowest number is the best score.

Item	NASA Rationale	NASA's Rank	Your Rank	Error Points	Team Rank	Error Points
Box of matches	No oxygen on moon to sustain flame; virtually worthless	15				
Food concentrate	Efficient means of supplying energy requirements	4				
50 feet of nylon rope	Useful in scaling cliffs, tying injured together	6				
Parachute silk	Protection from sun's rays	8				
Solar-powered portable heating unit	Not needed unless on dark side; won't work there because no sun	13				
Two .45-caliber pistols	Possible means of self-propulsion	11				
Case of dehydrated milk	Bulkier duplication of food concentrate	12				
Two 100-pound tanks of oxygen	Most pressing survival need	1				
Stellar map of moon's constellation	Primary means of navigation	3				
Self-inflating life raft	CO_2 bottle in raft may be used for propulsion	9				
Magnetic compass	Magnetic field on moon is not polarized; worthless for navigation	14				
5 gallons of water	Replacement of tremendous liquid loss on lighted side	2				
Signal flares	Distress signal when mother ship is sighted	10				
First-aid kit with injection	Needles for vitamins, medicines, etc.; will fit special aperture in NASA space suits	7				
Solar-powered FM receiver-transmitter	For communication with mother ship	5				
				Total		Total

STEP 9

Allow students to engage in groupwork activities without unnecessary interventions by you.

Rationale One reason for groupwork is to help students learn problem solving skills. Often, teachers are too quick to intervene when students appear stuck. Resist the temptation to solve groups' problems. Instead, allow them to struggle or even fail at a task, provided that you debrief with the group what worked and what didn't so they can learn from the experience.

What to Do Once groups have begun working, it's time for you to step aside and monitor the activity more discreetly. You may want to praise on-task behavior, record group progress for assessment, and note cooperative skills that groups are using. Curb any impulse to control group interaction and offer quick solutions. If students ask for substantive help, try to redirect them so they can solve the issues themselves. Accept only "team questions"— questions for which all group members have their hands in the air.

Allowing groups as much autonomy as possible encourages them to work out problems on their own.

Some conflict between group members is inevitable. Simply ask, *What seems to be the difficulty?* and let the students think of strategies for handling the conflict. Most groups can rise to this challenge. Some combinations of students are particularly volatile, but changing the composition of groups on a regular basis and rotating roles will help ensure that the conflict does not become chronic.

Your intervention may be needed if the problem seems to be created by one particularly difficult student. Observe that student closely. Exactly how is he or she behaving? How does the group respond? What interests, needs, and strengths does the student exhibit? Take the student aside and share your observations. Ask, *Are my observations correct? Is there a reason you are behaving this way? What could you do to make things run smoother? What could the group do? What could I do?* Often the student will be experiencing interpersonal conflict not only in the group, but with friends or family as well. Taking time to listen will probably make the student feel more comfortable in your class and willing to work on changing behavior.

After students have finished a groupwork activity, it's time for you to lead a discussion of the group process. Ask:

- How did your group interact?
- Which cooperative skills were exhibited the most?
- What did your group do well?
- What could you have improved?
- If another group of students were to do this same activity, what helpful suggestions would you make?

Helping students assess their own groupwork in this way will continue to build the effectiveness of their cooperative skills.

When Use this approach any time students are engaged in groupwork activities.

STEP 10

Discuss the three premises behind the TCI Approach with your students.

Rationale Students can become even more active and informed learners if you explain to them the rationale behind your teaching. Students are fascinated and appreciative—especially after they have experienced several activities—when they discover why you are teaching in this manner. The information will help them better understand you, the class, and their own abilities and strengths so they can benefit even more from this approach.

What to Do After you have finished your first or second unit of instruction, reveal to students the three premises behind the TCI Approach (as discussed in "Theory-Based Active Instruction," page 10). This explanation is crucial for two reasons. First, it informs students of the theories that guide your methods of instruction. More importantly, it validates the academic worth of all class members by pointing out that individuals have different abilities and unique talents. When all of these abilities and talents have an equal chance to contribute, learning together becomes a richer, more exciting experience.

Project a transparency of "The Three Premises Behind the TCI Approach" (page 160). Discuss each premise with your students, and have them give examples of ways in which each premise has been acknowledged and addressed in your class. By sharing this instructional framework with your students, you empower them to be in charge of their learning.

When Reveal these premises after students have had four to six weeks' experience with the TCI Approach.

"Using this method changed the atmosphere in my classroom almost immediately. As soon as my students realized how much I cared about them as people, the rigorous task of discipline dissolved almost totally in an environment of respect."

— Middle School Teacher

In a cooperative and tolerant environment, students lose their self-consciousness and participate freely in the sometimes unconventional multiple intelligence activities you use with the TCI Approach.

The Three Premises Behind the TCI Approach

Premise 1: Students learn best through multiple intelligences.

Howard Gardner believes that we all learn in different ways. Each of us is stronger in some of these types of intelligences than in others.

- You might be "word smart," or have linguistic intelligence.
- You might be "music smart," or have musical-rhythmic intelligence.
- You might be "number smart," or have logical-mathematical intelligence.
- You might be "picture smart," or have visual-spatial intelligence.
- You might be "body smart," or have body-kinesthetic intelligence.
- You might be "people smart," or have interpersonal intelligence.
- You might be "self smart," or have intrapersonal intelligence.

Premise 2: Cooperative interaction increases learning gains.

Elizabeth Cohen believes that working in a group helps people to

- get along with others.
- work with others to accomplish goals.
- learn concepts and how to solve problems.
- improve their talking and listening skills.

Premise 3: All students can learn via the spiral curriculum.

Jerome Bruner believes that everyone can learn any subject if

- lessons "spiral" from easier ideas to harder ideas.
- students learn harder ideas by discovering them in a step-by-step way.

Part 3

Using the Interactive Student Notebook

Using the Interactive Student Notebook _____

Introduction

Student notebooks are an essential part of any social studies course. Unfortunately, they are too often drab repositories of information filled with uninspired, unconnected, and poorly understood ideas. Interactive Student Notebooks, however, offer an exciting twist on the conventional social studies notebook. The first time you see one, you will be immediately struck by the colorful and varied expression within its pages. Words and diagrams, bullets and arrows, ink and pencil, a multitude of colors, highlighting—all reveal a unique personal style as students express their ideas, questions, feelings about and reactions to new content in a host of creative ways. No two Interactive Student Notebooks look the same.

At the same time, the Interactive Student Notebook provides a cohesive structure and serves as the organizational anchor for the multiple intelligence activities that occur in a TCI lesson. For each lesson, the Interactive Student Notebook centers on three key elements of the TCI Approach:

- **Preview Assignments** At the start of each lesson, short, intriguing assignments help students connect the upcoming lesson to their own experience, activating their prior knowledge. The purpose of these assignments, along with examples of the many different types, are found in "PreviewAssignment," page 22.
- **Graphically Organized Reading Notes** As the lesson unfolds, students use a section called Reading Notes to record, in a striking graphic format, main ideas and supporting details of what they are learning. Typically, all "testable" information can be found in this section. Many examples of the various formats suitable for this part of the notebook are presented in "Graphically Organized Reading Notes," page 96.
- **Processing Assignments** Students end each lesson with a Processing assignment—perhaps involving illustrated timelines, Venn diagrams, matrices, annotated maps, flowcharts, sensory figures, advertisements, visual metaphors, or persuasive letters—to synthesize and apply what they have learned. Many examples of these engaging assignments are found in "Processing Assignment," page 102.

Why Interactive Student Notebooks Engage Students

Teachers find that their students embrace the Interactive Student Notebook enthusiastically. "I used to hate taking notes and filling out worksheets in class," one student commented, "but I love working on my notebook because it's fun." Teachers also report that because the Interactive Student Notebook encourages a variety of forms of expression—personalized responses to the subject matter, artwork, graphics, timelines, maps, and song lyrics—there's more interest and more involvement by students, in addition to more learning and better retention. Here are some of the reasons Interactive Student Notebooks are found to engage students so thoroughly:

They reach out to students, inviting them to be active participants in their learning. Many students are accustomed to filling out blanks on a worksheet or laboriously copying teacher-written notes from the board or the overhead. The Interactive Student Notebook changes that. At the beginning of a lesson, students are "hooked" with a Preview assignment that taps into their own experiences and prior knowledge. Then students are encouraged to accurately record Reading Notes for a *purpose*—searching for implications or assumptions, identifying main ideas, providing supporting details, interpreting information. They will use this information during Processing assignments that challenge them to really *think* and apply what they have learned. As a result, students become more creative, more independent thinkers.

They encourage students to use a variety of intelligences, not just linguistic intelligence. Conventional student notebooks may work for motivated students with strong linguistic skills, but they do not work as well for students with other predominant intelligences. In the Interactive Student Notebook, students approach

Origin of the Interactive Student Notebook

The Interactive Student Notebook was initially developed in the 1970s by Lee Swenson and his colleagues at Aragon High School in San Mateo, California. Teachers at TCI, after using Interactive Student Notebooks in their classrooms and seeing how profoundly they improved instruction, contacted Lee in 1992 about adopting the Interactive Student Notebook as part of the TCI Approach. Lee then collaborated with teachers at TCI to refine his ideas by creating standard guidelines for students and teachers, and by expanding the variety of graphic organizers.

"Students like that the notebooks allow them the freedom and creativity to express themselves in a variety of ways. Parents continually tell me that they think it's fantastic that kids are relating social studies to their lives and writing about what they learn in their notebooks."

— High School Teacher

Students use their visual intelligence when they interpret information graphically in their notebooks. With colored markers and construction paper, they create vivid images that help them understand and remember key concepts—such as the attributes of Mexico's Porfirio Diaz (above left), and the demographic characteristics of modern Latin America (above right).

understanding in many ways. They can tap into their *visual* intelligence through such elements as graphs, maps, illustrations, pictowords, and visual metaphors; their *musical* intelligence by composing song lyrics or reacting to a piece of music; their *intrapersonal* intelligence by reflecting on the ways social studies topics affect them personally; their *interpersonal* intelligence by recording group discussions and group project notes; and their *logical-mathematical* intelligence through sequencing and the use of spectrums, graphs, and charts.

They help students to organize systematically as they learn. Students use their notebooks to record ideas about every social studies lesson. They use a variety of organizational techniques—topic headings, color-coding, different writing styles—to give coherence to what they learn. The notebook also helps students keep assignments together and in a logical order. Gone are the days of notes and assignments wadded up and stuffed in backpacks or lockers.

They become a portfolio of individual learning. These personal, creative notebooks become a record of each student's growth. Teachers, students, and even family members can review a student's progress in writing, thinking, and organizational skills.

Hints for Making Effective Interactive Student Notebooks

Teachers use the Interactive Student Notebook in a variety of forms. Some give their students the consumable workbook that is provided with TCI's core program materials. Teachers who elect to use this consumable can follow the sequence exactly as designed, having students complete the specified Preview, Reading Notes, and Processing assignment for each lesson. This is helpful to teachers who are new to TCI Approach, since they can rely on the published Interactive Student Notebook for support while they are learning to use the essential elements and strategies of the program.

Other teachers elect to supplement the printed workbook with their own handouts and materials that students bring in. Students use spiral-bound notebooks or three-ring binders to combine the materials, cutting and pasting as they create their own unique Interactive Student Notebooks. In this format, TCI materials serve as the backbone, but teachers have the flexibility to tailor instruction to suit their needs.

Help Students to See the Coherent Whole

The Interactive Student Notebook groups assignments by unit, so that students can see a logical flow from assignment to assignment and begin to understand the coherence of the unit. Their notebooks serve as a chronological record of their work and help reinforce the major concepts and themes in a unit.

This is where the parts of the integrated lesson come together—the Preview, the graphically organized Reading Notes, and the Processing assignment. Using this framework helps students see how everything connects.

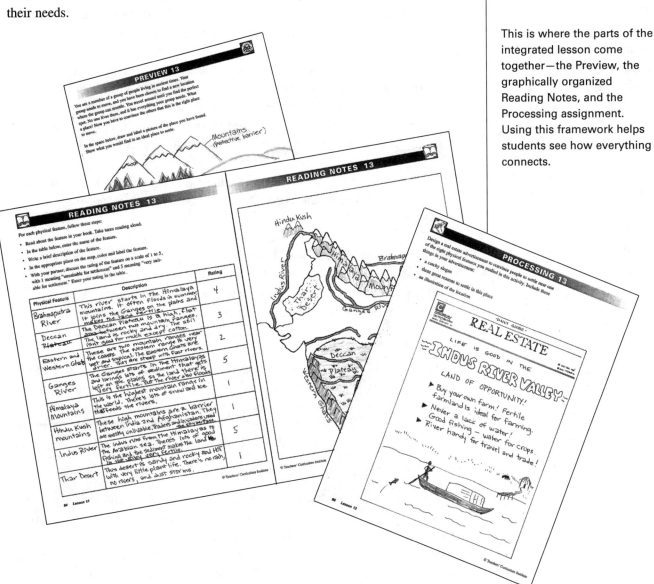

It Takes Time

Teaching students how to use Interactive Student Notebooks is a complex task. It takes patience, good modeling, and constant reinforcement. You will discover that your students' notebooks will improve dramatically over time.

"The notebook allows me to express my opinions about what we are learning. I usually don't get to do that in my other classes."

— Middle School Student

Still other teachers may be developing their own curricular materials based on the TCI Approach. They won't have a published notebook to start with, but they can follow the same structure, having students create spiral-bound Interactive Student Notebooks that include the teacher's own lesson Previews, graphic organizers for capturing content notes, and Processing assignments, plus any additional support materials. Creating this type of Interactive Student Notebook is labor-intensive, but many teachers are willing and eager to take on the task because of the tremendous success of this powerful organizational and instructional tool.

Regardless of the format you plan to use, the following hints will increase the effectiveness of your Interactive Student Notebooks and allow students' individual styles to flourish.

1. Supply materials that inspire creativity. An abundance of materials—colored pencils and markers, scissors, glue sticks, colored highlighters—will spark creativity for notebook assignments. Some teachers collect a class set of materials to keep in their room. These can be used by students who don't otherwise have the materials they need for in-class work on their notebook.

2. Let students create their own covers. When you introduce the Interactive Student Notebook, encourage students to embellish theirs with a colorful cover that in some way reflects the content you are teaching. This immediately sends students the message that the notebooks will be their own creations that they can take pride in—and it helps cut down on the number of lost notebooks during the year.

3. Personalize the notebooks with an author page. Have students create a page about themselves to include at the front of their notebooks. Their author page could include a portrait or photograph, as well as personal information or favorite quotes. (As needed, remind students that any content unsuitable at school is also unacceptable for use in notebooks.) With both a personalized cover and an author page, very few notebooks get lost.

Notebook covers can be as individual as your students. It's up to each teacher to specify which information is considered essential for the cover, such as student's name, course name, class period, date. Beyond that, the students' design treatment may take a wide variety of forms, from the simple to the complex, from the pictorial to the abstract.

Interactive Student Notebook Guidelines

What is the purpose of the Interactive Notebook?

The purpose of the Interactive Student Notebook is to enable you to be a creative, independent thinker and writer. Interactive notebooks will be used for class notes as well as for other activities in which you will be asked to express your own ideas and process the information presented in class.

What materials do I need?

- Spiral notebook—white paper, college-ruled, at least 100 pages
- Pencil
- Blue and black pens
- Glue stick and scissors
- Colored pens and pencils
- Highlighters
- Zipper pouch

What goes in my notebook?

Everything we do in class. We will use graphically organized visuals to help you take notes, structuring them so that key ideas are clear and supported by examples from class activities, discussion, or reading assignments. Your notebook will also be used for a variety of different activities to preview learning and process new content to demonstrate understanding. This is where you will record and express all of your well-considered ideas.

How can I earn an A on my notebook?

A student who expects to earn an A- or higher grade on the notebook will be one who keeps a complete, neat notebook, produces quality work, and has taken the time to consistently extend learning beyond classroom assignments. You will show this by including "Making Connections" entries, unassigned work that you complete in addition to our regular class assignments.

What do you mean by "Making Connections"?

For "Making Connections," you place articles, pictures, or cartoons (from magazines, newspapers, or the Internet) into your notebook, along with a 4–5 sentence summary and reflection on how the materials relate to our topic of study. You might also include original drawings. "Making Connections" entries should sharpen (rather than clutter) the visual appearance of your notebook.

How will my notebook be graded?

Notebooks will be graded on thoroughness, quality, organization, and visual appearance. You will know the value of each major notebook assignment when it is given. About 25 percent of your grade for the course will be based on the notebook.

An important part of your notebook is its visual appearance. Your notebook should be NEAT! Each entry should be title and dated. Your artistic talent should be visible throughout the notebook.

Notebooks will be checked periodically for completeness—usually about every 3–4 weeks, except for the first few weeks of class, when they will be checked more regularly. All class notes and notebook assignments should be included, even for days you were absent.

What happens if I am absent?

If you are absent, it is your responsibility to obtain notebook assignments from a classmate or from the Interactive Teacher Notebook.

Share this handout with your parent or guardian. When both of you have read this information, please sign your names below.

Student Signature _____   Parent Signature _____

4. Give clear guidelines for the notebooks. One of the most important steps for successful notebooks is to establish clear guidelines. Decide ahead of time what you expect your students to produce in their notebooks, and then clearly communicate your expectations. Most teachers create a list of criteria—how notebooks will be graded, what percentage of the class grade will depend on the notebooks—and ask students to attach that list to the inside cover of their notebooks. Some teachers even include directions for specific types of notebook assignments, class rules, and their grading policy.

You might also send a letter to students and families, explaining the purpose of the notebook and your expectations. In the sample guidelines shown on page 168, students *and* their parents are asked to sign the handout to show that they have read the guidelines and understand the purpose and importance of the Interactive Student Notebook.

5. Consider adding a table of contents. You may want students to create a running table of contents for their notebooks. This can be as simple as a list of completed assignments and page numbers, or it could include more complex information. Add your comments and scores for each assignment. This will help you immensely when it comes time to grade the notebooks.

Lost Notebooks?

Because students take a great deal of pride of ownership in their notebooks, typically very few are lost during a semester. Most teachers report that only a handful of students lose them each year. If your students do lose their notebooks, consider allowing them to make up a select number of assignments so they may receive partial credit.

This student's contents page lists each assignment completed and the page number where it can be found. A table of contents helps students stay organized, and helps you at grading time.

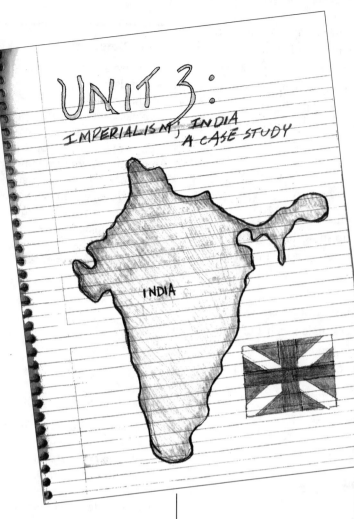

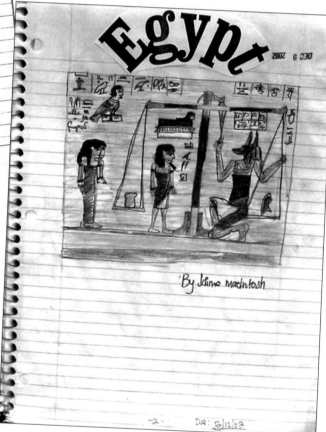

A simple title page design with a few bold images can be extremely effective.

6. Add unit title pages that echo the unit theme. For each unit you study, have students design a title page for that section of their Interactive Student Notebook. On this page they would write the title of the unit, and then find and affix pictures or draw illustrations to represent the unit's theme. This is an opportunity for students to preview the chapter, as well as to use their creative genius to personalize their notebooks.

How to Manage Interactive Student Notebooks

If you have four or five classes a day, each with up to 35 students, that means you could have 150 or more student notebooks to keep track of. Because so much of the students' work appears in these notebooks, you will need a system for assessing them. Ideally, you will both informally assess the notebooks on a regular basis, to give students immediate feedback, and also *formally* collect and grade the notebooks every three to four weeks.

An earlier section of this book, "How to Make Assessment of Student Notebooks Manageable" (pages 125–127), gives you further details and tips on effectively managing this task.

Create an "Interactive *Teacher* Notebook." Another management tool to help you monitor the use and the effectiveness of the Interactive Student Notebook throughout the year is an "Interactive *Teacher* Notebook." All you need is a master notebook in which you record each notebook assignment, attach student handouts, store copies of content notes, and make annotations on the activities for future reference—notes on how they went, which groups or individuals seemed to have trouble with them and why, and what questions really worked to prompt good critical thinking.

By keeping a master notebook, you have a visual record of what took place in class. If you incorporate details about the lesson objectives, standards addressed, materials needed, and procedures, the teacher notebook serves as your lesson-planning book as well. It is the ideal place to reflect on the outcome of lessons and to record ideas about how to make them more effective in the future.

The Interactive Teacher Notebook serves both the teacher and the students. For the teacher, this tool
- functions as the teacher's lesson-planning book.
- includes a table of contents that becomes the "official" record of assignments.
- provides a place to store extra materials and handouts.
- communicates special instructions for students who have been absent.
- serves as a journal to reflect on the effectiveness of activities and assignments and ways to improve them.

For students, the Interactive Teacher Notebook
- is a place they can find any information and assignments they missed during an absence.
- serves as a model of how assignments should be title, dated, and arranged.
- allows them to check the completeness of their own notebook.

Spotlight Student Notebooks

Showcase exceptional notebooks so students have the opportunity to gather ideas for improving their own notebooks. You might set up six or eight stations around the classroom, put an exceptional notebook at each, and conduct a "gallery walk." Allow students 15 or 20 minutes to roam around the room and collect ideas from the model notebooks.

Making the TCI Approach Your Own

How to Adapt Lessons to Meet Your Students' Needs

Introduction

In Part 4 of this book, we suggest ways to refine and adapt the TCI Approach to meet your individual classroom and student needs. In this first section, we focus on ideas for adapting lessons to meet the needs of your particular students. Subsequent sections discuss ways to hone your use of the multiple intelligence teaching strategies, and things to consider when you are designing your own units and lessons according to the TCI Approach.

As you read in Part 1, the TCI Approach is defined by three foundational premises and a series of instructional practices that allow students of all abilities to experience key social studies concepts. Whereas traditional instruction primarily rewards verbal-linguistic and logical-mathematical intelligences, the TCI Approach routinely reaches the other intelligences as well.

If you use TCI's published programs, you'll see that they're structured to support diverse learners. For example:

- Lessons consistently follow a sequence of steps—a motivational Preview, an engaging and memorable activity, graphically organized Reading Notes, and an innovative Processing assignment—which assures that even students with lesser linguistic skills have access to key social studies concepts.
- Students work in small groups of two, three, or four, often with defined roles that are tailored to their individual strengths.
- The Lesson Guide reminds teachers to model the steps necessary for successful completion of each task.
- Challenging, higher-level tasks are tackled one step at a time. Content is spiraled as students gather building blocks to create understanding.
- Teachers are given guidance in creating a cooperative, tolerant classroom environment that supports all students and encourages them to take risks.

Still, lessons based on the TCI approach may need to be further adapted to meet the unique and often wide-ranging needs of your students. After all, no one can identify these particular needs better than you. For example:

- You know which of your students are English language learners and may need additional language support.
- You know which students are reading and writing below grade level and may need support with reading assignments or written work.
- You know which students are easily distracted; which ones have difficulty communicating; which ones may be socially uncomfortable or have behavioral issues; which ones have physical disabilities that might inhibit their participation in certain types of activities.
- You also know which students could benefit from extra challenges that push them to use higher-order thinking skills.

Furthermore, you are in a position to assess each student's individual blend of strengths and limitations. For example, you may find that a student who struggles to string sentences together has stunning graphic talents and is able to express as much in a well-thought-out poster as other students do in a written essay.

The needs of your students will vary from class to class, and you must consider ways to tailor your lessons to meet the particular needs of each class. In this section, we offer a host of ways to adapt lessons based on the TCI Approach to meet different needs. As you consider these suggested adaptations, you will also see that a slight modification can sometimes serve a wide variety of students.

> *"I was looking for a way to inspire and engage reluctant students. This approach creates a desire for students to read on, find out, and understand."*
>
> — Middle School Teacher

Things You Can Do to Address Special Needs

Encourage Full Participation. Any time you feel that a student may be reluctant to participate in some activity—an act-it-out, an experiential exercise, a presentation of a groupwork project, a whole-group discussion—you need to find a way to ensure that student's inclusion. Consider these possible adaptations:

- Assign the reluctant student a "buddy" for help with preparation and to provide support and encouragement. Peer mentors, or helpers, can help with nearly any part of a lesson. For example, they can explain unknown vocabulary, provide guidance with a set of directions, answer questions about aspects of a game-like activity, help with organizational tasks, and so forth.

- For any minidrama, offer some nonspeaking or limited-speaking roles, allowing students to participate with movements or gestures. Or, adapt speaking roles by letting students use scripts or cue cards.

- For act-it-outs in Visual Discovery lessons, assign roles the night before so that students can rehearse what their character will say and do.

- When students are involved in role playing, such as taking on the role of delegates to a meeting or convention, assign mixed-ability pairs to split the responsibilities of a single role and help each other out.

- Incorporate manipulatives into activities to add a tactile component to a lesson. These manipulatives can be as simple as vocabulary cards to be matched with visual content, or cards with visual icons to aid in the placement of ideas or events along a spectrum.

- During a discussion, have students talk in pairs before you ask for a whole-group response. *In what ways did China's geography isolate it from other civilizations? Talk to your partner. Jot down your ideas. What did you and your partner come up with?* You can spend as little as 30–60 seconds on this, yet it gives students the chance to formulate their thoughts, to test their ideas, and to get the confidence to raise their hands. It also gives them a chance to revisit and reinforce the content, which is important for all students.

Provide Reading Support. Students who struggle with reading always benefit from some type of prereading experience. Some specific suggestions are given in the section "Considerate Text," page 86. Among these, do not overlook the value of providing focus questions, section by section, to give all students a purpose for reading and to help them discover the essential concepts being covered by the text. In addition, consider the following aids to reading both directions and expository text:

- Whenever possible, give directions in both written and oral form. For example, while explaining what students are to do, simultaneously show the directions on an overhead transparency. Or, ask one person in each small group to read the directions aloud.

- When directions are posted at stations, supply individual copies to students who need reading assistance. Highlight key words: *Read... Examine... List... Discuss... Record...* Draw a simple symbol next to each direction word, as a cue to its meaning: for *examine,* draw an eye; for *record,* draw a pencil.

Assign a "buddy" or partner to provide support and encouragement for a reluctant student. Peer mentors can help with nearly any part of a lesson.

- Have students create a set of vocabulary cards before reading a chapter. Provide a list of key terms or difficult vocabulary they will encounter in the reading. On an index card, students can write a word and its definition, and then draw a simple illustration to help them recall the meaning.

- As a prereading activity, have mixed-ability pairs scan the reading to develop vocabulary posters on letter-size paper. Each poster should display a single key term, an understandable definition, and a symbol representing the term. Hang these posters around the classroom as a reference for students as they read the chapter.

- Hang large poster paper on the wall to create a "word wall," which becomes an expanded glossary. While reading, students can go to this poster to write down words or phrases that they don't understand. You then write definitions directly on the poster—helping the student who had the question as well as anyone else who is struggling with the text.

- Make an audiotape recording of the textbook or of a series of placards or handouts, offering additional clarification of important terms and vocabulary.

Offer Help with the Reading Notes. In TCI's published programs, the Interactive Student Notebook has pages for students' Reading Notes. Here are some ways to simplify those Reading Notes when necessary:

- Provide *cloze* exercises (fill-in-the-blank sentences or paragraphs) to structure the students' note taking. When you are using TCI's published programs, use the Guide to Reading Notes in the Lesson Guide as a starting point and simply omit (or white out) key words and phrases, leaving blanks for students to fill in. For example, for notes on a section of reading about Alexander Hamilton, you would provide something like this:

Best Form of Government	Ideal Economy
Hamilton believed the country should be run by _____ , _____ , and public-spirited men.	Hamilton believed the ideal economy was one based on business, _____ , and trade. He also believed the nation needed a national bank to collect _____ , print _____ , and make loans to build factories and _____ .

- After each question, provide sentence starters for students:
  1. Why did the Greeks start colonies?
     Greek communities started colonies because they needed . . .
  2. Why did some Greek settlements trade?
     Greeks traded to get . . .
  3. What products did the colonies provide to settlements back home?
     Greek colonies provided . . .

- When the Reading Notes cover several sections of text in an identical format, make the students' work sequentially more difficult. For example:
  First section: Model what to do by giving appropriate responses.
  Second section: Provide cloze exercises.
  Third section: Provide sentence starters.
  Final section: Students provide the entire response.

- For Reading Notes organized in a matrix, provide the answers for one column and let students do the others.

- Provide a word bank with words or phrases students can use in their answers.

- Provide written answers to the questions in random order, for use as a "hint sheet."

Your students' strengths, needs, and limitations vary from class to class. Slight modifications and adaptations help ensure that all students are successfully engaged.

- Allow students to complete only part of the Reading Notes, and then have them copy the remainder either from a partner or from the Guide to Reading Notes in your Lesson Guide.

- Give students photocopies of the text pages they are reading. On these sheets, they circle or highlight words, phrases, and sentences that will help them complete their Reading Notes.

Make Modifications for Written Work. Any time a writing assignment is required, consider the following adaptations:

- Supply a more explicit list of criteria for students' writing, telling them precisely what they need to include.

- Break longer writing assignments into smaller segments with intermediate due dates. For additional support, give students feedback after each segment that will help them with subsequent work.

- Consider giving an alternative approach that might better meet the needs of some students. For example, you might have them
  — list bulleted words and phrases instead of writing a paragraph.
  — orally discuss their response with you, a peer, or an aide.
  — illustrate a response and label the drawing, rather than writing about it.
  — use word processing programs to type papers, and find digital images for their illustrations.

You can modify the format of Reading Notes to support both English language learners and students reading below grade level.

Modify the Processing Assignment. As explained in Part 1, the Processing assignment is a key element of the TCI Approach that helps students process and internalize the information they have learned in a lesson. Because these assignments challenge students to use multiple intelligences and higher-order thinking skills, you may need to modify them for some students.

- Consider reducing the number of requirements. For example:
  — Reduce the number of items to be placed on a timeline from ten to five.
  — Have them write three paragraphs instead of five, or write about fewer terms, or fewer characteristics.
  — Have them do two illustrations instead of four, or a single cartoon rather than a four-panel strip.

- Turn the work into a matching exercise:
  — Provide a set of items to cut and paste along a spectrum or a timeline.
  — Provide phrases students can use to place in a Venn diagram or to complete given analogies.
  — Provide headlines to match to pictured events.

- Offer alternative Processing assignments that let students play to their individual strengths. Refer to the "Processing Assignment" section (pages 102–117) to see the many possibilities.

Accommodate Students with Physical Challenges. Many of TCI's multiple intelligence activities require students to move freely around the room. If you have students for whom this is difficult, you need to be sure they are not excluded. For example, if the lesson involves students rotating from one station to

Teachers find that Processing assignments can be flexed, making them simpler or more sophisticated to match individual students' needs.

another to examine placards, you could instead have the sets of placards passed from group to group. This does not affect the integrity of the activity, and no one gets left out.

Support and Honor Cultural Diversity. As you present lessons, watch for idiomatic expressions or cultural references that might be unfamiliar to some students. At the same time, be aware of situations when you can draw on students' personal knowledge of other cultures.

- In a Preview of a lesson on the U.S. colonists' break with Britain, students are asked to describe a personal experience related to the phrase *It was the last straw.* Be sure that all students understand the meaning of that expression, and (in the case of nonnative speakers) can relate it to similar expressions in their native tongue.
- For a Processing assignment that asks students to find analogies between ancient Egyptian social classes and people or groups in our society, some students may not be familiar with the structure of American society. Pair these students with peer helpers, or let them complete the work using examples from their native countries.
- In a lesson on the wave of immigration the U.S. experienced between 1880 and 1920, skip the step where students interview role-played "immigrants" and instead allow class members to respond from their own life experiences.

Offer Extra Challenge. For those students who might benefit from extra challenge, you need to find ways to elevate and extend the activities in ways that push students to use higher-order thinking skills. Rather than simply asking for more work, or more writing, ask for a more sophisticated kind of writing, a higher level of thinking. For example:

- When the class is analyzing a historical painting, use an approach termed "Behind the Paintbrush" to raise the level of thinking and enrich the discussion. Ask students to step into the artist's shoes. *As the artist, what are you thinking as you create this picture? Why are you painting this scene in this way? What are you trying to show? What are your opinions about the event or the people you are depicting?* This type of question asks students to hypothesize about the artist's motivations, a step beyond analyzing the painting from the perspective of a viewer.
- Send students to the Internet to do additional research to extend and enrich any lesson. For some of the TCI programs, specific Internet Connections and enrichment projects are listed on TCI's Web site. For example, when students of ancient world history are learning about the early settlement of India, they complete a map showing India's main geographical features—rivers, mountains, deserts. To extend this work, students might find a virtual tour of India online, then annotate the map with facts they have learned about each region.

Modify the Assessment. Consider whether the format and delivery of your assessment will accurately gauge what your students know or if some modifications are required. Here are some ideas you might sometimes find appropriate:

- In a multiple-choice test, reduce the number of answer choices for each item from four to two—one right and one wrong.
- Have a peer or aide read the items aloud.
- Allow the student to respond orally, either with a tape recorder or with an aide or parent helper.
- Provide a word bank or list of phrases to provide additional support for open-ended responses, or to turn fill-in questions into a matching exercise.
- Send home copies of test questions ahead of time, in random order, for use as a study guide.
- Make the test "open book," allowing students to refer to their Reading Notes or the textbook during the assessment.

> *"I have great success reaching my limited English proficient students using this approach. Multiple intelligence lesson instruction that taps into the nonlinguistic intelligences allows these students to learn the content and then put English vocabulary to it."*
>
> — High School Teacher

How to Hone Your Use of the Multiple Intelligence Teaching Strategies

Students discover how the Continental Army finally defeated the British in the Revolutionary War as they participate in an orchestrated game of Capture the Flag. This Experiential Exercise helps students grasp the strengths and weaknesses of both sides of the conflict.

Introduction

As you learned in Part 1, the instructional practices that make up the TCI Approach allow students with diverse learning styles to experience social studies. A central component of the TCI Approach is the use of six multiple intelligence teaching strategies: Visual Discovery, Social Studies Skill Builders, Experiential Exercises, Writing for Understanding, Response Groups, and Problem Solving Groupwork. In Part 1 (pages 28–85), you learned the basic steps, along with the rationale, for using each of these strategies.

In this section, we offer an array of advanced tips for how to hone and enhance your use of these multiple intelligence teaching strategies. Through our work with teachers who have successfully implemented the TCI Approach for a number of years, we have identified specific tips and best practices that teachers have used as they have refined their teaching methods. While these tips may be instructive to a newcomer to the TCI Approach, they are expressly designed for the teacher who has used the TCI Approach in the classroom for a year or more and is ready for more sophisticated application of these teaching strategies.

Hone Your Use of Visual Discovery

Advanced TIPS

As described in Part 1 (see page 28), Visual Discovery is a teaching strategy that turns what is usually a passive, teacher-centered activity—lecturing—into a dynamic, participatory experience. After a Visual Discovery activity, students generally retain more information than they would from a traditional lecture. There are, however, ways to hone this strategy to make it even more powerful. This section explains how you can

- increase student interaction during spiral questioning.
- make act-it-outs more engaging and authentic.

Increase Student Interaction During Spiral Questioning

Asking spiral questions related to images sometimes produces low student interaction—the teacher asks questions, and a few students share their responses. Here are some strategies for making the process more interactive so that all students participate.

Think-Pair Share Have students individually come up with a response to a question and share it with another student or two before you ask for volunteers to share their responses with the entire class.

Touch the Image Invite eight to ten students to come up to the projected image and point out or touch a detail they found interesting or important. If you are asking students to interpret the image, they might first offer their interpretations, then point out or touch details to support their interpretation.

Eager to approach the screen, this student uses "magic" paper to point out details that support her interpretation of the projected image.

Visual Discovery activities use powerful images to teach social studies concepts. These students step into a political cartoon that reveals the hypocrisy in late-19th century attitudes toward immigrants to the United States.

Students use simple props to re-create this scene of slaves picking cotton in the South. You might consider playing a rousing spiritual in the background to create a more authentic atmosphere.

Record Answers in the Interactive Student Notebook Ask students to record in their notebooks their responses to a question. You can circulate and review (or check off) students' responses, and then ask volunteers to share their ideas.

Face-Off Assign half of the class one question, such as, *Where do you think this is happening?* while the other half works on another question, such as, *When do you think this is happening?* Have the students on each side mutually agree on a response and present it, along with evidence from the image that supports their response, to the other half of the class.

Write a Caption or Headline Your final question about an image can be to ask students to write a short caption that explains what is happening. Or, have them write a newspaper headline to summarize the pictured event. Have students share their captions or headlines with a neighbor, or ask volunteers to read them aloud to the entire class.

Become Inanimate Objects Ask students to assume the role of an inanimate object in the image and to consider what they have seen from the point of view of that object. For example, as the Statue of Liberty, what have they seen pass by? Or as the castle that Joan of Arc attacked, what do they see inside the walls? Outside the walls? Have students circulate around the classroom and share their responses with one another.

Make Act-it-Outs More Engaging and Authentic

Some images used as the basis of act-it-outs have only a few characters in the scene. One challenge in such cases is finding ways to involve more students in bringing the image to life. Here are some ways to involve the entire class during an act-it-out. These ideas can make the act-it-out more engaging for students in the audience and can often help to create a more authentic atmosphere.

Ask students to provide sound effects. Have the audience contribute sound effects at appropriate times during an act-it-out. For example, during an act-it-out of an image showing European emigrants leaving on a ship and waving good-bye to their families, students at their desks might make the sound of the ship's horn or of family members on the dock shouting their farewells. Later, during an act-it-out of an image of European immigrants going through medical inspections at Ellis Island, have the audience make sounds that the medical inspector might hear through his stethoscope: clear, healthy breathing from some immigrants; labored, congested coughing from others. Give students clear directions about which sound effects are appropriate and when to make them.

Have students check for accuracy. Alert the audience to watch act-it-outs critically, listening for accuracies and inaccuracies in the presentations. Before an act-it-out, tell students in the audience to keep two lists: statements they hear that are accurate, and statements they hear that are inaccurate. After the act-it-out, ask students to share one accurate and one inaccurate fact. Encourage them to acknowledge the actors' efforts and to be sensitive to their feelings.

Have students serve as reporters. After several act-it-outs in which you model the types of questions an on-the-scene reporter should ask, have students take the role of reporters and prepare questions to ask the actors. Have reporters follow this procedure for asking questions during the act-it-out: they stand, identify the newspaper they represent, and direct their questions to a specific character. Remind reporters that their job is not to trick or stump the figures, but to get information from them. Disallow questions that are inappropriate or that the actors cannot answer based on the information that has been covered on the subject.

Let the audience chant slogans. Suggest historically appropriate slogans for the audience to chant during an act-it-out. For example, during an act-it-out for an image showing Lenin addressing a crowd during the Russian Revolution, the watching class can chant, "Land, Bread, and Peace!" which was Lenin's rally cry for the revolution. After you have suggested slogans for several different act-it-outs, let students come up with an appropriate slogan to enhance a particular image.

Add background music by having the class hum relevant tunes. Having the audience hum at appropriate times during an act-it-out taps students' musical-rhythmic intelligence. For example, during an act-it-out of a lunch counter sit-in during the civil rights era, students could hum the tune of "We Shall Overcome."

Include crowd participation in the scene. For some events, it is appropriate to have the entire class come to the front of the room, surround the actors in the act-it-out, and serve as a crowd around the scene shown in the image. For example, the class might pretend to be a group of students watching the Red Guard parade through the streets of Communist China, workers participating in a strike, or bank clients lining up in front of a closed bank during the Great Depression.

Encourage students to react melodramatically. For some act-it-outs, you might assign students in the audience the role of either supporter or opponent of the event or figure depicted in the image. Then, when you are interviewing student actors during the act-it-out, have the rest of the class respond melodramatically to their comments, calling out things such as *Boo, Hiss, Ahhh,* or *Hurrah!* For example, during an act-it-out on Shays's Rebellion, half the class would represent the government and the other half would represent the rebellious farmers. When the student representing the farmers speaks, half the class will boo and half the class will cheer, recreating the tense and divided atmosphere that existed during the era of the Articles of Confederation.

Tell students they belong to the Screen Actors Guild. As members of the Screen Actors Guild, they must pay careful attention during the act-it-out and then vote on the actors who deserve the Oscars for best performance. Explain that members of the guild must make their vote based on these criteria: the accuracy of the actor's performance, how well they could hear and understand the actor, and the humor or emotion that the actor brought to the character.

"Acting out what I thought was going through these people's minds made it stick with me way past the test."

— High School Student

Here the teacher acts as an on-the-scene reporter, interviewing European immigrants about their hopes for a new life in America.

Hone Your Use of Social Studies Skill Builders

Advanced TIPS

As explained in Part 1 (see page 38), the Social Studies Skill Builder is a teaching strategy that allows students to learn and practice a new skill—such as mapping, categorizing, interpreting political cartoons, and graphing—through a dynamic, interactive activity rather than dry worksheets completed individually. Students receive feedback as they work on these fast-paced activities, allowing them to improve their skills rapidly and gain greater insights. In this section, you will read about ways to hone this strategy to make it even more effective. Specifically, you will learn how to

- review essential content and encourage critical thinking.
- use powerful wrap-up activities.

Review Essential Content and Encourage Critical Thinking

Some Social Studies Skill Builders require that students visit many stations or work with numerous placards to allow ample practice to master a skill, which can be time-consuming. When there isn't enough time for every student to visit all the stations or work with all the placards, you can use any of the following methods to ensure that students are exposed to all the content in the activity.

Have the class complete the student handout on a transparency. Call on different pairs to come up to the overhead and fill in one section of the handout until all sections have been completed. To save time when working with matrices, you can make a transparency of the matrix, cut it into strips, and give each pair a strip to complete. Then, call pairs to the overhead one at a time to place their transparency strip on top of a blank matrix.

Have pairs become station or placard "experts." When you see that time is running short, find out which pairs have completed (or nearly completed) their handout. Name them the "expert pair" for a particular station or placard, where they will share their information with classmates. For those pairs who have not completed most of the handout, split up the partners: one student will remain at a station to serve as an expert; the other goes around to the remaining stations or placards to learn from the resident experts. Have students circulate among the stations until their handouts are complete and then share their findings with their partners.

Have pairs take a "gallery walk." Another way to ensure that everyone gets all the content in the time remaining is to have students transfer their answers onto a piece of butcher paper placed next to each placard or station. This creates a written "gallery" of their responses. After at least one response has been recorded for every station or placard, have pairs go to the stations or placards for which they need more information. They can refer to the responses on the butcher paper to complete their handout. Students who have already completed their handout should circulate among the stations or placards as well, referring to the butcher paper to check, clarify, and, if necessary, modify their answers.

Social Studies Skill Builder activities use fast-paced engaging tasks to teach social studies skills.

Have pairs share information. Allow pairs of students to visit another pair to ask for information, clarification, or ideas—for one section of the handout only. Pairs may seek help from as many other pairs as necessary to complete their handout. Those pairs whose handouts are complete can serve as resources for pairs who need more information.

Have pairs engage in a "New York Stock Exchange." An engaging variation on pair sharing is to set up a Stock Exchange. As student pairs mingle around the classroom, one partner shouts the name of the placard about which the pair needs information, while the other partner shouts the name of a placard about which they can provide information. When students find another pair that can help them, they go off to the side of the room and share information. You could also conduct a quieter version of this, called Secret Sharing, in which students must whisper the names of the placards.

In order to allow all students access to all content, consider creating "expert" teams to assist students who have not yet completed the activity.

Use Powerful Wrap-up Activities

As explained in Part 1 (page 44), the final important step of Social Studies Skill Builders is the debriefing, or wrap-up. Here are several ideas for wrapping up activities in such a way that students apply higher-order thinking skills—evaluating, justifying, or synthesizing—to the content they have learned.

Human Spectrum After completing the Social Studies Skill Builder activity, use a 10- to 15-foot piece of masking tape to create a spectrum at the front of your classroom. Have pairs think about and discuss a question that forces them to synthesize or evaluate information from the activity. Then have each pair choose one student to stand along the spectrum to represent their response to the question. Facilitate a discussion in which the students who remain seated justify the position of their partner along the spectrum.

Example 1

After matching descriptions of eight key historical periods with corresponding maps and dates to construct a timeline of Middle Eastern history, have students place the periods along spectrums that address these questions:

When did this historical period take place?

3100 B.C.E.   1918 C.E.

Based on the reading and the map, how significant do you feel this period was for the Middle East?

Most significant   Least significant

"Not only is this strategy effective in teaching students new skills, but it also enables students to discuss high-level issues during the debriefing. After all the hands-on practice, students have a lot of information and opinions to share."

— Middle School Teacher

Have students record their groups' response on a projected spectrum. Students then debate and support their varied opinions.

Pairs serve as part of a blue-ribbon committee as they assess which contributions from ancient Greece were the most influential.

Example 2

After learning about reform movements of the mid–19th century and the role of women in those movements, have students debate the degree to which four of the grievances outlined in the Declaration of Sentiments have been redressed.

"He has monopolized (dominated) nearly all the profitable employments, and from those she is permitted to follow, she receives but a scanty remuneration (pay)." To what degree has this grievance been redressed?

Not redressed at all	Somewhat redressed	Totally redressed

Blue-Ribbon Committee After students have completed a Social Studies Skill Builder activity, explain that they are now members of a blue-ribbon (or expert) committee who will advise an important leader or organization—such as the president of the United States, the General Assembly of the United Nations, or the curator of a famous museum. Have pairs think about and discuss a question that forces them to synthesize or evaluate information from the activity. Facilitate a discussion in which the students offer their advice and explain and justify their position. In some cases you can assign each pair a particular position to argue; in other cases you might allow students to reach their own conclusions.

Example 1

After analyzing a series of placards representing achievements and inventions of the ancient Greeks, students take on the role of a blue-ribbon committee hired to consult on setting up a museum exhibit on ancient Greece. Ask pairs to select the achievement of the ancient Greeks they think has had the most impact on modern society and be prepared to explain why. Facilitate a class discussion in which pairs share and debate their viewpoints.

Students create a human bar graph to indicate their viewpoints on the effectiveness of World War I propaganda posters.

Example 2

After students analyze and graph data on eight different Latin American immigrant groups, have pairs take on the role of a blue-ribbon committee advising the president. Assign each pair of students one of the eight immigrant groups. Pairs use the immigration data and the reasons these groups came to the United States to formulate an argument for giving their group top priority in U.S. immigration policy. Hold a class discussion in which pairs share and debate their positions.

Human Bar Graphs When students have completed a Social Studies Skill Builder activity based on placards, post the placards along one wall of the classroom. Have pairs discuss a question that forces them to evaluate information from the activity in order to choose one of the placards. Then have one student from each pair come and stand in a single file line in front of the placard they chose. Have the students who remain seated analyze the human bar graphs their partners created by answering these questions:

> *Which placard was chosen by the most number of students? Why?*
> *Which placard did the least number of students choose? Why?*
> *What percentage of the class selected [name a placard]?*

Finally, have several students who are standing in the human bar graphs justify their answers. Facilitate a class discussion in which students debate their viewpoints.

Example 1

After students have analyzed a series of propaganda posters from World War I, post each of the placards along one wall and have pairs discuss which poster they think is most effective and why. Then have one student from each pair stand in a single-file line in front of the placard they chose. Have students analyze the human bar graphs and justify their answers.

Example 2

After students have analyzed a series of placards representing contributions of the Muslim culture to world civilization, post each of the placards along one wall. Have pairs discuss which placard they think represents the most important or influential contribution of the Muslim culture to world civilization. Then have one student from each pair stand in a single-file line in front of the placard they chose. Have students analyze the human bar graph and justify their answers.

Madison Avenue Sales Pitch Here's another way to inspire higher-level thinking skills during the debriefing. After pairs have completed the Social Studies Skill Builder, have students discuss a question that requires them to synthesize or evaluate information from the activity. Then ask pairs to write a short (20-second) sales pitch or design a mini advertising billboard that will convince others to reach the same conclusion. Allow pairs to mingle around the room, trying to sell their idea or perspective to other pairs. Afterward, ask the whole group to share whose sales pitch or billboard they found most convincing and why.

After completing a Social Studies Skill Builder about African art, this girl presents her "sales pitch" for the piece that she and her partner chose as the most representative of traditional African art.

Example 1

After students have identified and mapped sixteen important physiographic features of Latin America, assign each pair one feature and have them design a mini billboard which shows why that feature is the most important one in Latin America. Have students post their billboards around the room and give the class several minutes to view them all. Ask the class which billboard they find most convincing and why.

Example 2

After students have viewed placards of African art and identified the elements of traditional African art in each piece, have pairs discuss which piece they think is the best representation of traditional African art. They then write a 20-second sales pitch in which they explain why they think the piece they chose is the best representation. Taking the placard they chose, pairs mingle around the room and give their sales pitch. Afterward, ask the class whose sales pitch they found most convincing and why.

Example 3

After students have analyzed a series of political cartoons representing different American attitudes toward immigrants around 1900, have students discuss which cartoon they most agree with and why. Pairs write a 30-second editorial to support the cartoon they selected. Have pairs take their cartoon as they mingle around the room, sharing their editorial with other pairs. Afterward, ask the class whose editorial they found most convincing and why.

Hone Your Use of Experiential Exercises

The Experiential Exercise, as explained in Part 1 (see page 46), is a teaching strategy that taps into intrapersonal and body-kinesthetic intelligences and enables students to "experience" social studies concepts firsthand, with activities that make abstract ideas or remote events accessible and meaningful. Teachers using the TCI Approach consistently report that students tell them Experiential Exercises make learning fun and unforgettable. The suggestions in this section can help you hone this strategy to make it more powerful. Specifically, you will learn how to

- make Experiential Exercises more authentic.
- better connect Experiential Exercises to the content.

Make Experiential Exercises More Authentic

One of the best ways you can increase the value and power of Experiential Exercises is to make them more authentic. Often this requires making subtle changes to the way you deliver the activity. Following are examples of adaptations to Experiential Exercises that make them more authentic and thus more effective.

Activity: Experiencing the Assembly Line

This Experiential Exercise gives students a feeling for what it was like to work on an assembly line, as opposed to working as a skilled laborer or artisan. By re-creating work done by assembly line and comparing it to work done by independent craftspeople, students see firsthand the advantages and disadvantages of each mode of production. Students come away from this activity with a greater sensitivity to why workers often hated assembly-line work, and a new understanding of why this mode of production was profitable for factory owners.

"I heard about the real-life experiences my daughter was having in class. She was so involved and invested in the experiential activities that she wanted to share them with me."

— Parent of
Middle School Student

Experiential Exercises use short, memorable experiences to help students grasp social studies concepts. Here, working elbow to elbow, students feverishly reproduce drawings. Under the watchful eye of a demanding supervisor, each "worker" repeatedly draws just one small part of the whole, giving students an appreciation for the monotony and rigor of assembly-line work.

Adaptations

Make the classroom hot or cold. If possible, turn the temperature up or down so that the classroom is uncomfortably hot or cold. Explain to your student "workers" that as the factory manager, you must cut costs by turning off the heat or ventilation system.

Place workers in rows. Make the passing of the assembly-line product most difficult by seating students at desks set one in front of the other, rather than side by side. This way, workers cannot see or interact with one another. If possible, arrange the work-flow sequence so that the last worker in one row must leave his or her desk and walk to the front of the next row to pass along the product. This will frustrate and delay the assembly-line workers even more.

Fire unproductive workers. Fire a student worker who is talking too much or working too slowly. Pass the job of the fired worker to the next student on the line. Or, replace the worker with a student who has been standing outside the factory waiting for a job (perhaps a tardy student). Tell students that those who are working on the line at the end of the activity will receive extra credit.

Activity: The Unraveling of the Soviet Economy

In this Experiential Exercise, students experience the failures of the Soviet economy—inadequate materials, shortages of consumer goods, and worker apathy—that led to reforms under Gorbachev in the 1980s. Working in groups, students "produce" cars by cutting them out of paper. Regardless of how well they execute the task, all groups are rewarded equally with paper money representing rubles. After each of several rounds of work, students wait in line to buy candy from the teacher with their rubles. Few students reach the front of the line before the store closes. In the debriefing, the teacher helps students make comparisons between their experience and the failure of the Soviet economy.

Students experience one aspect of the failures of the Soviet economy as they wait in long lines to buy consumer goods, only to be frustrated by arbitrary closures.

Adaptations

Give some students inadequate or poor-quality work materials. Frustrate a few groups by supplying them with dried-up markers, paper already copied on one side (to hinder their ability to trace), and plastic scissors that do not work effectively. Give a few groups quality materials so that they are better able to meet the quota and do not grumble as loudly as the others.

Maintain a harsh, authoritarian persona. Your persona in this activity is critical. As the Director of Production, be authoritarian and lacking in empathy. Ignore some groups and show favoritism to others. Do not attend to the workers' complaints and grumblings.

"Scissors cut paper—I win." A childhood game is set up to demonstrate how Marxist theory benefits the working class. During the debriefing, students connect the historical content to their class-room experience.

Provide good candy, then bad candy. For the first round, let students exchange their rubles for quality candy most will really like, such as peanut-butter cups and chocolate kisses. For the second round, sell cheap, undesirable candy, but else-where in the room have a teacher's assistant (or a student) selling the expensive, good candy on the "black market." This black-market seller should demand twice the amount students paid during the first round, and should have a limited supply so it runs out quickly.

Activity: An Evening in the Plaza: Sharing Perspectives on Migration

This Experiential Exercise enables students to understand the different ways that rural Mexicans view migration to the United States. Students first work in pairs to learn about the life of one of eight villagers in Purísima, a town in central Mexico, and then discuss their views on migration during an "evening stroll" in the town plaza. During the stroll, pairs assume the roles of young villagers seek-ing advice and older villagers giving advice about the relative merits of migration to the United States. Then, pairs reverse roles and continue the stroll. Afterward, students reveal whether or not they would migrate and explain their decision.

Adaptations

Set the geographical context. To give students more visual references of the town, show them Purísima on a map of Mexico. Have students describe the geog-raphy of the area. Show images of other towns in central Mexico to help them visualize the buildings, plaza, climate, and people of Purísima.

Help students make connections to the "evening stroll." After describing the stroll as instructed in the Lesson Guide, ask the pairs of students to think of and describe something they do that is similar to the traditional stroll in Mexico, such as going to the mall or hanging out at a particular place.

Add props, music, or costumes. Bring in props that help create the look and feel of a Mexican town, such as silk plants, Mexican blankets, hanging paper lanterns (which can be easily made), and music.

Connect Experiential Exercises to the Content

Ensuring that students make the connection between the classroom activity and the content being studied is critical to the success of Experiential Exercises. Students need to recognize the similarities but also the differences. Always take time to debrief an experiential activity before continuing with the lesson. Following are several ways to assist students in organizing their thoughts as they connect their experiences to the events being simulated.

T-Chart Have students create a T-chart to identify connections between key content information and analogous aspects of the classroom activity. For example, after an activity in which students claim and reconfigure classroom furniture to understand the European "scramble for Africa" of the 1870s, students might complete a T-chart that looks like this:

Classroom Activity	*Historical Reality*
• Groups claimed desks, tables, and A-V equipment by placing labeled sticky notes on them.	• European countries claimed territory in Africa, without regard to tribal boundaries or existing cultures.
• Disputes broke out when groups removed someone else's sticky notes from items they had claimed.	• Disputes broke out between European countries when they claimed overlapping territory.
• Group 1 claimed far more items than the other groups because they had a head start.	• Britain claimed far more territory in Africa than other countries because it was industrialized before other European countries.

Complete the Sentence Have students complete sentences that connect key content information to analogous aspects of the classroom activity. For example, after the Experiential Exercise that simulates the anticommunist hysteria of the 1950s, you might ask students to complete a sentence like this:

Joe McCarthy and others accused some Americans of being communists, often without any evidence, just like in the classroom when... *Diego accused Kevin and Phoung of being "dots" even though he didn't know for sure that they were.*

Matrix Have students create a matrix to identify connections between key content information and analogous aspects of the classroom activity. For example, in an Experiential Exercise, students play Rock, Paper, Scissors to win tokens. "Wealthy students," who are given more tokens to start with, have an unfair advantage over "working class" students. As students experience the frustrations of unequal distribution of wealth, they propose changes to the game rules, and the teacher redistributes tokens equally to all. The experience provides a basis for understanding Marxist theory. To be sure that students make the connections between the classroom activity and the historical reality, you could have students complete a matrix (see next page).

	Classroom Activity: Rock, Scissors, Paper Game	Historical Information: Marxist Theory
Capitalism	Students have their own tokens, and not everyone starts with the same number. As students play the game, a few win lots of tokens, but most lose.	Individuals privately own industry. Freedom of competition results in unequal economic classes.
Class Struggle	Winners and lowers argue about whether the game is fair. Losers vote to change the rules of the game.	Upper and working class struggle over wealth. Working class revolts and takes over control of government.
Socialism	The teacher collects all tokens and redistributes them equally to all students.	Government takes over ownership of industry. Wealth created is distributed equally to all.

Annotated Images Make copies of an image related to the experience and have students annotate it with corresponding information from the classroom activity. For example, after the assembly-line activity that helps students understand workers' grievances during the Industrial Revolution, they might annotate an image such as the following:

1. Each assembly-line worker focuses on part of the job, just like each student only drew one part of the picture.

2. Workers don't talk to each other, just as in the classroom the teacher wouldn't let us talk to each other.

3. Workers at the front end of the assembly line don't see the finished product, just like students at the front of the classroom assembly line don't see the finished drawing.

Hone Your Use of Writing for Understanding

Writing for Understanding, as described in Part 1 (page 56), is a teaching strategy that taps into students' multiple intelligences, creating a memorable writing experience for all learners, including those whose greatest strengths are not linguistic. Writing for Understanding activities prompt students to write purposefully and in detail about social studies. With the ideas in this section, you can hone your use of the Writing for Understanding strategy to make it even more effective. You will learn how to

- conduct a "peer read-around."
- incorporate peer editing.
- use rubrics to evaluate student writing.

Writing for Understanding allows students to continue to learn key social studies concepts through writing assignments.

Conduct a Peer Read-Around

The peer read-around is an instructional tool that efficiently provides students with feedback on rough drafts of their writing assignments. This is similar to the peer-editing step of the writing process, with one important difference: here students are focused only on examples of good writing. By allowing students to read each other's work and identify the qualities of strong writing, you provide an opportunity for students to reflect on their own writing and to make structural and content revisions to their work. Follow these 12 steps to conduct a peer read-around in your classroom.

1. **Create balanced groups.** At the beginning of the school year or semester, set up peer read-around groups. Ask students to write a paragraph in response to a simple prompt, such as *What is your favorite subject in school and why?* Read through the paragraphs to determine who, based on the writing sample, are the strongest writers. Then create groups of four students, placing one of the stronger writers in each group. Balance the groups with students of various writing skills. Make a transparency showing group assignments. Keep the same peer read-around groups all semester so that students become accustomed to the process and have time to build trust as a group.

2. **Lead a class brainstorming session to identify qualities of an effective writing assignment.** After reviewing the requirements for a particular writing assignment, ask the class to brainstorm qualities that would be found in an effective piece of writing for this assignment. List these qualities on a transparency and have students copy the list into their notebooks. Expect that most of the items that students suggest will mirror your requirements for the assign-

Peer read-arounds allow students to indentify the qualities of strong writing, to reflect on their own writing, and to make revisions to their work.

ment, but encourage them to think beyond the requirements as well. You can suggest additional items yourself, especially if they are things that will help make students' written work more effective. However, the list should be generated primarily by the students.

3. **Have students bring in rough drafts.** When it is time for the peer read-around, tell students to bring in their rough drafts without their names on their papers, so their work will remain anonymous during the exercise. As students enter the classroom on the day of the peer read-around, collect their papers, write a number on each, and tell students what their number is. Use a black marker to block out any names written on the papers. Keep a record of which number you assign to each student.

4. **Put students into peer read-around groups and assign a leader for each group.** Project a transparency with group assignments and the expected class-room arrangement. Have students take their places in the groups, making sure that desks are in the correct formation. Assign a student leader for each group. Explain that the leader will pass out and collect papers, as well as take notes on which papers the group liked and why. You may want to rotate the role of leader after each group has read a full set of papers.

5. **Review the qualities of strong writing.** Remind students of the purpose of the peer read-around: to identify concrete examples of effective writing in each other's papers. Before students begin reading, review the list of qualities of an effective writing assignment they generated in step 2. Encourage students to look for these qualities in the papers they read. You may select just a few qualities for students to concentrate on, but allow them to comment on any other good qualities they see.

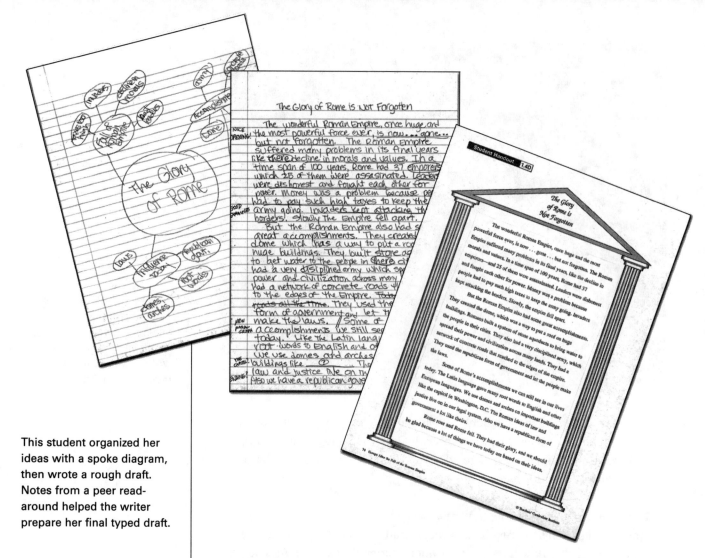

This student organized her ideas with a spoke diagram, then wrote a rough draft. Notes from a peer read-around helped the writer prepare her final typed draft.

6. **Model how to mark papers.** Place on a transparency the first paragraph of a paper from another class, or a sample rough draft you have written yourself (only one paragraph is necessary). Project the sample rough draft and have students read the paragraph silently. Then have students point out qualities of effective writing in the rough draft. As they point out these qualities, underline concrete examples on the transparency and write the name of the quality in the margin. For example, if someone notices the vivid language used in the second sentence...*pleading, sad, hungry eyes...,* underline those words and in the margin write *vivid language.* Explain that if students find further examples of the same quality later in the paper, they underline these and put check marks beside the original margin note.

7. **Pass out rough drafts to groups and have students read and mark each paper.** Give each leader a paper for each person in that group. When the papers have been distributed, tell students how many minutes they will have to read and mark the paper in front of them, then signal them to begin reading. After the allotted time, tell students to stop reading and pass the paper to the right. Continue this process until all group members have read all papers. (Note: If some students did not bring a rough draft, you have a couple of alternatives. You can either have them sit apart and work on their rough draft during this time, or you can pair them with each other—or with a student who

*"When I write, it helps me
to discover what I am
thinking about."*
— High School Student

has completed the draft—to include them in the reviewing process. You will know best which approach will most benefit the students in question.)

8. **Have groups choose the paper they like best and record its effective qualities.** As groups discuss which paper they liked best, have the group leader list specific examples telling why the group liked that one. For example, if the group agrees that they liked paper 6 because of the concrete evidence the writer gave to support his or her opinion, make sure the leader notes examples of that concrete evidence. The group can also identify and note specific qualities they liked in some of the other papers they read.

9. **Have groups pass their papers to another group.** After students have discussed the papers for a few minutes, groups pass their papers to another group. Ask group leaders to distribute the new set and repeat steps 7 and 8. Students should read at least two sets of papers; you can continue to repeat the passing of papers as appropriate or as time allows.

10. **Make a class list of outstanding papers and their qualities.** After each rough draft has been read by at least two groups, have group leaders report to the class the number of the paper their group liked best and the specific qualities they found effective in that paper. Push groups to give concrete examples, and keep track of group responses on a transparency. After each group has reported on the paper they liked the best, allow them to mention one or two qualities of effective writing, with accompanying examples, found in any of the other papers. If any group selects the same paper as another group, simply put a check next to that paper and add any qualities that the previous group did not mention.

11. **Add to the list of qualities of an effective writing assignment.** Using information from the class notes, make any significant additions to the list of qualities of effective writing that the class made during step 2. Have students add these qualities to the list in their notebook as well. Encourage them to find ways to incorporate these qualities in their final drafts.

12. **Return rough drafts and have students write final drafts**. Return rough drafts to the authors. Give students time in class or at home to review the comments on their papers and to revise their rough drafts by incorporating examples of the qualities of effective writing generated in the peer read-around activity.

Incorporate Peer Editing

A more traditional peer-editing activity involves peer-editing forms that students use to give and receive feedback during the writing process. The samples of peer-editing forms on the following pages were designed by teachers for specific Writing for Understanding activities. The forms vary in focus depending on the learning objectives. The first two serve as checklists for the requirements of the assignment, as well as opportunities to collect suggestions for improvement from classmates. The third peer-editing form is designed to help the author improve his or her use of imagery in a poem.

Peer-Editing Form for Editorial on the Industrial Revolution

Writer _____

Peer Editor _____

Read the editorial and look for the following requirements or writing qualities in the paper. If you answer no to a question, please explain your response.

1. Does the editorial have a headline that reflects the writer's view about the effects of the Industrial Revolution?

2. Does the editorial have an introduction (one paragraph) that describes the Industrial Revolution and states the writer's position on the overall effect on individuals and society?

3. Does the editorial include a paragraph or two that explain the positive effects of the Industrial Revolution on individuals and/or society?

4. Does the editorial include a paragraph or two that explain the negative effects of the Industrial Revolution on individuals and/or society?

5. Does the editorial include a paragraph or two that explain the writer's recommendations about how to address the negative effects of the Industrial Revolution?

6. Does the editorial include a drawing, graph, quote, or cartoon that illustrates one of the main ideas of the editorial?

7. Does the writer make reference to at least six aspects of the Industrial Revolution?

8. Is the editorial written in ink or typed?

9. Is the writing edited for grammar, punctuation, and spelling?

10. Does the editorial seem authentic—as if it were written in London in the 1830s?

Peer-Editing Form for a Letter About Mexico City

Writer _____

Peer Editor _____

Read the rough draft of the letter about Mexico City and check that the requirements have been met. If a requirement has not been met, describe what needs to be completed or revised.

Requirement	Complete?		Suggestions for Improvement
Date and salutation included	Yes	No	
Introduction with description of the city that uses at least five adjectives	Yes	No	
Description of at least five places visited, including interesting and memorable details for each place	Yes	No	
Description of the atmosphere for each of the five places	Yes	No	
Mention of discoveries	Yes	No	
Vivid references to at least three topics: history, culture, neighborhoods, environment	Yes	No	
Simple drawings or sketches that illustrate at least one site	Yes	No	
At least two pages in length; written in ink	Yes	No	
Correct spelling	Yes	No	

Peer-Editing Form for Haiku About Internment

Writer _____

Peer Editor _____

Read the rough draft of your classmate's poem and statement. Write answers to the questions.
Make sure your comments include suggestions for how to make the poem and the statement better.

1. What did you like best about the poem?

2. List examples of imagery, personification, similes, or metaphors that were particularly effective.

3. What, if anything, could the writer do to make this image even clearer? Be specific.

4. What phrase(s) or sentence(s) in the poet's statement help you understand the intent or meaning of the poem?

5. What could the writer add to the poet's statement to help you better understand the poem?

Use Rubrics to Evaluate Student Writing

Perhaps the hardest part of written assignments, as any teacher will tell you, is getting them graded. This task is actually a pleasure when you assign dynamic writing prompts like those in the Writing for Understanding activities, because the results are enjoyable to read. To make the process easier, you can develop rubrics to evaluate students' written work.

There are a wide variety of ways to set up such rubrics, depending on what you want to emphasize. Below are the directions for a specific Writing for Understanding activity—writing a letter from the World War I trenches—followed by three sample rubrics that show different ways you might evaluate student papers for this assignment. Some rubrics allow you to assign a point value to specific criteria; others are more holistic. Each form allows for both teacher assessment and student self-evaluation. Personal preference may dictate the type of rubric you choose; the choice could also depend on the general style of your district's writing assessments, or the format that you feel would best help your students understand the expectations for the assignment.

After vivid classroom experiences, students produce exceptional papers and have a real sense of accomplishment.

Assignment: Writing a Letter from the Trenches

The purpose of this writing assignment is to have students review the facts about World War I and to describe the salient aspects of trench warfare. Students assume the role of an American soldier fighting on the western front, and they write a letter home describing their experiences and their feelings about the war and the trenches. You give students these requirements for the assignment:

1. The letter should be **historically accurate.**
   State the causes of the war, the date, where the fighting is taking place, which nations are fighting, and why Americans are fighting in Europe.

2. The letter should describe the **conditions** in the trenches.
   Describe the strategy of trench warfare, the weapons being used, the landscape, what the food is like, and your living conditions.

3. The letter should reflect **empathy,** or feelings, about the war and trench warfare.
   How do you feel about this war? How do you feel about trench warfare? What emotions do you experience daily?

4. The letter should include a **map**—hand-drawn by you in the trench—showing where you are located.

5. The letter should be **authentic looking.** Because the letter is written from the trenches, it must be handwritten, but also legible. Include creative touches to add to the letter's authenticity, such as a tea or coffee stain for aging, or an addressed and stamped envelope.

6. **Extra effort** might include poetry, a description of leaflets, a reference to a specific site or battle, or a reference to some aspect not mentioned here.

Rubric Sample 1: Letter from the Trenches

Name_____

	Points Possible	Student Evaluation	Teacher Evaluation
1. Historical Accuracy	_____	_____	_____
• states causes of WWI and U.S. involvement—three reasons for causes of WWI and at least one reason for U.S. involvement are given			
• states alliances (minimum of five per side)			
• describes western front			
• includes map of western front—labeled countries			
• includes major physical features			
2. Description of Life in the Trenches	_____	_____	_____
• explains trench warfare			
• includes diagram of a trench			
• includes realistic description of daily life in trenches			
• includes details on chemical warfare, leaflets, food, and living conditions			
• states personal feelings about trench warfare			
3. Authenticity	_____	_____	_____
• letter looks real—antique and in black ink			
• letter sounds real—in first person present tense			
• includes additional touches for authenticity			
4. Spelling	_____	_____	_____
• letter has fewer than five spelling errors			
• spelling-check form is attached			
5. Rough draft attached	_____	_____	_____
6. Turned in on time	_____	_____	_____
Total Points	_____	_____	_____

Student Comments:

Teacher Comments:

Rubric Sample 2: Letter from the Trenches

5 Exceptional Letter

Letter has all the qualities stated for the standard letter below, plus the following:

- reflects outside research (perhaps includes a WWI poem, a story, a description of a specific battle, lyrics from a WWI song, quotes, a photo, etc.)
- has no more than one spelling mistake
- explains the causes of WWI and the reason(s) for U.S. involvement in no fewer than five sentences

4 Strong Letter

Letter has all the qualities for the standard letter stated below, plus the following:

- explains causes of WWI and U.S. involvement in the war in greater detail (at least three sentences)
- describes leaflets and chemical warfare
- includes a diagram of trenches
- has no more than three spelling mistakes

3 Standard Letter

Letter meets all requirements as stated in assignment:

- describes at least one cause of WWI and reason for U.S. involvement (no fewer than one sentence each)
- states alliances (who was fighting whom)
- describes the location of western front
- describes trench warfare and life in the trenches (at least three aspects)
- looks authentic (antique, black ink)
- includes map of where the fighting took place
- includes personal feelings about the war and trench warfare
- has no more than five spelling mistakes
- is turned in on time with rough draft and spelling-check form

2 Substandard Letter

Letter meets most of the requirements stated above, but is missing a few.

- may not be authentic looking
- may not be historically accurate in one or more ways
- may not include a map, information on trenches, causes of WWI, or reason for U.S. involvement
- may not have rough draft or spelling-check form attached
- may not have been turned in on time

1 Limited or No Letter

Letter does not meet most of the requirements stated above.

Rubric Sample 3: Letter from the Trenches

	1	2	3
Historical Accuracy	Letter may contain one or more inaccuracies about cause of the war, alliances, why the U.S. was involved, date, or location of fighting.	Letter includes discussion of causes, the date, where the fighting took place, which nations were fighting, and why the U.S. was fighting in Europe.	Letter includes thorough discussion of causes, the date, where the fighting took place, which nations were fighting, and why the U.S. was fighting in Europe. Letter reflects information from outside research not given in class.
Description of Trenches	Letter may not accurately describe trench warfare.	Letter accurately describes trench warfare strategy, weapons, landscape, food, and living conditions.	Letter thoroughly describes trench warfare strategy, weapons, landscape, food, and living conditions. It also describes leaflets, contains drawing of trenches, and has other aspects authentic to the conditions.
Empathy	Letter may not express emotion or feelings about the war or trench warfare.	Writer clearly states his or her feelings about the war and trench warfare.	Letter reflects convincingly on emotions and may include a poem or a song collected through outside research.
Map	Map may not be accurate and may not illustrate where a U.S. soldier would be fighting in WWI.	Letter includes a drawing or map of where the fighting is occurring.	Map illustrates entire front and names countries, physical features, towns, and cities.
Authenticity	There may be no attempt to make the letter look or sound authentic, such as using antique paper or black ink.	Letter looks old and is in black ink.	Letter is on antique paper, is in black ink, is in envelope, and otherwise looks and sounds real. It has additional authentic qualities such as a photo and a stamp.

Student Self Assessment: 1, 2, or 3 (circle one)

Teacher Assessment: 1, 2, or 3

Advanced

TIPS

Hone Your Use of Response Groups

As presented in Part 1 (page 66), the Response Group is a teaching strategy that gives students access to rich resources and the ideas of their classmates, both of which enrich class discussion and promote critical thinking. Teachers using the TCI Approach regularly comment that Response Group activities promote more involvement in class, that students' responses are more thoughtful and detailed than in conventional class discussion, and that students are listening to and respecting other's opinions. This section gives you ways to hone the Response Group strategy to make it even more effective. Specifically, you will learn how to

- score class discussions.
- conduct a "fishbowl" scored discussion to teach discussion skills.

Score Class Discussions

An excellent way to teach students to practice high-level discussion skills in their Response Groups is to score a class discussion. A scored discussion is one in which students receive points for displaying good command of a skill or appropriate group behavior and lose points for inadequate skills or inappropriate behavior. You (or in some cases, the students) score the discussion as it progresses and share the results at its conclusion.

Depending on your instructional objective, you might award points for accurately restating a previous comment, offering new evidence, or drawing someone into the discussion. A scored discussion can also help you monitor—and modify—student behavior during class discussions. That is, you could evaluate and score on-task behavior, polite responses, or other behavioral issues you want to address. The scored discussion is an alternative form of assessment and is relatively easy to execute. It is also extremely flexible; the type of scoring you do will likely vary from one class to the next.

Response Group activities challenge students to discuss controversial and complex issues.

Criteria for Scored Discussions Choose from the following criteria, in any combination, to meet your teaching objectives for group discussions. You may want to weight the point value of different criteria according to the relative importance of each. Have students focus on one to four criteria per discussion.

Positive Points
Acknowledging the previous speaker
Accurately restating the previous comment
Clearly stating an opinion
Clearly stating a fact
Using convincing evidence to support an argument
Making a relevant comment
Drawing another person into the discussion
Recognizing contradictions
Recognizing irrelevant comments
Using analogies to support an argument
Asking probing questions that further the discussion
Disagreeing in an agreeable way
Pointing out details in an image to support an opinion
Calling on the next presenter, by name, before sitting down
Speaking with a loud, clear voice

Negative Points
Interrupting speakers
Not paying attention or distracting others
Monopolizing the discussion
Making personal attacks or using put-downs
Deviating from the topic of discussion
Disagreeing in a disagreeable way

Some teachers use a scored-discussion tally sheet to monitor small-group behavior as students prepare for the class discussion. Are all group members participating? Are they respectful of each other's ideas? Are they helping to prepare the presenter for his or her role in the discussion?

Sample Scored-Discussion Tally Sheet

Group or student	Clearly states opinion	Offers convincing evidence	Deviates from topic	Total
1. Kelso/Jen/ Alvarado	+1 +1	+1 +1 +1	-1	4
2. Scoma/Avery/ Rundell	+1 +1 +1 +1 +1	+1 +1	-1 -1	5
3. McNeil/Decker/ Washington	+1 +1	+1		3
4. Robles/Schmit/ Karzai	+1 +1 +1	+1 +1 +1	-1	5
5.				
6.				

How to Use a Scored Discussion The following suggestions will help you execute a successful scored discussion.

1. **Determine the criteria.** Determine which scored-discussion criteria you want students to practice. If scored discussions are new for students, focus on one or two relatively easy skills, such as clearly stating an opinion and offering a new argument. You may also want to score for inappropriate behavior, such as interrupting speakers or not paying attention. As students become more familiar with scored discussion, use higher-level criteria, such as using convincing evidence to support an argument and using analogies to support an argument.

2. **Create a scored-discussion tally sheet.** The form of tally sheet will vary depending on the type of discussion and your teaching objective. For a Response Group discussion, you will need to set up a matrix that lists each group, plus each of the criteria you intend to score.

3. **Model the discussion skills to be scored.** Before students start their discussion, model the skills that will be scored and check to make sure all students understand what they are.

4. **Score the discussion.** As the presenter from each Response Group shares that group's ideas, score the discussion on a transparency of your prepared tally sheet. Scoring might consist of a simple plus/minus tally as you note positive and negative points. (Be sure to keep the overhead projector turned off at this time so that students focus on the discussion instead of your scoring.)

5. **Debrief the scored discussion.** After the discussion, reveal the scores and debrief the experience with students. Point out a few examples of when you gave points for the higher-level discussion skills that were exhibited.

Conduct a Fishbowl Scored Discussion

You can also help students improve on their discussion skills for Response Group activities by staging a "fishbowl" discussion. That is, one group holds a discussion in the center of the classroom—in the fishbowl—while you and the rest of the class observe and score the discussion. By observing a group discussion and learning to accurately identify and score high-level discussion skills, students will be better prepared to participate in a high-level discussion themselves.

Start with four student volunteers who are willing to discuss a topic while the rest of the class watches and scores them. Arrange the classroom as shown in the diagram, with the group of four in the center and the rest of the class seated in a large circle around them. Choose a discussion skill or two that you want students to learn—such as using convincing evidence to support an argument—and model it for the class. Then hand out a Scored-Discussion Tally Sheet. Have students start by listing the names of the students in the discussion group, and filling in the discussion skills they will be scoring. Model the scoring system you want students to use (plus/minus, checks, or points). Give the fishbowl group a topic to discuss while the class evaluates and scores the four students individually.

After several minutes, stop the discussion. Debrief the discussion with students by having them compare their scores for the students in the fishbowl. Have students post their score sheets on the wall, or create a matrix on a transparency and have them enter their tallies. Have students look for—and briefly discuss, if relevant—similarities and discrepancies among their scores.

This activity can be used at the beginning of the year to teach students the high-level discussion skills and behaviors that are necessary in a Response Group activity. It can also be used throughout the year to reinforce discussion skills or to introduce new ones.

Consider using a fishbowl scored discussion to model and teach the skills students need for a high-quality discussion.

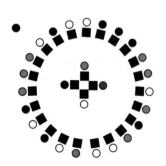

Hone Your Use of Problem Solving Groupwork

As explained in Part 1 (page 76), Problem Solving Groupwork is a strategy that involves students working in heterogeneous groups to complete challenging projects. Teachers particularly appreciate the fact that these activities contain a key ingredient for successful groupwork: The project requires the use of multiple abilities, so that every student in a group must contribute. This section gives you ways to hone the Problem Solving Groupwork strategy to make it even more effective, as well as more efficient. Specifically, you will learn how to

- make more efficient use of class time and increase content understanding.
- use groupwork checklists.
- assess groupwork efficiently.
- bring closure to groupwork activities.

Make More Efficient Use of Class Time and Increase Content Understanding

Teachers routinely list time as the primary obstacle to groupwork in the social studies classroom. Problem Solving Groupwork activities are well worth the time it takes to conduct them, but it is essential to maximize the efficient use of class time, resources, and student energies. Following are a number of ways to maximize efficiency and also increase student understanding of content during different stages of Problem Solving Groupwork activities.

Problem Solving Groupwork challenges students to complete engaging multiple-ability projects. These students are using a variety of resources as they begin to plan their group project.

1. **Prepare materials for the activity.**

   Ways to make more efficient use of class time
   - Create packets of handouts for each group before starting the activity. You save time by giving one packet to each group at the beginning, instead of handing out lots of different materials as the activity proceeds.
   - Copy any nonconsumable handouts onto colored paper and/or put them into sheet protectors. Tell students not to write on these handouts as you need use them for other classes, and collect them at the end of the activity for reuse.
   - Create hanging files for each class where groups can store any project handouts or materials overnight.
   - Collect (and have students contribute to) a box of simple costumes and props that students can use for performance-based groupwork activities.
   - Use long sheets of butcher paper to create simple costumes. For example, you can take a long strip (say, 6 feet long) and cut a hole in the middle for the actor's head. Drape the remaining paper over the front and back of the actor, sandwich-board style. Then, draw the costume onto the butcher paper.

   Ways to increase content understanding
   - Have a focus question for the activity that is prominent in activity materials and on student handouts, such as *Can people be trusted to govern themselves?* or *How were groups on the home front affected by World War II?* Review the activity materials to make sure that the focus question is incorporated throughout. If not, modify the handouts accordingly.

2. Groups learn the necessary background information to help them complete the project.

Ways to make more efficient use of class time

- Have students read any necessary background information for homework.
- If students are reading background information in class, pre-assign the numbers 1 through 4 to each person in the group. The number indicates the order in which students will take turns reading the information to the group.
- Have any additional background materials, such as primary resources, library books, or Web sites, available to groups from the beginning of the project, in your room if possible.

Ways to increase content understanding

- After students read background information, have them record initial responses to the focus question, based on what they have learned so far.

3. Groups plan and create their project.

Ways to make more efficient use of class time

- Set incremental deadlines for each step of the project.
- Check group progress at each incremental deadline, and tell groups that they cannot continue until you have checked off their work.
- Whenever possible, have students work on parts of the project for homework.

Ways to increase content understanding

- At the end of each class period, have groups share with the whole class any answers to the focus question that they have identified. Groups should listen for similarities to their own answers.
- Have all project materials (art and craft supplies, props, and costume materials) available to the groups during this stage to engage all learners, maximize interaction, and keep everyone working.

4. Groups present their project while other groups watch and listen.

Ways to make more efficient use of class time

- Enforce a strict time limit.
- Use presentation techniques that reduce overall presentation time. For example, have two or three groups present to each other, instead of having each group present to the whole class. For projects that are suited to display rather than performance (posters, newspapers, magazines), have audience groups do a "gallery walk" or a "docent-led" visit to stations, instead of having each group present their project to the class.

Ways to increase content understanding

- Have groups present to an authentic audience, such as students from a lower grade level or a group of parents. A more authentic audience raises the stakes for creating a product or performance that makes sense to both the audience and performers.
- Instead of having the group that is presenting tell the audience the topic of their presentation, have the audience guess the topic. Make sure the audience gives evidence from the presentation to support their guess. You might provide a list of the topics being presented to help narrow the possibilities.

- Have students in the audience respond to the focus question after each performance or presentation. This can be done in writing, by drawing a visual image in their notebooks, or in a small group discussion.

5. **Facilitate a whole-class review and synthesis of the lesson.**

Ways to make more efficient use of class time
- Assign the Processing assignment as homework.
- Have groups contribute to a class quiz. Each group writes one or two questions that focus on key content from their project. Combine all groups' questions into a class quiz.

While students work together on their project, the teacher circulates to monitor group progress, noting her observations on a checklist.

Ways to increase content understanding
Conduct a couple of quick review or synthesis activities, one in class and another for homework. Tie these to the focus question and incorporate different intelligences. Here are some examples:

- **Round robin** Each group takes a turn giving one answer to the focus question. Groups continue taking turns until they have exhausted their answers.
- **Human bar graph** The class brainstorms six or more key answers to the focus question, and you post those answers across the front of the class. Students stand in front of the answer they personally most agree with. You then facilitate an analysis of the bar graphs and a class discussion.
- **Spectrum** Create a spectrum related to the focus question—for example, a spectrum on which to place historical figures according to whether they believe Progressive Reforms went too far or Progressive Reforms did not go far enough. As one student stands on the spectrum, representing a particular figure, the class debates where the figure should be placed and why. Students keep a record of the spectrum in their notebooks.
- **Political cartoon** Students draw a cartoon to represent one or more answers to the focus question.
- **Learning log** Students write simple learning logs in which they explain what they learned about the topic by doing the assigned project.

6. **Evaluate the group projects.**

Ways to make more efficient use of class time
- Create a detailed rubric for evaluating projects.
- Make a checklist that is a streamlined version of the rubric, so you have an easy way to take notes during performances.
- Have each student complete Groupwork Brag Sheets (see page 121) to get information about the contributions of each group member.

Ways to increase content understanding
- Have students evaluate their own projects.
- Have students evaluate projects by nominating or voting for superlatives: Best Actor, Best Use of Props, Most Creative Presentation.

These students rehearse their minidrama on the forty-niners. When you break down the groupwork process into steps, a complex task seems more manageable to students. The first step ensures that all group members understand their roles.

Use Groupwork Checklists

During Problem Solving Groupwork activities, checklists can be beneficial for you and the students alike. You can start with standard checklists and modify them to keep track of more specific aspects of each step for a particular project. Using such a checklist helps students organize and manage their tasks and keep track of their progress, while also helping you to gauge and assess group progress.

Student Checklist Here, for example, is a student checklist for a groupwork project involving minidramas of life in the West. This is a teacher-modified version of the groupwork checklist that is provided with the published activity. As you see, the teacher has broken down and summarized the project tasks into seven steps. Notice that the checklist allows the teacher to set incremental deadlines to ensure that groups stay on task and accountable as they complete their work.

Student Checklist for "Minidramas for Life in the West"

Name: Sherrie
Period: 4
Minidrama Group: The Forty-Niners, Group 2
My Role: Screenwriter

Step 1
Have groups turn to Section 16.8 in the textbook. Make sure each group member knows his or her role:

Director Facilitates the group process to make sure the minidrama hangs together from start to finish. Leads the group's discussion. Helps coordinate all the parts of the performance and encourages all group members to participate. Acts in minidrama.

Screenwriter Writes a brief script that the actors can use to remember main ideas in their minidrama. Makes sure everyone gets a copy. Listens to the suggestions of the group and helps members work through their ideas. Continually reminds group members to bear in mind the question "Will students be able to clearly understand this aspect of life in the West by watching our minidrama?" Acts in minidrama.

Researcher Carefully examines text to find information that can be used in the minidrama. Seeks additional library resources if necessary. Makes sure the group uses the information on the topic accurately. Reads Section 16.8 aloud. Acts in minidrama.

Stage Manager Responsible for getting props, costumes, and sound effects for the minidrama. Figures out how to make scene changes quickly. Gets ideas and input for special effects from all group members. Devises ways to involve the audience when appropriate. Acts in minidrama.

Due: Beginning of the period

Step 2

Listen to the researcher read the handout aloud and examine the illustration. Then, write a paragraph summarizing in your notebook what you learned.

Due: Notebook paragraph due by the middle of the period today

Step 3

Brainstorm ideas for a minidrama that will show what happened before, during, and after the scene in the illustration. Assist the screenwriter in writing a brief script. You may use a tape recorder or record player.

Due: End of the period today

Step 4

Identify and gather props and additional resources to make the minidrama more authentic.

Due: Do for homework tonight

Step 5

Finish writing script and have the teacher approve it for accuracy.

Due: End of the period tomorrow

Step 6

Rehearse minidrama with your group. Make sure the actors know their entrances and exits. Use props in the rehearsal.

Due: In class on Wednesday

Step 7

Present minidrama with your group.
Due: Thursday

The incremental deadlines for each step allow both the student and the teacher to monitor the progress of the group.

Teacher Checklist As students work in their groups, you will want to use a parallel teacher checklist to monitor groups' progress and record observational notes for later evaluation. The following example (page 216), also for the minidramas on life in the West, works in conjunction with the student checklist shown here. You can see that the teacher checklist mirrors the student checklist, step for step. In the comments section, you can record anything that you think will be useful for evaluating the group's work

Assess Groupwork Efficiently

You need to assess Problem Solving Groupwork activities according to two criteria: (1) how well students worked within their group, and (2) how well the group project met explicit expectations. In addition to your observations of groups at work, you can use the Groupwork Brag Sheet (page 121) to gather information about how well individuals performed their tasks. An evaluation rubric can help you assess the final product or performance. The following sheets are sample evaluation tools you might use for the minidrama project on life in the West.

Teacher Checklist for "Minidramas for Life in the West"

Step	Due	Completed	Comments
1. Groups get handouts and determine roles.	Beginning of the period	Groups ☑1 ☑2 ☑3 ☑4 ☑5 ☑6 ☑7 ☑8	2 - Mario helping quiz group on their roles 4 - Inattentive: I had to redirect them
2. Groups read and record notes in their Interactive Student Notebooks.	Middle of period today	Groups ☑1 ☑2 ☑3 ☑4 ☑5 ⊘6 ☑7 ☑8	3 - Diem left early for office 4 - Excellent today!! All on track 6 Marilyn and Catherine have not completed NB assignment
3. Groups brainstorm ideas for minidrama and create outline for the story.	End of period today	Groups ⊘1 ☑2 ☑3 ☑4 ☑5 ⊘6 ☑7 ☑8	6 - Outline not complete for scene 3 1 - Late in completing this step
4. Groups identify and gather props and additional resources from library and at home.	Homework tonight Due Wed at start	Groups ☑1 ☑2 ☑3 ☑4 ☑5 ⊘6 ☑7 ☑8	5 - Check who is stage manager 2 - all members had good prop ideas! 1 - Better work and now on track
5. Groups complete script.	End of period tomorrow	Groups ☑1 ☑2 ◯3 ☑4 ☑5 ☑6 ☑7 ☑8	3 - Marilyn absent. Only Jackie brought materials. Talk to this group at end of class!
6. Groups rehearse minidrama.	In class on Wednesday	Groups ☑1 ☑2 ☑3 ☑4 ☑5 ☑6 ☑7 ☑8	5 - Bakari and Fernel already memorized parts 8 - Erin forgot her materials. Other groups rehearsing well
7. Groups present minidrama.	Thursday	Groups ☐1 ☐2 ☐3 ☐4 ☐5 ☐6 ☐7 ☐8	

Minidrama Evaluation

Name_____ Role_____

	Points Possible	Student Evaluation	Teacher Evaluation
1. Quality of Minidrama	_____	_____	_____

• Minidrama focused on the most important aspects of life for this group of people.
• Additional resources were used to accurately present life for this group.
• Minidrama was interesting and engaging for audience.

	Points Possible	Student Evaluation	Teacher Evaluation
2. Use of Nonverbal Elements	_____	_____	_____

• A variety of nonverbal elements such as props, costumes, sounds were used.
• Nonverbal elements created better understanding for audience.

	Points Possible	Student Evaluation	Teacher Evaluation
3. Effectiveness of Group Interaction	_____	_____	_____

• Group members worked consistently and purposefully.
• Group used cooperative skills to complete the minidrama.

	Points Possible	Student Evaluation	Teacher Evaluation
4. Individual Contribution	_____	_____	_____

• Shared equally in the planning, research, and performance.
• Effectively completed the responsibilities of your role.
• Gave a strong performance in the minidrama.

	Points Possible	Student Evaluation	Teacher Evaluation
5. Total Points	_____	_____	_____

Student Comments:

Teacher Comments:

Rubric for "Minidramas for Life in the West"

A – Exceptional
- Minidrama portrays *one or more* important experiences of the group being represented with no historical inaccuracies. Minidrama also includes *appropriate* humor or human emotion.
- Group does *additional* outside research and incorporates that information into their minidrama.
- Actors speak clearly and loudly for *entire* performance.
- Minidrama incorporates a variety of *creative* and *appropriate* costumes, props, and special effects.
- Group works cooperatively throughout *entire* project with *no* teacher interventions.

B – Above Average
- Minidrama portrays *one or more* important experiences of the group being represented, but has a *few* minor historical inaccuracies. Minidrama also includes *appropriate* humor or human emotion.
- Actors speak clearly and loudly for *entire* performance.
- Minidrama incorporates *creative* and *appropriate* costumes and props.
- Group works cooperatively throughout *entire* project with *no* teacher interventions.

C – Average
- Minidrama portrays *one* important experience of the group being represented, but has a *few* minor historical inaccuracies.
- Actors speak clearly and loudly for *most* of the performance, but it is *occasionally* hard to hear or understand actors.
- Minidrama incorporates *appropriate* costumes or props.
- Group works cooperatively *most* of the time with few interventions by teacher.

D – Below Average
- Experience that minidrama portrays is *not central* to the group being represented, and/or minidrama has *significant* historical inaccuracies.
- Hard to hear or understand actors for *much* of the performance.
- *No* appropriate props or costumes are incorporated in minidrama.
- Group has trouble working cooperatively; teacher intervenes *several* times.

F – Unacceptable
- Does not meet minimum requirements.

Bring Closure to Groupwork Activities

Once groups have completed their project, it is important to bring closure to the experience by asking them to reflect on their work together. Reflections are equally effective done orally or in writing. Give them one or more of the following prompts to guide their reflections:

One contribution that I made to the success of this group was...

One way I might improve as a group member next time would be to...

Our greatest strength as a group is...

One thing our group could improve upon is...

Advice we would give to a group doing this activity next year is...

The most significant thing I learned from this activity was...

A good metaphor for how our group worked together would be to say that our group was like...

This group should/should not work together again because...

"I get a kick out of watching groups present their products to the class. The pride some of them take in what they have produced is remarkable. Some students beam during their presentations."

— Middle School Teacher

How to Develop Curriculum Using the TCI Approach

Using the TCI Approach for course, unit, and lesson planning ensures that essential content is taught in a meaningful and engaging way.

Introduction

Curricular planning—determining what to teach in a course, designing units that cohere, and crafting individual lessons that engage students—is an essential element of effective instruction. In fact, it is a cornerstone of effectively implementing the TCI Approach in your classroom. In this section, we provide a host of tools to assist you in planning effective courses, designing cohesive units, and creating lessons based on the TCI Approach. The planning practices suggested in this section are rigorous and challenging, but when applied, they yield courses, units, and lessons that engage students in memorable learning—and enable students to achieve great results.

This section is designed both for teachers who use TCI's published materials and those who do not. While those who are using TCI's own programs are freed from developing curriculum from scratch, they still need to plan how to use the materials to support their particular course standards, how to shape coherent units, and how to modify or augment lessons to address their students' unique needs. And for those who are developing their own curricular materials, this section provides a wealth of ideas and models for crafting courses, units, and lessons that reflect the best practices of the TCI Approach.

Planning Effective Courses

Course planning encompasses an array of tasks: honing your expertise on the subject matter, searching for resources that will captivate students, organizing the content into elegant units. For many, state or local standards now dictate objectives and expectations for what is to be taught in each course, thus narrowing the teacher discretion in course planning. Still, you must plan courses to ensure that essential content is taught in meaningful, engaging, and time-sensitive ways.

Teachers who plan courses most effectively

- know the standards, essential content, skills, and objectives that must be taught.
- gather a wealth of rich resources—visual images, music, readings, activity ideas—to make the content more accessible for students.
- collaborate with their fellow teachers to generate or review new ideas about the course.
- plan a realistic master course calendar, making the difficult content choices to ensure that the units they choose are taught thoroughly.
- create a final semester or course assessment that both prepares students for any mandatory standardized testing and also allows students to show what they know about major themes and key standards.

Making a *realistic* course calendar is a step that is too often done without careful consideration. In planning any course, a teacher's first instinct—often in reaction to the daunting lists of standards—may be to think that "coverage" is the goal. However, mere "coverage" of content in a traditional fashion does not necessarily lead to meaningful learning and long-term retention. Realistic course planning involves finding a way to meld the coverage of standards with quality instruction. In this section we walk you through the steps of planning your course calendar and packing the maximum student learning into the all-too-short school year.

How to Develop a Realistic Course Calendar

Here is a six-step process for developing and maintaining a course calendar that will ensure you have adequate time to thoroughly teach the essential content for each unit. As an example, we show how one teacher set up a calendar for a 20th century U.S. history course.

Step 1. Determine the essential course content. Review the standards and content guidelines for the course. Identify the instructional units or content "chunks" that are essential for students to learn. In most cases, you will have to make difficult choices about what you can and cannot reasonably teach. Remember that the intent is to determine what you must and realistically can teach students *well,* as opposed to how much territory you can "cover."

The TCI Approach: A Summary Guide

While planning your curriculum, keep in mind these key features of the TCI Approach:

- Theory-Based Active Instruction
- Standards-Based Content
- Preview Assignment
- Multiple Intelligence Teaching Strategies
- Considerate Text
- Graphically Organized Reading Notes
- Processing Assignment
- Multiple Intelligence Assessments

For the sample course calendar shown (pages 223-224), the teacher has selected eight instructional units:

The Review Unit: 1700–1900
The Progressive Era
The United States Emerges as a World Power
The Roaring Twenties and the Great Depression
The United States in World War II
The Cold War
The Civil Rights Movement
Contemporary American Society

Step 2. Start with a school planning calendar and mark all noninstructional days. These will include school holidays, testing days, and staff development days, as well as any school celebrations, such as homecoming, that are likely to interrupt your instruction. Also consider the time it will take you, early in the year, to establish a cooperative, tolerant classroom environment. Note that on the sample calendar, the teacher has dedicated the first week of school to this and to a geography review.

Effective course planning is a rigorous task. However, when teachers design units that cohere, made rich with engaging lessons, then memorable learning occurs and students achieve great results.

Step 3. Count the available instructional days for the year. Once you have noted all the days you will be unable to teach content, count the number of actual instructional days you have left.

Step 4. Allocate instructional days for each unit. Review your list of essential units and allocate the available instructional days among them. You will likely face difficult choices at this step, too. For our sample, the teacher allotted 164 days of actual instruction as follows:

First Semester

The Review Unit: 1700–1900	15 days
The Progressive Era	20 days
The United States Emerges as a World Power	21 days
The Roaring Twenties and the Great Depression	25 days

Second Semester

The United States in World War II	19 days
The Cold War	24 days
The Civil Rights Movement	18 days
Contemporary American Society	22 days

Rather than trying to teach a comprehensive review unit at the beginning of the course, this teacher budgeted the instructional time to emphasize those units covering the 20th century.

Step 5. Note the start date for each unit on the course calendar. At this step, you will see when units will be interrupted by long breaks, such as winter vacation, or where the semester break falls, and can adjust your plans accordingly.

Step 6. Monitor your calendar as you teach the course. As you teach the first unit, keep in mind the planned start date of the second unit. To the best of your ability, pace your instruction so that you can start the second unit on time. Inevitably, there will be times when you need to slow the pace of instruction more than you intended, thus compromising the start dates of subsequent units. Just be conscious, when making such choices, of the impact on later units.

SEPTEMBER

Mon	Tues	Wed	Thur	Fri
	1	2 Cooperative, Tolerant Classroom and Geography	3	4
7 Labor Day	8 Start Review Unit: 1700–1900	9	10	11
14	15	16	17	17
21	22	23 Counselor Day	24	25
28	29	30 Start The Progressive Era		

OCTOBER

Mon	Tues	Wed	Thur	Fri
			1	2
5	6	7	8	9
12	13	14	15	16
19	20	21	22	23 Homecoming
26	27	28	29 Start U.S. Emerges as a World Power	30 Staff Development Day

NOVEMBER

Mon	Tues	Wed	Thur	Fri
2	3	4	5	6
9	10	11	12	13
16	17	18	19	20
23	24	25	26	27 Thanksgiving
30				

DECEMBER

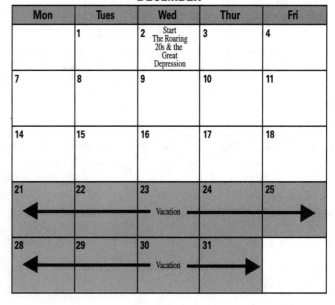

Mon	Tues	Wed	Thur	Fri
	1	2 Start The Roaring 20s & the Great Depression	3	4
7	8	9	10	11
14	15	16	17	18
21	22	23 Vacation	24	25
28	29	30 Vacation	31	

JANUARY

Mon	Tues	Wed	Thur	Fri
				1 Vacation
4	5	6	7	8
11	12	13	14	15
18 Martin Luther King Jr. Day	19	20	21	22 ←— Finals —→
25 Start The U.S. in WWII	26	27	28	29

FEBRUARY

Mon	Tues	Wed	Thur	Fri
1	2	3	4	5
8	9	10	11	12
15 President's Day	16	17	18	19
22 Start The Cold War	23	24	25	26 Staff Development Day

MARCH

Mon	Tues	Wed	Thur	Fri
1	2	3	4	5
8	9	10	11	12
15	16	17	18	19
22	23	24	25	26
29 Start The Civil Rights Movement	30	31		

APRIL

Mon	Tues	Wed	Thur	Fri
			1	2
5 ←—	6	7 Spring Vacation	8	9 —→
12	13	14	15	16
19	20	21 State Testing	22	23
26	27	28 Staff Development Day	29	30

MAY

Mon	Tues	Wed	Thur	Fri
3	4 Start Contemporary American Society	5 Cinco de Mayo	6	7
10	11	12	13	14
17	18	19	20	21
24 Memorial Day **31**	25	26	27	28

JUNE

Mon	Tues	Wed	Thur	Fri
	1	2	3	4
7 ←— Review —→	8	9 ←— Finals	10	11 —→
14	15	16	17	18
21	22	23	24	25
28	29	30		

Designing Cohesive Units

With a course plan in place, you are ready to turn your attention to the individual units that make up your course. Perhaps the biggest challenge you face in developing a good unit is finding a way to help students synthesize and evaluate the content you are presenting. This is a challenge that many teachers overlook in the interests of "covering" the topic. For example, to develop a history unit, teachers often choose an era to focus on: the Civil War, the Renaissance, the rise of Communist China. With their focus on trying to cover the topic, they often develop a series of lessons to convey essential information and important events as determined by the standards.

Seen in this way, a unit is like a container into which the teacher pours facts, events, and characters, with no particular impetus to help students explore how those pieces are related. While the teacher may have a solid understanding of a historical period and how the ideas or events are connected, students often do not. They may be able to regurgitate information—that is, to name, list, or describe various pieces in the container—but many have difficulty explaining how the parts of the unit cohere. As a result, students may leave the unit having gained impressions of the historical period, but lacking the understanding to grasp high-level concepts and to synthesize information.

The remedy to this "container" approach to instruction is to design each unit around what we call an *essential question:* a provocative question that prompts students to investigate, throughout the unit, the critical aspects of the topic. Many times these questions will be shaped and determined by the standards specific to a content area. After you introduce the essential question at the beginning of the unit, students reflect on it repeatedly as they gather evidence, explore various perspectives, and build their knowledge with purpose and focus. They are then able to synthesize and evaluate what they have learned to create a meaningful and convincing response to the question.

"Education is not the filling of a pail, but the lighting of a fire."
— William Butler Yeats

The process described in this section will help you identify good essential questions and craft an effective unit in any content area. The process as outlined assumes that you know all the standards, essential content, skills, and objectives that you must teach. It also assumes that, when possible, you will collaborate with fellow teachers to generate or review ideas about the unit you are developing.

Step 1. Develop an essential question for the unit. Determining a relevant and engaging question to pose to students at the beginning of a unit sounds deceptively simple. Even though it is just one single question, it is what defines the focus of your entire unit. Prior to crafting an essential question, it is imperative that you have already determined your unit topic, narrowed its scope and emphasis to reflect key standards and learning outcomes, and gathered resources you might include. The essential question, then, will help you determine which lessons and content should be included in the unit, and will also determine the focus of your assessment.

If a lesson or topic does not help students answer the essential question, it should not be included. Just as in the movies, if a scene does not move the plot forward, it ends up on the editing-room floor. Thus, the question helps you focus your efforts, make tough choices, and ensure that you—and ultimately your students— have a clear sense of how all the parts of the unit come together.

Criteria for a Good Essential Question Not all essential questions are equally effective. Here are some criteria to consider when determining the essential question for a unit:

Does it move students to a deeper understanding of the standards addressed in the unit? An essential question must be crafted so that it provides students an opportunity to reach a deeper understanding of key standards. If the focus of the question is too narrow, it may not push students to fully synthesize what they have learned. For example, for a unit on civil rights, the question *What roles did Malcolm X and Martin Luther King play during the civil rights movement?* certainly focuses on two key figures who are likely mentioned in your standards. However, it is too narrow to bring into play all the essential concepts and content you will cover in the unit, and students may respond by citing facts rather than synthesizing the information. A better question might be, *Was the civil rights movement successful?* This gives students the chance not only to tell what happened to whom and how, but also to evaluate the impact of those events.

Students prepare their "actor" for a press conference where historical figures will debate the essential question, *Can people be trusted to govern themselves?*

Is it provocative? The very wording of the essential question should provoke students to reflect and want to start responding. A cautious question will not entice students to argue, whereas a bold question sustains discussion over several weeks. For example, for a unit on the rise of democracy in Europe, you might consider the question, *What are the advantages and disadvantages of democratic government?* A more engaging question to elicit the same ideas might be, *Can people be trusted to govern themselves?*

Provocatively phrased essential questions will engage students and elicit varied responses.

Is the question stated simply and clearly? The simpler the question, the better. For a unit on World War I, you might be tempted to pose a lengthy question that obviously covers several key points: *Considering the motivations and circumstances that led up to the war, the carnage that ensued, and the Versailles Peace Treaty, was World War I fought for good reason?* A simpler question with the same thrust might be, *Was World War I a just war?*

Is it arguable from different points of view? If an essential question is to be truly effective, students must be able to answer it in more than one way. If they cannot argue different sides of the question, or if the evidence presented leans too heavily to one side, there is little point in posing the question. No one wants to participate in a debate that is fixed; if it is, students will lose interest and fall back on regurgitating information. For example, consider the question, *Why was American imperialism at the turn of the century wrong?* A better question that lends itself to argument would be, *When is it appropriate for the United States to intervene in the affairs of other nations?* Pose an arguable question, and let the students make up their own minds. The objective is for students to learn the skills of using evidence, forming sound arguments, and generating their own knowledge.

Does the question prompt students to synthesize and evaluate information? The question should encourage students to see the big picture, weigh evidence, and form an argument. For example, a question like *Were the 1920s really "roaring" and the 1930s really "depressing"?* encourages students to synthesize and evaluate information from the unit and generate their own conclusions.

Is it easily broken down into teachable sections? Craft the essential question so that it can be broken down into smaller, more manageable parts. These parts, or sections, should allow students to reflect on the question, explore it from different angles, and gather evidence for their answer. For example, the question *Was World War I a just war?* could be divided into sections on *Just Causes, Just Means of Warfare,* and *A Just Peace.*

The table on the following page lists some examples of essential questions for both U.S. and World History.

United States History	World History
Review of the Early United States: *"The period between 1760 and 1865 was created by the elite, for the elite."* Do you agree or disagree?	Early Humans: *What makes us human?*
The Constitution: *Can people be trusted to govern themselves?*	Ancient Mesopotamia: *What does it mean to be civilized?*
Manifest Destiny: *Was manifest destiny just?*	Ancient Egypt: *"Contrary to popular belief, Egypt was actually not among the most important ancient civilizations."* Do you agree or disagree?
The Civil War: *Should the North and the South reconcile their rocky marriage or divorce?* Or, *Did the Civil War create a more perfect union?*	The Roots of Western Civilization: Hebrews, Greeks, and Romans: *What is the best set of rules for people to live by?*
The Industrial Revolution and the Progressives: *Do you agree or disagree with Calvin Coolidge's quote, "What's good for business is good for America"?* Or, *Is progress good?*	The Fall of the Roman Empire: *Is the United States now in the position that the Roman Empire was in during its final years?*
Immigration: *Is immigration a benefit or a detriment to the United States?*	Imperial China and Feudal Japan: *Was imperial China really more advanced than feudal Japan and Europe?*
The 1920s and the Great Depression: *Were the 1920s really "roaring" and the 1930s really "depressing"?* Or, *"The 1920s were to the 1930s like a wild party is to the day after the party."* Do you agree or disagree?	Empires and Kingdoms of Sub-Saharan Africa: *Did contact with non-African civilizations (Europe and the Middle East) help or hurt the kingdoms and empires of sub-Saharan Africa?*
World War II: *Was World War II really a "good war" for the United States?*	Civilizations of the Americas: *"The Spanish conquest marked the beginning of a dark age in the history of the Americas."* Do you agree or disagree?
The Cold War: *Should the United States be praised or condemned for its efforts in the Cold War?*	The Rise of Democracy in Western Europe: *Can people be trusted to govern themselves?*
The Civil Rights Movement: *Was the civil rights movement a "smashing" success?* Or, *Should Americans use nonviolence or "any means necessary" to rectify social injustice?*	The Rise and Fall of the Soviet Union: *Did Communism improve life?*
	Modern Africa: *What unifies modern Africans?*
Women's Rights: *"Since the 1800s, women have not made significant progress in obtaining equality with men."* Do you agree or disagree?	The Modern Middle East: *What is the best way to achieve peace in the Middle East?*
	Modern China and Japan: *Did life in the modern era improve in China and Japan?*

Step 2. Design a unit "opener" activity. Once you have determined your essential question for the unit, design a kick-off activity for the first lesson that introduces the essential question, piques student interest, and challenges students to draw initial conclusions. For example, you might use quotes, provocative propositions, or musical or visual prompts. Following are examples for each of these ways of introducing a unit and its essential question.

Quotes Introduce the essential question with a famous quote. Have students discuss whether they agree or disagree with the quote. Make it clear that they are free to change their minds as the unit unfolds.

Example
For a unit on the U. S. Constitution, you might want to introduce the essential question *Can people be trusted to govern themselves?* You could have students write down and respond to the following quote from Alexander Hamilton:

> *The people are turbulent and changing, they seldom judge or determine right. Given therefore to the first (upper) class a...permanent share in the government...they will ever maintain good government.*

Provocative Propositions Present the essential question in the form of a provocative proposition and have students take an initial stand on it. They can revise their initial stand as they gather more information throughout the unit.

Example
To introduce a unit on World War II, write the following proposition on the board: *For the United States, World War II was a "good war."* Inform students that they will evaluate the accuracy of this statement. To help students set criteria for evaluating the statement, have them copy the matrix below in their notebooks, including the three column headings and the three factors to consider. Then have them discuss each remaining section of the matrix with a partner and write down appropriate ideas and responses (like the examples shown in the first row). Afterward, hold a brief discussion of students' responses. Encourage students to add ideas to their matrices during the discussion.

In an opener for a unit on the Rise and Fall of the Soviet Union, the teacher uses several images that provide evidence on more than one side of the essential question, *Did life improve in the Soviet Era?* Students record initial responses and questions they would like to investigate to draw a more informed conclusion.

Factors to Consider	Examples Supporting Statement	Examples Not Supporting Statement
Reasons for entering war	*defending homeland against invasion*	*trying to expand territory for selfish gain*
Conduct of military		
Conduct on the home front (treatment of foreign-born citizens, issues of free speech, contributions of civilians)		

Musical Prompts Begin the unit by playing an appropriate music selection or two to help introduce the essential question. Encourage students to give an initial response to the question after listening to the music.

Example
To introduce the essential question for a unit on the Roaring Twenties and the Great Depression, have students listen to music associated with those two eras. You might play "The Charleston" for the 1920s and "Brother Can You Spare a Dime?" for the 1930s. As they listen to each selection, have students record their impressions of the decade in their notebooks. Have them identify the mood of the piece and make some guesses as to the general mood of the nation at the time. For each selection, have students share some of their impressions. Then explain that people typically view the 1920s as a decade filled with energy, excitement, and fun, and that they see the 1930s as depressing. Point out that in this unit, students will test the accuracy of these impressions and answer this question: *To what extent were the 1920s truly "roaring" and the 1930s truly "depressing"?*

Visual Prompts Open the unit by showing selected images to help introduce the essential question. Encourage students to give an initial response to the question after viewing the images.

Example
For a unit on the Cold War, provide a brief overview. Explain that in the upcoming unit, the class will study the important concepts, events, and people that fueled the Cold War, and will evaluate actions taken by the United States to answer this unit question: *Should the United States be praised or condemned for its actions during the Cold War?*

Then place students in mixed-ability pairs for image viewing and have them create a T-chart like this:

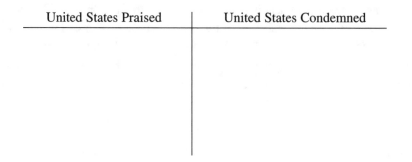

United States Praised	United States Condemned

South Vietnamese Refugees

Berlin Airlift

Soviet Missile Sites in Cuba

Soldiers in the Korean War

Project four strong visual images related to the Cold War. Focusing on visual details in each image, students formulate hypothetical arguments that support either praise or condemnation of the United States for the depicted event. For each image, encourage students to try to develop at least one argument on both sides of the T-chart. After students have recorded arguments for all four images, project one of the images again. Hold a class discussion with students using the hypothetical arguments in their T-charts to fuel the debate. Play the role of devil's advocate if most students argue only one side of the T-chart.

Step 3. Determine the sections of the unit. Use the essential question as a guide when you determine the main sections of the unit. These sections, each containing a series of lessons, should provide a clear organization for students as they gather and weigh evidence from a variety of perspectives, all related to the essential question.

For example, consider how you might divide that unit on the Cold War with the essential question, *Should the United States be praised or condemned for its efforts in the Cold War?* You look for teachable chunks, usually chronological or thematic, that will help students answer the question. One possible set of three sections (which will be explored further in the following pages) would be the early Cold War, a case study of the Vietnam War, and the later Cold War years. You could ask students to respond to the essential question after each section as their perspective becomes broader.

You might also offer specific section questions—slight variations on the essential question—to help students focus their evidence gathering. For example, for the first section you might ask, *Should the United States be praised for its efforts in the early years of the Cold War?* For the following sections: *Should the United States be praised for its efforts in Vietnam? For its efforts in the later years of the Cold War?* In this way, students' work in the sections gives them benchmarks for reflecting on the essential question and building blocks for their final response to it. Students can draw on their section evaluations as they make their final evaluation at the end of the unit.

Step 4. Identify lesson content that covers key standards and provides evidence on the essential question from different points of view.
Having identified your main sections for the unit, you must now determine what lessons to teach in each section. From your course calendar, you know how much time you have allotted for the unit. You probably won't have time to cover everything you would like. At this point, you will need to review which topics the standards expect you to address. While considering the standards, you should view them through the lens of your essential question for the unit: What lessons will both address key standards *and* enable students to explore the essential question from different points of view?

To better understand how you might make decisions about which lessons to include—or not to include—in a unit, let's take a look at one California teacher's calendar and curricular plan for a unit on the Cold War. (See her calendar in the Sample Unit Plan, pages 242–243.) As this teacher's calendar shows, she has allotted 24 instructional days to the Cold War unit. Following is her reasoning for planning the lessons you see in that calendar. Keep in mind that lesson content for this unit will vary from place to place, depending on what the state and local standards define as essential knowledge and skills.

California standards require that students be able to trace the origins and geopolitical consequences (foreign and domestic) of the Cold War and containment policy, including the McCarthy era and blacklisting; the Truman Doctrine; the Berlin Blockade; the Korean War; the Bay of Pigs Invasion and the Cuban Missile

Crisis; atomic testing, the "mutual assured destruction" doctrine, and disarmament policies; the Vietnam War; and Latin American policy. The teacher's challenge is to turn this essential content into coherent and memorable classroom instruction within her 24-day unit plan.

In previous years, this teacher had not covered either Korea or Latin America in her Cold War unit, electing instead to do an in-depth study of the Vietnam War, which she believed was a powerful way to highlight increasingly complex views about U.S. efforts in the Cold War. However, with an eye to the standards, she finds it necessary to shorten the Vietnam portion somewhat in order to introduce content on Korea and Latin America.

A lesson on Korea naturally falls into the section on the early Cold War. However, where to place Latin America in the unit is not so easily decided. On the one hand, it could work well in the early Cold War section, because movements toward communism in Latin American were in part a reaction to American imperialism, with roots in the 19th century. On the other hand, it could be folded into the late Cold War section, because Soviet/Cuban influence was more apparent in Latin America in the later stages of the Cold War. This year, the teacher decides to include a lesson on U.S. involvement in Latin America during the late Cold War years. This is a decision she may revisit next year.

Aware that she wants to provide evidence for both sides of the essential question, she starts the unit with "Cold War Terms." This lesson sets up the perspectives of the bipolar world, the different value systems of the two sides, and the development of the Cold War as viewed by the two superpowers. She then takes a look at the Korean conflict, along with the anticommunist hysteria of the McCarthy era, to help students grasp the sentiments of the time. She plans an entire lesson on the Cuban Missile Crisis, a dramatic and representative Cold War conflict in which the United States and the Soviet Union pushed themselves to the brink of nuclear war.

For the section on Vietnam, the teacher plans ways for students to explore various perspectives: those of antiwar protesters, the military, politicians in favor of the war, and the South Vietnamese. Through "Writing Songs About the Vietnam War" and writing oral histories with the help of people who lived through that era, students continue to think about the essential question for the unit. A lesson exploring the My Lai massacre could be illuminating, but the teacher ultimately deems it too one-sided and redundant with her other activities, so does not include it.

She does decide to show the movie *Dear America: Letters Home from Vietnam*, because this documentary shows the multiple perspectives of soldiers who fought the war: patriotic, caring, tired, frightened, confused, disillusioned. The movie makes the perspectives very human and real for students. The teacher also plans to bring in guest speakers on the Vietnam War, making sure they will represent different points of view.

As she moves toward the later years of the Cold War, she includes a lesson on the nuclear arms race, plus a look at the U.S. and Soviet involvement in revolutions in Latin America, particularly in the 1970s and 1980s. She will close the unit with an analysis of events that brought the Cold War to an end, followed by a debate to review the unit, and then the unit test.

Step 5. Plan assignments for the Interactive Student Notebook that will support the essential question. The Interactive Student Notebook assignments for each lesson should lead students to continually reevaluate their position on the essential question as the unit unfolds. Each time students reflect on the question, they will have new information to integrate into their position. While you are planning your unit, begin to think about notebook assignments that will help students to identify and explain changes in their opinions and discover areas in which they need to gather more evidence.

For example, for a lesson in the early Cold War section of your unit, you might plan to have students organize their reading notes on a series of timelines. On these timelines, they will record events in the development of the Cold War—such as the Marshall Plan—and will also consider whether the country or countries involved should be praised or condemned for their actions. For your lesson on the Cuban Missile Crisis, the processing assignment in the notebook might be a spectrum on which students indicate the extent to which they think the U.S. response should be praised or condemned, with a paragraph justifying their ideas. And after hearing multiple perspectives on the Vietnam War—soldiers, antiwar protesters, U.S. politicians, the South Vietnamese—students might capture the different arguments in a T-chart, one side praising the United States, the other condemning. In each case, the Interactive Notebook assignment helps students further reflect on the essential question for the unit.

Step 6. Create an appropriate multiple intelligence assessment for the unit. As we explain in "Multiple Intelligence Assessments" (page 118), an effective assessment process in social studies involves activities in which students use their various intelligences to both demonstrate and further their understanding of key concepts in authentic ways. Now you must consider how these multiple intelligence assessment techniques will play out in a unit assessment that revolves around your essential question.

You have a range of options for assessment; whichever method you select, students should have the opportunity to respond to the essential question for the unit. You might choose a more traditional paper-and-pencil test in multiple-choice format, perhaps combined with a number of less traditional, justified multiple-choice items. But in addition, make sure you give students an opportunity to address the essential question in a substantive way. Here are two examples of how this might work.

- For the Cold War unit, you might offer a series of political cartoons, asking students to choose one that supports their position. They would then incorporate their analysis of this image, along with historical evidence, into their position statement on the essential question.

Rich resources from the unit can be used as assessment tools. Students might be required to explain if this political cartoon captures the spirit of the Cold War, using specific historical examples to support their position.

- You might challenge students to respond to the essential question with the following writing prompt:

Pretend you are an editorial writer for the New York Times. Write an opinion piece that completes this statement: *The United States should be praised [or condemned] for its efforts in the Cold War because....* Your editorial must include the following:

— a clear thesis statement
— discussion of the contrasting ideologies of the superpowers, including four of the following: capitalism, socialism, democracy, totalitarianism, equality, individualism, freedom, collectivism
— information to support your position that includes five of the following: Yalta, the Marshall Plan, the Berlin blockade, NATO, the Korean War, the Vietnam War, détente, the revolution in Nicaragua, the Truman Doctrine, McCarthyism
— a strong concluding paragraph

Alternatively, you might assign a Culminating Project that allows students to show in great depth their response to the essential question. A suitable Culminating Project for the Cold War unit, for example, might challenge student pairs to create a visual metaphor that represents the role of the United States in the Cold War and clearly shows their response to the question, *Should the United States be praised or condemned for its role in the Cold War?* There are many possible metaphors—the United States seen as a police officer on a school campus, as a bully on the playground, as a referee in a basketball game, or as a gunfighter in the Wild West. In an evaluation rubric, spell out the requirements: which comparisons students are to make, which ideologies and events should be represented, how much explanation students are expected to provide.

Creating an appropriate assessment is a key part of the unit planning process for this reason: When you know in advance precisely how you will be assessing students at the end the unit, you can then plan activities and Interactive Student Notebook assignments throughout the unit—writing editorials, creating political cartoons—that not only foreshadow the final unit assessment, but also directly help students prepare for it.

In this Culminating Project, students work in pairs to create a visual metaphor that represents the United States in the Cold War and demonstrates their position on the essential question, *Should the United States be praised or condemned for its role in the Cold War?*

Cold War Playground

Friends of Bully (NATO allies)

Bully (United States)

Bully's Competitor (Soviet Union)

Monkey Bars
Escalating Cold War Tensions

Bully's Motto (American Capitalism)

Slingshot (Conventional Weapon)

USA

USSR

VIETNAM

KOREA

HIROSHIMA

YALTA

Injured Student (Cold War Enemies)

Ball (The World)

Bat (Military Strength)

Creating Lessons Based on the TCI Approach

Once you have your unit plan in order, it's time to consider the day-by-day lessons through which you will deliver your instruction. If you have TCI published programs, you may have all the lessons you need, or you may want to add a lesson here and there to address specific state standards. Or, it may that your district wants an entire course—such as state history—to be based on the TCI Approach, and you need all new lessons.

This section will support your work in creating dynamic lessons. To some extent, it is a reminder of information that you have read elsewhere in this book. The tasks involved echo much of what you have already done in creating a unit plan: You must review the standards for the essential information that must be taught. You must create each of the separate assignments and activities that are identified as part of the TCI Approach. You need to keep in mind the essential question that guides your unit plan. And you need to consider how to pace your activities to maximize instructional time.

In addition, each lesson must contain these elements of the TCI Approach:

Theory-Based, Active Instruction Make sure that your lessons involve active learning and reflect these three foundational premises: (1) Howard Gardner's theory that students learn best through multiple intelligences, (2) Elizabeth Cohen's theory that cooperative interaction increases learning gains, and (3) Jerome Bruner's theory that all students can learn if they are taught via the spiral curriculum.

Standards-Based Content Identify the standards and objectives your lesson will address. Determine if these work in conjunction with your essential question for the unit.

Preview Assignment Write out the directions for a short, engaging assignment in the Interactive Student Notebook that previews lesson content, sparks interest, activates students' prior knowledge, taps a wide range of intelligences, and prepares students to tackle new concepts. Many ways to approach this part of the lesson are suggested in the section "Preview Assignment" (page 22).

Multiple Intelligence Teaching Strategies Determine which teaching strategy will work best with the content of the lesson. The six multiple intelligence strategies employed in the TCI Approach are explained in detail in Part 1 of this book (pages 28–85). Following are guidelines to help you determine which of the multiple intelligence teaching strategies to use in your lesson, along with the important design elements to include with each strategy.

Pay careful attention to the elements of the TCI Approach as you create assignments. The use of multiple intelligence teaching strategies helps you create a student centered learning environment.

Visual Discovery Think "Visual discovery of information and concepts."

Visual Discovery

Use the Visual Discovery strategy when …

- you want to introduce new content.
- you need to cover a relatively large amount of content in a student-centered way.
- you want to explain complex events.
- you have access to rich, powerful images.

Make sure your Visual Discovery lesson has these design elements:

- from four to six carefully selected images
- a content focus for each image
- four or five spiraled questions for each image that help lead students to discover key content
- materials (role cards, props) for dynamic act-it-outs for one or two images
- techniques for class participation in act-it-outs (optional)

Social Studies Skill Builder Think "Game-like, repeated practice of a skill, based on content."

Social Studies Skill Builder

Use the Social Studies Skill Builder strategy when …

- a skill can be used as a vehicle to teach relevant content.
- multiple examples of engaging materials, such as propaganda posters or primary source images, are available on a single topic.
- you want to teach about the breadth of information on a single topic.

Make sure your Social Studies Skill Builder lesson has these design elements:

- an identified target skill
- a sufficient number of stations (usually 12–18) so that all pairs can work at the same time. You might duplicate some stations to create the ideal number for the size of your class.
- materials for each station (political cartoons, geography questions, artifacts from Industrial Revolution, or the like)
- a student handout on which to record information
- a plan to ensure that all students are exposed to all the content if time runs out
- ideas for how to wrap up the activity (human spectrum, blue-ribbon committee, or the like)

Experiential Exercise Think "Live it, feel it, understand it."

Experiential Exercise

Use the Experiential Exercise strategy when …

- your teaching objective centers on a topic that can be tapped into through the intrapersonal and/or body-kinesthetic intelligences.
- you want to re-create the feelings of a key event quickly and simply.
- you need to capture a moment or feeling that is central to a unit so that you can refer to it throughout the remainder of the unit.

Make sure your Experiential Exercise lesson has these design elements:

- a key event or concept to be experienced or re-created
- simple materials to conduct the Experiential Exercise
- ideas or materials that will make the Experiential Exercise more authentic
- a technique to help students connect the Experiential Exercise to key social studies concepts

Writing for Understanding

Use the Writing for Understanding strategy when …
- you have an idea for a multiple intelligence experience that can serve as a writing prompt
- you want to enable students to analyze, synthesize, and reach a deeper understanding of a topic they have been studying.
- you want to allow students to step into the shoes of some individual or group.

Make sure your Writing for Understanding lesson has these design elements:
- a rich prewriting activity
- directions for the writing assignment
- an evaluation rubric
- directions for a peer read-around activity (optional; see page 196)

Writing for Understanding
Think "Rich, creative writing that furthers learning."

Response Group

Use the Response Group strategy when…
- you want to teach controversial topics that elicit animated discussion.
- rich materials—political cartoons, music, or primary sources—are available for students to analyze, discuss, and debate.
- you want students to debate events or issues from a variety of perspectives.
- you want students assume a specific role to solve historical or contemporary problems.

Make sure your Response Group lesson has these design elements:
- two to four provocative critical thinking questions
- background information for each question
- an artifact—such as an image, song, or primary source document—to serve as a prompt for each question
- criteria and tally sheet for a scored discussion (optional; see page 208)

Response Group Think "Highly-structured, lively, student-centered class discussions."

Problem Solving Groupwork

Use the Problem Solving Groupwork strategy when …
- you want to teach higher-level analytical skills.
- you want students to synthesize and apply new content.
- you want students to explore multiple perspectives on an event.
- you have a variety of materials on a single topic—primary sources, literature, documents from multiple perspectives.
- you have an objective that can be addressed through a project involving small groups.

Make sure your Problem Solving Groupwork lesson has these design elements:
- a complex task, requiring multiple intelligences—designing a monument, poster, or newspaper, staging a press conference or minidrama, and so forth
- distinct roles for each group member
- a checklist of tasks or steps to follow
- specific background materials for each group
- an evaluation sheet or rubric

Problem Solving Groupwork
Think "Problem solving with an instructional product—panel, poster, monument, minidramas."

After deciding on an appropriate multiple intelligence activity, you need to do four more things to support your lesson:

Considerate Text Identify or modify readings for the lesson so that you can provide students with text that is considerate, or "reader-friendly." Considerate text has a clearly organized structure, "chunking" of concepts, a manageable length, careful vocabulary development, and clear, helpful, images and graphic organizers. (Refer to the section "Considerate Text," page 86, for further information.) Primary source reading material will not always contain considerate text, and you will need to think about how best to support readers in such instances. At the same time, consider whether your reading materials for the lesson provide information from different points of view, encouraging students to evaluate and formulate their stance on the essential question for the unit.

Graphically Organized Reading Notes Identify the essential content you want students to record in their notebooks for a particular lesson, and establish the graphic format that will best help them organize and understand that information from the readings and/or classroom activities. Many ideas for effective graphic organizers can be found in the section "Graphically Organized Reading Notes" (page 96). Be prepared to guide students in setting up these organizers in their notebooks, and don't forget to consider such details as whether a particular format—perhaps a long timeline—might work better on a side-turned notebook page.

Processing Assignment Write out the directions for a Processing assignment in the Interactive Student Notebook that taps multiple intelligences and involves higher-order thinking skills. This task should ask students to synthesize and actively apply what they learned in the lesson so that you can assess their understanding. Check to see if your assignment supports the essential question for the unit. Many engaging ways to approach this part of the lesson are suggested in the section "Processing Assignment," page 102.

Multiple Intelligence Assessment
Create end-of-lesson tests or Culminating Projects that honor students' multiple intelligences. Whatever format you choose, your lesson assessment should continue to support your essential question for the unit. Remember, too, that in the TCI Approach, assessment does not happen just at the end of a lesson; you can regularly assess students' understanding through their work in daily activities. Refer to the section "Multiple Intelligence Assessments" (page 118) for ideas on assessing various kinds of groupwork and writing assignments, and for tips on managing the assessment of student notebooks.

Sample Unit Plan

The following pages contain excerpts from a teacher's plan for a Cold War unit centered around the essential question, *Should the United States be praised or condemned for its role in the Cold War?* Included are possible Interactive Student Notebook assignments for several lessons from the unit. This sample serves to illustrate the discussion of unit and lesson planning and can be used as a model for planning units of your own. The following checklist, used in conjunction with the sample pages, will remind you of the important criteria for each part of a unit.

Essential Question for the Unit

❑ Is clearly connected to key standard(s)

❑ Is engaging and provocative

❑ Is stated simply and clearly

❑ Is arguable from different points of view

❑ Requires students to synthesize and evaluate information

❑ Deals with issues to which students have direct access and interest

Unit Opener

❑ Introduces the essential question for the unit

❑ Piques students' interest

❑ Requires students to engage with the question and draw initial conclusions

Unit Sections

❑ Provide a clear, logical organization for the unit

❑ Allow students to see the content from a variety of perspectives

❑ Give students an opportunity to rethink the essential question after each section

Assessment Tool

❑ Requires the use of multiple intelligences

❑ Connects to essential content, concepts, and understandings

❑ Asks students to take a stand on the essential question

❑ Requires students to synthesize all of the learning from the unit

Unit Calendar

❑ Is a realistic length, given the school year schedule and the importance of the unit's content

❑ Includes the lesson title, multiple intelligence strategy, and summary for each day

❑ Indicates which standards are addressed

❑ Shows lessons using a variety of multiple intelligence strategies and activities

❑ Shows activities that provide evidence for both sides of the essential question

Interactive Student Notebook

Preview

❑ Makes content more relevant or accessible by creating a bridge between what students know and what they are about to learn

❑ Can be completed in 5–10 minutes

Graphically Organized Reading Notes

❑ Utilize an appropriate graphic organizer

❑ May connect in some way to the preview assignment

Processing

❑ May connect to content from graphically organized notes

❑ Requires students to use higher-order thinking skills

❑ Uses multiple intelligences

❑ Connects to the essential question whenever possible

Sample Unit Plan

The teacher starts by identifying the essential question for the unit, the smaller chunks or sections of the unit, and her plan for a final assessment, all in view of the standards that she intends to address. Although she opts for a multiple intelligence assessment this year, she also formulates a plan for a possible Culminating Project, which she might use another time she presents this unit.

The Cold War

Essential Question

Should the United States be praised or condemned for its role in the Cold War?

Sections

- The Early Cold War
- A Case Study of the Vietnam War
- The Later Cold War Years

Assessment

Multiple intelligence asesssment

Alternative Culminating Project: Metaphor poster

Requirements

1. Title that includes the metaphor you chose (The role of the United States in the Cold War was like...)
2. Metaphorical visuals with historical labels for at least nine of the important events covered in this unit.
3. One-sentence explanations for each historical item that tell how it is like the metaphorical visual you have created to represent it.
4. One statement of how the role of the United States in the Cold War was *not* like the metaphor you chose.

Standards

11.9.3   Trace the origins and geopolitical consequences (foreign and domestic) of the Cold War and containment policy.

11.9.4   List the effects of foreign policy on domestic policies and vice versa (e.g., protests during the war in Vietnam, the "nuclear freeze" movement).

11.9.5   Analyze the role of the Reagan administration and other factors in the victory of the West in the Cold War.

Sample Unit Opener

The teacher plans a unit opener that introduces the unit and hooks students into the essential question on the first day of the unit.

1. Give the students a brief overview of the Cold War by reading the following selection.

    After World War II, the differing interests and ideologies of the United States and the Soviet Union led to mutual suspicion, hostility, and eventually indirect conflict that lasted for over 40 years. This conflict is called the Cold War. Although the two superpowers never engaged in direct military actions against one another, they competed with and confronted each other in a variety of other ways. The Soviet Union and the United States created opposing alliance systems in Europe; competed for influence among emerging nations in Asia, Africa, and Latin America; engaged in nuclear arms and space races, and supported opposing forces—directly or indirectly—in wars from Afghanistan to Nicaragua to Vietnam.

2. Next, place students in pairs and have them draw a T-chart with the headings "United States Praised" and "United States Condemned."

United States Praised	United States Condemned
•	•
•	•

3. Explain that students will see four different pictures that relate to the Cold War. Their task is to use visual details from the images to formulate hypothetical arguments as to why the United States should be praised or condemned for what appears to be happening. For each image, encourage students to develop at least one argument for each side of the T-chart. *Note:* Alternatively assign each pair one side of the T-chart and require them to defend that position with their arguments.

4. Project transparencies 1.2E, 1.2F, 2.2E, 3.2F. Give pairs a few minutes to analyze each image and discuss and write down one or more potential arguments in the T-chart.

5. After students have created hypothetical arguments for each of the four images, review the transparencies one at a time. For each, facilitate a short debate/discussion as to whether the United States should be praised or condemned for the events depicted. Students should use the hypothetical arguments they wrote in their T-charts to fuel the debate from two perspectives. Be prepared to play the role of devil's advocate if all or most students are arguing just one side of the T-chart.

Sample Unit Calendar

This sample unit calendar shows how the teacher arranged her Cold War unit across the allotted 24 days, using the essential question and the standards to guide her choice of lessons. She outlines the focus of the Preview, the activity, and the Processing assignment for each lesson.

Monday	Tuesday	Wednesday	Thursday	Friday
Unit Opener Respond to images from the unit, pose questions, and discuss the essential question. **Processing:** Take an initial stand on the question.	**Cold War Terms** **Preview:** Conflict in values **Activity:** Basic terms such as *socialism, capitalism, totalitarianism* (pp. 345-51) **Processing:** Billboard of Soviet/U.S. values	**The Early Cold War** **Preview:** From friend to enemy **Activity:** (Visual Discovery) Overview of the early Cold War. **Processing:** Illustrated timeline of early Cold War events. For each event, take a stand on the essential question.	Counselors coming in **No Class**	
McCarthyism **Preview:** Have you ever been falsely accused? **Activity:** (Experiential Exercise) Experience the suspicion of the McCarthy era **Processing:** Pictoword of McCarthyism	**Korean Conflict** **Preview:** Is there such a thing as a forgotten war? **Activity:** (Skill Builder) Timeline of key people and events in Korean conflict—make trade cards. **Processing:** Political cartoon		**The Cuban Missile Crisis** **Preview:** Would the U.S. ever be justified in using nuclear weapons? **Activity:** (Response Group) Respond to stages of Cuban Missile Crisis. Record responses. **Processing:** Persuasive paragraph: Should U.S. response to the Cuban Missile Crisis be praised or condemned?	**Introduce Vietnam War Oral History** **Preview:** What questions would you like to ask someone who lived through the Vietnam War era? **Activity:** Review past examples of oral histories. Record questions. **Processing:** Prepare interview questions for various groups affected by the war.

Monday	Tuesday	Wednesday	Thursday	Friday
The Vietnam War **Preview:** Mind Map—record ideas, images, words, symbols related to Vietnam War. **Activity:** (Visual Discovery) Key people and events of Vietnam War. **Processing:** Banner of Protest or Support		**Dear America: Letters Home from Vietnam** **Preview:** Rate any Vietnam War movie. **Activity:** View documentary. Use T-chart to record observations. **Processing:** Rate documentary; take stand on essential question, using letters as evidence.	**Writing Songs About the Vietnam War** **Preview:** Respond to "Ballad of the Green Beret." **Activity:** (Writing for Understanding) Vietnam War—responses, experiences, feeling from multiple perspectives. **Processing:** Complete song and prepare to present on following day.	
Vietnam War Guest Speakers **Preview:** Prepare three questions to ask the guest speakers. **Activity:** Record information during talks. **Processing:** How did the various speakers stand on the essential question?	**Sharing Oral Histories** **Preview:** What makes an oral presentation successful? **Activity:** Share and record findings from oral histories. **Processing:** Take a stand on the Vietnam War.	**Latin America** **Preview:** Respond to excerpt from *Inevitable Revolutions* about Nicaragua. **Activity:** (Response Group) Apply significant policies (Monroe Doctrine, Roosevelt corollary, Wilson corollary, Truman Doctrine) to U.S.-Nicaragua relations. **Processing:** Political cartoon of Cold War impact on Nicaraguan history.		**Missile Madness** **Preview:** Define *nuclear arms race*. **Activity:** (Experiential Exercise) Illustrated timeline of events in nuclear arms race. **Processing:** Summarize news article. Search library or Internet.
The End of the Cold War **Preview:** Do the ends justify the means? **Activity:** (Skill Builder) Analyze and record events that led to the end of the Cold War. **Processing:** Create a metaphor or analogy explaining two of the events.		**Review for Unit Test** Address the essential question by creating spectrums with ten events, annotated explanations.	**Debate Essential Question** Class debate by sections: Early Cold War, Vietnam War, Later Cold War Years. Take overall stand on question.	**Multiple Intelligence Assessment*** * If you elect to assess with a Culminating Project instead, allow class time to prepare and showcase projects.

Sample Assignments for the Interactive Student Notebook

The following samples show the Preview, the graphic organizer for students' notes, and the Processing assignment that the teacher plans for these lessons.

Lesson: Cold War Terms

Preview—Conflict in Values

Put the following terms and visuals into two categories: *Communists; the West; the East; capitalist; Reds; the Free World*

Reading Notes—Cold War Terms

Carefully examine the illustration, written information, and quotes on Student Handouts 1.1A–1.1H. Then discuss with your partner which term you think each illustration depicts, record the letter of the Student Handout next to the corresponding term, and write an explanation. Finally, copy the quote you think best represents the term.

Term	Student Handout	Why do you think this illustration depicts the term?	Quote that best represents the term
socialism			
democracy			
totalitarianism			
freedom			
equality			
individualism			
collectivism			

Processing—Soviet or U.S. Billboard

Design a billboard promoting four American or Soviet values you learned about in this activity. The billboard should use visual symbols and a few words to promote the values of one superpower. At the bottom of the billboard, scrawl some graffiti that a person from the other country might write in response to seeing the billboard. (No inappropriate language!)

Lesson: The Cuban Missile Crisis

Preview—Use of Nuclear Weapons

Write a paragraph response to the following question:
Would the United States ever be justified in using nuclear weapons?

Reading Notes—The Cuban Missile Crisis: You Make the Call

Carefully read the Top Secret Briefing and then discuss the critical thinking question at the bottom. List key evidence from the Top Secret Briefing below, according to whether the information supports or refutes the essential question.

The United States should be praised	The United States should be condemned

Processing—Take a Stand on the Essential Question

Create a spectrum like the one below and place an X on it to indicate the extent to which you think the United States should be praised or condemned for its role in the Cuban Missile Crisis. Below the spectrum, write a paragraph to defend your placement.

The United States
should be praised

The United States
should be condemned

I believe the United States should be . . .

Lesson: The Vietnam War

Preview—Mind Map

Trace the silhouette of your own head. Inside the silhouette, record any ideas, images, words, symbols, or personal connections you have, related to the Vietnam War.

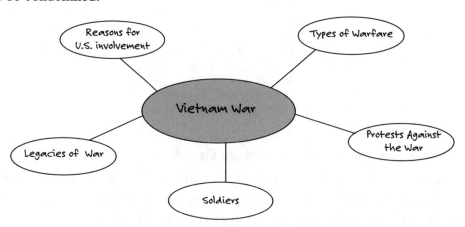

• My uncle Jim fought doesn't like to talk about it.

• I heard that Vietnam was the only war that the United States lost.

• I visited the Vietnam War Memorial once. I saw some people crying.

• My friend and I watched "Platoon." The war in Vietnam looked horrible.

Reading Notes—The Vietnam War: A Visual History

Copy the spoke diagram below and, as you analyze each transparency image, record important information next to the appropriate spoke. For homework, highlight with one color all information that supports the proposition that the United States should be praised, and with another color, all evidence that supports the proposition that the United States should be condemned.

Reasons for U.S. involvement — Types of Warfare — Vietnam War — Protests Against the War — Soldiers — Legacies of War

Processing—Banner of Protest or Support

Design a banner that you would carry to a rally to protest or support the Vietnam War. On the left side, draw a picture or symbol and write a short, catchy slogan that represents your stand on the essential question, thinking in terms of the Vietnam War. On the rest of the banner, list at least three arguments to support your stand. Be sure to use concrete information from your notes for your arguments.

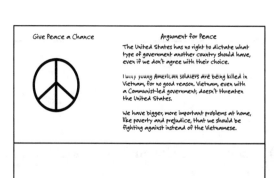

Give Peace a Chance

Argument for Peace

The United States has no right to dictate what type of government another country should have, even if we don't agree with their choice.

Too many young American soldiers are being killed in Vietnam, for no good reason. Vietnam, even with a Communist-led government, doesn't threaten the United States.

We have bigger, more important problems at home, like poverty and prejudice, that we should be fighting against instead of the Vietnamese.

Lesson: Missile Madness

Preview—What Is a Race?

Based on our "race" in the classroom, write the definition of the term *nuclear arms race.*

Reading Notes—Missile Madness

After reading Student Handout 3.1A, *A Short History of the Nuclear Arms Race,* create an illustrated timeline of 5–7 key events in the nuclear arms race. Place each event on the correct year of the timeline, label it, draw an appropriate symbol for the event, and write a one- or two-sentence summary of the event.

 1945 The United States uses atomic weapons to end the war against Japan.

1950

Processing—Missile Madness…Update

Do research in the library or on the Internet to find at least one news article from the last year which discusses the topic of nuclear weapons. Summarize the main points of the article and give your opinion on whether the U.S. role in the situation discussed in the article should be praised or condemned.

Part 5

Program Overviews and Sample Lessons

History Alive! The Ancient World _____

Program Components

- **Lesson Guides:** with classroom activities, reproducible sheets, assessment tools
- **Overhead Transparency Book:** color images to enhance visual literacy
- **Placard Set:** picture cards for use with the activities
- **Audio CD:** music, audio effects, dramatic readings
- **Student Edition:** with colorful, considerate text
- **Interactive Student Notebook**

History Alive! The Ancient World is one of TCI's core programs for middle school social studies. Each lesson is built around an interactive classroom activity, based on one of six strategies that are the hallmark of the TCI Approach. This section contains two sample lessons from that program. Sample 1 demonstrates a Social Studies Skill Builder; Sample 2 is a Problem Solving Groupwork activity.

Sample 1 Lesson 5, "Was Ancient Sumer a Civilization?" from Unit 1, *Early Humans and the Rise of Civilization*

Sample 2 Lesson 9, "Daily Life in Ancient Egypt" from Unit 2, *Ancient Egypt and the Near East*

Contents of *History Alive! The Ancient World*

Was Ancient Sumer a Civilization?

Overview

In this lesson, students first read about characteristics of civilization in a **Social Studies Skill Builder**. They use their new knowledge to analyze artifacts from ancient Sumer to determine whether ancient Sumer was a civilization. Then, in a Processing assignment, they find contemporary artifacts to use as evidence of civilization today.

Objectives

Students will

- identify characteristics of civilization.
- analyze artifacts from ancient Sumer and explain how they are examples of the various characteristics of civilization.
- identify modern-day artifacts that are examples of characteristics of civilization.

Materials

- *History Alive! The Ancient World*
- Interactive Student Notebooks
- Transparencies 5A and 5B
- Information Master 5A (several copies on card stock)
- Information Master 5B (1 transparency)
- Placards 5A–5H (2 sets)
- CD Track 6
- transparent tape

Preview

Have students turn to Preview 5 in their Interactive Student Notebooks. Review the directions with them, and answer any questions they have. After they have completed their diagrams describing characteristics of a "highly civilized" society, have them share their ideas with a partner, or have several volunteers briefly share their work with the class. Explain to students that in the following activity, they will investigate whether ancient Sumer had the characteristics of civilization.

Graphic Organizer

1 Have students read Section 5.1 of *History Alive! The Ancient World.* Have them identify what they will learn about in this chapter. Make sure they understand the meanings of the boldfaced key terms, which are defined in the Glossary. (**Note:** You may want to have students use the Prereading Handout on page xviii of the Lesson Guide to conduct a prereading of the chapter.)

2 Introduce the graphic organizer. Have students examine the illustration on page 41. Ask, *What kind of diagram is this? What is the main topic of this spoke diagram? What characteristics of civilization are shown on this spoke diagram?*

Reading for Understanding

Have students read Section 5.2 in their books. When they are finished, ask, *What characteristics of civilization will we learn about in this chapter? What everyday objects might be examples of these characteristics? What kinds of things might ancient Sumerians have left behind that could be examples of these characteristics?*

Social Studies Skill Builder

1 Prepare your classroom for the activity. Follow these steps:

- Post the two sets of *Placards 5A–5G: Artifacts from Ancient Sumer* on the walls along opposite sides of the room.
- Post the two copies of *Placard 5H: Artifact from Ancient Sumer* together. Place the CD player near them, and cue the CD to Track 6, "Essence Arabe."
- Create several dice for the activity using *Information Master 5A: Die Template.* Place the dice in a central location.

2 Put student into mixed-ability pairs. You may want to create a class seating chart on a transparency to show students who their partners are and where to sit.

3 **Explain the objective of the activity.** Tell students that in this activity they will learn about characteristics of civilization. They will determine whether ancient Sumer had each characteristic by analyzing artifacts that archeologists have unearthed.

4 **Explain the activity.** Have students open their Interactive Student Notebooks to Reading Notes 5. Project a transparency of *Information Master 5B: Steps for Analyzing Artifacts* and review the steps for completing the activity. Answer any questions students have.

5 **Practice the steps for analyzing an ancient Sumerian artifact as a class.** Ask students to read Section 5.3, which is about ensuring a stable food supply, and have pairs complete the steps on Information Master 5B. Encourage them to find *as many artifacts as possible* that are examples of this characteristic of civilization. Then have volunteers share their ideas from their Reading Notes with the class.

6 **Conduct the Social Studies Skill Builder.** Project Information Master 5B during the activity as reference. Have pairs come to you to have their work checked for the first two sections of the Reading Notes they complete. If they are following directions accurately, consider circulating around the room to spot-check work rather than checking each pair's work for every section of the Reading Notes. Tell students to play CD Track 6 when they inspect Placard 5H.

7 **Conduct a wrap-up activity.** This wrap-up activity will allow students to share their ideas and emphasize that a single artifact can provide evidence for more than one characteristic of civilization. After most pairs have learned about most of the characteristics of civilization, follow these steps for the wrap-up activity "Last One Standing":

- Have each pair determine who will be their first "stander."
- Select one of the artifact placards at random and show it to the class.
- Have pairs check their Reading Notes to see if they used this artifact as evidence of *one or more* of the characteristics of civilization. If so, their stander should stand up.
- Ask a couple of standers to share their explanation of how this artifact is evidence for *one* characteristic of civilization.
- Next, ask the standers who used this artifact as evidence for *two or more* characteristics to remain standing while the others sit down. Ask a couple of them to share how this artifact is evidence for a different characteristic of civilization.
- Continue this process until one student is the "last one standing."
- Select a new placard and repeat the activity. (**Note:** It is sufficient to do this for only a few of the eight placards.)

Processing

Review the instructions for completing Processing 5 in the Interactive Student Notebook. Answer any questions students have. When students have finished their spoke diagrams, have them share some of their modern examples of characteristics of civilization in a class discussion.

Internet Connections

For more information on Unit 1: Early Humans and the Rise of Civilization, including primary- and secondary-source materials, refer students to Internet resources for *History Alive! The Ancient World* at www.historyalive.com/connections.html. You will also find an on-line enrichment project for the unit at this site.

Assessment

Masters for assessment appear on the next three pages. Project *Transparency 5A: The Standard of Ur* and *Transparency 5B: Overlay for Assessment 5* for students to view while they complete the third section of the assessment.

1. C   2. A   3. B   4. B   5. C

6. D   7. A   8. B

9. *inner circle:* ziggurat, merchants, priests, slaves (belonging to upper classes); *middle circle:* craftspeople, government officials; *outer circle:* farmers, farms, irrigation ditches

10. The bulleted points can provide a rubric for this item.

Fill in the bubble beside the best answer to each question.

1. Ancient Sumerians invented irrigation systems and plows. What did these two inventions help provide?

  Ⓐ a system of government

  Ⓑ a partner with whom to trade

  Ⓒ a steady supply of food

  Ⓓ an honor for the gods

2. What evidence shows that Sumerian society developed after the Stone Age?

  Ⓐ copper blades

  Ⓑ painted pottery

  Ⓒ wooden plows

  Ⓓ mud houses

3. What ancient Sumerian most likely spoke the words below?

  "I live in a two-story house near the center of the city. I like to throw parties where my guests eat from gold plates and drink from gold cups."

  Ⓐ a farmer

  Ⓑ a merchant

  Ⓒ a craftsperson

  Ⓓ a government official

4. Which statement shows how Sumerian religion and government were connected?

  Ⓐ Sumerians believed that merchants sold goods for the king.

  Ⓑ Sumerians believed that the king got power from the gods.

  Ⓒ Sumerians recorded their prayers on clay tablets.

  Ⓓ Sumerians recorded the movements of the planets.

5. The Sumerians invented something that made it possible for their armies to use chariots. What was it?

  Ⓐ harnesses

  Ⓑ swords

  Ⓒ wheels

  Ⓓ horseshoes

6. What evidence shows that Sumerians were not prehistoric?

  Ⓐ ziggurats

  Ⓑ statues

  Ⓒ irrigation ditches

  Ⓓ written laws

7. Whose duty was it to do these jobs: build temples, lead the army, and enforce laws?

  Ⓐ the king's

  Ⓑ the priests'

  Ⓒ the scribes'

  Ⓓ the governors'

8. The artifact pictured below is evidence of what part of Sumerian civilization?

  Ⓐ religion

  Ⓑ government

  Ⓒ the arts

  Ⓓ technology

Use your knowledge of social studies to complete the item below.

9. The circles below represent a Sumerian city. The inner circle is the center of the city. The two outer circles show more distant parts of the city. Put each item from the Word Bank on the part of the city where it belongs.

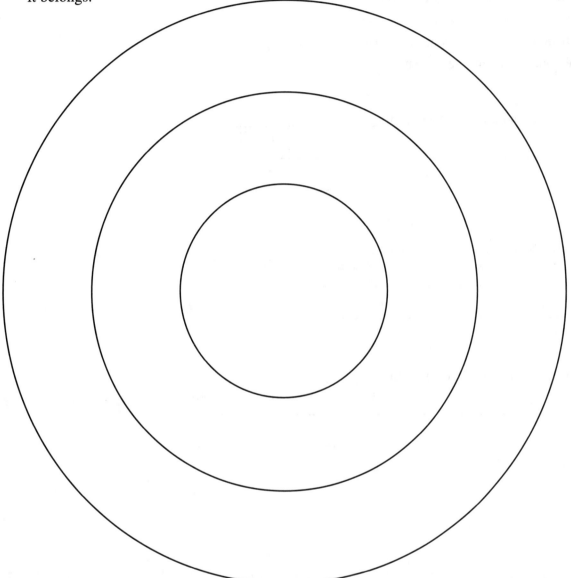

Word Bank		
craftspeople	government officials	priests
farmers	irrigation ditches	slaves
farms	merchants	ziggurat

Follow the directions to complete the item below.

10. The Standard of Ur is the most famous artifact ever recovered from ancient Sumer. Carefully examine the Standard of Ur on the transparency. Notice that some parts of it have been circled and numbered.

- Select three numbered parts that you think represent different characteristics of civilization.

- In each sentence below, identify one of the numbered parts you selected and complete the sentence.

Part _____ of the Standard of Ur represents _____
                                                       (characteristic of civilization)

because _____

_____.

Part _____ of the Standard of Ur represents _____
                                                       (characteristic of civilization)

because _____

_____.

Part _____ of the Standard of Ur represents _____
                                                       (characteristic of civilization)

because _____

_____.

To create a die, copy this page onto card stock. Cut the template along the solid lines, fold it along the dashed lines, and tape it together to create a cube.

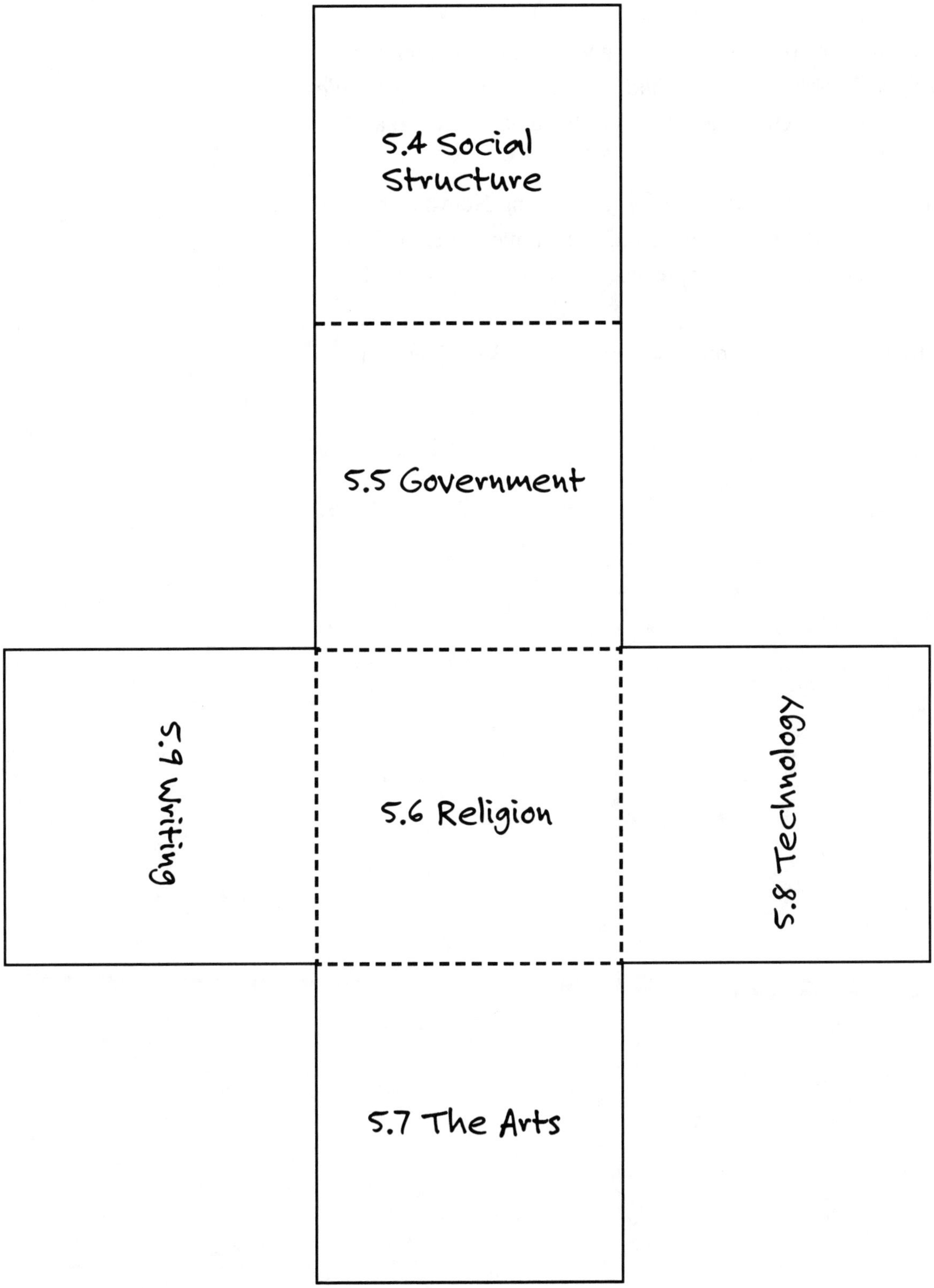

5.4 Social
Structure

5.5 Government

5.9 Writing

5.6 Religion

5.8 Technology

5.7 The Arts

Follow these steps to analyze the artifacts from ancient Sumer:

1. Roll one of the dice to determine which characteristic of civilization you will read about. If you have already read this section, roll again.

2. Read the corresponding section in Chapter 5 of *History Alive! The Ancient World.*

3. Carefully examine the artifacts posted around the room and read the accompanying archeologist's notes. Find *as many artifacts as possible* that are examples of the characteristic of civilization you just read about.

4. Complete the corresponding section of your Reading Notes. *For each artifact you choose,* remember to make a simple sketch and to complete the sentence about how it relates to that characteristic of civilization.

5. Bring your Reading Notes to your teacher to be checked. Then start over at Step 1.

After reading one section of Chapter 5 in *History Alive! The Ancient World* and analyzing all the artifacts from ancient Sumer, follow these steps:

1. Find the oval in the diagrams on pages 32–35 that corresponds to the section you read.

2. In the space around that oval, make a simple drawing of *each artifact* you analyzed that you think is an example of that characteristic of civilization.

3. Next to each drawing, complete this sentence: *(Name of artifact) relates to this characteristic of civilization because….*

4. Complete the spoke diagram by connecting each drawing with a line to the oval.

Possible answers:

5.3 Stable Food Supply

The cuneiform tablet relates to this characteristic of civilization because it tells that the Sumerians raised barley.

The seal showing plowing relates to this characteristic of civilization because it shows Sumerians preparing fields.

The clay tablet relates to this characteristic of civilization because it indicates a class of scribes and workers.

This seal of the king appointing a governor relates to this characteristic of civilization because it shows a government class.

The statue of a chariot relates to this characteristic of civilization because it shows a military class.

The gold cup relates to this characteristic of civilization because it indicates a craftsman and upper class.

The lyre relates to this characteristic of civilization because it indicates a class of musicians.

5.4 Social Structure

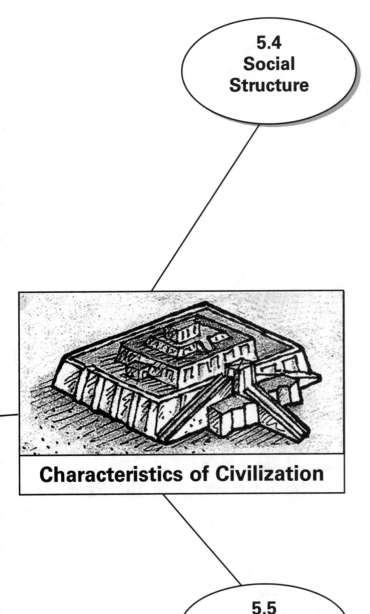

Characteristics of Civilization

5.5 Government

The clay tablet relates to this characteristic of civilization because it shows that government officials distributed grain.

The stone seal relates to this characteristic of civilization because it indicates there were government artisans, governors, and a king.

The copper statue relates to this characteristic of civilization because it shows there was an army.

The statue of a king carrying a basket relates to this characteristic of civilization because it illustrates there was a king.

The lyre relates to this characteristic of civilization because it indicates there was a queen.

Possible answers:

5.6 Religion

The statue of a married couple relates to this characteristic of civilization because it was found in a shrine and might have been a gift to the gods.

The statue of a king carrying a basket relates to this characteristic of civilization because it indicates that one of the king's duties was to build temples and shows that Sumerians had many gods.

The stone seal relates to this characteristic of civilization because it shows two gods.

Characteristics of Civilization

5.7 The Arts

The statue of a married couple relates to this characteristic of civilization because it shows there were skilled sculptors.

The gold cup relates to this characteristic of civilization because it shows there were skilled metalworkers.

The statue of a king carrying a basket relates to this characteristic of civilization because it shows they had architects for the temples.

The lyre relates to this characteristic of civilization because it shows Sumerians had music.

5.8 Technology

The copper statue of a chariot relates to this characteristic of civilization because it shows the Sumerians developed the wheel.

5.9 Writing

The clay tablet relates to this characteristic of civilization because it has writing on it.

The stone seal relates to this characteristic of civilization because it has writing on it.

The statue of a king carrying a basket relates to this characteristic of civilization because it has writing on it.

Scientists sometimes describe a society or group of humans as "highly civilized." What do you think this means?

Fill in the empty spokes of the diagram below with words that describe characteristics of a society that is highly civilized. For each spoke, draw and label a simple example of that description. One spoke is completed for you.

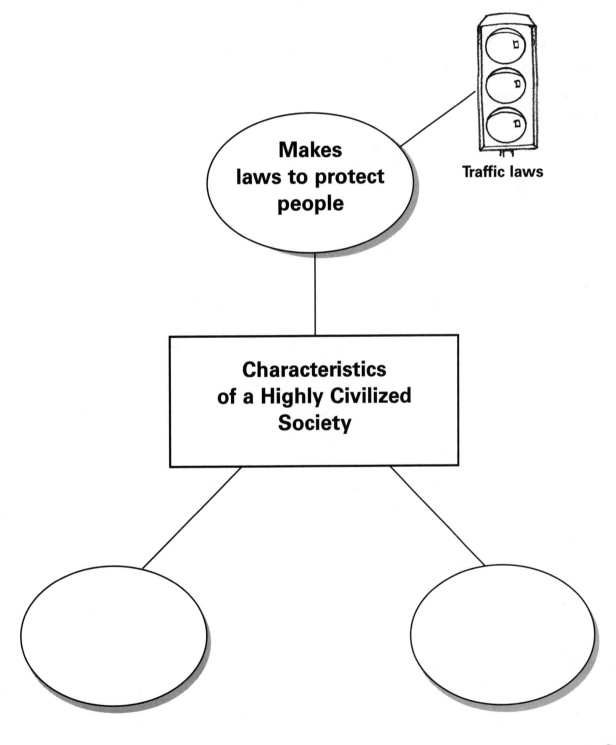

Makes laws to protect people

Traffic laws

Characteristics of a Highly Civilized Society

After reading one section of Chapter 5 in *History Alive! The Ancient World* and analyzing all the artifacts from ancient Sumer, follow these steps:

1. Find the oval in the diagrams on this and the following three pages that corresponds to the section you read.

2. In the space around that oval, make a simple drawing of *each artifact* you analyzed that you think is an example of that characteristic of civilization.

3. Next to each drawing, complete this sentence: *(Name of artifact) relates to this characteristic of civilization because....*

4. Complete the spoke diagram by connecting each drawing with a line to the oval.

**5.3
Stable Food
Supply**

5.4
Social
Structure

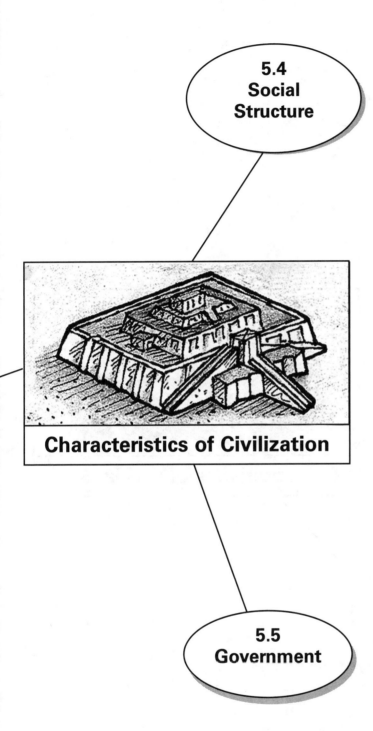

Characteristics of Civilization

5.5
Government

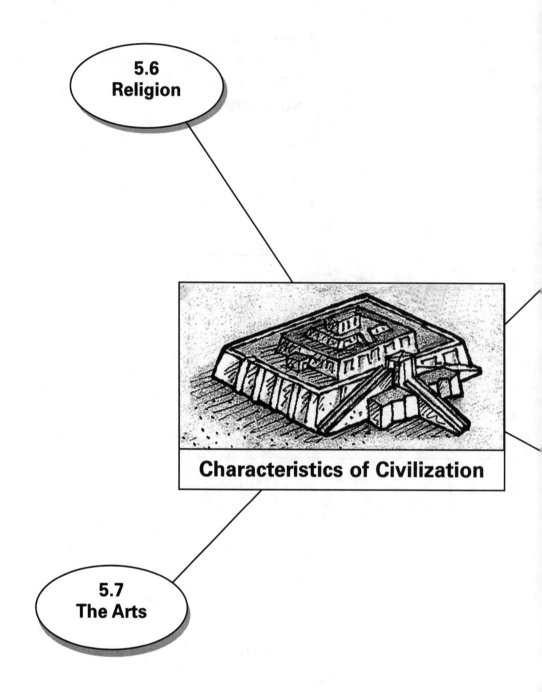

5.6
Religion

Characteristics of Civilization

5.7
The Arts

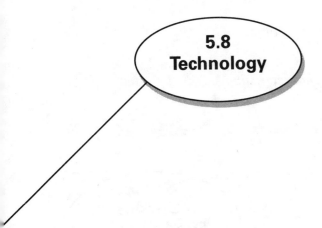

5.8
Technology

5.9
Writing

Complete the spoke diagram below by drawing or finding pictures of modern items that are examples of each characteristic of civilization. For each picture, follow these steps:

1. Glue or draw the picture next to the characteristic to which you think it is related.

2. Complete this sentence: *(Name of artifact) relates to this characteristic of civilization because….*

3. Draw a line connecting the picture to the oval.

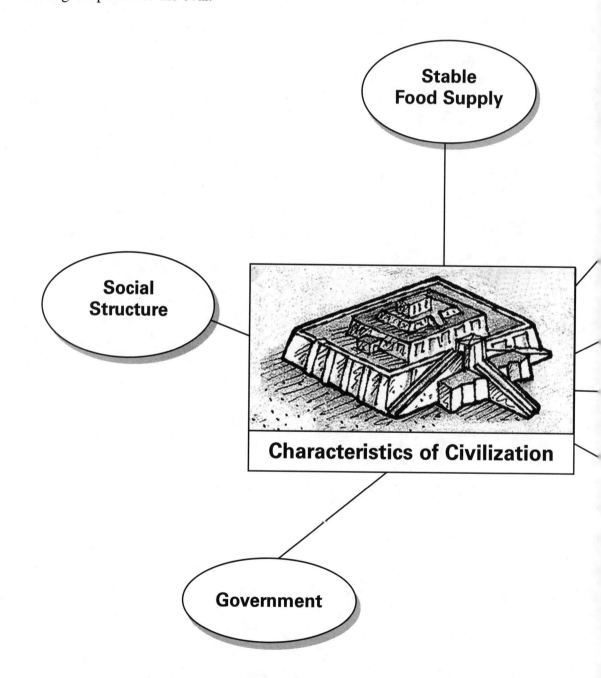

Sample 1

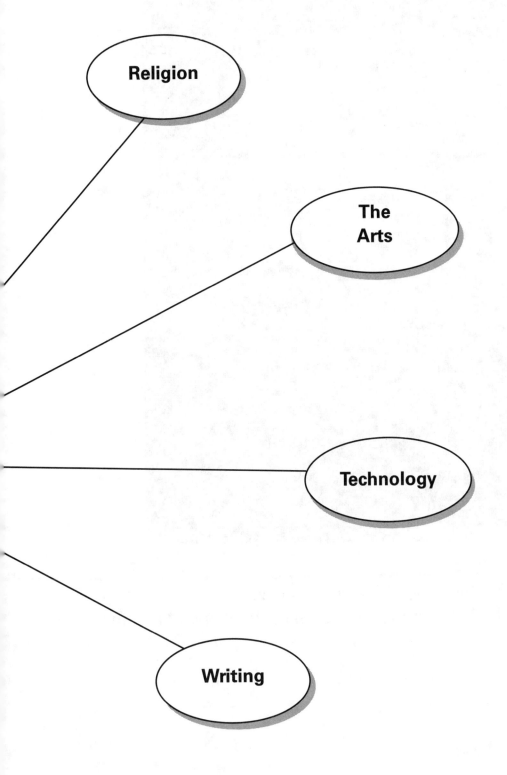

Religion

The
Arts

Technology

Writing

Archeologist's notes: On this clay tablet, scribes from the Temple of Bau recorded the amount of barley (a grain) that each of the workers and their families will receive.

Archeologist's notes: This small statue of a married couple was found in the rubble of a religious shrine. The original statue had eyes made of shells and semiprecious stones. It was probably left at the shrine as a gift to the gods.

Archeologist's notes: This impression was made from a stone seal. It shows two gods. One god has a hand in the shape of a scorpion. The other is using a plow.

Sample 1

Archeologist's notes: This clay seal shows King Ur-Nammu (seated) appointing Hashhamer as one of his governors. The cuneiform inscription on the seal says, "Ur-Nammu, the mighty hero, king of Ur; Hashhamer, the governor of Ishkun-Sin, his servant."

This carved stone seal was rolled across a slab of clay to create the scene shown above.

Archeologist's notes: This small copper statue shows a Sumerian chariot being pulled by four donkeys. This kind of chariot was probably used by Sumerian soldiers.

278 Sample Lesson from *History Alive! The Ancient World*

© Teachers' Curriculum Institute

Sample 1

Archeologist's notes: This gold cup was created by Sumerian artisans, probably to be used at banquets. These banquets were generally for the members of the upper classes of Sumerian society.

Archeologist's notes: This bronze statue shows King Ur-Nammu carrying a basket of bricks on his head. This probably represents the fact that one of the king's main responsibilities was to build and maintain the temples, even though he didn't actually do the work himself. The inscription around the body of the statue records the restoration of the temple of Inana, the patron god of Uruk.

Archeologist's notes: This lyre—a stringed musical instrument—was decorated with gold and semiprecious stones. It was found in the tomb of a Sumerian queen. Royal musicians may have played this instrument to entertain the queen and her court. The music you hear is similar to the kind of music the queen might have listened to.

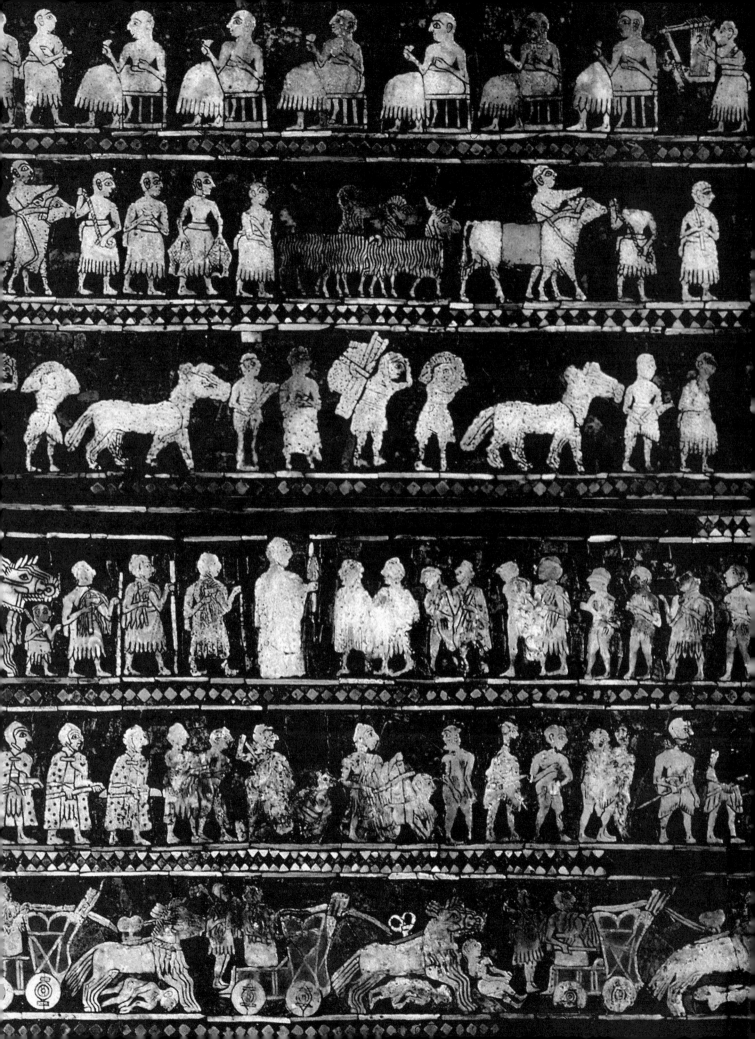

Was Ancient Sumer a Civilization?

5.1 Introduction

In the last chapter, you read about the rise of Sumerian city-states. In this chapter, you'll take a closer look at Sumerian **culture**. Like an archeologist, you'll consider evidence to try to answer a question about the distant past. The question is this: Was Sumer a **civilization**?

Until about 150 years ago, archeologists had no idea that the Sumerian people had lived at all. Then, in the mid 1800s, archeologists began finding artifacts in the area we call Mesopotamia. They dug up tablets, pottery, and the ruins of cities. They were surprised to find writing in a language they had never seen before.

By studying artifacts, archeologists have learned a lot about Sumer. One artifact is called the "Standard of Ur." It was found where the ancient city of Ur once stood. You can see the standard on the opposite page. It is made of wood and decorated with pieces of shell and lapis lazuli, a semi-precious blue stone. It shows Sumerians in times of peace and war. Artifacts like this one can tell us a great deal about daily life in ancient Sumer.

We now know that the Sumerians had a complex society. Some of the things they invented, like the plow and writing, are still in use today. But can we call Sumer a civilization? Let's consider the evidence.

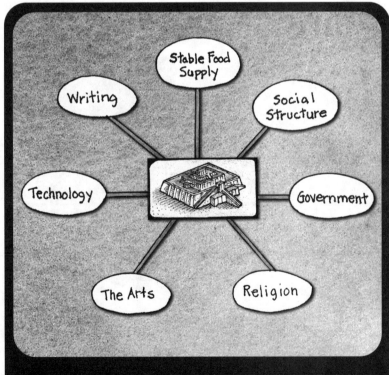

Use this spoke diagram as a graphic organizer to help you think about the characteristics of civilization.

5.2 Characteristics of Civilization

As you learned in the last chapter, Sumer was a challenging place to live. It had hot summers, little rain, and rivers that flooded the plains. Yet the Sumerians overcame these challenges. They built complex irrigation systems and large cities. By 3000 B.C.E., most Sumerians lived in powerful city-states like Ur, Lagash, and Uruk. But can we say that the Sumerians had created a civilization?

To answer this question, we need to think about what *civilization* means. What characteristics make a culture a civilization? Historians name several such characteristics, including these:

- a *stable food supply,* so that the people of a society have the food they need to survive
- a **social structure** with different social levels and jobs
- a *system of government,* so that life in the society is orderly
- a *religious system,* which involves a set of beliefs and forms of worship
- a *highly developed culture* that includes arts such as painting, architecture, music, and literature
- *advances in* **technology**
- a highly developed written *language*

Did Sumer have these characteristics? Let's find out what the evidence can tell us.

social structure the way a civilization is organized

technology the use of tools and other inventions for practical purposes

These two artifacts—one modern and one ancient Sumerian—are both examples of one characteristic of a civilization. Can you name the characteristic?

5.3 Stable Food Supply

Civilizations need a stable food supply. A complex society can thrive only if its members have the food they need to survive.

Sumerians invented two things to help them create a stable food supply. You already know about one of these inventions—their complex irrigation systems. The Sumerians built networks of canals, dams, and reservoirs to provide their crops with a regular supply of water.

Their second invention was the plow. A plow is a tool for tilling (turning) the soil to prepare it for planting. Before the plow was invented, farmers used animal horns or pointed sticks to poke holes in the earth. Then they would plant seeds in the holes. This was a very slow way to farm. Farmers needed a faster way to prepare the land for planting.

The Sumerians made the first plow out of wood. One end was bent for cutting into the ground to turn the soil. Farmers pushed and pulled the plow along the ground themselves, or they used animals such as oxen to pull it.

Sumerians invented the plow. Today, families in Iraq (ancient Sumer) still farm the land using ox-drawn plows.

This man and child are standing in the ruins of the ancient city of Uruk.

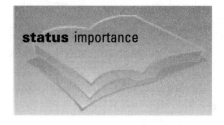

status importance

5.4 Social Structure

Civilizations have a complex organization, or social structure. A social structure includes different jobs and social levels. People at higher levels have greater **status** than others.

Archeologists have found evidence that several classes of people lived in Sumer. At the top was an upper class, which included priests and land owners. These people had the largest and most luxurious homes, near the center of the city. Their houses were two stories high. Evidence suggests they had whitewashed mud walls.

In the middle was the common class. This included merchants and craftspeople. The craftspeople included highly skilled metalworkers. They worked with such metals as gold, silver, tin, lead, copper, and bronze. With these materials, they made swords and arrowheads for the army. They made tools like plows and hoes for farmers. They also made luxury items, such as mirrors and jewelry, for the upper class.

The common class also included farmers and fishermen. They lived in small, mud-brick houses at the edge of the city. Farmers often worked to build or repair the irrigation systems. In times of war, they were forced to serve in the army.

At the very bottom of the social structure were slaves. They lived in their owners' homes and had no property of their own.

5.5 Government

All civilizations have a system of government to direct people's behavior and help make life orderly. Sumerian city-states were ruled by kings. The Sumerians believed that gods ruled the heavens and chose kings to rule on Earth. This belief made their kings very powerful.

Sumerian kings enforced the laws and collected taxes. They built temples and made sure irrigation systems were maintained.

A king also led his city-state's army. All the city-states needed armies because they were constantly fighting over land boundaries and the use of water. Leading the army was one of the king's most important jobs.

A Sumerian army included both professional soldiers and temporary citizen-soldiers. Some were foot soldiers. Others drove **chariots,** wheeled vehicles pulled by horses.

Kings had officials under them to help them with their duties. Governors ruled over outlying towns. **Scribes** helped record laws. The Sumerians were the first people to develop a system of written laws.

One special group of officials patrolled the canals. They looked for damage and made sure farmers didn't take water illegally.

chariot a two-wheeled vehicle pulled by a horse
scribe a person who writes

A king looks out from his palace walls over the city-state he rules.

5.6 Religion

Throughout history, all civilizations have had a religious system. A religious system involves a set of beliefs, usually in a god or gods. It also includes forms of worship.

Sumerians built temples and towers to express their religious beliefs. It was the king's duty to build and maintain these structures.

Sumerian religious towers were called **ziggurats**. They were made of mud bricks and located near temples. Ziggurats were so large they could be seen from 20 miles away. Some were as high as eight stories and as wide as 200 feet. It took hundreds of people to build one of these towers. Scholars have learned a lot about Sumerian beliefs by studying ziggurats.

Ziggurats were very important to the Sumerian religion. The Sumerians believed that the gods lived in the towers, and they built special temples at the top for them. Outside the ziggurat, they attached a long staircase so the gods could climb down to Earth. Kings and priests stood inside the towers to ask for the gods' blessings.

Sumerian statues also expressed their religious beliefs. Many of these statues were detailed and lifelike. They showed people worshipping the gods, often with their eyes gazing upward. The Sumerians believed that the gods were pleased when people showed them devotion, or love and obedience.

Sumerians had many kinds of religious ceremonies. Often musicians played at these ceremonies. Some ceremonies may have involved human sacrifice, the ritual killing of a person as an offering to the gods.

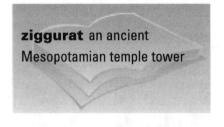

ziggurat an ancient Mesopotamian temple tower

This is a reconstruction of the ziggurat that once rose over the ancient city of Ur.

5.7 The Arts

All civilizations have a highly developed culture, including the arts. Arts include creative forms of expression such as painting, architecture, and music.

There were many kinds of artists and craftspeople in Sumer. Sumerian metalworkers made practical objects, like weapons and cups. They also made decorative items, such as mirrors and jewelry. Sumerian architects designed temples and ziggurats.

Music was another important art in Sumer. The Sumerians believed that music brought joy to the gods and people alike. Musicians played instruments and sang during temple ceremonies. They wrote love songs and entertained guests at feasts.

Musicians played many instruments, including drums and pipes. One favorite was a small harp called a *lyre*. Lyres were wooden instruments made of a sound box and strings. A wooden bar held the strings in place at the top. Lyre makers often decorated their instruments with precious stones and carvings made of horn. These decorations show how much the Sumerians valued music.

This fancy lyre has the head of a bull decorating its sound box. A musician would strum the strings to play musical notes.

5.8 Technology

All civilizations create new forms of technology, or practical tools and inventions. The Sumerians made several technological advances.

The Sumerians' most important invention was the wheel. The earliest examples of the wheel date back to 3500 B.C.E. Sumerian potters, or pottery makers, used wheels as a surface for shaping clay into pots. Potters' wheels spun, flat side up, on an axle. Sumerians discovered that a wheel that was flipped onto its edge could be rolled forward. They used this discovery to create wheeled carts for farmers and chariots for the army. They built the wheels by clamping pieces of wood together.

It would be hard to imagine a more powerful invention than the wheel. Before the wheel, people had to drag their goods on flat-bottomed carts called *sledges*. The sledges often got stuck in mud, and they couldn't support heavy loads. Wheeled carts made it much easier to move goods over long distances. Oxen could pull three times more weight on wheeled carts than they could on sledges.

Another technological advance was the **arch**. Sumerian arches were inverted (upside down) U- or V-shaped structures built above doorways. To build arches, the Sumerians stacked bricks made of clay and straw so that they rose in steps from the walls until they met in the center.

Arches added strength and beauty to Sumerian buildings. They became a common feature of temple entrances and upper-class homes. Some historians say the arch is the Sumerians' greatest architectural achievement.

This model shows a wheeled chariot used in the Sumerian army. They were pulled by a horse while a soldier stood behind the shield.

arch an upside-down U- or V-shaped structure that supports weight above it, as in a doorway

5.9 Writing

A final characteristic of civilizations is a highly developed written language. The Sumerians created a written language called **cuneiform**. This name comes from the Latin word for "wedge." The Sumerians used a wedge-shaped stylus (a sharp, pointed tool) to etch their writing in clay tablets.

Sumerians developed cuneiform around 2400 B.C.E. The earliest examples of cuneiform show that it was used to record information about the goods Sumerians exchanged with one another. At first, they may have used as many as 2,000 symbols to stand for ideas and sounds. Over time, they were able to reduce this number to about 700.

Cuneiform was based on an earlier, simpler form of writing that used pictographs. **Pictographs** are symbols that stand for real objects, such as a snake or water. Scribes drew the symbols with a sharpened reed on wet clay. When the clay dried, the marks became a permanent record.

cuneiform writing that uses wedge-shaped characters
pictograph a symbol that stands for an object

Sample 1

This relief sculpture shows scribes using a clay tablet and stylus.

5.10 Chapter Summary

Was Sumerian culture a civilization? It had all the characteristics you read about at the start of this chapter. The people of Sumer created a stable food supply. Their society had a complex social structure. They had a system of government, headed by kings. They had a religious system with priests, temples, and ziggurats. They had highly developed arts, technologies, and written language. For these reasons, historians call Sumer one of the world's first civilizations.

Sumerian civilization lasted about 1,500 years, from 3500 to 2000 B.C.E. What happened to the Sumerians? What new cultures developed in Mesopotamia? In the next chapter, you'll find out.

Daily Life in Ancient Egypt

Overview

In this lesson, students learn what life was like for five social classes in ancient Egypt. In a **Problem Solving Groupwork** activity, they read about the ancient Egyptian social pyramid. Then they work in groups to create interactive dramatizations—using props, costumes, and audience involvement—that bring to life typical scenes from daily life in ancient Egypt. Finally, students compare social classes in ancient Egypt to groups in contemporary society.

Objectives

Students will

- explain the social pyramid of ancient Egyptian society.
- bring to life a typical scene from the daily life of a social class in ancient Egypt.
- identify key aspects of daily life of various social classes in ancient Egyptian society.

Materials

- *History Alive! The Ancient World*
- Interactive Student Notebooks
- Transparencies 9A–9E
- Student Handouts 9A–9E
- CD Tracks 16 and 17

Preview

Have students complete Preview 9 in their Interactive Student Notebooks. Review the directions with them, and answer any questions. After they complete the Preview, have several volunteers share their answers. Tell students that, in this lesson, they will be exploring the various levels of society in ancient Egypt.

Graphic Organizer

1 Introduce Chapter 9 in *History Alive! The Ancient World.* Have students read Section 9.1. Make sure they understand the meanings of the boldfaced key terms, which are defined in the Glossary. (**Note:** You may want to have students use the Prereading Handout on page xviii of the Lesson Guide to conduct a prereading of the chapter.)

2 Introduce the graphic organizer. Have students examine the graphic organizer on page 81. Ask, *What is this shape? What might the symbols on the different levels of the pyramid represent? For any one of the symbols on the pyramid, which social class in ancient Egypt do you think it represents? Why do you think the levels at the top of the pyramid are smaller while those at the bottom are larger? Select one of the social classes on this pyramid. What do you think daily life was like for someone in that class?*

Reading for Understanding

Have students read Section 9.2, which explains ancient Egypt's social pyramid. After they have read the section, ask, *Name the various classes in Egypt's social pyramid. In what ways was ancient Egypt's society similar to the society of your school? In what ways was it different? Do you think a pyramid is an appropriate way to represent ancient Egypt's social structure? Why or why not?*

Problem Solving Groupwork

1 Put students in mixed-ability groups of four. Minimally, create five groups so that each of five social classes in ancient Egypt— government officials, priests, scribes, artisans, and peasants—will be represented in the dramatizations. Create a transparency that shows students who is in their group and where to sit.

2 Introduce the activity. Explain to groups that in this activity they will become experts on one social class in ancient Egypt. They will work together to create an interactive dramatization that brings to life a typical scene from the daily life of that social class. The dramatization will have props and costumes and must involve members of the audience.

3 Assign each group of students to one of five social classes in ancient Egyptian society. Government officials, priests, scribes, artisans, and peasants should be represented.

4 Distribute materials. Pass out one of *Student Handouts 9A–9E: Creating a Dramatization About the Daily Life of [Ancient Egyptian Social Class]* and one of *Transparencies 9A–9E* to each group of students according to the topic they have been assigned. Briefly review the steps for creating an interactive dramatization, and answer any questions. (**Note:** Encourage students to sound out the Egyptian words as best they can.)

5 Monitor groups as they create their interactive dramatizations. Allow them adequate time—at least two class periods—to prepare. Monitor their progress by checking their work and initialing Student Handout 9 as they complete each step. Pay special attention to Step 3 on the handout, making sure each group incorporates all six items listed into their dramatization. The groups representing government officials and peasants will need access to CD Track 16, "Khet (The Physical Body)," and CD Track 17, "Peasants' Harvesting Chant," respectively, before and during their dramatizations.

6 Arrange the classroom for presentations. Arrange a stage area in front with an overhead projector centrally located. Make sure everyone can see the projection screen or wall.

7 Project *Transparency 9A: Government Officials,* and have the first group present their dramatization. Make sure the group involves at least four members of the audience. (**Note:** Consider having each group act as the visitors for another group's dramatization.)

8 Have students record key information from the dramatization. After the performance, have students turn to Reading Notes 9 in their Interactive Student Notebooks and record information from the dramatization in the appropriate section of their Reading Notes.

9 Repeat Steps 7 and 8 until all groups have presented their dramatizations. (**Note:** The six items listed in Step 3 on the handout make an easy evaluation checklist for each presentation. Consider also evaluating for these two items: all actors can be seen and heard clearly; costumes and props are creative and appropriate.)

10 Have students check and add information to their Reading Notes. Once the presentations are complete, have groups read Section 9.3 of *History Alive! The Ancient World,* check the accuracy of their Reading Notes, and add one or two pieces of important information from the text.

Afterward, have volunteers share their notes with the class. Repeat this process for Sections 9.4 to 9.7. (**Note:** You can have students begin this as homework after the first day of presentations, and check information at the beginning of the next class period as a strategy for reviewing the previous day's content.)

11 Wrap up the activity. Base the discussion on such questions as,
• What words would you use to describe life in ancient Egypt?
• If you had lived in ancient Egyptian times, in which social class would you have wanted to be? Why?
• In what ways was life in ancient Egypt similar to today? In what ways was it different?

Processing

Have students complete Processing 9 in their Interactive Student Notebooks. Review the directions with them, and answer any questions.

Internet Connections

For more information on Unit 2: Ancient Egypt and the Near East, including primary- and secondary-source materials, refer students to Internet Resources for *History Alive! The Ancient World* at www.historyalive.com/connections.html. You will also find an on-line enrichment project for the unit at this site.

Assessment

Masters for assessment appear on the next three pages.

1. C   2. A   3. C   4. B   5. D

6. A   7. D   8. C

9. Possible answers: *Government officials, work:* advised pharaoh; *Food:* meat, dried fruit, cakes, wine; *Fun:* lush banquets with entertainment
Peasants, work: farming, labor on royal projects; *Food:* bread, beer, fish, lentils; *Fun:* harvest festivals, river game
In common: love of family, men as head of household, important burial rites

10. The bulleted points can provide a rubric for this item.

Fill in the bubble beside the best answer to each question.

1. The pharaoh was at the top of Egypt's social pyramid. Moving down the pyramid, what is the order of the classes listed below, from highest to lowest?

    1. artisans
    2. government officials
    3. peasants
    4. priests
    5. scribes

    Ⓐ 2, 5, 4, 1, 3
    Ⓑ 4, 5, 2, 3, 1
    Ⓒ 2, 4, 5, 1, 3
    Ⓓ 1, 2, 4, 5, 3

2. What does the social pyramid show about Egypt's social classes?

    Ⓐ The fewest number of people were in the highest classes.
    Ⓑ There were more rich than poor people in Egypt.
    Ⓒ The largest number of people were in the artisan classes.
    Ⓓ There were many people advising the pharaoh.

3. This list describes the jobs of people in which social class?

    • decided difficult court cases
    • collected taxes
    • led the army

    Ⓐ scribes
    Ⓑ artisans
    Ⓒ government officials
    Ⓓ pharaoh

4. Why did ancient Egypt believe having social classes was a good idea?

    Ⓐ They believed there wasn't enough money for everyone.
    Ⓑ They believed society worked when people knew their roles.
    Ⓒ They believed Egypt should focus on Egyptians rather than fight wars.
    Ⓓ They believed there would not be enough farmers without a class system.

5. If you were a peasant and wanted to raise your status, what one route might be open to you?

    Ⓐ to marry an official
    Ⓑ to work for the rich
    Ⓒ to take care of a temple
    Ⓓ to become a scribe

6. An ancient Egyptian schoolteacher once said, "A youngster's ear is on his back." What did he mean when he spoke those words?

    Ⓐ Children listen only if they're beaten.
    Ⓑ Children never look at their teachers.
    Ⓒ Children learn only by listening.
    Ⓓ Children never sit still during school.

7. It took a long time to become a scribe because

    Ⓐ it was difficult to write on papyrus.
    Ⓑ there were so few teachers to train people.
    Ⓒ it was difficult to find time to study.
    Ⓓ there were so many hieroglyphs to learn.

8. It is surprising that members of which group had as many rights as they did in ancient Egypt?

    Ⓐ the poor
    Ⓑ the uneducated
    Ⓒ women
    Ⓓ children

Use your knowledge of social studies to answer the questions below.

9. Members of different social classes led very different lives in many ways. However, in some ways, all the social classes were alike. Use the Venn diagram to compare and contrast the lives of government officials and peasants. Fill in the diagram, describing each group's work, food, and fun. Also identify three similarities between the groups.

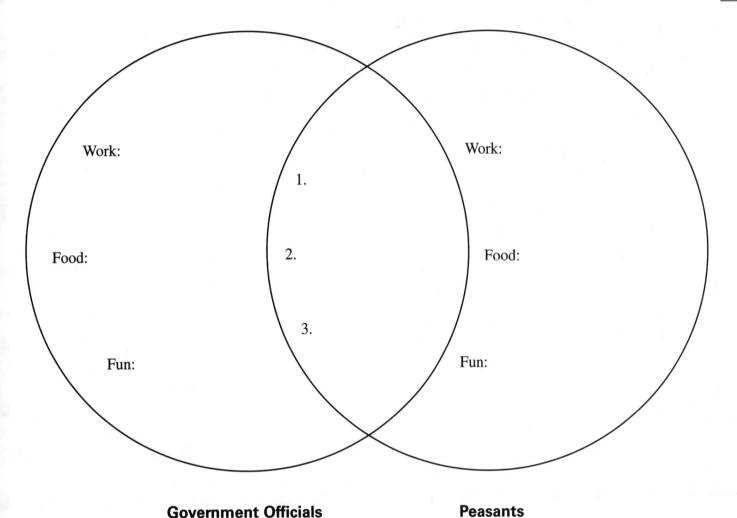

Work:

Food:

Fun:

1.

2.

3.

Work:

Food:

Fun:

Government Officials

Peasants

Use your knowledge of social studies to complete the item below.

10. You have decided to become a screenwriter (someone who writes movie scripts). Imagine you are writing a scene that will appear in a movie that takes place in ancient Egypt. Your scene will show viewers what life was like in two different social classes. In the space below, write a dialogue between two people of different social classes. Follow these guidelines:

    - Set the scene by describing
        —who the two people are.
        —the location where the dialogue takes place.
        —what the two people are doing at the time of the dialogue.
    - Through your dialogue and the people's actions, be sure you show
        —two differences between the people.
        —one way the people are similar.

Work with your group to create an interactive dramatization about the daily life of Egyptian government officials.

_____ **Step 1: Assign roles.** Review the roles below, and divide them up among the members of your group. Make sure everyone understands his or her responsibilities. Everyone will participate in the dramatization.

Historian You will lead the group during Step 2. Make sure the dramatization includes important historical information.

Director You will lead the group during Step 3. Make sure the dramatization includes all required elements and that everyone is involved.

Special Effects Designer You will lead the group during Step 4. Make sure the dramatization is as realistic as possible.

Host You will lead the group during Step 5. During the dramatization, invite visitors to participate and answer any questions they have.

_____ **Step 2: Learn about Egyptian government officials.** Take turns reading aloud from Section 9.3 of _History Alive! The Ancient World_. Afterward, the Historian leads a group discussion of the questions below. Use this information to complete the corresponding section of Reading Notes 9 in your Interactive Student Notebook.

• After the pharaoh, who were three important officials in the government of ancient Egypt? What were their major responsibilities?

• What was the seating arrangement at banquets?

• What kinds of food and drink were served at banquets?

• What typical forms of entertainment occurred at banquets?

_____ **Step 3: Plan your interactive dramatization.** The Director leads a group discussion of ideas for a five-minute interactive dramatization. Your dramatization must include every group member and at least four members of the audience. It should bring to life the scene on your transparency of a banquet at the home of an important government official. It should also share the important information from your completed Reading Notes. Your dramatization must include these parts:

1. Have a servant greet the visitors. The servant should tell the visitors from which social class of ancient Egypt the host and other banquet guests are from and then escort the visitors into the banquet room. Have the host welcome guests and visitors with an appropriate greeting.

2. Explain to the visitors about the seating arrangement at banquets, and have them sit in appropriate places. Have other members of the banquet party "show off" their perfumed hair, jewelry, and linen garments.

3. Describe the typical diet of the upper class, and have the servant offer food and drink to each guest.

4. Have the host say, "Regard one you know like one you don't know, one near you like one far from you," and explain why this is good advice from the vizier. Have the other guests describe their positions and responsibilities in the government of Egypt.

5. Have a musician play some music to entertain guests and visitors (your teacher has a CD recording for you to use). Encourage the visitors to clap along with the music. Describe other forms of entertainment that occur at banquets.

6. Ask if your visitors have any questions, and answer them. Thank your visitors for coming and say goodbye using the ancient Egyptian word, *Senebti*.

_____ **Step 4: Brainstorm ideas for costumes, props, and special effects.** The Special Effects Designer leads the group in brainstorming ideas for costumes, props, and other special effects to make the dramatization more realistic. (During your presentation, the transparency will be projected on the screen behind your group.)

_____ **Step 5: Rehearse your dramatization.** The Host leads the group in rehearsing your interactive dramatization. As you rehearse, the Host should make sure that

• each group member is actively participating in the dramatization.

• all actors speak their lines loudly, clearly, and at the right time.

• actors use their costumes and props appropriately.

• the Special Effects Designer knows the cues for any special effects.

• all actors know when and how the visitors will participate in the dramatization.

Work with your group to create an interactive dramatization about the daily life of Egyptian priests.

_____ **Step 1: Assign roles.** Review the roles below, and divide them up among the members of your group. Make sure everyone understands his or her responsibilities. Everyone will participate in the dramatization.

Historian You will lead the group during Step 2. Make sure the dramatization includes important historical information.

Director You will lead the group during Step 3. Make sure the dramatization includes all required elements and that everyone is involved.

Special Effects Designer You will lead the group during Step 4. Make sure the dramatization is as realistic as possible.

Host You will lead the group during Step 5. During the dramatization, invite visitors to participate and answer any questions they have.

_____ **Step 2: Learn about Egyptian priests.** Take turns reading aloud from Section 9.4 of _History Alive! The Ancient World_. Afterward, the Historian leads a group discussion of the questions below. Use this information to complete the corresponding section of Reading Notes 9 in your Interactive Student Notebook.

- What did Egyptians think happens to people after they die? Why did they bury things with people?

- What are the key steps Egyptian priests followed to embalm a body?

- Besides embalming bodies, what else did priests do in Egyptian society? What was the role of women priests?

- Why couldn't a priest eat fish, wear wool, or bathe fewer than three times a day?

_____ **Step 3: Plan your interactive dramatization.** The Director leads a group discussion of ideas for a five-minute interactive dramatization. Your dramatization must include every group member and at least four members of the audience. It should bring to life the scene on your transparency of priests embalming the body of a dead person. It should also share the important information from your completed Reading Notes. Your dramatization must include these parts:

1. Greet your visitors by using the ancient Egyptian welcome of _Em hotep nefer_. Introduce yourselves to your visitors, and invite them

inside. Tell them from which social class in ancient Egyptian society you come.

2. Explain what Egyptians think happens to people after they die. Show your visitors some of the things that will be buried along with this person's body, and explain why Egyptians think these things are important.

3. Describe the key steps followed to embalm a body. Have visitors help you complete one of these steps. Be sure to explain why the heart is left in the body and what you believe happens to it later.

4. Explain some of the other things priests do in Egyptian society, including the role of women.

5. Say, "As a priest, I can't eat fish or wear wool, and I must bathe at least three times a day," and explain why.

6. Ask if your visitors have any questions, and answer them. Thank your visitors for coming and say goodbye using the ancient Egyptian word, *Senebti.*

_____ **Step 4: Brainstorm ideas for costumes, props, and special effects.** The Special Effects Designer leads the group in brainstorming ideas for costumes, props, and other special effects to make the dramatization more realistic. (During your presentation, the transparency will be projected on the screen behind your group.)

_____ **Step 5: Rehearse your dramatization.** The Host leads the group in rehearsing your interactive dramatization. As you rehearse, the Host should make sure that

- each group member is actively participating in the dramatization.
- all actors speak their lines loudly, clearly, and at the right time.
- actors use their costumes and props appropriately.
- the Special Effects Designer knows the cues for any special effects.
- all actors know when and how the visitors will participate in the dramatization.

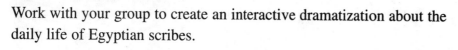

Work with your group to create an interactive dramatization about the daily life of Egyptian scribes.

_____ **Step 1: Assign roles.** Review the roles below, and divide them up among the members of your group. Make sure everyone understands his or her responsibilities. Everyone will participate in the dramatization.

Historian You will lead the group during Step 2. Make sure the dramatization includes important historical information.

Director You will lead the group during Step 3. Make sure the dramatization includes all required elements and that everyone is involved.

Special Effects Designer You will lead the group during Step 4. Make sure the dramatization is as realistic as possible.

Host You will lead the group during Step 5. During the dramatization, invite visitors to participate and answer any questions they have.

_____ **Step 2: Learn about Egyptian scribes.** Take turns reading aloud from Section 9.5 of *History Alive! The Ancient World*. Afterward, the Historian leads a group discussion of the questions below. Use this information to complete the corresponding section of Reading Notes 9 in your Interactive Student Notebook.

• What was the purpose of scribe schools? Who studied there and for how long?

• What were the typical tools and materials scribes used?

• What would a scribe schoolteacher mean when he said, "A youngster's ear is on his back; he only listens to the man who beats him"?

• Why were scribes important in ancient Egypt?

• What was one advantage of being a scribe?

_____ **Step 3: Plan your interactive dramatization.** The Director leads a group discussion of ideas for a five-minute interactive dramatization. Your dramatization must include every group member and at least four members of the audience. It should bring to life the scene on your transparency of students at a school for scribes. It should also share the important information from your completed Reading Notes. Your dramatization must include these parts:

1. Greet your visitors using the ancient Egyptian welcome of *Ak em hotep*. Introduce yourselves to your visitors, and invite them to join

304 Sample Lesson from *History Alive! The Ancient World*

© Teachers' Curriculum Institute

you inside the school. Tell them from which social class in ancient Egyptian society you come.

2. Give your visitors a tour of the scribe school classroom. Explain the purpose of scribe schools, who studies there, and for how many years they study.

3. Show your visitors the typical tools and materials that scribes use. Have them watch a student use these tools. Then let your visitors have a try.

4. Explain to your visitors what happens when a student doesn't pay attention to the teacher. Say, "A youngster's ear is on his back; he only listens to the man who beats him," and explain what you mean.

5. Tell your visitors about the importance of scribes in Egyptian society, the different kinds of work they do and some of the advantages of life as a scribe.

6. Ask if your visitors have any questions, and answer them. Thank your visitors for coming and say goodbye using the ancient Egyptian word, *Senebti.*

_____ **Step 4: Brainstorm ideas for costumes, props, and special effects.** The Special Effects Designer leads the group in brainstorming ideas for costumes, props, and other special effects to make the dramatization more realistic. (During your presentation, the transparency will be projected on the screen behind your group.)

_____ **Step 5: Rehearse your dramatization.** The Host leads the group in rehearsing your interactive dramatization. As you rehearse, the Host should make sure that

- each group member is actively participating in the dramatization.

- all actors speak their lines loudly, clearly, and at the right time.

- actors use their costumes and props appropriately.

- the Special Effects Designer knows the cues for any special effects.

- all actors know when and how the visitors will participate in the dramatization.

Work with your group to create an interactive dramatization about the daily life of Egyptian artisans.

_____ **Step 1: Assign roles.** Review the roles below, and divide them up among the members of your group. Make sure everyone understands his or her responsibilities. Everyone will participate in the dramatization.

Historian You will lead the group during Step 2. Make sure the dramatization includes important historical information.

Director You will lead the group during Step 3. Make sure the dramatization includes all required elements and that everyone is involved.

Special Effects Designer You will lead the group during Step 4. Make sure the dramatization is as realistic as possible.

Host You will lead the group during Step 5. During the dramatization, invite visitors to participate and answer any questions they have.

_____ **Step 2: Learn about Egyptian artisans.** Take turns reading aloud from Section 9.6 of *History Alive! The Ancient World*. Afterward, the Historian leads a group discussion of the questions below. Use this information to complete the corresponding section of Reading Notes 9 in your Interactive Student Notebook.

• What kinds of work did artisans do in ancient Egypt?

• What tools did stone carvers use? Why was their work so difficult?

• Did artisans get credit from the upper classes for the work they did? Explain.

• What were the living conditions like for most artisans?

_____ **Step 3: Plan your interactive dramatization.** The Director leads a group discussion of ideas for a five-minute interactive dramatization. Your dramatization must include every group member and at least four members of the audience. It should bring to life the scene on your transparency of artisans working on a sculpture. It should also share the important information from your completed Reading Notes. Your dramatization must include these parts:

1. Greet your visitors using the ancient Egyptian greeting of *Yii em hotep*. Introduce yourselves to your visitors, and invite them to join you inside the worksite. Tell them from which social class in ancient Egyptian society you come.

2. Describe some of the kinds of work that artisans do in ancient Egypt, including what the artisans at this site are creating.

3. Let the visitors examine the tools you are using and, if appropriate, try some of the work you are doing at the worksite. Make sure they understand why the stone carvers' work is so difficult.

4. Have the visitors listen in on a debate between two artisans about whether artisans get credit from the upper classes for the work they do.

5. Tell your visitors about the homes you live in when you are not working.

6. Ask if your visitors have any questions, and answer them. Thank your visitors for coming and say goodbye using the ancient Egyptian word, *Senebti.*

_____ **Step 4: Brainstorm ideas for costumes, props, and special effects.** The Special Effects Designer leads the group in brainstorming ideas for costumes, props, and other special effects to make the dramatization more realistic. (During your presentation, the transparency will be projected on the screen behind your group.)

_____ **Step 5: Rehearse your dramatization.** The Host leads the group in rehearsing your interactive dramatization. As you rehearse, the Host should make sure that

• each group member is actively participating in the dramatization.

• all actors speak their lines loudly, clearly, and at the right time.

• actors use their costumes and props appropriately.

• the Special Effects Designer knows the cues for any special effects.

• all actors know when and how the visitors will participate in the dramatization.

Work with your group to create an interactive dramatization about the daily life of Egyptian peasants.

_____ **Step 1: Assign roles.** Review the roles below, and divide them up among the members of your group. Make sure everyone understands his or her responsibilities. Everyone will participate in the dramatization.

Historian You will lead the group during Step 2. Make sure the dramatization includes important historical information.

Director You will lead the group during Step 3. Make sure the dramatization includes all required elements and that everyone is involved.

Special Effects Designer You will lead the group during Step 4. Make sure the dramatization is as realistic as possible.

Host You will lead the group during Step 5. During the dramatization, invite visitors to participate and answer any questions they have.

_____ **Step 2: Learn about Egyptian peasants.** Take turns reading aloud from Section 9.7 of *History Alive! The Ancient World*. Afterward, the Historian leads a group discussion of the questions below. Use this information to complete the corresponding section of Reading Notes 9 in your Interactive Student Notebook.

• What were the three seasons in Egypt? What kind of work did peasants do during each season?

• What role did music play in the work of peasants?

• What were possible punishments or rewards for peasants during harvesttime?

• What was the typical diet of peasants in ancient Egypt?

_____ **Step 3: Plan your interactive dramatization.** The Director leads a group discussion of ideas for a five-minute interactive dramatization. Your dramatization must include every group member and at least four members of the audience. It should bring to life the scene on your transparency of peasants working in the fields during harvesttime. It should also share the important information from your completed Reading Notes. Your dramatization must include these parts:

1. Greet your visitors using the ancient Egyptian greeting of *Yeh*. Introduce yourselves to your visitors, and invite them to join you in the

fields. Tell them from which social class in ancient Egyptian society you come.

2. Tell your visitors about the three seasons in Egypt and the kind of work you do during each season. Be sure to explain the jobs of peasant men and women during harvesttime.

3. Describe how you use music and chants to help pass the time while working. Have your visitors work alongside and chant with you (your teacher has a CD recording that will help you).

4. Explain to your visitors the possible punishments and rewards for peasants during harvesttime.

5. Describe the typical diet of peasants in ancient Egypt, and offer your visitors some of the food you brought with you. Tell them what you do for fun.

6. Ask if your visitors have any questions, and answer them. Thank your visitors for coming and say goodbye using the ancient Egyptian word, *Senebti*.

_____ **Step 4: Brainstorm ideas for costumes, props, and special effects.** The Special Effects Designer leads the group in brainstorming ideas for costumes, props, and other special effects to make the dramatization more realistic. (During your presentation, the transparency will be projected on the screen behind your group.)

_____ **Step 5: Rehearse your dramatization.** The Host leads the group in rehearsing your interactive dramatization. As you rehearse, the Host should make sure that

- each group member is actively participating in the dramatization.

- all actors speak their lines loudly, clearly, and at the right time.

- actors use their costumes and props appropriately.

- the Special Effects Designer knows the cues for any special effects.

- all actors know when and how the visitors will participate in the dramatization.

Read Sections 9.3–9.7 in *History Alive! The Ancient World*. For each section, write four things you learned about daily life for the members of that social class.

Possible answers:

Pharaoh ————

9.3 Government Officials

- The vizier served as chief judge and appointed and supervised other officials.
- The chief treasurer collected taxes in the form of such things as grain, cows, and beer.
- The general of the armies advised the pharaoh and helped make alliances.
- Government officials lived a life of luxury, including banquets with exotic foods and entertainment.

9.4 Priests

- Priests followed many rules, such as bathing several times a day.
- Priests had different jobs, such as advising the

9.5 Scribes

- Becoming a scribe was one of the few ways men could rise to a higher social class.
- Students spent 12 years or more in the scribe schools.

9.6 Artisans

- Egyptian artisans included carpenters, jewelers, leather- and metalworkers, painters, potters, sculptors, and weavers.
- Artisans rarely received recognition from the upper classes for their work.

9.7 Peasant Farmers

- Peasant life revolved around three seasons: flooding season, planting season, and harvest season.
- Peasants often sang songs to help pass the long hours working in the fields.

Sample 2

pharaoh and
supervising ceremonies.
- Priests oversaw the
important task of
embalming dead bodies.

- Life in scribe schools was difficult, and
teachers often beat their students.
- Scribes used pens made from reeds, paper
made from papyrus, writing tablets, and two
ink wells

- Stone carving was difficult work because artisans worked
with hard rock such as granite.
- Artisans and their families lived in modest, rectangular homes
that were barely 10 yards long.

- The diet of peasants was simple: bread, beer, some vegetables, and
maybe fish.
- During harvesttime, peasants were allowed to gather and keep leftover grain,
but they also could be beaten if they had a poor harvest.

Copy the name of each individual or group listed below onto the level of the pyramid where you think it belongs. For each name, write a short sentence to explain why you placed it at that level on the pyramid.

| Students | Principal | Teachers | Student Council | Office Staff |

Sample 2

My School's Social Pyramid

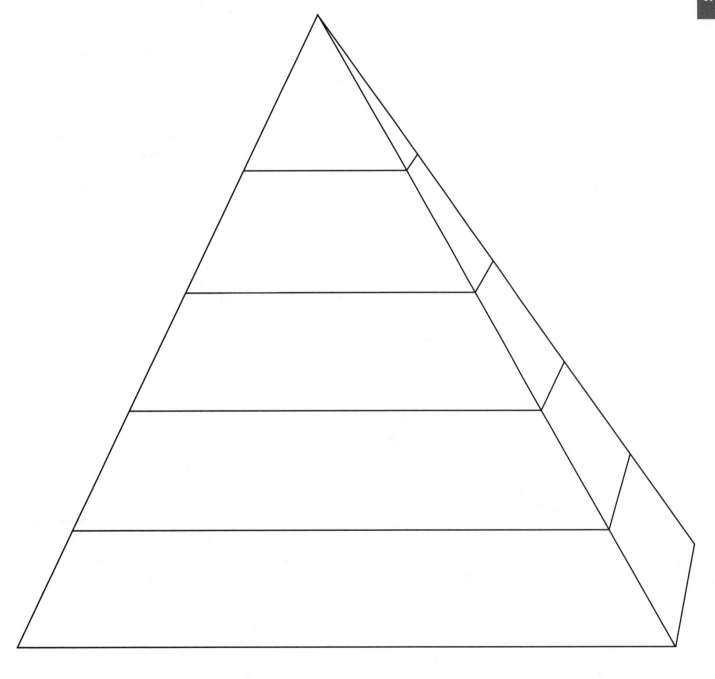

Read Sections 9.3–9.7 in *History Alive! The Ancient World*. For each section, write four things you learned about daily life for the members of that social class.

Pharaoh ————

9.3 Government Officials
-
-
-
-

9.4 Priests
-
-

9.5 Scribes
-
-

9.6 Artisans
-
-

9.7 Peasant Farmers
-
-

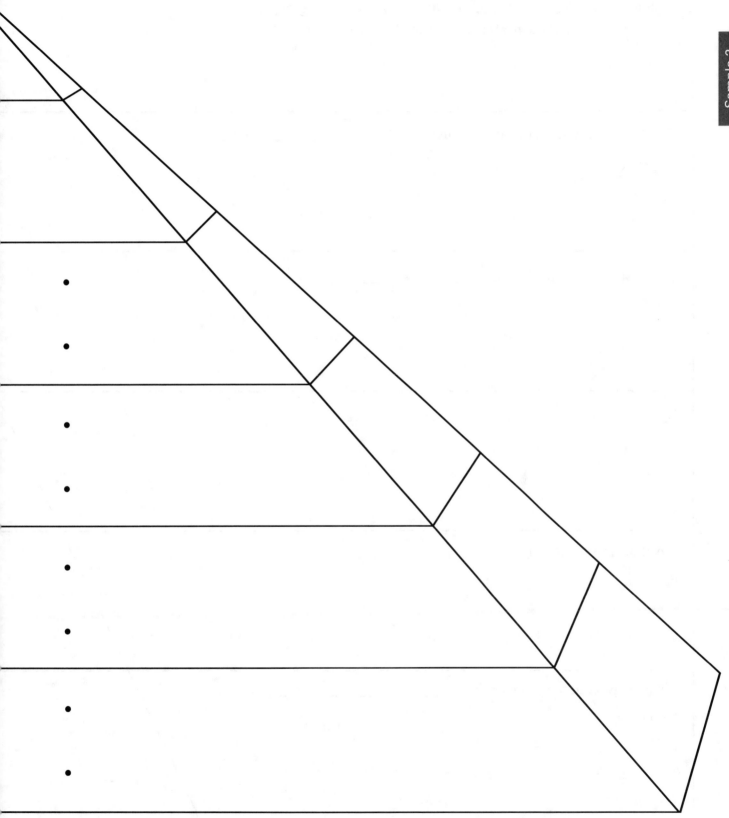

Complete the social pyramid below by identifying a person or group in our society that is like each of the ancient Egyptian social classes listed. Explain how the modern group is similar to the ancient Egyptian social class. Finally, draw or glue an image of the modern person or group into the appropriate level of the pyramid. An example is done for you.

Egyptian government officials were like _____

because…

Egyptian priests were most like _____

because…

Egyptian scribes were like _____

because…

Egyptian artisans were like _____

because…

Egyptian peasant farmers were like _____

because…

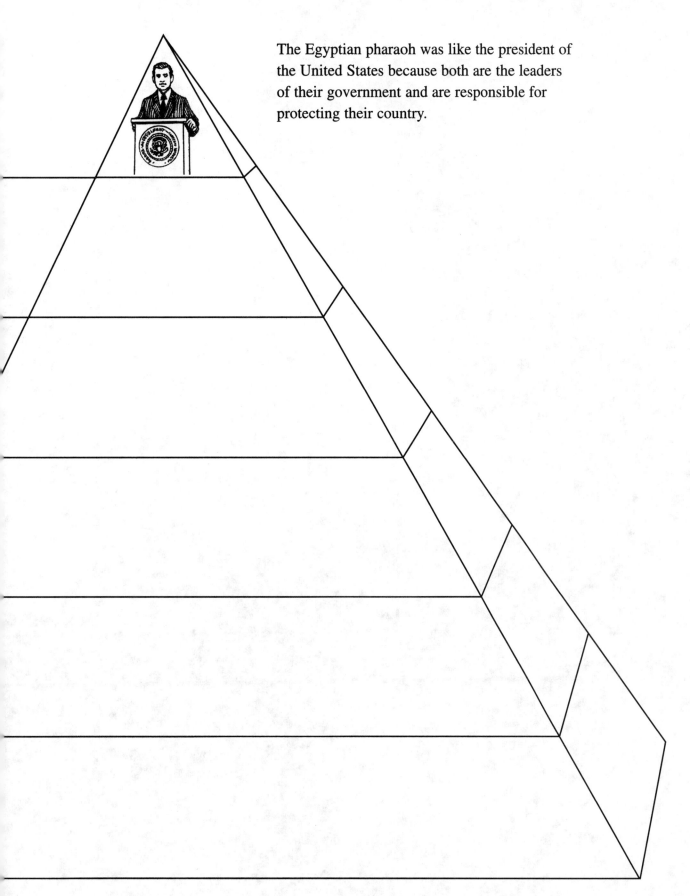

The Egyptian pharaoh was like the president of the United States because both are the leaders of their government and are responsible for protecting their country.

CHAPTER 9

Daily Life in Ancient Egypt

9.1 Introduction

In Chapter 8, you learned about four Egyptian pharaohs. In this chapter, you will meet other members of Egyptian society. You'll learn what life was like for Egyptians during the New Kingdom (about 1600 to 1100 B.C.E.).

Each year, when the Nile River flooded its banks, all of Egypt celebrated the Opet Festival. Work in the fields stopped while the people joined in a festival honoring the pharaoh and his patron, the god Amon-Re.

Almost everyone in Egyptian society took part in the festival. Priests decorated a statue of the god with jewelry. They put the statue in a shrine and placed the shrine on a ceremonial boat called a *barque*. The beautifully decorated boat was made by artisans, or craftspeople. High government officials competed for the honor of carrying the barque on poles through town. Peasant farmers lined the streets to watch the procession. Scribes made a written record of the celebration.

The Opet Festival brought all these groups together. But in everyday life, they belonged to very different **social classes**. These classes made up a **social pyramid,** with the pharaoh at the top and peasants at the bottom. In between were government officials, priests, scribes, and artisans. The daily life of each class was quite different.

In this chapter, you will learn more about Egypt's social pyramid. Then you'll explore the work and daily life of the various classes in Egyptian society.

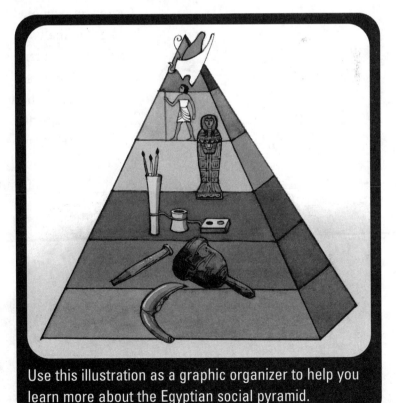

Use this illustration as a graphic organizer to help you learn more about the Egyptian social pyramid.

artisan a craftsperson

peasant a person who does farmwork for wealthy landowners

9.2 Ancient Egypt's Social Pyramid

Egyptian society was structured like a pyramid. At the very top of this social pyramid was the pharaoh, Egypt's supreme ruler. Below the pharaoh were several layers of social classes. The classes near the top of the pyramid had the fewest people and enjoyed the highest status. The classes nearer the bottom had more people and lower status.

Egypt's Social Classes

Government officials and priests belonged to the top two classes in the social pyramid under the pharaoh. They were the most powerful groups in Egypt.

Government officials carried out the orders of the pharaoh. Most of them came from noble families. They were powerful and wealthy, and they enjoyed a high quality of life.

Priests were also a powerful group, because religion touched every part of people's daily lives. The priests were in charge of the temples and religious rituals. They also oversaw the important ceremonies surrounding death and burial.

Next on the social pyramid were scribes. The scribes held a respected position in society. They recorded information for government and religious leaders. It took many years of schooling to become a scribe.

Artisans occupied the next layer of the social pyramid. This group included craftspeople like carpenters, metalworkers, painters, sculptors, and stone carvers. Artisans were highly skilled, but they had little social status.

At the bottom of the social pyramid were the **peasants**. They were the largest social class. Peasants worked the land, providing Egypt with a steady food supply. When they weren't farming, they worked on the pharaoh's massive building projects.

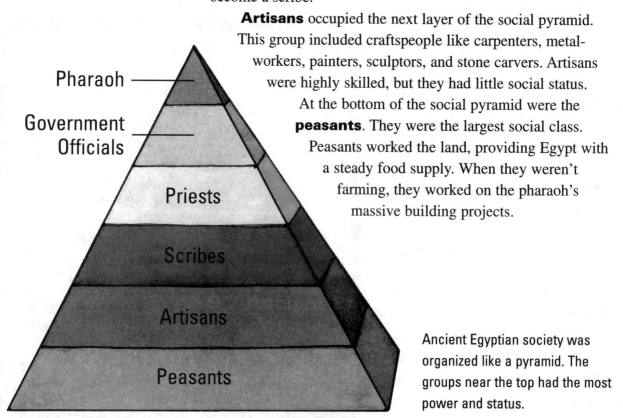

Pharaoh
Government Officials
Priests
Scribes
Artisans
Peasants

Ancient Egyptian society was organized like a pyramid. The groups near the top had the most power and status.

Sample 2

Egyptian women enjoyed more freedom and rights than most women in the ancient world. A few women even became pharaohs.

Life in Egypt's Social Classes

Egypt's social pyramid was fairly rigid. People usually belonged to the same social class as their parents. Most people had little chance to move to a higher class. People in different classes had some things in common, but in other ways their lives were quite different.

Egyptians in all social classes cherished family life. Most Egyptians married within their social group. Children were highly valued.

Men and women had different roles within the family. Men were the heads of their households. They worked to support the family. Fathers often trained their sons from an early age to take on their line of work. Women typically managed the home and raised the children. Noblewomen had servants or slaves to help them. Lower-class women had to do the work themselves.

Men were in charge of Egyptian society, but women enjoyed more freedom and rights than most women in the ancient world. They could own land and run businesses. They could ask for divorces and represent themselves in legal matters. Some women in the middle and upper classes worked as doctors, government officials, or priestesses. Both women and men enjoyed a better quality of life the higher they were on the social pyramid.

The Egyptians believed that their class system created a stable, well-ordered society. Each group had its own role to play. Let's take a look at the duties and daily lives of the various social classes during the time of the New Kingdom.

9.3 Government Officials

Government officials belonged to the highest class on Egypt's social pyramid, after the pharaoh. Their job was to assist the pharaoh in his or her role as supreme ruler of Egypt.

Government officials usually came from the pharaoh's family or other upper-class families. Most of them inherited their positions from family members. However, trusted servants from the royal court sometimes rose to power.

Important Government Officials

Three important officials were the vizier, the chief treasurer, and the general of the armies. Each had his own duties.

The **vizier** had more power than anyone except the pharaoh. The vizier advised the pharaoh and carried out his commands. He appointed and supervised most of the other government officials.

The vizier also served as a kind of chief judge. Judges often brought him their toughest cases. A vizier was expected to be fair and not show special favor to either side in a dispute. One vizier had this advice for those who would follow him: "Regard one you know like one you don't know, one near you like one far from you." In works of art, viziers often were shown wearing white, the color of neutrality.

The chief treasurer looked after the government's wealth. His main duty was to collect taxes. Egypt's economy was based on goods rather than money. People paid their taxes in grain, cows, cloth, silver, and even beer.

After the pharaoh, the general of the armies was the top military commander in Egypt. He advised the pharaoh in matters of war and national security, such as how to protect Egypt's borders from invaders. He also helped the pharaoh make **alliances** with other kingdoms.

This is a statue of Imhotep, an early and powerful vizier in ancient Egypt. Imhotep was famous for his role in designing and building great monuments.

Lives of Luxury

High government officials led lives of luxury. Most were nobles who had great wealth, fine homes, and plenty of time to socialize.

The lavish banquets enjoyed by these wealthy Egyptians illustrate their luxurious lifestyle. A good host made every effort to provide the best food. Cooks roasted ducks, geese, pigeons, quail, antelope, wild sheep, and goats. Dishes were piled high with figs, dates, grapes, and coconuts. Bread, cakes, honey, and plenty of beer and wine completed the meal.

Guests at banquets dressed in fine linen clothing. Both men and women wore perfume. The women often wore ropes of beads. They painted their nails, lined their eyes with makeup, and wore lipstick.

At the start of a banquet, the guests usually offered the host long blessings. They wished the host many riches, great happiness, a long life, and good health. The host often simply responded with "Welcome, welcome," or "Bread and beer," as a way of saying, "Come and eat!"

The feast began with men and women sitting on opposite sides of the room. Important guests were given chairs with high backs. Everyone else sat on stools or cushions. Servants, who were nearly all women, waited on the guests. There were no forks or spoons, so people ate with their fingers.

While the guests ate, musicians, dancers, and acrobats provided entertainment. Most of the musicians were women. They played flutes, harps, rattles, and lutes (a guitarlike instrument). Guests often clapped along with the music.

This painting shows women at a banquet.

9.4 Priests

Like government officials, priests were powerful and highly respected in Egyptian society. A large network of priests served under the pharaoh, who was considered the highest-ranked priest of all.

The Duties of Priests

Priests had different jobs. The High Priest advised the pharaoh and oversaw all religious ceremonies. Temple priests were in charge of the many temples scattered throughout Egypt. Other priests handled more common concerns and requests. They gave advice and performed healings.

Women were allowed to be priestesses in Egypt. They were generally considered to be equal to male priests. Their main duty was to oversee temples that were devoted to music and dancing.

Temple priests played an

Priests shaved their heads as an act of cleanliness and to show their religious purity.

especially important role in Egyptian religion. Every temple was home to an Egyptian god or gods. A temple priest's main job was to take care of the god.

A temple's god was thought to live in a statue. The statue was housed in a holy room called a *sanctuary*. Only a priest who had purified (cleansed) himself could enter the sanctuary. There were many things a priest had to do in order to be purified. He had to avoid certain foods, such as fish, that were associated with the lower classes. He had to cleanse his body by bathing three or four times a day in holy pools. He also had to shave off his body hair. And he had to wear clothes made of linen cloth, because animal products like leather and wool were considered unclean. Once he was purified, the priest could perform his sacred duties.

The Priests' Role in Burial Practices

Priests had a special role to play in burial practices. Egyptians believed in a life after death. They thought the spirits of the dead needed their bodies in the afterlife. For this reason, they preserved bodies from decay through **embalming**. Priests oversaw this sacred work.

The embalming process had many steps. First, the embalmers removed the body's organs, such as the brain, lungs, and liver. They used hooks to pull the brain out through the nostrils. Only the heart was left in the body. Egyptians believed that the gods used the heart to judge a dead person's soul.

The organs were packed in jars to preserve them. The organs and body were dried out with a special salt called *natron*.

After about 70 days, the embalmers washed and oiled the body. Then they wrapped it in hundreds of yards of linen. They decorated the wrapped body, or mummy, with jewelry and protective charms. Often they placed a mask over the head. Finally, they spread a black, gooey gum over the body and wrapped it a final time.

The mummy was then ready for burial. The mummy was placed in a wooden box which was then put inside a large stone coffin, called a **sarcophagus**. Because the ancient Egyptians believed that the afterlife was much like life in this world, the box or coffin was buried along with other items. These included food and drink, furniture, statues, gold, jewelry, clothes, games, and mirrors.

Not all Egyptians could afford such complicated burials. But even poor Egyptians wrapped their dead in cloth and buried them with jars of beer, loaves of bread, and other items they thought would be needed in the afterlife.

The process of embalming a body produced a mummy, such as those shown here.

embalm to treat a dead body with preservatives to prevent it from decaying

sarcophagus a large stone coffin

9.5 Scribes

Scribes were one level below priests in the social pyramid. Scribes were Egypt's official writers and record keepers. They were highly respected and well paid. Most scribes worked for the government. Others worked for priests or nobles.

Only men were allowed to be scribes. They came from all classes of society. Becoming a scribe was one of the few ways that men could rise above their parents' social class.

Scribe Schools

Boys who wanted to become scribes had to attend scribe school. The schools were run by priests. Most students came from artisan or merchant families. A very few came from the peasant class.

Schooling started around the age of five. Students typically spent 12 years or more learning **hieroglyphs,** the symbols used in the Egyptian system of writing. The system was very complicated. Most students first mastered a simpler form of writing and then worked their way up to hieroglyphs.

Students had to memorize over 700 hieroglyphs. They spent as many as four years copying the signs over and over. They practiced their writing on pieces of wood, flakes of stone, and even broken bits of pottery. When they were good enough, they were allowed to write on papyrus, a type of paper made from the papyrus plant.

This engraving shows students in a scribe school working at their writing.

Students in scribe schools did not have an easy life. Classes sometimes lasted from dawn until sunset. Teachers were strict and often treated their students harshly. They frequently yelled at students for being lazy or not paying attention. Beatings were common. One stern schoolmaster wrote, "A youngster's ear is on his back; he only listens to the man who beats him."

The Work of the Scribes

Ancient Egyptians made all kinds of records, so scribes held a wide variety of jobs. They kept records of the grain and food supply. When a government **census** counted the people living in Egypt, they recorded the results. Some scribes calculated and collected taxes. Legal scribes recorded court cases and helped enforce laws. Military scribes kept track of the army's soldiers and food supply, and the number of enemies killed in battle.

Every scribe used the same tools. For pens, a scribe used finely sharpened reeds. For paper, he used a sheet of papyrus laid out on a writing tablet. The tablets were made of wood or stone. Each tablet contained two wells, one for black ink and one for red ink. A small container held water that was used to wet the ink.

A scribe carried his tools with him wherever he traveled. His tablet hung from a cord slung over his shoulder. Leather bags and cases attached to the tablet held his other tools.

Scribes also carried rolls of papyrus. This paper was a remarkable invention of the Egyptians. To make it, they first cut the inner part of the papyrus plant into strips and soaked the strips in water for several days until they were soft. Then they laid the strips out in a crisscross pattern between two sheets of cloth. The papyrus strips were pressed together until the cloth had absorbed all the water. Finally, the papyrus strips were pressed one more time to form a sheet of paper.

census an official count of the population or number of people living in an area

This relief shows two scribes. Only men were allowed to be scribes, although women were sometimes taught to read and write.

Stone carvers were some of the most skilled workers in the artisan class.

9.6 Artisans

Below the scribes on the social pyramid were the artisans. Egypt's artisans were highly skilled laborers who created some of the most beautiful art objects in the ancient world. Yet, unlike scribes, they rarely got the respect they deserved. Only the select few who became master craftsmen were sometimes honored for their work.

Types of Artisans

Artisans specialized in any one of a number of crafts. Workers in this class included carpenters, jewelers, leatherworkers, metalworkers, painters, potters, sculptors, and weavers. Artisans made many beautiful objects, including stunning jewelry and elegant furniture. Painters portrayed scenes of Egyptian daily life. Most artisans were men, but some women wove fabric, beaded clothing, and made perfume.

The most skilled artisans were the stone carvers. They produced the statues, engravings, and reliefs found in Egyptian temples, tombs, and monuments.

Stone carvers played an important role in tomb building. The belief in an afterlife inspired wealthy Egyptians to order elaborate tombs for themselves. Stone carvers helped equip the tombs with artwork to honor and preserve the dead. They created statues of the deceased, highly detailed wall engravings, and stone coffins.

Stone carving was hard, time-consuming work. The carvers often worked with very hard rock, such as granite. They used a hard type of rock called *dolerite* to pound out the object's initial shape. Next, they refined the shape and carved in details using stone tools and copper chisels. Then they smoothed and polished the object using quartz sand. Painters often added color to the finished product.

This painting shows different kinds of artisans at work. Look carefully. What do you see?

The Daily Life and Work of Artisans

Artisans were a class in the middle of Egyptian society. They and their families lived in modest homes. Their houses were usually rectangular and barely 10 yards long. Three rooms stretched from front to back. The first room was used either as a workroom or to house animals. The living room came next. The final room was divided into a kitchen and a bedroom. The roof was sometimes used as a place to work or sleep.

Artisans typically worked side by side in large workshops. They usually worked for 10 days at a stretch before taking time off. The workers depended entirely on their employers for food. In hard times when food was in short supply, artisans often went hungry.

Pharaohs called upon hundreds of artisans at a time to work on royal projects. Artisans created the fine artwork that often covered temples, royal tombs, and other monuments. They worked in large groups to complete engravings, paintings, and hieroglyphics.

Despite artisans' skill and creativity, the upper classes often viewed them as little more than common laborers. Even the most talented artists were almost never allowed to sign their work. But some artists did receive recognition. Employers sometimes threw a banquet for their favorite artist. Occasionally they honored an artist by letting him portray himself in a painting or an engraving.

This painting shows a peasant farmer and his wife sowing their land. Peasants worked hard to supply Egyptians with food.

9.7 Peasants

Peasants made up the lowest and largest class in Egypt's social pyramid. They were generally considered unskilled laborers. Yet Egyptian society depended on their work. Peasants grew the crops that supplied everyone with food. When they weren't busy working the fields, they helped build monuments like the pyramids.

The Three Seasons of the Nile

Peasant life revolved around the Nile River and its three seasons: the flooding season, the planting season, and the harvest season.

The flooding season lasted from June to September. During this time, the Nile overran its banks and fertilized the fields. Farmers had to wait for the waters to go down before they could work the fields. In the meantime, they labored on royal projects, such as building pyramids and temples.

In October, the planting season began and farmers sowed their fields with seeds. The biggest crops were wheat and barley, which were used to make bread and beer.

Peasants worked in pairs to sow the fields. The farmer softened the earth with a plow pulled by cattle. A second person, often the farmer's wife, followed behind to scatter the seeds. Throughout the season, farmers carefully irrigated the land.

The harvest season began in March. Usually the farmer's entire family helped with the harvest. The men cut down the plants with sickles (metal blades with short wooden handles). Then the women and children gathered the tall stalks of grain.

During harvesttime, everyone worked from dawn to dusk. Peasants often sang songs to make the long hours of labor go more quickly. Sometimes musicians played in the fields while the workers sang.

The Daily Lives of Peasants

Peasants had the fewest comforts of any of the social classes. They lived in simple houses made of mud bricks. Their furniture was usually limited to woven mats.

The peasants' diet was simple. A typical meal might include onions, cucumbers, fish, homemade bread, and water or beer. Peas and lentils were also common. Unlike the upper classes, peasants rarely ate meat. In times of **famine,** they often had to boil tough papyrus plants for food.

Peasants spent most of their lives working, but they did have some time for fun. Men enjoyed a river game that involved knocking each other off papyrus rafts. Holidays were celebrated before planting and after the harvest. Peasants also took part in festivals honoring the Egyptian gods.

An important time of year for peasants was the end of the harvest season. As a reward for their hard work, they were allowed to gather up as much leftover grain as they could and keep it for food. But they could also be punished for a poor harvest.

Farmers had to pay taxes in the form of crops. If a farmer's harvest came up short and he couldn't pay the required tax, he was brutally beaten.

famine a severe shortage of food

This painting shows peasants cutting and gathering the wheat harvest.

9.8 Chapter Summary

In this chapter, you learned about Egypt's social pyramid. Each social class had its own role to play in society. You learned about the work and daily lives of government officials, priests, scribes, artisans, and peasants. In the next chapter, you will travel south along the Nile and explore the civilization of Kush.

History Alive! The United States

Program Components

- **Lesson Guides:** with classroom activities, reproducible sheets, assessment tools
- **Overhead Transparency Book:** color images to enhance visual literacy
- **Placard Set:** picture cards for use with the activities
- **Audio CD:** music, audio effects, dramatic readings
- **Interactive Student Notebook**
- **Interactive Timeline**
- **Student Edition:** with colorful, considerate text
- **Interactive Desk Map**

History Alive! The United States is another one of TCI's core programs for middle school social studies. Each lesson is built around an interactive classroom activity, based on one of six strategies that are the hallmark of the TCI Approach. This section contains three sample lessons from that program. Sample 3 is a Visual Discovery activity; Sample 4 is a Response Group activity; and Sample 5 is an Experiential Exercise.

Contents of *History Alive! The United States*

Andrew Jackson and the Growth of American Democracy

Overview

In this lesson, students learn about the growth of democracy during the Jacksonian Era. In a **Visual Discovery** activity, students analyze images and read information to assess Jackson's presidency from the perspectives of four groups: the common man, states' rights supporters, the rich and well-born, and Native Americans. Afterward, students apply their learning in a Processing assignment.

Objectives

Students will be able to

- analyze songs and images to identify key differences between the Federal Period and the Jacksonian Era.
- write summaries of key events of the Jacksonian Era.
- critique Andrew Jackson's presidency from the perspectives of the common man, states' rights supporters, the rich and well-born, and Native Americans.
- create commemorative plaques and "Wanted" posters that depict the positive and negative impacts of Andrew Jackson's presidency.

Materials

- Graphic Organizer Placard 14
- Transparency 14A–14H
- CD Track 5, "The President's March"
- CD Track 6, "The Hunters of Kentucky"
- Student Handout 14 (1 per group)
- Map Transparency 14

Preview

1 Project *Transparency 14A: President and Mrs. Washington at a Presidential Reception,* **and review the directions for Preview 14.** Tell students to answer the first set of Image Analysis Questions on page 91 of their Interactive Student Notebooks. When they have finished, ask several students to share their answers. Student responses should include some or all of the following key points:

- All the people are in fancy attire. They appear to be rich.
- Washington and the other figures appear stiff and formal. For example, many of the women are wearing fancy dresses, and some of the men are wearing powdered wigs.
- Words that describe Washington and the people at the banquet include *serious, stiff, unemotional, heroic,* and *brooding.*

2 Have students analyze the song "The President's March." Tell students they will listen to a song that was probably played at Washington's inauguration. Play CD Track 5 and have students record answers to the first set of Song Analysis Questions in their Interactive Student Notebooks. Have them share their answers. Student responses should include some or all of the following key points:

- The song makes one feel proud and reverent.
- Three words that describe the song are *classical, formal,* and *slow.*
- The president was a reserved and dignified man who remained aloof from others.

3 Have students analyze *Transparency 14B: Jackson Stops to Greet the People after His Election in 1828.* Project Transparency 14B, and have students answer the second set of Image Analysis Questions on page 92 of their Interactive Student Notebooks. Have them share their answers. Student responses should include some or all of the following key points:

- Jackson appears to appeal to a broader cross section of people. Some are well dressed, while others appear to be working class. Still, there are no people of color, and the president is white and male.
- Words that describe Jackson and his followers include *happy, adoring, diverse,* and *common.* (**Note:** Jackson has stopped in a public place, near the tavern and the post office.)

4 Have students analyze the song "The Hunters of Kentucky." Tell students that they will listen to a song that was written for Andrew Jackson's 1828 presidential campaign. Explain that it celebrates Jackson's military leadership in the War of 1812, when Jackson led Kentucky sharpshooters to victory against the British. Play CD Track 6 and have students record answers to the second set of Song Analysis Questions. Have them share their answers. Student responses should include some or all of the following key points:

- The song makes one feel upbeat and excited.
- Three words that describe the song are *folksy, fast,* and *fun.*
- The president was an informal, friendly man who enjoyed being with common people.

Sample 3

5 Have students contrast the images and songs. After students have completed the final Preview questions, ask them to share their responses. Then tell them that the period from the 1820s to the 1840s was a time of great political change. During this time, more and more people became involved in the democratic process. Explain that students can see this change in the livelier, more inclusive music and images of the period. President Andrew Jackson was at the center of the political changes of the 1820s to the 1840s. In fact, the entire era, or time period, is named after him—the Jacksonian Era.

Graphic Organizer

1 Introduce Chapter 14 in *History Alive! The United States*. Tell students they will learn more about the political changes that occurred during the Jacksonian Era. Have them read Section 14.1. Remind them that important terms appear in colored type (teal). Each term is defined in the Glossary.

2 Introduce the graphic organizer on page 189. Ask the following questions: *What do you see here? Who is the man in the center? What different groups, represented by single faces, are looking at him? Based on what you know about Jackson, which groups are most likely to have favored Jackson? Which groups are least likely to have favored Jackson?* Explain that students will use this graphic organizer to assess the Jackson presidency from the perspectives of four groups: the common man, states' rights supporters, the rich and well-born, and Native Americans.

Visual Discovery

1 Arrange the classroom. Place students in mixed-ability groups of four. Prepare an overhead transparency that shows students with whom they will sit and how to arrange their desks.

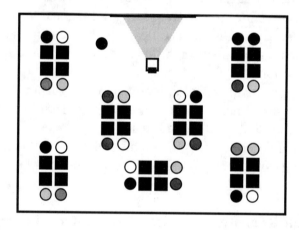

2 Have students analyze *Transparency 14C: Jackson's Inaugural Party.* Explain that students will analyze six transparencies to understand Jacksonian democracy and to assess Andrew Jackson's presidency. Project Transparency 14C, and ask these questions:

- What do you see here?
- Why do you think all these people have gathered at the White House?
- What three adjectives best describe the appearance and actions of the crowd?

Ask students to turn to Reading Notes 14 on page 93 of their Interactive Student Notebooks. Review the directions. Have students read Section 14.2 and complete the corresponding sections of their Reading Notes. (**Note:** You may want to record notes as a class, or allow students to work in pairs to complete this task.) After students have completed their notes, have them share their responses. Use Guide to Reading Notes 14 to review the main points with the class.

Finally, have students reexamine Transparency 14C. Encourage them to use what they learned in Section 14.2 to answer these questions:
- Why are so many people gathered at the White House?
- Which Americans do you think were happy about the election of Andrew Jackson?
- Which Americans do you think were unhappy about Jackson's election?

3 Pass out *Student Handout 14: Creating Act-It-Outs on Jacksonian Democracy*, and have students create and perform an act-it-out. Follow these steps:
- Tell students they will have five minutes to prepare for an act-it-out that will bring to life the scene shown in the transparency.
- Assign each group one of the characters for the act-it-out. Make sure students understand that they are responsible for portraying only the character you have assigned to their group.
- Tell students to use the guidelines on Student Handout 14 to prepare for the act-it-out. Review the directions with the class.
- When all groups are ready, choose two students to step into the projected image and take on the two roles.
- Assume the role of reporter and interview the characters, asking questions like those they discussed in their groups.

4 Have students analyze *Transparency 14D: From the Frontier to the White House*. Project Transparency 14D and ask these questions:
- Who do you see here?
- These images tell the story of how Jackson became president. If you were to tell the story, what other important events would you include?
- Based on these images, do you think Jackson was well qualified to be president?

Have students read Section 14.3 and complete the corresponding Reading Notes. After completing their notes, have them share their responses. Use the Guide to Reading Notes to review the main points with the class.

Have students reexamine Transparency 14D. Encourage them to use what they learned in Section 14.3 to answer these questions:
- What details about Jackson's background for the presidency are not included in these images?
- If you were to complete the story of Jackson's rise to the presidency in pictures, what other images would you include?
- Was Jackson well qualified to be president? Why or why not?

5 Have students analyze *Transparency 14E: Jackson's Approach to Governing*. Project Transparency 14E, and ask these questions:
- What do you see here?
- Who is pictured at the top of the image?
- Why do you think Jackson is pictured in this way?
- What is he doing?

Have students read Section 14.4 and complete the corresponding Reading Notes. After completing their notes, have them share their responses. Use the Guide to Reading Notes to review the main points with the class.

Have students reexamine Transparency 14E. Explain that the people at the bottom of this image are seeking political office. Encourage students to use what they learned in Section 14.4 to answer these questions:

- What is the cartoonist's opinion of the people seeking political office?
- What is the cartoonist's opinion of Andrew Jackson?
- Do you agree with the cartoonist? Why or why not?

6 **Have students analyze** *Transparency 14F: The Nullification Crisis.* Project Transparency 14F and ask these questions:
- What do you see in this cartoon?
- What is the man near the top of the staircase doing?
- What are the labels on each step? What does each label mean?
- Why is the man on the right pulling on another man's coattails?
- What is lying at the bottom of the staircase?

Have students read Section 14.5 and complete the corresponding Reading Notes. After students have completed their notes, have them share their responses. Use the Guide to Reading Notes to review the main points with the class.

Have students reexamine Transparency 14F. Tell them that the man near the top of the stairs is John C. Calhoun, and Andrew Jackson is pictured on the right pulling on the coattails of another figure. Encourage them to use what they learned in Section 14.5 to answer these questions:
- What does the cartoonist imply that John C. Calhoun wants?
- Why did the cartoonist label each step as he did?
- What does the cartoonist show Andrew Jackson trying to do?
- Why is the Constitution pictured as it is, lying at the bottom of the stairs?
- What is the cartoonist's intended message?
- Do you agree with the message? Why or why not?

7 **Have students analyze** *Transparency 14G: Jackson Battles the Bank of the United States.* Project Transparency 14G, and ask these questions:
- What do you see in this cartoon?
- What do you think is happening?

Have students read Section 14.6 and complete the corresponding Reading Notes. After completing their notes, have them share their responses. Use the Guide to Reading Notes to review the main points with the class.

Have students reexamine Transparency 14G. Explain that Andrew Jackson is pictured on the left, Nicholas Biddle is pictured in a top hat at the center, and the heads represent the 24 Bank directors. Encourage students to use what they learned in Section 14.6 to answer these questions:

- What does Jackson have in his hand? What is he trying to do?
- What danger does the snake represent?
- What is the cartoonist's intended message?
- Do you agree with the message? Why or why not?

8 Have students analyze *Transparency 14H: Jackson's Indian Policy.* Project Transparency 14H, and ask these questions:
- What is happening in this picture?
- Where might these people be going?
- Describe their facial expressions. How do you think they feel?

Have students read Section 14.7 and complete the corresponding Reading Notes. After students have completed their notes, have them share their responses. Use the Guide to Reading Notes to review the main points with the class.

Have students reexamine Transparency 14H. Encourage them to use what they learned in Section 14.7 to answer these questions:
- Where are these people going?
- Who has sent them there?
- Why is this happening?
- Are the Native Americans being treated fairly? Why or why not?

9 Have students answer the questions about the Trail of Tears that appear on the Geography Challenge on page 198 of *History Alive! The United States.*

10 Repeat Step 3 to have students create and perform an act-it-out about the Trail of Tears.

Processing
Have students complete the Processing assignment on page 99 of their Interactive Student Notebooks.

Internet Connections
For students wanting additional enrichment, refer them to the Internet Project for Lesson 14 at www.historyalive.com/connections.html.

Assessment
A blackline master for the assessment follows on pages 82–85.

1. B	3. A	5. D	7. B	9. D	11. D	13. C	15. C	17. C
2. C	4. C	6. A	8. B	10. C	12. B	14. A	16. A	18. B

19. The bulleted points can provide a rubric for this item.

Choose the letter of the best answer for each question.

1. Why did three times as many people vote in the presidential election of 1828 as voted in 1824?

   A. By 1828, women had gained the right to vote in some states, while no women could vote in 1824.

   B. By 1828, voting laws had been changed in most states to give all white men the right to vote.

   C. The United States had twice as many states in 1828 as it had in 1824.

   D. The candidates running for president in 1828 were more interesting that those running in 1824.

2. Andrew Jackson's election victory in 1828 depended on support from

   A. the rich and well-born.

   B. Native Americans.

   C. the common people.

   D. state's rights supporters.

3. Jackson's practice of rewarding political supporters with government jobs became know as

   A. the spoils system.

   B. Jacksonian democracy.

   C. mudslinging.

   D. a corrupt bargain.

4. The Nullification Crisis was triggered by strong opposition to the

   A. Force Bill.

   B. Indian Removal Act.

   C. Tariff of Abominations.

   D. Bank of the United States

5. Jackson's handling of the Nullification Crisis was most upsetting to

   A. the rich and well-born.

   B. Native Americans.

   C. the common people.

   D. state's rights supporters.

6. Who was most upset by Jackson's crusade to destroy the Bank of the United States?

   A. the rich and well-born

   B. Native Americans

   C. the common people

   D. state's rights supporters

7. Why did many whites call the Creek, Cherokee, Chickasaw, Choctaw, and Seminole the "Five Civilized Tribes"?

   A. These groups had never gone to war against whites.

   B. These groups had learned and adopted many white ways.

   C. These groups had won the right to elect representatives to Congress.

   D. These groups had agreed to leave their homelands peacefully.

8. Which group was most hurt by Jackson's removal policy?

   A. the rich and well-born

   B. Native Americans

   C. the common people

   D. state's rights supporters

Use the images and your knowledge of social studies to answer the questions below.

9. This painting shows Andrew Jackson as

A. a crusader for states rights.

B. a champion of the spoils system.

C. the protector of Native Americans.

D. the hero of the Battle of New Orleans.

10. The artist painted Jackson as a

A. charming ladies' man.

B. battling, frontier lawyer.

C. strong, determined leader.

D. hot-tempered dueler.

11. Who would have been most likely to buy this painting?

A. a Cherokee chief

B. a director of the Bank of the United States

C. a South Carolina nullifier

D. a western farmer

12. What event is depicted in this image?

A. The Trail of Tears

B. Andrew Jackson's inauguration

C. The Nullification Crisis

D. President Jackson's bank battle

13. The building in the image is the

A. South Carolina capitol.

B. Bank of the United States.

C. White House.

D. birthplace of Andrew Jackson.

14. Most of the people shown in the image are

A. farmers and workers and their families.

B. members of the Five Civilized Tribes.

C. wealthy bankers and merchants.

D. Tariff of Abominations protesters.

Sample 3

Read the passage below. Then read each question and choose the best answer based on the passage.

Sequoyah was born in Taskigi, Tennessee, probably the son of an English trader and a Cherokee mother. As a young man he moved to Georgia, where he worked as a silversmith. There a customer suggested that he sign his work, like white silversmiths did. Not knowing how to write, Sequoyah visited a local farmer who showed him how to spell his name. At that point Sequoyah began to toy with the idea of a Cherokee writing system.

While serving with U.S. Army during the War of 1812, Sequoyah became convinced of the need for a written Cherokee language. He and other Cherokees were unable to write letters home, read military orders, or make a written record of events. A few years later he completed his "Talking Leaves"—an 85-letter alphabet that represent all the syllables of the Cherokee language.

Word spread quickly of Sequoyah's invention. In 1821, the Cherokee Nation adopted Sequoyah's alphabet as their own. Within months, thousands of Cherokee were literate. Meanwhile, the Cherokee began publishing newspapers and books in their own language. The giant sequoia trees and Sequoia National Park in California are both named after this man, who has been called by one scholar perhaps the most remarkable man who has ever lived on Georgia soil.

15. Which event happened first in the passage?

   A. Sequoyah developed an alphabet.

   B. Sequoyah was asked to sign his work.

   C. Sequoyah moved to Georgia.

   D. Sequoyah fought in the War of 1812.

16. In this passage, the word *literate* means

   A. able to read.

   B. familiar with books and literature.

   C. well-written.

   D. competent or knowledgeable.

17. Which **OPINION** is found in the passage?

   A. Sequoyah was the greatest Cherokee who ever lived.

   B. The sequoia tree is a fitting memorial to Sequoyah.

   C. Sequoyah is the most remarkable man who ever lived in Georgia.

   D. Sequoyah's 85-letter alphabet is too long to learn.

18. This passage is an example of

   A. a primary source written by an eyewitness to an event.

   B. a secondary source written by a historian about an event.

   C. a piece of fiction written about an event that never happened.

   D. an opinion piece written to express the author's views.

Follow the directions to complete the item below.

Note to Teacher: Project Transparency 14C for students.

19. Examine the image your teacher is projecting. Respond to the four prompts below:

- Which president's inaugural party is this a picture of? How can you tell?

- Why are the people reacting like this to the president's inauguration?

- For which accomplishment(s) do you think this president should be praised? Why?

- What group(s) would probably not praise this president? Why not?

Directions: You will work in a small group to bring to life two images from Andrew Jackson's presidency. Your teacher will select one member from your group to play the part of your assigned character. A reporter will interview characters that appear in the two images. Follow the directions in each section to create your act-it-out.

Act-It-Out 1: Jackson's Inaugural Party

To prepare for the act-it-out on Jackson's inaugural party, follow these steps:

Step 1: Circle the character your group has been assigned.

Farmer on the frontier   Banker from Philadelphia

Step 2: Discuss the questions below. Make sure that everyone in your group can answer each question so that everyone is prepared to be the actor.
* How do you view Jackson's inaugural party?
* What hopes do you have for Jackson's presidency?
* What fears do you have about Jackson's presidency?
* If you have a chance to meet Jackson at the party, what will you say to him?

Step 3: Discuss how the person who is chosen to perform can make the character come alive. Use visual and written information to brainstorm ways to make the characterization realistic. Make or collect simple props to use during the act-it-out.

Act-It-Out 2: The Trail of Tears

To prepare for the act-it-out on the Trail of Tears, follow these steps:

Step 1: Circle the character your group has been assigned.

White Georgian who recently settled   Elderly Native American
on former Indian land

                                         Native American teenager

Andrew Jackson

                                         Native American mother of three

Armed soldier escorting Cherokees
to Indian Territory   Young Native American warrior

Step 2: Discuss the questions below. Make sure that everyone in your group can answer each question so that everyone is prepared to be the actor.
* Why are Indians being removed from their homelands?
* Is the policy of Indian removal fair? Why or why not?
* How has the policy changed your life?
* What do you think should happen now?

Step 3: Discuss how the person who is chosen to perform can make the character come alive. Use visual and written information to brainstorm ways to make the characterization realistic. Make or collect simple props to use during the act-it-out.

Directions: After you read each section in your text, record notes as directed.

14.2 The Inauguration of Andrew Jackson

Write a paragraph summary of this section that includes these terms: *democracy, common man, vote, rich and well-born*.

*During the election of 1828, the United States experienced a growth in **democracy**. In this election, the **common man** could **vote** for the first time. Before this, only white men who owned property could **vote**. Many people wildly celebrated Jackson's inauguration at the White House. They believed he was the champion of the **common man**. They also believed that Jackson would reduce the power of monied interests. The **rich and well-born** were not so sure Jackson was the best person to be president.*

Add facial expressions and speech bubbles to the drawing below to reflect what the common man and the rich and well-born felt and thought about Jackson's rise from the frontier to the White House.

Facial expressions and comments will vary. The face on the right should express approval. The face on the left should express disapproval.

Directions: After you read each section in your text, record notes as directed.

14.3 From the Frontier to the White House

Write a paragraph summary of this section that includes these terms: *Battle of New Orleans, Democratic Party, corrupt bargain, self-made man.*

*Andrew Jackson grew up in poverty. He was truly a **self-made man**. He became a lawyer, then a planter, then a military hero, and, finally, the president of the United States. Jackson was well known for his victory in the **Battle of New Orleans**. Jackson lost the election of 1824 in the so-called **"corrupt bargain"** when Henry Clay was accused of trading his support for Adams for a job as secretary of state. Jackson's supporters founded a new **Democratic Party** to represent the common people. In 1828, Jackson was elected president.*

Add facial expressions and speech bubbles to the drawing below to reflect what the common man and the rich and well-born felt and thought about Jackson's rise from the frontier to the White House.

Facial expressions and comments will vary. The face on the right should express approval. The face on the left should express disapproval.

Directions: After you read each section in your text, record notes as directed.

14.4 Jackson's Approach to Governing

Write a paragraph summary of this section that includes these terms: *kitchen cabinet, spoils system, civil servant*.

*Jackson's approach to governing was controversial. He relied more on his friends in the "**kitchen cabinet**" than he did on the regular cabinet. He also tried to reform the government. He believed that government workers should "go back to making a living as other people do." He replaced about 10% of **civil servants**. Jackson rewarded his followers in the Democratic Party with government jobs. His opponents called this the "**spoils system**," from the saying "to the victor belong the spoils of war."*

Add facial expressions and speech bubbles to the drawing below to reflect how the common man and the rich and well-born felt and thought about Jackson's approach to governing.

Facial expressions and comments will vary. The face on the right should express approval. The face on the left should express disapproval.

Sample 3

Directions: After you read each section in your text, record notes as directed.

14.5 The Nullification Crisis

Write a paragraph summary of this section that includes these terms: *tariffs, states' rights, South Carolina, John C. Calhoun.*

Tariffs were a source of unhappiness and hardship in some states and a source of joy in others. Southern states suffered because of tariffs. When a high tariff was passed in 1828, citizens in South Carolina were outraged. They believed the federal government had gone too far, and they threatened to secede. John C. Calhoun was a champion of South Carolina's states' rights position. He tried to have the tariffs repealed, and argued in favor of nullification. Jackson threatened to send in federal troops, and the crisis ended.

Add a facial expression and a speech bubble to the drawing below to reflect what a states' rights believer thought about the nullification crisis.

Facial expressions and comments will vary, but should express disapproval.

Directions: After you read each section in your text, record notes as directed.

14.6 Jackson Battles the Bank of the United States

Write a paragraph summary that includes these terms: *Nicholas Biddle, Henry Clay, farmers, Bank of the United States.*

*The **Bank of the United States** was a controversial institution during Jackson's time. Jackson believed that the Bank served only the rich. The Bank's director, **Nicholas Biddle,** represented everything that Jackson hated. He was not only rich, but well-born. The government had large deposits in the Bank. **Henry Clay,** one of Jackson's chief political opponents, tried to use the Bank controversy to defeat Jackson in 1832. With the support of poor **farmers**, Jackson defeated Clay and killed the Bank.*

Add facial expressions and speech bubbles to the drawing below to reflect how the common people and the rich and well-born felt and thought about Jackson's battle with the Bank of the United States.

Facial expressions and comments will vary. The face on the right should express approval. The face on the left should express disapproval.

Directions: After you read each section in your text, record notes as directed.

14.7 Jackson's Indian Policy

Write a paragraph summary of this section that includes these terms: *Cherokees, Black Hawk, Trail of Tears*.

*Jackson believed that the Indians should move west to make room for white settlers. He urged Congress to pass the Indian Removal Act of 1830. Even Native Americans such as the **Cherokees**, who adopted white ways, passed a constitution, and learned to read and write were forced to move west. Some groups, like those led by **Black Hawk** in Illinois, resisted with arms. Their resistance did not work. They were forced to march in the **Trail of Tears** to Indian territory. Many died. Only the Florida Seminoles had any luck resisting removal.*

Add facial expressions and speech bubbles to the drawing below to reflect how Native Americans and the common man felt and thought about Jackson's Indian policy.

Facial expressions and comments will vary. The face on the right should express approval. The face on the left should express disapproval.

Directions: Examine the transparency your teacher projects, and answer the Image Analysis Questions. Share your answers with the class. Then listen to the corresponding song, and answer the Song Analysis Questions. Finally, compare the images and songs. Be prepared to share your answers with the class.

The Federal Period: 1790s

Image Analysis Questions

Based on this painting of President George Washington at a banquet, what were some characteristics of the people who ran the government during the Federal Period? What three words best describe them?

Song Analysis Questions

Listen to the song "The President's March." How does this song make you feel? What are three words that might be used to describe the song? What does the song tell you about our first president?

Sample 3

Directions: Examine the transparency your teacher projects, and answer the Image Analysis Questions. Share your answers with the class. Then listen to the corresponding song, and answer the Song Analysis Questions. Finally, compare the images and songs. Be prepared to share your answers with the class.

The Jacksonian Era: 1820s to 1840s

Image Analysis Questions

Based on this painting of Andrew Jackson meeting the public, what were some characteristics of the people who ran the government during the Jacksonian Era? What three words best describe Jackson and his supporters?

Song Analysis Questions

Listen to the song "The Hunters of Kentucky." The song was written for Andrew Jackson's 1828 presidential campaign. How does the song make you feel? What are three words that might be used to describe the song? What does the song tell you about our sixth president?

Contrasting Images and Songs

Based on the images and songs you have analyzed, how do you think the Jacksonian Era was different from the Federal Period? What do you think accounts for the differences?

© Teachers' Curriculum Institute

Directions: After you read each section in your text, record notes as directed.

14.2 The Inauguration of Andrew Jackson

Write a paragraph summary of this section that includes these terms: *democracy, common man, vote, rich and well-born.*

Add facial expressions and speech bubbles to the drawing below to reflect what the common man and the rich and well-born felt and thought about Jackson's rise from the frontier to the White House.

Sample 3

Directions: After you read each section in your text, record notes as directed.

14.3 From the Frontier to the White House

Write a paragraph summary of this section that includes these terms: *Battle of New Orleans, Democratic Party, corrupt bargain, self-made man.*

Add facial expressions and speech bubbles to the drawing below to reflect what the common man and the rich and well-born felt and thought about Jackson's rise from the frontier to the White House.

Directions: After you read each section in your text, record notes as directed.

14.4 Jackson's Approach to Governing

Write a paragraph summary of this section that includes these terms: *kitchen cabinet, spoils system, civil servant*.

Add facial expressions and speech bubbles to the drawing below to reflect how the common man and the rich and well-born felt and thought about Jackson's approach to governing.

Directions: After you read each section in your text, record notes as directed.

14.5 The Nullification Crisis

Write a paragraph summary of this section that includes these terms: *tariffs, states' rights, South Carolina, John C. Calhoun.*

Add a facial expression and a speech bubble to the drawing below to reflect what a states' rights believer thought about the nullification crisis.

Directions: After you read each section in your text, record notes as directed.

14.6 Jackson Battles the Bank of the United States

Write a paragraph summary that includes these terms: *Nicholas Biddle, Henry Clay, farmers, Bank of the United States.*

Add facial expressions and speech bubbles to the drawing below to reflect how the common people and the rich and well-born felt and thought about Jackson's battle with the Bank of the United States.

READING NOTES 14

Directions: After you read each section in your text, record notes as directed.

14.7 Jackson's Indian Policy

Write a paragraph summary of this section that includes these terms: *Cherokees, Black Hawk, Trail of Tears.*

Add facial expressions and speech bubbles to the drawing below to reflect how Native Americans and the common man felt and thought about Jackson's Indian policy.

Directions: Use the information you learned in this activity to evaluate Andrew Jackson's impact on American society. Create a hero's commemorative plaque for Jackson that emphasizes his positive contributions to American democracy, and a "Wanted" poster that shows his negative impact on American democracy. Make sure you include

- two sketches of Andrew Jackson.
- two sentences stating why Jackson should be praised (below the commemorative plaque).
- two sentences stating why Jackson should be condemned (below the "Wanted" poster).
- a one-paragraph answer to the following question: In your opinion, was Andrew Jackson more of a villain or a hero?

Andrew Jackson
A National Hero

WANTED
Andrew Jackson

Sample 3

What do you think these voters are talking about?

What type of candidate might these voters vote for?

What type of candidate might these voters vote for?

14

Andrew Jackson and the Growth of American Democracy

14.1 Introduction

The presidential campaign of 1828 was one of the dirtiest in American history. The election pitted John Quincy Adams, the nation's sixth president, against Andrew Jackson, the popular hero of the Battle of New Orleans.

During the campaign, both sides hurled reckless accusations at each other, a practice called *mudslinging*. Adams was called a "Sabbath-breaker" for traveling on Sunday. He was falsely accused of being an alcoholic. He was accused of using "public money" to purchase "gambling furniture" for the White House. In reality, he had used his own money to purchase a billiard table. Strangely, his opponents missed the one truth that might have shocked most Americans of the day. The very formal and proper Adams had a habit of swimming naked in the Potomac River.

The president's supporters lashed back. They called Jackson a crude and ignorant man who was not fit to be president. They also raked up old scandals about his wife, Rachel. She was accused of marrying Jackson while she was still knowingly wed to her first husband (not true). One newspaper even charged Jackson's mother with immoral behavior (not true). Jackson was called "Old Hickory" by his troops because he was as tough as "the hardest wood in creation." But when he read these lies, he broke down and cried.

When the votes were counted, Jackson was clearly the people's choice. But he was not the choice of the rich and **well-born** people who were used to running the country—the planters, merchants, bankers, and lawyers. "Nobody knows what he will do," wrote Senator Daniel Webster gloomily. "My fear is stronger than my hope."

Jackson proved to be a controversial president. In this chapter, you will discover how he was viewed by several groups of Americans, including not only the rich and well-born, but also the common people, Native Americans, and supporters of states' rights.

Graphic Organizer: Character Portraits
You will draw facial expressions on the figures to record various groups' reactions to Andrew Jackson's presidency.

People of every color, age, and class mobbed the White House to see Andrew Jackson take his oath of office. One observer claimed that the scene was like the invasion of barbarians into Rome.

14.2 The Inauguration of Andrew Jackson

On March 4, 1829, more than 10,000 people from every state crowded into Washington, D.C., to witness the inauguration of their hero. The visitors overwhelmed local hotels, sleeping five to a bed and drinking the city dry of whiskey. "I have never seen such a crowd here before," observed Senator Webster. "Persons have come 500 miles to see General Jackson, and they really seem to think the country has been rescued from some…disaster."

Many of the people flocking into the capital were first-time voters. Until the 1820s, the right to vote had been limited to the rich and well-born. Only white men with property, it was said, had the education and experience to vote wisely.

The new states forming west of the Appalachians challenged this argument. Along the frontier, all men—rich or poor, educated or not— shared the same opportunities and dangers. They believed they should also share the same rights, including the right to vote.

With the western states leading the way, voting laws were changed to give the "common man" the right to vote. This expansion of democracy did not yet include African Americans, Native Americans, or women. Still, over one million Americans voted in 1828, more than three times as many as voted in 1824.

Many of these new voters did believe that they had rescued the country from disaster. In their view, the national government had been taken over by corrupt "monied interests"—that is, the rich. During his campaign, Jackson had promised to throw these rascals out and return the government to "the people."

According to eyewitness Margaret Bayard Smith, Jackson's inauguration was "an imposing and majestic spectacle." Afterward, a huge crowd followed Jackson to the White House to celebrate. As the crowd surged in, the celebration turned into a near riot.

"Ladies fainted, men were seen with bloody noses, and such a scene of confusion took place as is impossible to describe," wrote Smith. Jackson was nearly "pressed to death and suffocated by the people" before escaping out a back door. "But it was the people's day, and the people's president," Smith concluded. "And the people would rule."

14.3 From the Frontier to the White House

The "people's president" was the first "**self-made** man" to occupy the White House. Jackson was born in 1767, on the South Carolina frontier. His father died before he was born, leaving Jackson, his mother, and two brothers in poverty. Young Andrew loved sports more than schoolwork. He also had a hot temper. He would pick a fight at the drop of a hat, a friend recalled, and "he'd drop the hat himself."

The American Revolution ended Jackson's childhood. When he was just 13, Jackson joined the local militia and was captured by the British. One day, a British officer ordered Jackson to polish his boots. "Sir," he replied boldly, "I am a prisoner of war and demand to be treated as such." The outraged officer lashed out with his sword, slicing the boy's head and hand. Jackson carried the scars to his grave.

The Frontier Lawyer After the war, Jackson decided to become a lawyer. He went to work in a law office in Salisbury, North Carolina. He quickly became known as "the most roaring, rollicking, game-cocking, horse-racing, card-playing, mischievous fellow" in town. The wonder is that he learned any law at all.

In 1788, Jackson headed west to Nashville, Tennessee, to practice law. At that time, Nashville was a tiny clump of rough cabins and tents beside the Cumberland River. But the town grew quickly, and Jackson's practice grew with it. He soon earned enough money to buy land and slaves and set himself up as a gentleman planter.

Despite his success, Jackson never outgrew his hot temper. A slave trader named Charles Dickinson found this out when he called Jackson

Sample 3

Andrew Jackson was born in this cabin in a small, rural South Carolina town. He received little formal education, but in his teens he studied law to become a lawyer.

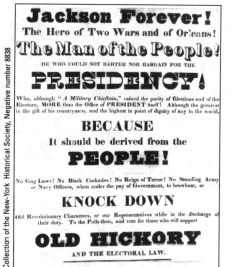

Jackson is shown here at the Battle of New Orleans, where he became a national hero after defeating the British.

"a worthless scoundrel" and insulted his wife, Rachel. Enraged, Jackson challenged Dickinson to a duel (fight) with pistols, even though the slave trader was said to be the best shot in Tennessee. At that time, duels were accepted as a way of settling disputes between gentlemen.

Dickinson shot first, hitting Jackson in the chest. Jackson stiffened, raised his pistol, and fired a single shot. Dickinson fell dead to the ground.

"My God," a friend exclaimed on spotting Jackson's wound. "He missed your heart only by an inch." In fact, Dickinson's bullet was lodged so close to Jackson's heart that doctors were not able to remove it. "I would have hit him," replied Jackson, "if he'd shot me through the brain!"

The People's Choice Jackson entered politics in Tennessee, serving in both the House and Senate. But he did not become widely known until the Battle of New Orleans during the War of 1812. His glorious defense of the city made "Old Hickory" a national hero.

In 1824, the hero of New Orleans ran for president against three other candidates—Henry Clay, William Crawford, and John Quincy Adams. Jackson won the most popular votes, and the most electoral votes as well. But he did not have enough electoral votes for a majority. When no candidate has an electoral majority, the House of Representatives chooses a president from the three leading candidates.

Clay, who had come in fourth, urged his supporters in the House to back Adams. That support gave Adams enough votes to become president. Adams then chose Clay to be his secretary of state.

Bringing Clay into Adams' cabinet made sense, because the two men shared many of the same goals. Jackson's supporters, however, accused Adams and Clay of making a "corrupt bargain" to rob their hero of his rightful election. And they promised revenge in 1828.

Jackson's supporters used the time between elections to build a new political organization that came to be called the Democratic Party, the name it still wears today. This new party, they promised, would represent ordinary farmers, workers, and the poor, not the rich and well-born who had taken control of the Republican Party.

Jackson's supporters worked feverishly to reach the nation's new voters. Besides hurling insults at Adams, they organized huge parades, picnics, and rallies. At these events, supporters sang "The Hunters of Kentucky"—the nation's first campaign song—and cheered for Old Hickory. They wore Jackson badges, carried hickory sticks, and chanted catchy campaign slogans like "Adams can write, but Jackson can fight."

The result was a great victory for Jackson. But it was also a victory for the idea that the common people should control their government. This idea became known as Jacksonian Democracy.

This campaign poster shows the theme of Jackson's presidential campaign. His supporters claimed that if Jackson were elected, government would finally be in the hands of ordinary people, not just the rich and well-born.

14.4 Jackson's Approach to Governing

Jackson approached governing much as he had approached leading an army. He listened to others, but then he did exactly what he thought was right.

The Kitchen Cabinet Unlike earlier presidents, Jackson did not rely on his cabinet for advice. He made most of his decisions with the help of trusted friends and political supporters. These advisors were said to meet with him in the White House kitchen. For this reason, they were known as the "kitchen cabinet."

The rich and well-born looked at the "kitchen cabinet" with deep suspicion. In their eyes, the men around the president were not the proper sort to be running the country. One congressman accused Amos Kendall, Jackson's closest advisor, of being "the President's…lying machine!" Jackson ignored such charges and continued to turn for advice to men he trusted.

The Spoils System Jackson's critics were even more upset by his decision to replace many Republican officeholders with loyal Democrats. Most of these **civil servants** viewed their posts as lifetime jobs. Jackson disagreed. Rotating people in office was more democratic than lifetime service, he said, because it gave more people a chance to serve their government. After a few years in office, civil servants should "go back to making a living as other people do."

Jackson's opponents called the practice of rewarding political supporters with jobs the **spoils system**. This term came from the saying that "to the victor belong the spoils [prizes] of war." They also exaggerated the number of Republicans removed from office. Only about 10 percent of all civil servants were replaced, and many who were dismissed from their jobs deserved to be. One was an official who had stolen $10,000 from the Treasury. When he begged Jackson to let him stay in office, the president replied, "Sir, I would turn out my own father under the same circumstances."

But Jackson could put patriotism above party loyalty. One dismissed postmaster started to undress to show the president his wounds from the Revolutionary War. Jackson snapped, "Put your coat on at once, sir!" The next day, the postmaster got his job back.

civil servants: employees of the government

spoils system: the practice of rewarding political supporters with government jobs

In this cartoon, titled "Office Hunters for the Year 1834," Andrew Jackson is a puppet master. He is pulling strings attached to people who want to be appointed to public offices. What is the cartoonist's opinion of Jackson?

14.5 The Nullification Crisis

Jackson's approach to governing was tested by an issue that threatened to break up the United States. In 1828, Congress passed a law raising **tariffs,** or taxes, on imported goods such as cloth and glass. The idea was to encourage the growth of manufacturing. Higher tariffs meant higher prices for imported factory goods. American manufacturers could then outsell their foreign competitors.

Northern states, humming with new factories, favored the new tariff law. But southerners called it the Tariff of Abominations (horrors).

Southerners opposed tariffs for several reasons. Tariffs raised the prices they paid for factory goods. High tariffs also discouraged trade among nations. Since much of the South's cotton was exported to other countries, planters worried that tariffs would hurt cotton sales.

In this cartoon, John C. Calhoun is the figure at the top of the staircase. Calhoun, who believed that states have the right to nullify, or reject, federal laws, is reaching toward a crown. The crown is a symbol of his desire for power. Andrew Jackson is pulling on the coattails of a Calhoun supporter. He wants to prevent Calhoun from trampling on the Constitution and destroying the Union.

Many southerners also believed that a law passed to favor one group—in this case, northern manufacturers—was unconstitutional. Based on this belief, John C. Calhoun, Jackson's vice president, called on southern states to declare the tariff "null and void," or illegal and not to be honored.

Jackson understood southerners' concerns. In 1832, he signed a new law that lowered tariffs—but not enough to satisfy the most extreme supporters of states' rights in South Carolina. Led by Calhoun, they boldly proclaimed South Carolina's right to nullify, or reject, both the 1828 and 1832 tariff laws. Such an action was called *nullification*. South Carolinians even threatened to **secede**—withdraw their state from the United States—if the national government tried to enforce the tariff laws.

Jackson was outraged. "If one drop of blood be shed there in defiance of the laws of the United States," he raged, "I will hang the first man of them I can get my hands on from the first tree I can find." He called on Congress to pass the Force Bill, which allowed him to use the federal army to collect tariffs if needed. At the same time, Congress passed a compromise bill that lowered tariffs still further.

Faced with such firm opposition, South Carolina backed down and the nullification crisis ended. However, the tensions between the North and the South would increase in the years ahead.

14.6 Jackson Battles the Bank of the United States

Jackson saw himself as the defender of the people, and never more so than in his battle with the Bank of the United States. The Bank was a private business that had been chartered by Congress for 20 years in 1816. The federal government owned one fifth of the Bank and deposited its money there.

Jackson distrusted the Bank and its president, Nicholas Biddle. Biddle was everything that Jackson was not—a wealthy, well-born, highly educated, widely traveled, well-mannered lawyer, politician, and banker. Still, Jackson might have waited to slay "the monster," as he called it, until the Bank's charter came up for renewal in 1836. But Henry Clay forced the issue.

Clay, who planned to run for president against Jackson in 1832, pushed a bill through Congress that renewed the Bank's charter four years early. Clay figured that if Jackson signed the bill, he would lose votes from farmers who shared his dislike of banks. But if Jackson vetoed the bill, he would lose votes from business-people who depended on the Bank for loans. What Clay forgot was that there were many more poor farmers to cast votes than there were bankers, merchants, and manufacturers.

The president vetoed the recharter bill. In his veto message, he called the Bank an unconstitutional monopoly and said that it existed mainly to make the rich richer. The voters seemed to agree. Jackson was reelected by a large majority.

Rather than let the Bank die when its charter ran out, Jackson decided to hasten its end by starving it to death. In 1833, he ordered the secretary of the treasury to remove all federal deposits from the Bank. These funds were then deposited in state banks. Jackson's enemies called these banks "pet banks" because they were run by the president's supporters.

Delegations of businessmen came to Washington to beg Jackson not to kill the Bank. Jackson responded bluntly, "It is folly to talk to me thus." He would rather suffer tortures, he said, than see "the monster" rechartered. Slaying the Bank, Jackson believed, was a victory for democracy—and for the common people—who were its greatest strength.

Andrew Jackson, on the left, is attacking the many-headed Bank of the United States with a veto stick. Nicholas Biddle is in the center wearing a top hat. The many heads represent the 24 state directors of the Bank. Vice President Van Buren is choking Massachusetts and Delaware.

14.7 Jackson's Indian Policy

By the time Jackson became president, only 125,000 Native Americans still lived east of the Mississippi River. Warfare and disease had greatly reduced the number of Indians in the East. Others had sold their lands and moved across the Mississippi. One of Jackson's goals was to remove the remaining Indians to a new Indian Territory in the West.

Most of the eastern Indians lived in the South. They belonged to five groups, called *tribes* by whites: the Creek, Cherokee, Chickasaw, Choctaw, and Seminole. Hoping to remain in their homelands, these Indians had adopted many white ways. Most had given up hunting to become farmers. Many had learned to read and write. The Cherokee even had their own written language, a newspaper, and a constitution modeled on the U.S. Constitution. Whites called these Indians the "Five Civilized Tribes." While the Five Civilized Tribes may have hoped to live in peace with their neighbors, whites did not share this goal. As the cotton kingdom spread westward, wealthy planters and poor settlers alike looked greedily at Indian homelands. The Indians, they decided, had to go.

Sequoyah, pictured above, was a Cherokee Indian who developed an 86-letter alphabet for the Cherokee language. The alphabet contained both Roman letters and symbols that Sequoyah created. In spite of the fact that these Native Americans developed what many whites considered an advanced civilization, wealthy planters and poor settlers were still determined to force them out and seize their lands.

The Indian Removal Act In 1830, urged on by President Jackson, Congress passed the Indian Removal Act. This law allowed the president to make treaties in which Native Americans in the East traded their lands for new territory on the Great Plains. The president wrote this letter to the Creeks, hoping to persuade them to move willingly:

Friends and brothers, listen. Where you now are, you and my white children are too near to each other to live in harmony and peace.... Beyond the great river Mississippi...your father has provided a country large enough for all of you, and he advises you to remove to it. There your white brothers will not trouble you...and you can live upon it as long as the grass grows or the water runs, in peace and plenty. The land beyond the Mississippi belongs to the President and no one else, and he will give it to you forever.

Some groups agreed to move west voluntarily. Others resisted, usually with tragic results. This was true of the Sac and Fox of Illinois. Led by a chief named Black Hawk, the Sac and Fox fought removal for two years. Black Hawk's War ended in 1832 with the slaughter of most of his warriors. As he was taken off in chains, the chief told his captors:

"Black Hawk is an Indian. He has done nothing for which an Indian ought to be ashamed. He has fought for his countrymen, the squaws [women] and papooses [young children], against white men

who came, year after year, to cheat them of and take away their land.
You know the cause of our making war. It is known to all white men.
They ought to be ashamed of it."

The Trail of Tears Many whites were ashamed. Washington was flooded with protests over the treatment of Indians. Still the work of removal continued. Thousands of Creeks who refused to leave Alabama were rounded up and marched west in handcuffs. "To see the remnant of a once mighty people fettered and chained together and forced to depart from the land of their fathers," wrote an Alabama journalist, "is of itself enough to move the stoutest heart."

More than 17,000 Cherokee were dragged from their homes in Georgia and herded west by federal troops. Four thousand died during their long walk to Indian Territory. Those who survived remembered that terrible journey as their "Trail of Tears." A soldier who took part in the Cherokee removal called it "the cruelest work I ever knew."

Led by a young chief named Osceola, the Seminoles of Florida resisted removal for ten years. Their long struggle was the most costly Indian war ever fought in the United States. A number of Seminoles were finally sent to Indian Territory. But others found refuge (safety) in the Florida swamps. Their descendants still live in the state today.

When Jackson left office, he was proud of having "solved" the Indian problem for good. "I feel conscious of having done my duty to my red children," he said. But as you will learn in the next two chapters, Jackson had simply moved the conflict between Indians and whites across the mighty Mississippi.

This artist painted an unrealistic picture of the Trail of Tears. Most of the Cherokees had no horses or warm blankets. They were dragged from their homes and allowed to take only the clothes they had on. Many died as they walked barefoot for hundreds of miles.

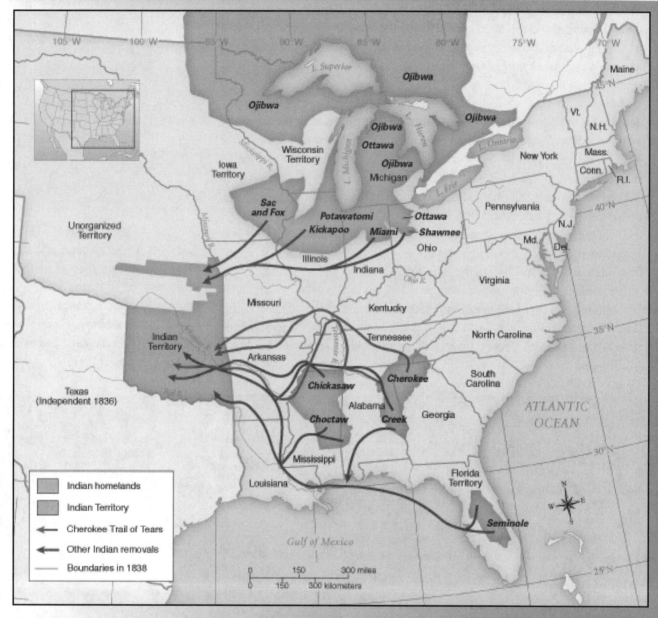

1. From which states were Indians removed?

2. To what future state were they moved?

3. How does the size of Indian Territory compare to the size of their homelands?

4. How far were Indians forced to travel to reach Indian Territory?

5. Which Native American tribe was involved in the Trail of Tears?

6. How many other tribes were forced into Indian Territory?

7. In what direction were Indians pushed? Why were they pushed in this direction?

14.8 Chapter Summary

In this chapter, you read about the presidency of Andrew Jackson. You used character portraits to evaluate Jackson's presidency from the perspective of different groups.

First-time voters, many of them farmers and frontiersmen, flocked to the polls to help elect Andrew Jackson in 1828. Jackson's supporters celebrated his election as a victory for the "common man" over the rich, well-born, and powerful. Jackson, after all, was a self-made man who rose from poverty to become president of the United States.

As president, Jackson fought a number of battles for "the people"—and rewarded his friends and supporters at the same time. For advice, he relied on his "kitchen cabinet," rather than the official cabinet. He replaced a number of Republican civil servants with Democrats. And he waged war on the powerful Bank of the United States.

A controversy over higher tariffs led to the nullification crisis, in which South Carolinians threatened to separate from the United States. Although Jackson forced them to back down, the crisis was an early sign of developing tensions between northern and southern states.

Jackson's Indian policy was simple: move the eastern Indians across the Mississippi to make room for whites. The Indian Removal Act caused great suffering for thousands of Native Americans. Furthermore, Jackson had only moved the conflict between whites and Indians to the West, not solved it. For, as you will read in the next chapter, the West was just where many white Americans were looking for new opportunities and the chance to expand their way of life across the continent.

Andrew Jackson was America's first frontier president. He came to office with great popular support. His supporters viewed him as a president of the people. His enemies saw him as a president hoping to become a king.

An Era of Reform

Overview

In this lesson, students learn about reform movements of the mid–nineteenth century and the role of women in those movements. Students read in *History Alive! The United States* and take notes about various reform movements of the period, including prison reform, educational reform, anti-slavery efforts, and the women's rights movement. Then, in a **Response Group** activity, students debate the degree to which four of the grievances outlined in

the Declaration of Sentiments have been redressed. Finally, students apply their knowledge in a Processing assignment.

Objectives

Students will be able to

- identify important reform movements of the mid–nineteenth century.
- describe the role of women in those movements.
- identify the purpose of the Seneca Falls Convention and key grievances outlined in the Declaration of Sentiments.
- use facts and personal experiences to debate the degree to which four such grievances have been redressed today.

Materials

- Graphic Organizer Placard 18
- CD Track 8, "Let Us All Speak Our Minds"
- Transparency 18
- Student Handout 18 (1 per student)
- Student Information 18 (copied onto a transparency)

Preview

Play CD Track 8, "Let Us All Speak Our Minds," and have students follow along with the lyrics on page 122 of their Interactive Student Notebooks. Afterward, have them complete the Preview assignment on page 123. Ask several students to share their answers with the class.

Graphic Organizer

1 Have students read Section 18.1 in History Alive! The United States. Remind students that important terms appear in colored type (teal). Each term is defined in the Glossary. After students have completed the reading, ask the following questions: *Who was Sojourner Truth? How did she answer those who said women were weaker? What are some of the other reform movements that began during this period?*

2 Have students look at the graphic organizer on page 245 of History Alive! The United States. Ask the following questions: *What do you see? Why are they carrying signs? Why do you think they are protesting?* Tell students that they will use this graphic organizer to help them learn about reform movements of the mid–nineteenth century.

Reading

1 Have students read Sections 18.2 through 18.7 and complete the Reading Notes on pages 124 and 125 of their Interactive Student Notebooks. Tell students that they will now read information about the key figures and events of the reform movements of the mid–nineteenth century. Review the directions for Reading Notes 18. Be sure students understand the word *grievance* (a complaint against an unfair condition). After students have completed the Reading Notes, use Guide to Reading Notes 18 to discuss the information with the class.

2 Project Transparency 18: Mary S. Anthony's Scrapbook. Explain that this image is a page from a scrapbook kept by Mary S. Anthony, Susan B. Anthony's sister. Mary Anthony wanted to record the achievements women made during the nineteenth century. Ask students to identify women from their reading and summarize their achievements. Students should recognize the achievements of Lucretia Mott, Elizabeth Cady Stanton, Lucy Stone, Susan B. Anthony, and Dorothea Dix. Other important women who appear on this page of the album are Julia Ward Howe, who wrote "The Battle Hymn of the Republic"; Martha C. Wright and Jean Brooks Greenleaf, presidents of the New York State Suffrage Association; Anna Shaw, first woman minister of the Methodist Protestant Church; and Elizabeth Boyton Harbert, who was involved in both the temperance and suffrage movements.

Response Group

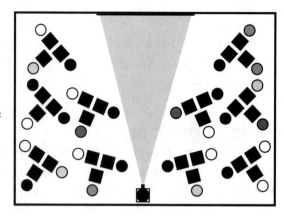

1 Place students in mixed-ability groups of three or four. You may want to prepare a transparency before class that shows students with whom they will work and where they will sit. They should arrange their desks so that group members can talk among themselves and clearly see the overhead projector screen. (**Note:** Because this activity centers on gender issues, try to create gender-balanced groups.)

2 Introduce the activity. Have students turn to *Activity Notes 18: Critical-Thinking Prompts for Women's Issues,* on pages 126–129 in their Interactive Student Notebooks. Tell students they will examine and discuss four excerpts from the Declaration of Sentiments. Review the three steps groups will follow for each excerpt. Make sure students understand the term *redress* (correction of an unfair condition). Pass out *Student Handout 18: Fact Sheet on Women in the United States Today.* Tell students they will use these facts, as well as their own experiences, to help answer the critical-thinking prompts on the Activity Notes.

3 Have students complete the Activity Notes for Excerpt A. Stop students after Step 1, and have several groups share their rewritten excerpts. Make sure students understand the directions for Step 2, and remind them that they must have facts from the handout—or information from their own experiences—to defend their entries on the spectrum.

4 Appoint a presenter for each group. Explain that the role of presenter will rotate with each excerpt so that everyone in the group will be the presenter at least once.

5 Assign each group a number, and have students share their decisions on a transparency of Student Information 18: Class Spectrum. Place the transparency on the overhead projector, but do not turn the projector on. Have someone from each group come up and write their group number on the transparency on the appropriate place along the spectrum. Then turn on the projector, and reveal to the class the different opinions of the various groups as shown on the spectrum.

6 Call on presenters to explain their spectrum placement to the class. Require presenters to use this phrase when they begin: "*(Name of previous presenter), our group disagrees/agrees with your group's placement because….*" Encourage lively debate by calling on presenters whose answers differ from those previously expressed. End discussion when all new ideas have been voiced.

7 Repeat Steps 3–7 for Excerpts B–D. Remember to select a new presenter for each set of critical-thinking prompts.

8 Debrief the activity. Ask students to respond to the following questions:

- In what areas have women made the most progress since the Seneca Falls Convention? Why have they made so much progress in these areas?
- In what areas have women made the least progress since the Seneca Falls Convention? Why have they made so little progress in these areas?
- What actions are women and men taking today to continue to redress the grievances in the Declaration of Sentiments?

Processing

Have students complete the Processing assignment on page 130 of their Interactive Student Notebooks.

Internet Connections

For more information on leaders of the women's rights movement and the current status of women, refer students to Internet Resources for Lesson 18 at www.historyalive.com/connections.html.

Assessment

A blackline master for the assessment follows on pages 146–149.

1. A	3. C	5. B	7. D	9. D	11. B	13. A	15. C	17. A
2. D	4. A	6. C	8. B	10. D	12. B	14. B	16. B	18. D

19. The bulleted points can provide a rubric for this item.

Choose the letter of the best answer for each question.

1. Americans who became abolitionists wanted to end
   A. slavery.
   B. discrimination against women.
   C. immigration.
   D. imprisonment for debt.

2. Angelina and Sarah Grimke led the way for other women to
   A. gain admission to colleges.
   B. work for the same pay as men.
   C. vote and hold public office.
   D. speak out in public on issues.

3. What motto did Frederick Douglass choose for his abolitionist newspaper, the *North Star*?
   A. "Be ashamed to die until you have won some victory."
   B. "I will be harsh as truth."
   C. "Right is of no sex—Truth is of no color."
   D. "All men and women are created equal."

4. Radicals in the abolition movement
   A. hoped to inspire slave revolts to end slavery.
   B. favored the gradual ending of slavery.
   C. sought a quick but peaceful end to slavery.
   D. did not care about slavery in the South.

5. Before the reform movement led by Horace Mann,
   A. few women had the right to vote.
   B. most children did not attend school.
   C. debtors were often thrown in jail.
   D. sinners did not expect to be forgiven.

6. Which group benefited **MOST** from early efforts to establish public schools?
   A. African American boys
   B. African American girls
   C. European American boys
   D. European American girls

7. The Second Great Awakening was a
   A. period of new scientific thinking.
   B. disease that caused sleeplessness.
   C. campaign for public education.
   D. religious revival movement.

8. The Seneca Falls Declaration of Sentiments was modeled on the
   A. Monroe Doctrine.
   B. Declaration of Independence.
   C. Bill of Rights.
   D. Missouri Compromise.

9. One effect of the Second Great Awakening was to
   A. increase prejudice against sinners.
   B. encourage people to move west.
   C. bring out the vote for Andrew Jackson.
   D. inspire reformers to improve society.

Use the chronology and your knowledge of social studies to answer the questions below.

1820s Second Great Awakening sweeps the nation

1829 Andrew Jackson is inaugurated as the "People's President"

1831 William Lloyd Garrison begins publishing the *Liberator*

1833 The American Anti-Slavery Society is established

1837 Oberlin College becomes the first college in the nation to accept women

1837 Elijah Lovejoy is killed by an anti-abolitionist mob in Illinois
Horace Mann becomes secretary of the Massachusetts Board of Education

1838 Frederick Douglass escapes from slavery

1840 Lucretia Mott and Elizabeth Cady Stanton are barred from the World Anti-Slavery Convention

1841 Dorothea Dix makes her first visit to a prison

1845 Frederick Douglass publishes his autobiography

1848 First women's rights convention is held at Seneca Falls, New York

1849 After years of being turned down by colleges, Dr. Blackwell graduates from medical school

1851 Sojourner Truth addresses women's rights meeting

Sample 4

10. What would be the best title for this chronology?
   A. The Second Great Awakening
   B. Jacksonian Democracy
   C. The Civil Rights Movement
   D. Revival and Reform

11. From the chronology, a reader might infer that
   A. the majority of abolitionists were women.
   B. the women's rights movement grew out of other reform movements.
   C. Frederick Douglass began the abolition movement.
   D. Andrew Jackson supported the abolition movement.

12. Why did Dr. Blackwell have such a difficult time getting into medical school?
   A. Blackwell was an African American.
   B. Blackwell was a woman.
   C. Blackwell was a Native American.
   D. Blackwell was an abolitionist.

13. The chronology suggests that
   A. women were not able to participate fully in the anti-slavery movement.
   B. Elijah Lovejoy helped Frederick Douglass to escape from slavery.
   C. men were barred from attending the Seneca Falls Convention.
   D. Oberlin was the first college to accept African Americans.

Read the passage below. Then read each question and choose the best answer based on the passage.

"Gentlemen: I come to present the strong claims of suffering humanity. I come to place before the Legislature of Massachusetts the condition of the miserable, the desolate, the outcast.... I proceed, gentlemen, briefly to call your attention to the *present* state of insane persons confined within this Commonwealth, in *cages, closets, cellars, stalls, pens! Chained, naked, beaten with rods, and lashed* into obedience. I offer the following extracts from my notebook and journal....

"*Lincoln:* A woman in a cage. *Medford:* One idiotic subject chained, and one in a close stall for seventeen years. *Pepperell:* One often doubly chained, hand and foot; another violent; several peaceable now. *Brookfield:* One man caged, comfortable. *Granville:* One often closely confined, now losing the use of his limbs from want of exercise. *Charlemont:* One man caged. *Savoy:* One man caged. *Lenox:* Two in the jail, against whose unfit condition there the jailer protests."

14. This report was written by
   A. Sojourner Truth.
   B. Dorothea Dix.
   C. Lucretia Mott.
   D. Elizabeth Cady Stanton.

15. The report was presented to the
   A. Massachusetts Anti-Slavery Society.
   B. Seneca Falls Convention.
   C. Massachusetts legislature.
   D. House of Representatives.

16. The term *desolate* has several meanings. As used in this report, the word *desolate* means
   A. barren and lifeless.
   B. neglected and alone.
   C. without warmth.
   D. empty of people.

17. What claim does the author make?
   A. The mentally ill are often treated in an inhumane manner.
   B. Lawmakers should be ashamed of their treatment of the mentally ill.
   C. The mentally ill are responsible for the way they are treated.
   D. Being around mentally ill people makes others uncomfortable.

18. What evidence does the author use to support her claim?
   A. Stories told to her by people who are mentally ill.
   B. Newspaper reports on treatment of the mentally ill.
   C. Sermons on how society should treat the less fortunate.
   D. Conditions she saw and described in her journal.

Follow the directions to complete the item below.

19. Design a museum exhibit that showcases four of the important issues that you studied from the Era of Reform. Your exhibit should include the following:

   • drawings of four historical artifacts, each representing one of the important reform issues you studied

   • a plaque for each of the four artifacts that explains what the artifact is and how it is related to the reform issue it represents

   • an appropriate title for your exhibit

- Women have the right to vote in every state.

- In the 1996 elections, 53.4% of the voters were women.

- 3 of 50 U.S. governors are women.

- 9 of 100 U.S. Senators and 56 of 435 House of Representatives members are women.

- There has never been a female president or vice president; only once has a major political party nominated a woman as a candidate for the vice presidency.

- Two of the nine Supreme Court justices are women.

- In 1972, 26% of Americans said they would not vote for a woman for president. In 1996, 6% of Americans said they would not vote for a woman for president.

- In 1999, women earned approximately 79 cents for every dollar men earned.

- The average lifetime earnings for a 50-year-old woman is $496,000, while the average lifetime earnings for a 50-year-old man is $1.1 million.

- In 1999, of the 500 largest businesses in America, 11.9% of the top officers were women, up from 8.7% in 1994.

- In 1983, 15% of lawyers were women. In 1995, 26% of lawyers were women.

- In 1983, 16% of doctors were women. In 1995, 24% of doctors were women.

- In 1995, the average annual salary for male computer operators was $26,000. For female computer operators, the average annual salary was $19,084.

- In 1995, the average annual salary of female elementary school teachers was $32,292. For male elementary school teachers, the average annual salary was $33,800.

- In 1998, 69.1% of the women graduating from high school went on to college, compared with 62.4% of the men.

- In 1994, the number of women taking math and science courses equaled or surpassed the number of men taking those courses.

- In 1970, 1 in 27 girls played high school sports. In 1995, 1 in 3 girls played high school sports.

- The number of single-parent families headed by women increased from 2,619,000 in 1960 to 7,874,000 in 1997.

- In 1995, 54% of single-parent families headed by women were living below the poverty line.

380 Sample Lesson from *History Alive! The United States*

© Teachers' Curriculum Institute

Class Spectrum

Sample 4

Totally Redressed

Somewhat Redressed

Not Redressed at All

Directions: Read Sections 18.2 through 18.7. Follow these steps to take notes on each section: 1) Find the figure below whose sign's symbol best matches the information you read. 2) Create an appropriate slogan for the reform movement associated with that figure. 3) Write the slogan next to the symbol on the sign.

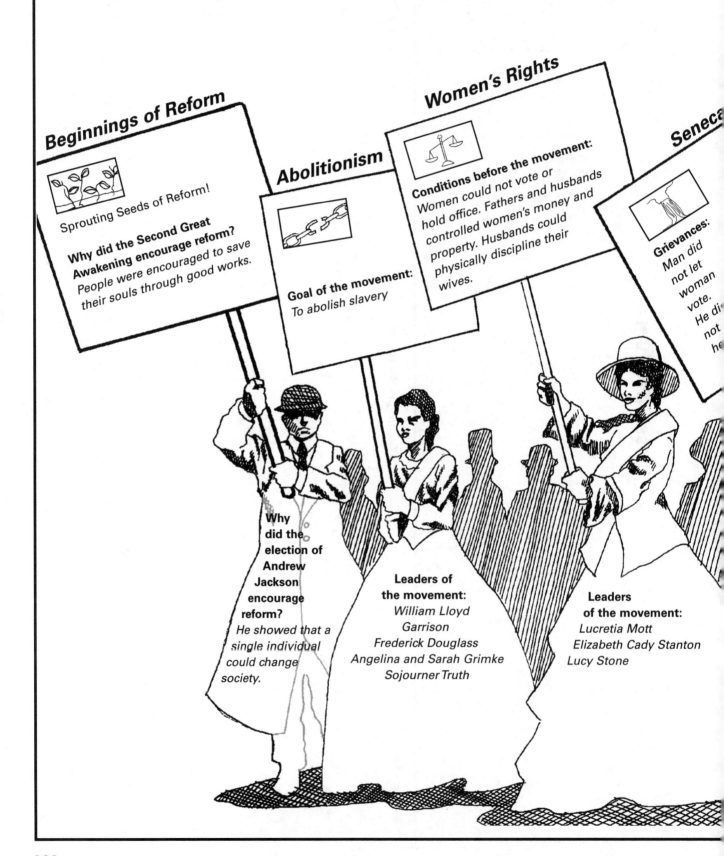

Beginnings of Reform

Sprouting Seeds of Reform!

Why did the Second Great Awakening encourage reform?
People were encouraged to save their souls through good works.

Abolitionism

Goal of the movement:
To abolish slavery

Women's Rights

Conditions before the movement:
Women could not vote or hold office. Fathers and husbands controlled women's money and property. Husbands could physically discipline their wives.

Seneca

Grievances:
Man did not let woman vote. He di not h

Why did the election of Andrew Jackson encourage reform?
He showed that a single individual could change society.

Leaders of the movement:
William Lloyd Garrison
Frederick Douglass
Angelina and Sarah Grimke
Sojourner Truth

Leaders of the movement:
Lucretia Mott
Elizabeth Cady Stanton
Lucy Stone

4) Write the name of the reform movement or event near the figure. 5) Write notes about the reform movement in the appropriate sections. (The first figure is partially completed for you.)

Education Reform

Conditions before reform:
Few areas had public schools.
Schoolrooms were overcrowded.
Teachers had limited education and received little pay.
Most children didn't go to school.

Prison Reform

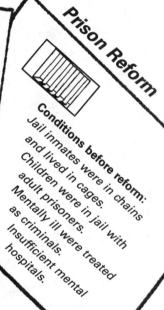

Conditions before reform:
Jail inmates were in chains and lived in cages.
Children were in jail with adult prisoners.
Mentally ill were treated as criminals.
Insufficient mental hospitals.

property rights, even to her own wages. He did not allow her to practice professions like medicine and law.

Sample 4

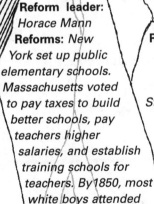

Reform leader:
Horace Mann
Reforms: *New York set up public elementary schools. Massachusetts voted to pay taxes to build better schools, pay teachers higher salaries, and establish training schools for teachers. By 1850, most white boys attended free public schools. Public universities accepted women.*

Reform leader:
Dorothea Dix
Reforms:
*New asylums.
State governments stopped placing debtors in prison.
Special justice systems for children.
Cruel punishments outlawed.*

Advances achieved:
*New York gave women control over property and wages.
Massachusetts and Indiana passed more liberal divorce laws.
Elizabeth Blackwell started her own hospital.
Women eventually were given the right to vote.*

Directions: Listen to the song "Let Us All Speak Our Minds." Follow along with the lyrics below. Afterward, answer the questions on the next page.

Analyzing "Let Us All Speak Our Minds"

Men tell us 'tis fit that wives should submit

To their husbands submissively, weakly;

Tho' whatever they say, their wives should obey

Unquestioning, stupidly, meekly.

Our husbands would make us their own dictum take

Without ever a wherefore or why for it.

But I don't and I can't and I won't and I shan't,

No, I will speak my mind if I die for it.

For we know it's all fudge to say man's the best judge

Of what should be and shouldn't, and so on.

That woman should bow, nor attempt to say how

She considers that matters should go on.

I never yet gave up myself thus a slave,

However my husband might try for it;

For I can't and I won't and I shan't and I don't,

But I will speak my mind if I die for it.

And all ladies, I hope, who've with husbands to cope,

With the rights of the sex will not trifle.

We all, if we choose, our tongues but to use,

Can all opposition soon stifle;

Let man, if he will, then bid us be still

And silent, a price he'll pay high for it.

For we won't and we can't and we don't and we shan't,

Let us all speak our minds if we die for it.

LUCRETIA MOTT.   JULIA WARD HOWE.   SUSAN B. ANTHONY.   DOROTHEA LYNDE DIX.

1. What is the mood of the song's melody? What emotions are expressed in the lyrics? Do the melody and lyrics seem to go together? Why or why not?

2. Why do you think women like those pictured above would write and sing a song like this?

3. Do you think this song's message still has meaning today? Why or why not?

Directions: Read Sections 18.2 through 18.7. Follow these steps to take notes on each section: 1) Find the figure below whose sign's symbol best matches the information you read. 2) Create an appropriate slogan for the reform movement associated with that figure. 3) Write the slogan next to the symbol on the sign.

Sprouting Seeds of Reform!

Why did the Second Great Awakening encourage reform? People were encouraged to save their souls through good works.

Goal of the movement:

Conditions before the movement:

Grievances:

Why did the election of Andrew Jackson encourage reform? *He showed that a single individual could change society.*

Leaders of the movement:

Leaders of the movement:

4) Write the name of the reform movement or event near the figure. 5) Write notes about the reform movement in the appropriate sections. (The first figure is partially completed for you.)

Conditions before reform:

Conditions before reform:

Reform leader:

Reforms:

Reform leader:

Reforms:

Advances achieved:

Sample 4

Critical-Thinking Prompts for Women's Issues

Excerpt A

"He has never permitted her to exercise her inalienable [undeniable] right to the elective franchise [vote]. He has compelled her to submit to laws, in the formation of which she had no voice."

1. Rewrite the above excerpt from the Declaration of Sentiments, using simpler language that a classmate would understand.

2. Discuss in your group the degree to which this grievance has been redressed today. Place an X on the spectrum below to represent your group's decision.

Not Redressed at All   Somewhat Redressed   Totally Redressed

3. List facts and information your group used to come to your decision.

Excerpt B

"He has monopolized [dominated] nearly all the profitable employments, and from those she is permitted to follow, she receives but a scanty remuneration [pay]."

1. Rewrite the above excerpt from the Declaration of Sentiments, using simpler language a classmate would understand.

2. Discuss in your group the degree to which this grievance has been redressed today. Place an X on the spectrum below to represent your group's decision.

Not Redressed at All   Somewhat Redressed   Totally Redressed

3. List facts and information your group used to come to your decision.

Sample 4

Critical-Thinking Prompts for Women's Issues

Excerpt C

"He has denied her the facilities for obtaining a thorough education, all colleges being closed against her."

1. Rewrite the above excerpt from the Declaration of Sentiments, using simpler language a classmate would understand.

2. Discuss in your group the degree to which this grievance has been redressed today. Place an X on the spectrum below to represent your group's decision.

|---------------------------|------------------------|--------------------------|

Not Redressed at All   Somewhat Redressed   Totally Redressed

3. List facts and information your group used to come to your decision.

ACTIVITY NOTES 18

Critical-Thinking Prompts for Women's Issues

Excerpt D

"He has created a false sense of public sentiment by giving to the world a different code of morals for men and women."

1. Rewrite the above excerpt from the Declaration of Sentiments, using simpler language a classmate would understand.

2. Discuss in your group the degree to which this grievance has been redressed today. Place an X on the spectrum below to represent your group's decision.

Not Redressed at All   Somewhat Redressed   Totally Redressed

3. List facts and information your group used to come to your decision.

Sample 4

Directions: Write a letter to Elizabeth Cady Stanton that updates her on how much progress women have made in America today. Your letter should include the following:

Letter to a Woman Reformer

- date and proper salutation (i.e., "Dear Ms. Stanton...")
- an update on the degree to which two grievances outlined in the Declaration of Sentiments have been redressed today
- at least three facts or pieces of information to support each of your updates
- a conclusion summarizing your opinion regarding where women have made the greatest progress and where work still needs to be done
- a memento from the Seneca Falls Convention, such as a program, button, or poster. Make sure the memento includes the date and location of the convention, names of the key organizers, and the main reason for the convention

LUCRETIA MOTT.

ELIZABETH CADY STANTON.

LUCY STONE.

JULIA WARD HOWE.

SUSAN B. ANTHONY.

MRS. MARTHA C. WRIGHT.
First President N. Y. State Suffrage
Association. Elected 1860.

MRS. JEAN BROOKS GREENLEAF.
Fourth President N. Y. State Suffrage
Assn. Served 6 years, 1890-96.

REV. ANNA H. SHAW.

MRS. ELIZABETH BOYNTON HAR-
BERT.

Rev. Anna H. Shaw

A. D. R.
C 1887
AC 62?4 A.D.3

DOROTHEA LYNDE DIX.

This page, from a scrapbook kept by
Mary S. Anthony, pictures women who
led various reform movements.

18

An Era of Reform

18.1 Introduction

In 1851, a group of people gathered in a church to discuss the rights of women. A tall African American woman made her way through the crowd and sat down. Her name was Sojourner Truth. Back when she was a slave, she had learned to pay careful attention to white people. Now she listened as whites discussed whether women should have the same rights as men.

Sojourner heard one minister after another explain that women didn't need more rights because they weren't smart or strong enough to do much besides raise children. Women, they argued, needed help from men. One man summed it up by saying, "Women are weak."

With that, the former slave had heard enough. She rose slowly to her stately height of six feet and walked to the pulpit. The room grew quiet as everyone waited for her to speak.

"The man over there says women need to be helped into carriages and lifted over ditches and over puddles, and have the best places everywhere," she began. "Nobody helped me into carriages or over puddles, or gives me the best place."

Her voice rose to a thunderous pitch. "And ain't I a woman? Look at my arm! I have plowed and planted and gathered into barns, and no man could head [outdo] me—and ain't I a woman? I could work as much and eat as much as a man—when I could get it—and bear the lash as well! I have borne thirteen children, and seen most of 'em sold into slavery, and when I cried out with my mother's grief, none but Jesus heard me—and ain't I a woman?"

When she finished, people applauded. Some cried. One witness said, "She had taken us up in her strong arms and carried us safely."

As a woman and a former slave, Sojourner Truth represented two of the great reform movements in America in the 1800s. Between about 1820 and 1850, American **reformers** devoted themselves to such causes as ending slavery, promoting women's rights, and improving education. As you will read in this chapter, women like Sojourner Truth not only participated in these movements, but emerged as powerful leaders.

Graphic Organizer: Illustration
You will use this illustration to learn about the Era of Reform.

18.2 Planting the Seeds of Reform

Second Great Awakening:
A revival of religious feeling and belief in the 1820s and 1830s. The First Great Awakening swept through the American colonies in the 1700s.

It was fitting that the meeting attended by Sojourner Truth took place in a church. Many of the impulses to reform American society began with new religious movements.

The Second Great Awakening One such movement was the **Second Great Awakening** of the 1820s and 1830s. Day after day, people gathered in big white tents to hear a message of hope. "Repent and you shall be saved," preachers cried. Their listeners prayed, shouted, and sang hymns. Sometimes they cried for hours or fell down in frenzies.

Like the First Great Awakening during colonial days, this religious movement fired people's emotions and inspired them to become better Christians. But it also offered something new. In the past, most Christian ministers had said that people didn't control their own fates. God had already decided who would be saved and who would suffer eternal punishment. Therefore, there was little reason to perform good deeds like helping the poor.

In the early 1800s, however, preachers told their flocks that everyone could gain forgiveness for their sins. And one way to be saved was to do good works. Christians, they said, could build "heaven on Earth."

Preachers at religious meetings, such as the one pictured below, proclaimed that people could earn salvation by doing good works. This message encouraged many people to work to improve society.

The Granger Collection, New York

This optimistic message attracted enthusiastic followers throughout the West and North. The movement inspired many women to become preachers and missionaries. And it gave men and women alike a reason to work for the improvement of society.

Optimistic Ideas Other optimistic, nonreligious ideas also inspired Americans during this time. Writers urged people to follow their own hearts to improve their lives. One of the most famous was Henry David Thoreau. "If a man does not keep pace with his companions," wrote Thoreau, "perhaps it is because he hears a different drummer. Let him step to the music he hears."

To many people, the election of Andrew Jackson as president in 1828 was proof that individuals could change society for the better. Born in a backwoods settlement, Jackson had never attended college. Yet he had achieved fame as a soldier and Indian fighter, and eventually became president. His supporters rejoiced that ordinary people could participate in democracy and even rise to positions of leadership.

18.3 Reforming the Treatment of Prisoners and the Mentally Ill

One day in 1841, a Boston woman named Dorothea Dix agreed to teach Sunday school at a jail. Dix believed that she was simply doing her Christian duty. She didn't plan on starting a reform movement. But what she witnessed that day changed her life forever.

Observing Horrors Dix was horrified by what she found. Many inmates were bound in chains and locked in cages. Children who had been accused of minor thefts were jailed with adult criminals. Were conditions this bad everywhere? she wondered.

To find out, Dix visited hundreds of jails and prisons throughout Massachusetts. She also visited debtors' prisons, or jails for people who owed money. At about this time, more than 75,000 Americans were in debtors' prisons. Most of them owed less than 20 dollars. While they were locked up, they could not earn money to repay their debts. As a result, they remained imprisoned for years.

The Plight of the Mentally Ill What shocked Dix most of all was the way mentally ill people were treated. Most people who were judged "insane" were locked away in dirty, crowded prison cells. If they misbehaved, they were whipped. Dix and other reformers believed that insanity should be treated as a disease, not a crime.

Horrified by what she saw during a visit to a local jail, Dorothea Dix worked tirelessly to improve conditions for prisoners and the mentally ill.

Before the reforms brought about by Dorothea Dix's work, many people were put in prison simply because they owed money. Most of them owed less than 20 dollars.

Massachusetts did have one hospital for the mentally ill, called an *asylum*. Sending the mentally ill there was much better than putting them in prison. They needed treatment and care, not punishment. But only the wealthy could afford to send a family member to the asylum. Even so, it was filled to overflowing. The state needed more mental hospitals.

Dix believed that such conditions existed mostly because people didn't know about them. For two years, she quietly gathered firsthand information about the horrors she had seen. Then she prepared a detailed report for the Massachusetts state legislature. "I come as the advocate of helpless, forgotten, insane, and idiotic men and women," she said. "I proceed, gentlemen, to briefly call your attention to the present state of insane persons, confined…in cages, closets, cellars, stalls, pens! Chained, naked, beaten with rods, and lashed into obedience."

Establishing Better Conditions

Shocked by Dix's report, the lawmakers ordered thousands of copies to be printed and distributed. They also voted to create public asylums for the mentally ill.

Inspired by her success in Massachusetts, Dix visited prisons in other states as well. After she prepared reports demanding justice for the mentally ill, those states also created special mental hospitals.

Dix continued working on behalf of prisoners and the mentally ill for the rest of her life. By the time she died in 1887, state governments no longer put debtors in prison. Most had created special justice systems for children in trouble. And many had outlawed cruel punishments, such as branding people with hot irons.

Dix demonstrated that reformers, including women, could lead society to make significant changes. But to do so they needed courage, dedication, and a willingness to speak out in public against injustices.

18.4 Improving Education

Asecond reform movement that won support in the 1800s was the effort to make education available to more children. The man who led this movement was Horace Mann, "the father of American public schools."

The Need for Public Schools As a boy in Massachusetts in the early 1800s, Horace Mann attended school only ten weeks a year. The rest of the time, he had to work on the family farm.

Mann was lucky to have even this limited chance to attend school. In Massachusetts, Puritans had established town schools. Few other areas had **public schools**—schools paid for by taxes. Wealthy parents sent their children to private school or hired tutors at home. On the frontier, 60 children might attend a part-time, one-room school. Their teachers had limited education and received little pay. Most children simply did not go to school at all.

In the cities, some poor children stole, destroyed property, and set fires. Reformers believed that education would help these children escape poverty and become good citizens. Influenced by its big cities, New York set up public elementary schools in every town as early as the 1820s.

Meanwhile, in Massachusetts, Horace Mann became the state's supervisor of education. In towns and villages, he spoke out on the need for public schools. "Our means of education," he stated, "are the grand machinery by which the 'raw material' of human nature can be worked up into inventors and discoverers, into skilled artisans and scientific farmers."

Citizens in Massachusetts responded to Mann's message. They voted to pay taxes to build better schools, to pay teachers higher salaries, and to establish special training schools for teachers.

An Unfinished Reform By 1850, many states in the North and West used Mann's ideas. Soon most white children, especially boys, attended free public schools.

But America still did not offer education to everyone. Most high schools and colleges did not admit girls. States as far north as Illinois passed laws to keep African Americans out of public schools.

Prior to the reforms in public education led by Horace Mann, most children did not attend school. Those that did usually had to suffer overcrowded classrooms, like the one shown below, and poorly trained teachers.

The Granger Collection, New York

Sample 4

abolitionists: people who favored abolition, the ending of slavery

When towns did allow African Americans to attend school, most made them go to separate schools that received less money. In the South, few girls and no African Americans could attend public schools.

Education for girls and women did make some progress. In 1837, Ohio's Oberlin College became the first college to admit women as well as men. When states started the first public universities in the 1860s, most accepted female students.

African Americans, however, had few options. When Prudence Crandall admitted an African American girl to her girls' school in Connecticut, white parents took their children out of the school. Crandall responded by having all African American students. Enraged, white people threw stones at the school and had Crandall jailed. After two years, she was forced to close her school.

Horace Mann realized that much more needed to be done to increase educational opportunity for women and African Americans. He became the first president of a new college for men and women, Antioch College in Ohio. There, he urged his students to become involved in improving society. "Be ashamed to die," he told them, "until you have won some victory for humanity."

Sojourner Truth, a former slave, gave speeches throughout the North against slavery and, later, in favor of women's rights.

18.5 Fighting Slavery

In 1835, a poster appeared on walls throughout Washington, D.C. The poster showed two drawings. One drawing, labeled "The Land of the Free," showed the founding fathers reading the Declaration of Independence. The other, labeled "The Home of the Oppressed," showed slaves trudging past the Capitol building, the home of Congress. The poster posed a challenging question: How could America, the "land of the free," still allow slavery? By the 1830s, growing numbers of people were asking this question. They were called **abolitionists**.

The Struggle Begins Some Americans had opposed slavery even in Revolutionary War times. Quakers stopped owning slaves in 1776. By 1792, every state as far south as Virginia had anti-slavery societies.

Once the slave trade ended in 1808, northern shipping communities had no more interest in slaves. Still, northern factory owners liked the cheap cotton that the South provided. Although slavery ended in the North by the early 1800s, many northerners still accepted southern slavery.

Unlike their neighbors, abolitionists wanted to end slavery. But they did not always agree about how to do it. Radicals tried to inspire slaves to rise up in revolt. Others wanted to find a peaceful way to end slavery immediately. Moderates wanted to give slaveholders time to develop farming methods that didn't rely on slave labor.

From the early days, both blacks and whites worked in the abolition movement, sometimes together, sometimes separately. Black activists often maintained their independence. One African American journalist wrote, "As long as we let them think and act for us...they will outwardly treat us as men, while in their hearts they still hold us as slaves."

In 1831, a deeply religious white man, William Lloyd Garrison, started a fiery abolitionist newspaper, the *Liberator*. Braving the disapproval of many northerners, Garrison demanded the immediate freeing of all slaves. "I will be as harsh as truth," he wrote. "I will not retreat a single inch—and I will be heard." Angry pro-slavery groups destroyed Garrison's printing press and burned his house.

Frederick Douglass Speaks Out One day, Garrison heard an escaped slave, Frederick Douglass, speaking to a meeting of abolitionists. Over six feet tall, Douglass spoke with a voice like thunder. When he described the cruel treatment of slave children, people cried. When he made fun of ministers who told slaves to love slavery, people laughed. When he finished, Garrison jumped up and cried, "Shall such a man be held a slave in a Christian land?" The crowd called out, "No! No! No!"

Frederick Douglass quickly became a leader in the abolitionist movement. His autobiography (the story of his life) became an instant bestseller. A brilliant, independent thinker, Douglass eventually started his own newspaper, *North Star*. Its motto read, "Right is of no sex—Truth is of no color—God is the father of us all, and we are all Brethren."

Women Get Involved Many women were inspired by the religious reform movement to become involved in the fight against slavery. Like other abolitionists, they sometimes faced violence. When a young woman named Angelina Grimke spoke against slavery, an anti-abolition mob threw stones. When she kept speaking, they burned the building.

Angelina and her sister Sarah had been raised in a South Carolina slaveholding family. After traveling North and becoming Quakers, they saw slavery in a new way. The two sisters began speaking out about the poverty and pain of slavery. At first they spoke only to other women, but soon they were speaking to large groups of men and women throughout the North. The Grimkes led the way for other women to speak in public.

Some abolitionists, like Sojourner Truth, were former slaves. Truth had always been strongly spiritual and had preached throughout the North at religious meetings and on street corners. But when she met Douglass and Garrison, their enthusiasm inspired her to speak out about slavery. An outstanding speaker, Truth argued that God would end slavery peacefully.

Abolitionists were a minority, even in the North. But their efforts, and the violence directed against them, helped change northerners' attitudes toward slavery. In addition, the anti-slavery fight helped pave the way for the next great reform movement, the struggle for women's rights.

Wilson Chinn, a branded slave from Louisiana, poses with the irons used to chain him.

In this painting, women are represented in traditional ways—shy, in the background, or serving men. During the Era of Reform, many women began to work to change and expand the way women were viewed.

18.6 Equal Rights for Women

Women abolitionists were in a strange position. They were trying to convince lawmakers to make slavery illegal, yet they themselves could not vote or hold office. They worked to raise money for the movement, yet their own money and property were controlled by their fathers and husbands. They spoke out against slave beatings, yet their husbands could discipline them whenever they wanted.

Even wealthy women like the Grimke sisters started to see that women and slaves had much in common. "What then can woman do for the slave," asked Angelina, "when she herself is under the feet of man and shamed into silence?"

The Struggle Begins The organized movement for women's rights was sparked by the friendship between Lucretia Mott and Elizabeth Cady Stanton. The two women met in 1840 at the World Anti-Slavery Convention in London. When they arrived, they were outraged to discover that women were not allowed to speak at the meeting. The men who ran the convention even made women sit in the balcony, behind a curtain!

The men's decision may have backfired, because it was in the balcony that Mott and Stanton met. At first glance, the two women seemed quite different. Mott was 47 years old, the mother of four children, and an active reformer. Inspired by the Grimke sisters and her own Quaker faith, she had preached against slavery in both white and black churches. She had also helped Prudence Crandall try to recruit students for a school for black girls.

Stanton was 25 years old and newly married. She had never spoken in public. As a young girl, she had overheard women beg her father, a judge, to protect them from husbands who had beaten them. He had to tell them that there was no law against it. Later, she attended Troy Female Seminary, the nation's first high school for girls. She knew from her studies in history that America did not treat women fairly. When she met Lucretia Mott in London, she readily agreed that something had to be done about the injustices suffered by women.

Unequal Treatment of Women Even a fine education like Stanton's did not assure women equal treatment. When Lucy Stone graduated from Oberlin College, the faculty invited her to write a speech. But a man would have to give the speech, since the school would not allow women to speak in public! Stone refused. After graduation, she spoke out for women's rights. Because women could not vote, she refused to pay property taxes. "Woman suffer taxation," she said, "and yet have no representation."

Stone's sister-in-law, Elizabeth Blackwell, wanted to be a doctor. She knew mathematics, science, and history. She had even been tutored by a helpful doctor. Yet she was rejected by 29 medical schools before one finally accepted her. She graduated at the top of her class, becoming the country's first female doctor. Still, no hospitals or doctors would agree to work with her.

To overcome such barriers, women would have to work together. By the time Elizabeth Cady Stanton and Lucretia Mott left London, they had decided "to hold a convention…and form a society to advocate the rights of women."

18.7 The Seneca Falls Convention and the Declaration of Sentiments

Eight years passed before Stanton and Mott met again. Over afternoon tea at the home of Mott's sister, they decided to send a notice to the local newspaper announcing a women's convention in Seneca Falls, New York. The organized movement for women's rights was about to begin.

The Declaration of Sentiments On July 19, 1848, almost 300 people, including 40 men, arrived for the Seneca Falls Convention. Many were abolitionists, Quakers, or other reformers. Some were local housewives, farmers, and factory workers.

The convention organizers modeled their proposal for women's rights, the **Declaration of Sentiments,** on the Declaration of Independence. "We hold these truths to be self-evident," the document began, "that all men and women are created equal."

Just as the Declaration of Independence listed King George's acts of tyranny over the colonists, the new declaration listed acts of tyranny by men over women. Man did not let woman vote. He did not give her property rights, even to her own wages. He did not allow her to practice professions like medicine and law.

Declaration of Sentiments: A formal statement of injustices suffered by women, written by the organizers of the Seneca Falls Convention. *Sentiments* means "beliefs" or "convictions."

Elizabeth Cady Stanton was one of the organizers of the Seneca Falls Convention. The image below shows her reading the Declaration of Sentiments to the participants at the convention.

Stanton's presentation of the declaration at the convention was her first speech. A few other women also summoned the courage to speak. One of them, Charlotte Woodward, was a 19-year-old factory worker. "Every fiber of my being," she said, "rebelled [against] all the hours that I sat and sewed gloves for a miserable pittance which, after it was earned, could never be mine."

Debate about the Right to Vote The convention passed resolutions in favor of correcting these injustices. Then Stanton proposed that women demand the right to vote. For many, this step was too big. Even Mott cried, "Thou will make us ridiculous! We must go slowly."

At this point, Stanton received powerful support from another participant at the convention, Frederick Douglass. Everyone who believed that black men should have the right to vote, Douglass argued, must also favor giving black women the right to vote. And that meant all women should have this precious right. Inspired by Douglass's speech, the convention voted narrowly to approve this last resolution.

Elizabeth Cady Stanton (above) and Elizabeth Blackwell (below) were two leaders in the early struggle for women's rights.

The Legacy of Seneca Falls The Seneca Falls Convention helped to create an organized campaign for women's rights. Sojourner Truth, who would later mesmerize an audience by asking defiantly, "Ain't I a woman?" became an active campaigner in the movement.

Elizabeth Cady Stanton didn't like speaking at conventions, but she could write moving speeches. Fortunately, she made friends with Susan B. Anthony, a refomer with a flair for public speaking.

While Stanton stayed in Seneca Falls to raise her children, Anthony traveled from town to town, speaking for women's rights. Of their lifelong teamwork, Stanton said, "I forged the thunderbolts, she fired them."

Slowly, reformers for women's rights made progress. New York gave women control over their property and wages. Massachusetts and Indiana passed more liberal divorce laws. Elizabeth Blackwell started her own hospital, including a medical school to train other female doctors.

Other reforms would take decades to become reality. Of all the women who signed the declaration at Seneca Falls, just one would live to vote for president legally—Charlotte Woodward.

18.8 Chapter Summary

In this chapter, you read about the reform movements that swept through the United States between about 1820 and 1850. You used an illustration of a protest march to learn about these reforms.

Many reformers were inspired by the Second Great Awakening, which taught Christians to perform good works in order to be saved. Other reformers were inspired by writers, such as Henry David Thoreau, and by the spirit of participation created by Andrew Jackson's presidency.

Dorothea Dix was a pioneer in the movement to reform the treatment of prisoners and the mentally ill. The movement to make education freely available to all was led by Horace Mann.

Women played a key role in the movement to abolish slavery. Former slaves, like Frederick Douglass and Sojourner Truth, added powerful voices to the movement.

The fight to end slavery helped spark the struggle for women's rights. The organized movement for women's rights began with the Seneca Falls Convention and its Declaration of Sentiments.

In the next chapter, you will learn that the reformers' efforts to improve the lives of slaves were unsuccessful.

In 1998, Hilary Rodham Clinton spoke at the 150th anniversary of the Seneca Falls Convention. In her speech, she said, "Much of who women are…today can be traced to the courage, vision, and dedication of the pioneers who came together at Seneca Falls. Now it is our responsibility to finish the work they began."

Sample 4

The Rise of Industry

Overview

In this lesson, students learn about the rapid rise of industrialism in the United States at the turn of the century, and labor's response to it. First, students participate in an **Experiential Exercise** that re-creates the experience of working on an assembly line. Then they read about industrialism and the Triangle Shirtwaist Factory fire in *History Alive! The United States*, and take notes about how the historical events connect to their experience working on an "assembly line." Finally, students apply their learning in a Processing assignment.

Objectives

Students will be able to
- identify factors leading to the rise of industrialism and urbanization.
- experience assembly-line work and describe the conditions for assembly-line workers.
- explain why labor unions emerged to protect workers' interests.

Materials

- Graphic Organizer Placard 24
- Student Information 24A and 24B (1 copy)
- Student Information 24C (copied onto an overhead transparency)
- Student Information 24D (1 copy)
- CD Track 27, "Factory Sounds"
- plain white paper, 8 1/2" x 11", (1 sheet per student)
- scrap paper, 11" x 8 1/2" (100 sheets, cut in half)
- stubby crayons, one per student
- plain white paper, 8 1/2" x 11" (300–400 sheets
- sharpened pencils (1 per student)
- Map Transparency 24

Preview

There is no Preview for this lesson. The Experiential Exercise functions as the Preview.

Experiential Exercise

(**Note:** In this activity, you will simulate the behavior of a harsh factory supervisor, verbally exhorting students, subjecting them to difficult conditions, and destroying "unsatisfactory" work. It is critical that you have a cooperative-learning environment in your classroom and a strong rapport with your students because they may feel vulnerable, uncertain, or upset by the activity. Allow ample time to debrief the activity.)

1 Have students create their own designs for a woman's blouse. Distribute a sheet of plain white paper to each student. Explain that students will have three to five minutes to draw a picture of a woman's blouse. Instruct them to use the whole page for their drawing. Explain that even though their work time is limited, they should create the most stylish, detailed blouses that they can. (This represents students working as individual artisans in cottage industries. At the end of the Experiential Exercise, you can compare these drawings with those produced on the assembly line.)

2 Have students assume the role of employees in two garment factories. Choose approximately three students to observe from the side of the room. Explain that they will play the role of immigrants and will participate later (in Step 7). Divide the remaining students into two groups. Have them place their desks in two facing rows, about six inches apart, as shown in the classroom map. Post *Student Information 24A: Tri Company* in front of one row, and *Student Information 24B: Angle Company* in front of the other.

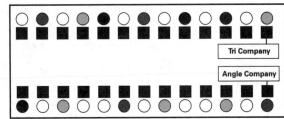

3 Project *Student Information 24C: Making Standard Woman's Shirtwaist Blouse*, and explain the new method of production. Tell students they will now draw the woman's shirtwaist blouse as many times as they can in 20 minutes. Explain that each student will specialize in one feature of the blouse. Have students in each group number off from 1 to 18. Make sure that all group members understand which blouse feature they are supposed to draw. Explain these rules:
- There will be absolutely no talking, laughing, or horseplay during production.
- Laborers who work hard and according to the guidelines will receive ten points.
- Employees of the "company" that creates the largest number of high-quality facsimiles will each receive five bonus points.

4 Tell students to begin assembly-line production. Pass out crayons. Give Worker One on each team approximately 100 half-sheets of scrap paper. Instruct students to quickly draw their assigned blouse features and pass the paper on to the next student in the row. Take on the role of production supervisor. Urge the employees to speed up, to concentrate, and to work harder. Make frequent loud demands, such as "Keep production moving!" and "Don't slow down!"

Sample 5

5 **After five minutes, announce that technological advances have been invented that will help workers make better blouses.** Distribute sharpened pencils to each worker, and give each Worker One 150–200 full sheets of plain white paper. (The new pencils and the larger sheets of paper represent the technological advancements of the Industrial Revolution.) Resume assembly-line work.

6 **After five minutes, announce that "Tri Company" and "Angle Company" are merging.** Explain that as owner of Tri Company, you want to increase production, decrease overhead costs, and make more profit, so you will buy the Angle Company and create a new, larger business, called the Triangle Company. Remove Student Information 24A and 24B, and post *Student Information 24D: Triangle Company.* (This step represents the growth of big business during the Industrial Revolution.) Tell the workers that to increase productivity and efficiency, and to encourage competition, the assembly line with the greatest number of high-quality facsimiles at the end of the lesson will receive ten bonus points instead of five. Resume assembly-line work.

7 **After five minutes, announce that you will be moving the Triangle Company to the city, for better access to workers, markets, and transportation.** Tell the workers that space in the city is expensive, so the workrooms in the new factory will be smaller for the same number of workers. Have the students in each row move their desks together so that there is no space between them. (This represents the urbanization that occurred during the Industrial Revolution.) Resume assembly-line work. If/when workers begin to slow down or do poor work, ask the "immigrants" (who are looking on), "Would you like to earn some points? These workers cost ten points but are doing a poor job. I'll fire them if you're willing to work for five points." If the immigrants hesitate, remind them that they need to feed their families. Have each immigrant replace a worker. (This step represents the use of cheap immigrant labor during the Industrial Revolution.)

8 **As workers continue to produce "shirtwaists," make the working conditions deteriorate.** Play CD Track 27, "Factory Sounds," as loudly as possible. (The track is 45 seconds long. Set the CD player on "repeat 1" to have the track play continuously.) Turn down the lights and, if possible, adjust the room temperature to be uncomfortably hot or cold. Continue to make loud demands, such as "Work faster!" and "I demand high quality!" (These actions represent the poor conditions workers were subjected to during the Industrial Revolution.)

9 **Expect students to begin to complain or even to "revolt."** Act as quality control supervisor, and dispose of any drawings that don't "measure up." Monitor the workers carefully, and punish those who misbehave by destroying their finished products and "barking" commands, such as "No talking! Pay attention to your work! Don't waste time laughing!" If students begin to talk about a strike, allow this to build and spread. If necessary, secretly encourage a student or two to say "strike!" (This represents the emergence of labor unions during the Industrial Revolution.)

10 **After about 20 minutes, stop the assembly lines.** Have two students count the number of finished products. Compare finished products with the model blouse and with the "cottage industry" blouse, from Step 1.

11 Debrief the exercise. Ask students: *Did you enjoy this activity? What did you like or dislike about it? What feelings did you experience during this activity?* Expect them to identify feelings of frustration, stress, tedium, alienation, and even anger and physical discomfort. Acknowledge these feelings, and allow students adequate time to express them. This is a crucial part of the debriefing process.

Graphic Organizer

1 Introduce Chapter 24 in *History Alive! The United States.* Tell students they will now learn about the rise of industrialism in the United States at the turn of the century, and labor's response to it. Explain that they will read an account of an infamous landmark in American history, the Triangle Shirtwaist Factory fire, and how it influenced the society, politics, and economy of the period. Have students read Section 24.1.

2 Introduce the graphic organizer on page 341. Ask the following questions: *What do you see? What are the people doing? What technology, new for that time, are the workers using? What makes these working conditions difficult?* Explain that students will use this graphic organizer to understand why industrialization expanded after the Civil War and the problems workers encountered as a result of this expansion.

Reading

1 Have students respond to the Geography Challenge questions on page 349. Explain that students will now learn about the factors that led to the industrial expansion following the Civil War.

2 Have students read Sections 24.2 through 24.6. Direct them to turn to pages 6–9 in their Interactive Student Notebooks. As they read the sections and complete Reading Notes 24, encourage them to think about how their experience in the earlier exercise connects to the history. You may want to complete the Reading Notes for Section 24.2 as a class. Use Guide to Reading Notes 24 to check students' work.

Processing

1 Place students in pairs and prepare them to role-play a dialog between labor and management. Have one student in each pair assume the role of a factory owner. Have the other student assume the role of a worker. Tell students they will respond to a series of prompts about factory conditions and will role-play a conversation that would likely occur between a factory owner and a worker. Emphasize that students must stay in character. Explain that this exercise will prepare them for their Processing assignment.

2 Have pairs engage in the dialog. Read Prompt 1, and have students playing the role of the worker repeat it. Then have pairs engage in a dialog for about one minute. Encourage students to bring up points from the reading and their Reading Notes. Repeat this process for each of the prompts.

Prompt 1: *Worker:* Why is the pay so low in this factory?

Prompt 2: *Owner:* Why do you put your personal interests over the good of the company?

Prompt 3: *Worker:* Why is work here so boring and repetitive?

Prompt 4: *Owner:* If you don't like the job you're doing, why don't you get a better job?

Prompt 5: *Worker:* What are you going to do about the dangerous work conditions?

Prompt 6: *Owner:* Why is our factory being outproduced by our competitors?

Prompt 7: *Worker:* Why won't management allow unionization?

Prompt 8: *Owner:* Why do you keep threatening to strike?

3 **Have students complete the Processing assignment on page 10 of their Interactive Student Notebooks.**

Internet Connections
For more information on the Triangle Shirtwaist Factory and on the labor movement, refer students to Internet Resources for Lesson 24 at www.historyalive.com/connections.html.

Assessment
A blackline master for the assessment follows on pages 39–41.

| 1. C | 3. A | 5. B | 7. A | 9. D | 11. B | 13. D | 15. B |

| 2. A | 4. D | 6. C | 8. B | 10. C | 12. A | 14. A |

16. The bulleted points can provide a rubric for this item.

Choose the letter of the best answer for each question.

1. Who said "Steel is king!" and made it happen?
   A. John D. Rockefeller
   B. Thomas Edison
   C. Andrew Carnegie
   D. Alexander Graham Bell

2. A corporation is a
   A. business that it owned by many investors.
   B. group of businesses formed to reduce competition.
   C. company that controls all production and sales of a product.
   D. partnership between two business people working together.

3. What attracted people to America's rapidly growing cities in the late 1800s?
   A. job opportunities
   B tenement houses
   C. electric lighting
   D. art museums

4. Most city factory workers lived in
   A. homes that they owned.
   B. ten-story skyscrapers.
   C. spacious suburbs.
   D. crowded slum neighborhoods.

5. The wages offered many factory workers were so low that
   A. people would not take those jobs.
   B. everyone in the family had to work.
   C. one wage earner could support a family.
   D. no one was able to make a profit.

6. What invention made it practical to locate factories at the top of ten-story skyscrapers in the late 1800s?
   A. the electric light bulb
   B. the telephone
   C. the electric elevator
   D. the sewing machine

7. As businesses grew bigger after the Civil War, labor unions were organized to represent the interests of
   A. workers.
   B. investors.
   C. managers.
   D. customers.

8. In the 1909 "Uprising of the 20,000," striking garment workers in New York City won
   A. free lunches.
   B. better wages.
   C. safer factories.
   D. paid vacations.

9. What simple change might have prevented the death of some of the 149 workers who perished in the Triangle Shirtwaist Factory fire?
   A. allowing workers to join unions
   B. building safer passenger elevators
   C. using fire-resistant fabrics
   D. keeping factory doors unlocked

Sample 5

Use the cartoon and your knowledge of social studies to answer the questions below.

10. The setting of this cartoon is the
    A. White House.
    B. Supreme Court.
    C. U.S. Senate.
    D. Bank of the United States.

11. Who do the small men sitting in front represent?
    A. wealthy bankers
    B. U.S. senators
    C. federal judges
    D. cabinet members

12. Who do the men who look like giant moneybags represent?
    A. business trusts
    B. the Standard Oil trust
    C. business investors
    D. labor union organizers

13. The large men are shown using a special entrance at the right for
    A. senators.
    B. the people.
    C. the president.
    D. monopolies.

14. Which caption best fits the cartoon?
    A. "Government by and for the trusts!"
    B. "In the trusts we trust!"
    C. "The United States of Trusts!"
    D. "Put your trust in the Senate!"

15. What is the cartoonist's message?
    A. Trusts have made the nation richer.
    B. Trusts are corrupting our government.
    C. Trusts make business more efficient.
    D. Trusts protect the free enterprise system.

412 Sample Lesson from *History Alive! The United States*

© Teachers' Curriculum Institute

Follow the directions to complete the item below.

16. Draw the heads and faces of four people affected by the rise of industry in the early 1900s: a factory owner, a factory worker, a union organizer, and a consumer. Make sure each drawing includes the following:

   • a simple piece of clothing, like a hat, scarf or necktie that is appropriate for each person.

   • a facial expression for each person that accurately reflects how they might feel about the rise of industry.

   • a thought bubble for each person that accurately reflects what that person might think about the rise of industry and why.

TRI Company

ANGLE Company

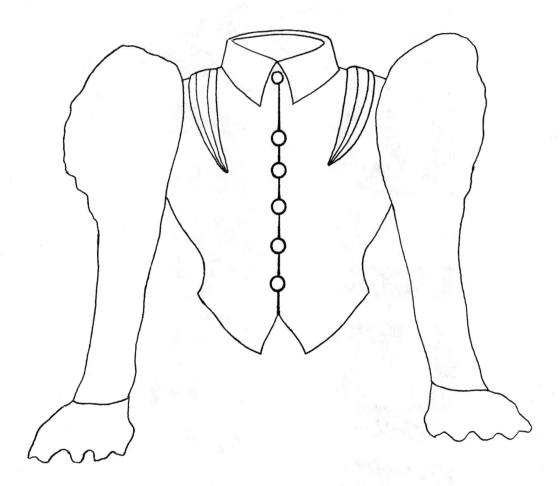

Worker 1: Collar

Worker 2: Collar button (button #1)

Worker 3: Outline of body of blouse

Worker 4: Left sleeve

Worker 5: Left cuff

Worker 6: Right sleeve

Worker 7: Right cuff

Worker 8: Button #2

Worker 9: Button #3

Worker 10: Button #4

Worker 11: Button #5

Worker 12: Button #6

Worker 13: First pleat on right side

Worker 14: First pleat on left side

Worker 15: Second pleat on right side

Worker 16: Second pleat on left side

Worker 17: Third pleat on right side

Worker 18: Third pleat on left side

TRIANGLE Company

Directions: Read Sections 24.2 through 24.6 in *History Alive! The United States.* Answer the questions that correspond to each section.

24.2 Improved Technology

What technological advances did you experience while on the assembly line?

sharp pencils, full-sized sheets of paper

What technological advances and new production methods helped industries expand in this period?

steel, electric light bulb, electrical power station, electric motor, telephone, division of labor for production of goods

What technological advances were used in the Triangle Factory?

electric motors, division of labor, electronic freight elevators, telephone

24.3 The Rise of Big Business

How did your teacher turn your classroom factory into a big business?

combined Tri Company and Angle Company

How did men like Rockefeller and Carnegie make their businesses bigger?

through corporations (businesses owned by investors) and trusts (groups of corporations run by a single board of directors)

How big was the Triangle Factory?

It was the largest shirtwaist factory in the country.

Sample 5

Directions: Read Sections 24.2 through 24.6 in *History Alive! The United States.* Answer the questions that correspond to each section.

24.4 The Growth of Cities

What changed when your factory "moved" to the city?

It became crowded.
Immigrants replaced workers and agreed to work for fewer points.

What groups of people moved to the city? What was their life like there?

Immigrants and rural Americans flocked to the cities where they lived in crowded, unclean, and dangerous tenements.

Why was the Asch Building unsafe for the workers in the Triangle Factory?

It had only two narrow staircases. Doors opened inward, not outward.

24.5 Working Conditions

What were working conditions like on the classroom assembly line?

noisy, poor lighting, uncomfortable temperature, teacher made unreasonable demands

What were working conditions like in factories?

low wages, child labor, crowded conditions, uncomfortable temperatures, fire danger

What were working conditions like in the Triangle Factory?

low wages, long hours, workers charged for supplies, prohibited from leaving the factory floor to go to the toilet or for a drink, machines crowded together, fire danger

24.6 Labor Unions

What methods did workers in your class use to get better working conditions?

suggested striking

What did labor unions do to improve working conditions? How did employers react to labor unions?

Unions went on strike. Employers fired union workers and hired guards to protect strikebreakers.

What happened at the Triangle Factory when owners refused to bargain with unions for better working conditions?

146 workers died because they could not escape a fire that started in the factory.

Sample 5

Directions: Read Sections 24.2 through 24.6 in *History Alive! The United States.* Answer the questions that correspond to each section.

24.2 Improved Technology

What technological advances did you experience while on the assembly line?

What technological advances and new production methods helped industries expand in this period?

What technological advances were used in the Triangle Factory?

24.3 The Rise of Big Business

How did your teacher turn your classroom factory into a big business?

How did men like Rockefeller and Carnegie make their businesses bigger?

How big was the Triangle Factory?

Sample 5

Directions: Read Sections 24.2 through 24.6 in *History Alive! The United States.* Answer the questions that correspond to each section.

24.4 The Growth of Cities

What changed when your factory "moved" to the city?

What groups of people moved to the city? What was their life like there?

Why was the Asch Building unsafe for the workers in the Triangle Factory?

24.5 Working Conditions

What were working conditions like on the classroom assembly line?

What were working conditions like in factories?

What were working conditions like in the Triangle Factory?

24.6 Labor Unions

What methods did workers in your class use to get better working conditions?

What did labor unions do to improve working conditions? How did employers react to labor unions?

What happened at the Triangle Factory when owners refused to bargain with unions for better working conditions?

Sample 5

Directions: Write a dialogue between a factory owner and a worker that might have taken place in 1900. Your dialogue must:
- begin with these opening lines:
  - Worker: We on the assembly line aren't happy.
  - Owner: Well, what's your beef?
  - Worker: I've got a list of complaints, and I want to know your response. To begin with…
- contain at least four concerns that workers had at the turn of the century.
- contain accurate responses by the factory owner to each of the worker's concerns.
- use the following terms: *assembly line, working conditions, labor* (or *trade*) *union, strike, profit.*
- use language that reflects the passionate feelings held by workers and owners.
- be free from spelling and grammatical errors.

What do you think this man's job is?

How do you think this woman feels about her job?

24

The Rise of Industry

24.1 Introduction

The tragedy started late in the afternoon on March 25, 1911. The quitting bell had just sounded in New York City's Triangle Shirtwaist Factory. Nearly 500 employees, most of them young immigrant women, headed toward the exit. It was Saturday, and they were looking forward to a day off with family and friends.

One woman sniffed the air. Something was burning! Another spotted flames leaping out of a pile of cloth scraps. Before she could react, the wooden table above the fabric was ablaze. From there the flames jumped to the paper fabric patterns hanging above the table. Flaming bits of paper and fabric whirled around the room, setting other tables on fire.

The room filled with smoke, and the air became so hot that it burst the windows. Fresh air poured into the room, sending the flames even higher. Fingers of the blaze started to scorch workers' clothing and hair.

"I heard somebody cry, 'Fire!' I left everything and ran for the door," recalled one woman. "The door was locked and immediately there was a great jam of girls before it." She could see at once that, "If we couldn't get out, we would all be roasted alive."

Such factories and their dangers were a relatively new part of life in the United States. You read in Chapter 13 how the Industrial Revolution began. After the Civil War, new inventions and business methods allowed Americans to create industry on a much larger scale than ever before. Unfortunately, this industrial progress brought not only economic benefits, but also tragedies to the United States. The nation's new mills and factories produced a wondrous assortment of goods that made life better for many. But the people who were employed in these new industries often lived and worked in the most miserable, even dangerous, conditions.

In this chapter, you will read the rest of the story of the Triangle Shirtwaist Factory fire. You will also read how, by 1900, the United States became the world's leading industrial nation.

Graphic Organizer: Illustration
You will use this illustration to learn more about the expansion of industry and the effects of this expansion on workers.

24.2 Improved Technology

By the 1860s, many of the factors necessary for the rapid **industrialization** of the United States were already in place. Machines had taken over much of the work once done by hand. Work had moved from homes to factories. Railroads had begun to connect customers and manufacturers with an efficient transportation system.

After the Civil War, new inventions and improved technology prompted the growth of new industries. Some of these innovations, or new ideas, helped businesses to grow and become more efficient. Others made daily life easier for many Americans.

The Granger Collection, New York

Sparks fly in a steel-manufacturing plant as molten metal meets cold air in the Kelly-Bessemer process. The process cleaned the steel of impurities.

The Age of Steel Before the Civil War, the nation's railroads ran on iron rails that wore out quickly. Railroad owners knew that rails made of steel—a mixture of iron, carbon, and sometimes other metals—were stronger and would last longer. Steel, however, was difficult and costly to make.

In 1872, a Scottish immigrant named Andrew Carnegie went to England to study a less expensive method of making steel, invented by Henry Bessemer. Carnegie owned a company that made iron bridges for railroads. But he knew that his bridges would be better if made out of steel. Carnegie was so impressed by the Bessemer process that he brought it back to the United States. "The day of iron has passed," he announced. "Steel is king!"

Carnegie was right. Within a decade, steel was replacing iron in rails, locomotives, and bridges. Other industries also took advantage of less expensive steel. Steel nails, needles, and knives became common household items.

Many steel companies competed fiercely to supply steel for such products. To remain the leader, Carnegie hired scientists to improve the quality of his company's steel. He employed good managers to make his steel mills run efficiently. His recipe for success was, "Adopt every improvement, have the best machinery, and know the most."

To keep costs low, Carnegie set out to control every step in the steel-making process. He purchased iron mines to supply his ore, coal fields to fire his furnaces, and railroads to ship his finished steel to customers.

To reduce his competition, Carnegie also bought up several rival steel companies. He then combined them all to form the giant Carnegie Steel Company. By 1900, Carnegie Steel produced a quarter of the nation's steel.

Electric Power During this era, inventor Thomas Edison helped to transform electricity from a scientific curiosity into a practical source of light and power. In 1876, Edison opened an "invention factory" in New Jersey. With a team of workers, he set out to create a "minor" invention every few days and a "big thing every six months or so."

Edison succeeded brilliantly. His workshop turned out the first practical electric lightbulb, the phonograph, the motion picture projector, and many other inventions.

In 1882, Edison built the first electrical power station and distribution system in New York City. His team invented everything the system required, including generators, regulators, meters, switches, light sockets, fuse boxes, and underground electric cables. When he finally turned the generator on, electricity began to flow to homes, stores, and factories. The age of electricity had begun.

By 1900, some 25 million lightbulbs were glowing across the country. In many factories, electric motors were replacing waterwheels and steam engines as sources of power. New electric-powered devices, such as washing machines and vacuum cleaners, were making housework easier.

The Telephone The telephone was invented by a Scottish immigrant named Alexander Graham Bell. In 1876, as he was getting ready to test his "talking machine," Bell spilled acid on himself. "Watson, come here, I want you," he commanded his assistant. Watson, who was in another room, heard every word over a telephone.

Bell's invention worked. It worked so well that, by 1915, Americans were communicating with one another over nine million telephones. All these telephones made American industry more efficient and competitive. They allowed suppliers, producers, sellers, and customers to communicate quickly and easily.

New Production Methods New methods of organizing work were also making business more efficient. Factory owners adopted Eli Whitney's idea of assembling a wide variety of products from interchangeable parts. They also used the assembly line. In a shoe factory, for example, one worker operated a heel-cutting machine. Another operated a sole-cutting machine. Another made shoelaces. Still other workers assembled, labeled, and packaged the shoes.

With this assembly-line process, workers produced more goods per day at less cost. As prices dropped, more Americans could afford to buy manufactured products. More customers meant more factories. By 1900, almost four times as many Americans worked in factories as had a generation earlier.

The Collection of the New-York Historical Society, negative number 2946

Electric lines form a criss-crossed canopy over this city street. Thomas Edison's invention of the lightbulb in the 1880s spurred tremendous growth in the electric industry.

Sample 5

The Triangle Factory

The Triangle Shirtwaist Factory was just one of many new businesses that took advantage of improved technology to mass-produce a quality product at a good price. The Triangle Factory specialized in a style of women's blouse known as a *shirtwaist*. A shirtwaist had puffy sleeves, a neat collar, front buttons, and a snug waist. Women liked shirtwaists so much that by 1909, New York City had more than 500 factories that made only such blouses.

Sam Bernstein, the production manager at the Triangle Shirtwaist Factory, loved watching his workers use up-to-date tools and production methods. Each person at the cutting tables had a special steel knife. This knife could slice through many layers of fabric at a time, cutting dozens of sleeves, then fronts, then backs. That was the way to get things done in a modern factory!

From the next floor of the building, Bernstein could hear the whirring of 240 sewing machines. The machines were neatly laid out in 16 tightly packed rows. Flexible belts connected each machine to a rotating axle running down each row just above the floor. This axle, which was spun by an electric motor, delivered power to each machine. The machines clattered loudly as women sewed the pieces of shirtwaists together.

Piles of finished blouses were then lifted to the floor above by electric freight elevators. There, two rows of workers gave the shirtwaists a final pressing. Finally, shipping clerks packed the shirtwaists into boxes for shipment.

Usually, the factory almost ran itself. But if a problem occurred, the company's switchboard operator could reach Bernstein by telephone on any of the three floors of the factory.

Sewing machines, shirtmakers, bobbins, and piles of cloth crowd this factory. Imagine working here in the heat of summer.

24.3 The Rise of Big Business

When Carnegie opened his first factory in 1865, most businesses were still owned by one person or a few partners. Because the owners' funds were limited, businesses were small. Owners knew their employees and often treated them like family.

Growth of Corporations A partnership might work well for a garment, or clothing, factory. But big businesses, such as railroads, needed much more capital—money to start a business—than a few partners could provide. To raise larger sums, entrepreneurs—people who start new businesses—set up **corporations.** A corporation is a business that is owned by many investors, or people who help pay its initial expenses.

A corporation raises funds by selling stock, or shares in a business. The investors who buy the stock are known as *stockholders*. In return for their investment, stockholders hope to receive dividends, or a share of the corporation's profits.

The money invested by the stockholders is used to build the business. To make sure their money is used properly, stockholders elect a board of directors. The people on the board of directors oversee the running of the corporation.

After the Civil War, corporations attracted large amounts of money from investors. By the 1880s, thousand of corporations were doing business across the United States.

Rockefeller's Oil Trust A giant in the oil business, John D. Rockefeller introduced another form of business organization known as the **trust.** A trust is a group of corporations run by a single board of directors.

Rockefeller invested in his first oil refinery in 1862, at the age of 23. At that time, petroleum, or oil found underground, was just becoming a valuable resource. Oil refineries purify petroleum into fuel oil. During the nineteenth century, oil was used to light homes, cook food, and run engines and generators.

Before long, many small refineries were competing fiercely in the oil business. The amount of oil produced by these firms rose and fell wildly, along with prices. Rockefeller saw this as wasteful and inefficient. To reduce competition, he did everything he could to drive his rivals out of business. Those companies he could not destroy, he bought.

Like Carnegie, Rockefeller took control of every step of his business. He bought oil fields along with railroads, pipelines, and ships to move his oil. He built his own warehouses and even made his own oil barrels for storing oil products. By 1880, Rockefeller controlled 95 percent of the nation's oil refining.

To manage his many businesses, Rockefeller combined them into the Standard Oil Trust. The trust made the oil industry more efficient than ever before. But, as a **monopoly,** it had the power to control oil prices. This worried people who depended on oil in their homes and businesses.

Following Rockefeller's example, entrepreneurs created trusts in other businesses such as railroads, meatpacking, sugar, whiskey, and tobacco.

J. P. Morgan, pictured above, was to banking and finance what Carnegie and Rockefeller were to steel and oil. In 1901, Morgan used his financial resources to buy Carnegie's steel company. Morgan founded U.S. Steel, America's first billion-dollar corporation.

The "people's entrance" to the United States Senate is "closed" in this turn-of-the-century cartoon. According to the cartoonist, the Senate was controlled by business trusts, depicted here as giant, bloated moneybags.

The business leaders who controlled these huge trusts became fabulously wealthy. Because most had made their fortunes by crushing their competitors, critics called them "robber barons."

The Evils of Trusts The growth of trusts alarmed many Americans. They saw these monopolies as a threat to the free-enterprise system. This system depends on free competition among businesses to provide the public quality products at fair prices. A monopoly, people argued, has little reason to improve its products or to keep prices low because it has no competition.

People also worried about the influence of trusts on the political process. Wealthy entrepreneurs, they complained, were using their enormous wealth to buy elections and corrupt public officials. As the *Chicago Tribune* warned, "liberty and monopoly cannot live together."

The Triangle Factory

The Triangle Shirtwaist Factory would never be the size of U.S. Steel or Standard Oil. However, it was the largest shirtwaist factory in the country. The two men who owned the factory, Max Blanck and Isaac Harris, were known in the garment industry as "the shirtwaist kings."

The owners worked well together. While Max Blanck entertained buyers from stores to convince them to carry Triangle products, Isaac Harris ran the factory. Harris kept up with garment production, machinery maintenance, and work flow. He did not, however, try to keep up with his workforce. The factory had too many workers for him to get to know them all personally.

The shirtwaist business made Blanck and Harris very wealthy. They drove fancy cars and enjoyed comforts that their workers could only dream about. Both had worked hard in a competitive business and probably felt that they had earned their success.

24.4 The Growth of Cities

Industrialization brought with it **urbanization,** or city growth. Most of the nation's new industries were located in cities. Immigrants and rural Americans flocked to these industrial centers looking for jobs. Chicago, for example, more than tripled its population between 1880 and 1900.

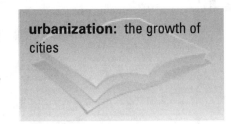

urbanization: the growth of cities

Urban Tenements As cities swelled with workers, demand for cheap housing exploded. To meet this demand, developers threw up cheap apartment buildings called *tenements.* One person described tenements as "great prison-like structures of brick, with narrow doors and windows, cramped passages and steep, rickety stairs." By 1900, about two thirds of New Yorkers lived in such buildings.

A poor family might occupy just one or two rooms in a tenement, usually with no heat or water. Friends or family often took in newcomers who arrived in cities without money for rent. As a result, tenement neighborhoods were some of the most heavily populated areas on Earth.

Tenements were unclean and even dangerous places to live. Only a few rooms had windows to provide light and fresh air. The rest were dark and airless. In some tenements, the only source of water was a single faucet in a courtyard. Many lacked sewer services. In such conditions, diseases such as typhoid and cholera spread quickly, killing infants and young children. Fire was another constant worry.

Cities Expand Upward As cities expanded, urban land costs shot up. In New York, land that had sold for $80 in 1804 was selling for $8,000 by 1880. Such prices inspired builders to construct more building space on less land by going upward. Using lightweight steel beams to support walls and ceilings, builders constructed skyscrapers that rose ten or more stories into the air. Electric elevators whisked people and freight effortlessly from floor to floor.

Businesspeople rented space in city skyscrapers for their offices and factories. Factory owners preferred the top floors. Rents were cheaper higher up, and the natural light was better, saving owners money on electric lighting. The cost of insurance was low as well because steel buildings were thought to be fireproof. By the early 1900s, more than half of New York City's workers labored above the seventh floor.

City Excitement For all their problems, cities were also exciting places to live. City stores were filled with products never seen on a farm. City dwellers enjoyed all sorts of entertainment from operas and art museums to dance halls and sporting events. When writer Hamlin Garland

A family in a New York City tenement in the early 1900s. Cramped, dirty, dark, and crowded, tenements spread disease and misery among their inhabitants.

The ten-story Asch Building in New York City had only two staircases, even though the city required at least three for safety reasons.

came to Chicago with his brother, he found that, "Everything interested us.… Nothing was commonplace; nothing was ugly to us."

The Triangle Factory

Blanck and Harris located their thriving shirtwaist business on the top three floors of the ten-story Asch Building in New York City. They chose this space partly because of the morning sunlight that streamed in through its large windows. Their landlord, Joseph Asch, boasted that when construction was completed in 1901, "the architects claimed my building was ahead of any other building of its kind which had previously been constructed."

It may have been ahead of other buildings, but the Asch Building was not perfect. It had only two staircases, even though the city building code required three. The city had agreed to count the building's fire escape as the third staircase. But the fire escape ended at the second floor. Nor was the Asch Building well designed for evacuation during an emergency. Its staircases were narrow. Instead of opening outward to let people escape easily, the building's doors opened inward. Despite scares from several small fires in the building, Asch had not bothered to fix these problems.

The Triangle Factory's workforce was made up mainly of young immigrant women, most of them Italians and Jews from Eastern Europe. Even if they had been aware of these safety problems, they would have hesitated to demand improvements for fear of being fired. Often their jobs provided their family's only income.

Like most factory workers, Triangle employees could only afford housing in crowded slums. "I lived in a two-room tenement with my mother and two sisters and the bedroom had no windows," recalled one employee. "There was nothing to look forward to."

Geography Challenge

United States Industries in 1890

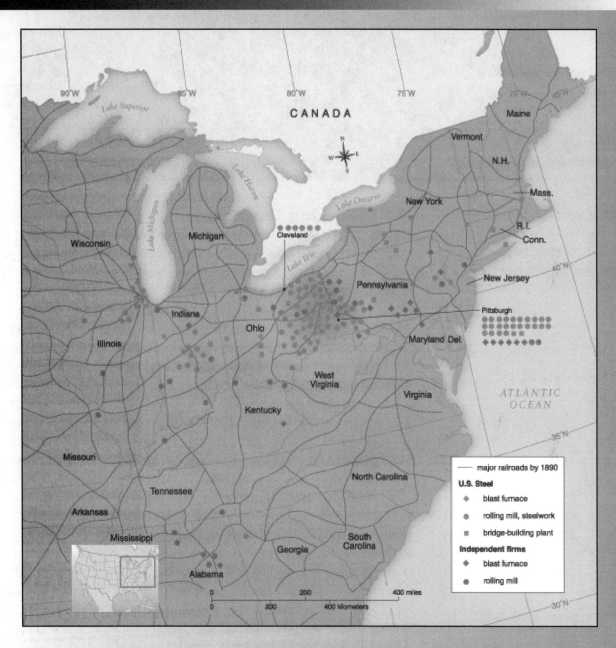

1. Identify at least four interesting details on this map.

2. What two cities were the centers of steel production?

3. How many U.S. Steel factories were located in Cleveland? In Pittsburg? How many independent factories were located in these two cities?

4. What do you believe were some of the effects of U.S. Steel's monopoly over steel production in these two cities?

A young girl stands between looms in a textile factory. At the turn of the century, millions of children worked long hours in mines, mills, and factories.

24.5 Working Conditions

Working conditions in most industries were appalling. Gone were the days when business owners knew and cared about the people who worked for them. Men like Carnegie and Rockefeller knew little about their workers.

Working Families Gone too were the days when factory workers could expect decent pay. With so many people looking for jobs, business owners could pay low wages. Many wages were so low that men could not support their families. To get by, wives and children had to work as well, usually at even lower wages.

Most factory women earned about $1 to $3 per day. If business was slow, wages dropped. A boss might not pay a new worker anything until she had learned her job. Then he would charge her for the sewing machine she worked on. If a worker complained, she could easily be replaced with a new one, perhaps for less money.

Millions of young children worked in mines, mills, and factories. A newspaper reported that young boys hired by coal miners to separate lumps of coal from rocks, "go to work…at seven o'clock in the morning and work till it is too dark to see any longer. For this they get $1 to $3 a week." They also got curved spines from bending over piles of coal all day.

Inside Factories Mills and factories were hot in summer and cold in winter. To keep costs low, owners crowded workers together.

Of all working dangers, fire claimed the most lives. In New York, tall buildings often lacked fire escapes. New York City's fire chief wanted buildings to have fire escapes and sprinkler systems that could put out fires quickly. But factory owners objected to such added expenses.

New York City did require that factory doors "open outwardly" and "shall not be locked" so workers might escape quickly in case of fire. The law was not enforced, however. In 1910, some 94 percent of all factory doors in the city opened inward instead of outward.

The Triangle Factory

Saturday was payday at the Triangle Shirtwaist Factory. Most workers earned only $9 per week, with the most experienced making up to $12. The younger workers, some only 13 years old, earned just $6 per week for sewing on buttons all day. The very youngest earned even less. Worker Pauline Newman recalled:

"We were young, eight, nine, ten years old.… The hours were from 7:30 in the morning to 6:30 at night when it wasn't busy. When the [busy] season was on we worked until 9 o'clock. No overtime pay, not even supper money.… My wages were $1.50 for a seven-day week."

Of course, these pay rates were what workers earned before deductions. The company charged its employees for the thread and electricity they used, for the chairs they sat on, and even for using Triangle's coat lockers.

Everybody was expected to work at least 59 hours a week. This included every Saturday, plus occasional Sundays. To keep workers from claiming overtime pay, the managers sometimes set the clock back. To keep workers from being "interrupted," the heavy steel doors to the hall and stairs remained locked until closing time.

To make sure workers didn't steal any shirtwaists, fabric, or lace, the factory built a narrow corridor leading to the elevators. Every day at quitting time, employees filed through this corridor one at a time so that a watchman could inspect each woman's handbag.

Working at Triangle was unhealthy, uncomfortable, and unsafe. Managers seldom let workers leave the factory floor to use the toilet or drink from the dirty tap in the hallway. In the crowded sewing room, women could barely squeeze by each other's machines. The wooden chairs behind the machines often lacked backs to support the sewers while they worked. When all the machines were in use, the noise could be deafening.

Fire hazards abounded. Even though the city prohibited smoking, the factory rarely enforced that rule. Workers stuffed leftover fabric into wooden bins where it sat for months just waiting for a misplaced spark to set it ablaze. The Asch Building's only fire protection was a few hundred pails of water scattered throughout its ten floors.

An inspector points to a bolted door in the Triangle Shirtwaist Factory. The inspection came too late for the women who lost their lives in the fire. Tragically, the factory owners had locked the door to keep workers on the job.

24.6 Labor Units

As a teenager, Rose Schneiderman found work in a cap factory. After three years, she later wrote, "it began to dawn on me that we girls needed an organization. We were helpless; no one girl dared stand up for anything alone."

Workers like Rose Schneiderman had been forming unions since the 1830s. These early labor organizations were **trade unions**. They organized workers in the same trade, or job, to fight for better wages and working conditions. Sometimes these unions went out on strike, refusing to work until their employers agreed to meet their demands.

Knights of Labor In 1869, Uriah Stephens organized a new union known as the Knights of Labor. Stephens hoped to unite "men and women of every craft, creed, and color" into "one common brotherhood." The Knights led several successful strikes against telegraph and railroad companies. With such victories, the union grew to over 700,000 members.

In 1886, nearly 200,000 workers went on strike nationwide to demand an eight-hour workday. During a rally at Haymarket Square in Chicago, someone threw a bomb at police. The police shot back, injuring many workers. Four workers were sentenced to death for the bombing, even though no evidence tied them to the bomb.

Fearing more violence, employers fired anyone associated with the Knights. Membership dropped quickly, and the organization faded away.

American Federation of Labor As the Knights declined, a group of local trade unions formed the American Federation of Labor (AFL). Instead of strikes, the AFL used collective bargaining to reach its goals. In collective bargaining, union representatives meet with employers to try to reach agreement on such issues as wages.

Despite the AFL's peaceful approach, many employers made their

Strikes often pitted the police against labor organizers. This image shows a policeman being shot on Haymarket Square in Chicago during a strike of the Knights of Labor in 1886. A short time later, a dynamite bomb killed or injured several dozen persons, including police.

The Granger Collection, New York

workers sign pledges not to join unions. They also fired union members and exchanged lists of such "troublemakers" with other employers.

The Homestead Strike Some bosses used force to defeat unions. When workers struck at a Carnegie steel plant in Homestead, Pennsylvania, Henry Clay Frick, Carnegie's partner, refused to talk about their demands. Instead Frick made plans to reopen his plant with non-union workers. To protect these strikebreakers, he hired 300 armed guards.

When the guards arrived in Homestead, they faced an angry crowd of strikers. A battle broke out in which both guards and strikers died. Still Frick went ahead with his plan. When the Homestead plant reopened with strikebreakers, the union collapsed in defeat.

Women Organize Such tactics kept many women from joining unions, but not Rose Schneiderman. Upset by pay cuts, Schneiderman organized the women in her factory as part of the National Board of United Cloth Hat and Cap Makers. Soon after she joined the union, she wrote,

Sample 5

"A strike was declared in five of the biggest factories. There are 30 factories in the city. About 100 girls went out. The result was a victory, which netted us—I mean the girls—$2 increase in our wages on the average…. But all was not lovely by any means, for the bosses were not at all pleased with their beating and had determined to fight us again."

The largest women's union was the International Ladies' Garment Workers' Union (ILGWU), which represented women in clothing factories. In 1909, thousands of New York City garment workers walked off their jobs to protest poor working conditions and low pay. As the strike grew, so did public sympathy for the young women. The newspapers called this movement "The Uprising of the 20,000."

The strike ended months later when employers agreed to a shorter workweek and better pay. They also ended fees for the use of factory equipment. The employers refused, however, to meet the workers' demands for safety improvements. Most garment factories remained unsafe.

Shirtwaist workers display strike leaflets for a newspaper photographer. Strikers wanted shorter hours, higher pay, and safer working conditions.

The Triangle Factory
About 5,000 workers from the Triangle Shirtwaist Factory were part of the ILGWU strike of 1909. Their demands included unlocked doors during working hours and safer fire escapes in the Asch Building.

Rather than meet those demands, Blanck and Harris responded by locking the strikers out of the factory and advertising for replacements. "If the union had won, we would have been safe," said striker Rose Safran. "But the bosses defeated us and we didn't get the open doors or the better fire escapes." Because of that defeat, 146 workers would die needlessly.

The cause of the fire that swept through the Triangle Shirtwaist Factory in 1911 was never known. But suddenly people on the eighth floor began to cry, "Fire!" Within minutes, the entire floor was a "mass of flames." Escaping workers rushed to the stairs or pushed their way into the two small elevators. The stairs, however, were soon ablaze, and the elevators stopped running.

On the tenth floor, Mary Alter was warned of the fire by telephone. Harris and Bernstein led everyone out onto the roof. People from neighboring buildings stretched ladders between the rooftops to help the workers on the roof escape.

Workers on the ninth floor had no warning. The fire just appeared. Some women died immediately. Firemen later found them as "skeletons bending over sewing machines." Those who had time to escape found themselves trapped by the locked factory door. In desperation, they rushed to the windows and began to jump.

The crowd that gathered outside the Asch Building watched in horror as girls began to fall out of the sky—"fire streaming back from their hair and dresses." Their bodies hit the pavement with sickening thuds.

Firefighters arrived quickly, but had trouble bringing their equipment close to the building because of the bodies on the pavement. Not that it mattered. There was little the firemen could do. Their ladders were not tall enough to reach beyond the sixth floor. Their safety nets were just as useless. The workers fell with such force, said one fireman, that they "went right through the life nets."

At the public funeral for the Triangle victims, garment workers marched under a banner proclaiming, "We demand fire protection." As she marched, Rose Schneiderman glanced up at the buildings lining the funeral procession. "There they were. Girls right at the top of hundreds of Buildings, looking down on us," she recalled. "The structures were no different from the Asch Building...many were in a far worse condition."

Mourners stand shoulder to shoulder in the rain to honor the women who died in the Triangle Shirtwaist Factory fire. One hundred forty-six girls and women were killed or fell to their deaths in the preventable tragedy.

Honoring the Triangle victims

24.7 Chapter Summary

In this chapter, you read about the rapid industrialization of the United States and how this progress influenced the way average people earned their livings. You also read an account of an infamous event in history—the Triangle Shirtwaist Factory fire. You used an illustration to learn about the expansion of industry and the effects of this expansion on workers.

New inventions and ideas made it possible for businesses to grow in size and efficiency. While these innovations allowed more Americans to afford manufactured items, there was a hidden price to pay. With the rise of big business through corporations, trusts, and monopolies, the wealthy got wealthier and the poor got poorer.

As cities grew, factories rose ten or more stories above the ground, and people from all over came looking for jobs. People lived in crowded, unclean, and dangerous tenement buildings. Men, women, and children worked long hours for low wages in crowded, unsafe factories. Doors were kept locked, and workers could not leave their stations without permission. Most worked in miserable conditions.

Workers didn't dare speak up for fear of losing their jobs. By joining trade unions, they could fight as a group for better wages and working conditions. When organized workers went on strike, factory owners often responded with violence or by simply hiring other workers. Unfortunately, it took the horrors of the Triangle Factory fire to make the dangers of factory life real to the American public.

In the next chapter, you will read about how the many immigrants that worked in these factories viewed their lives in America.

This cartoon shows the women of the Triangle Shirtwaist Factory desperately trying to open one of the few exit doors. A man dressed in a suit decorated with dollar signs holds the door closed. The cartoonist believes that the women died because of the greed of factory owners.

TCI's Supplemental Programs

Program Components

- **Lesson Guides:** with classroom activities, reproducible sheets
- **Overhead Transparency Book:** color images to enhance visual literacy
- **Placard Set:** picture cards for use with the activities
- **Audio CD:** music, audio effects, dramatic readings

In addition to the core programs, TCI offers a series of supplemental programs for use in middle and high school history classes. These programs are configured to suit a wide range of course needs. Although there are no student textbooks, each program of six units contains complete instructions and resources for implementing a full-year program with 70–90 dynamic activities. Each activity is based on one of the six strategies that are the hallmark of the TCI Approach. This section contains sample activities from two of the supplemental programs. Sample 6 is an Experiential Exercise; Sample 7 is a Writing for Understanding activity.

Contents of TCI's Supplemental Programs

United States History to 1900
Six units with 90 lessons

Geography of America from Past to Present
Colonial Life and the American Revolution
The Constitution in a New Nation
Manifest Destiny in a Growing Nation
The Civil War and Reconstruction
The Rise of Industrial America

Twentieth Century United States History
Six units with 70 lessons

The United States Coming of Age: 1890–1920
The Roaring Twenties and the Great Depression
The United States in World War II
The Cold War
The Civil Rights Movement
Contemporary American Society

Ancient World History
Six units with 80 lessons

Early Humans
Ancient Egypt and the Near East
Ancient India
Ancient China
Ancient Greece
Ancient Rome

World History from 500 to 1700
Six units with 80 lessons

Europe After the Fall of the Roman Empire
The Rise of Islam
Empires and Kingdoms of Sub-Saharan Africa
Imperial China and Feudal Japan
Europe's Transition to the Modern World
Civilizations of the Americas

Modern World History
Six units with 80 lessons

Western Europe in the Modern World
The Rise and Fall of the Soviet Union
Communist China and Modern Japan
Modern Latin America
Modern Africa
The Modern Middle East

The Scramble for Territory

Experiential Exercise

Overview

In this **Experiential Exercise** groups of students claim possession of classroom furniture as they attempt to reconfigure the classroom in order to understand the European "scramble for Africa" of the 1870s. Students are told that they will provide input on a new classroom configuration. The teacher breaks students into small groups and gives each group written directions telling them to create a map of their proposed arrangement, to create and replicate a simple group symbol on small pieces of paper, and to affix the paper to classroom furniture to claim as theirs. Once students realize they must race to claim furniture, groups scramble to stake claims to desks, tables, and chairs. Afterward, the teacher debriefs the experience, making comparisons between students' race to claim furniture and European countries' scramble for African territory.

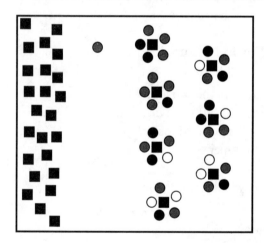

Procedures at a Glance

Tell students that you want to reconfigure the classroom and that you want their input on how to do it. Place students into groups of five. Pass out **Student Handout 3.1A** to one group, and pass out **Student Handout 3.1B** to the remaining groups. Do not let groups know they are receiving different handouts. Tell groups to follow the directions on the handout precisely. Remain uninvolved as students in the various groups begin claiming furniture. Expect that students from the group that received **Student Handout 3.1A**—which directs students to claim furniture before creating a new classroom map—will begin claiming furniture first, which may trigger a race to claim furniture. Allow the "scramble" to go on until most of the furniture is claimed. Afterward, hold a class discussion to debrief the experience. Project Transparencies 3.1A and 3.1B, and help make the connection between what students did and the scramble among European countries for African territories in the 1870s.

Procedures in Detail

1. This activity is designed to introduce students to the scramble for African territories that took place among European countries in the late 1800s by allowing students to "claim" classroom furniture as they attempt to reconfigure the classroom. (**Note:** This activity shows the European perspective on the scramble for territory. Unit 5 of TCI's High School Modern World History Program, entitled *Modern Africa,* contains African perspectives on European colonialism.)

2. Before class, move all but seven desks to one side of the room. Place the other seven desks apart on the other side of the room, as shown on the previous page. At the beginning of class, tell students you would like to rearrange the classroom and you want their input on ideas for new configurations. Place students into groups of five, and have each group huddle around one of the seven desks. Tell groups you would like each to submit a proposal for a new class configuration.

3. Pass out **Student Handout 3.1A:** Planning a New Classroom Arrangement to one of the groups, and pass out **Student Handout 3.1B:** Planning a New Classroom Arrangement to the rest of the groups. These handouts contain the following set of steps, but in different sequences:

   • Decide on a name for your group.
   • Create a simple flag to represent your group. Draw it on your index cards.
   • Create a map that shows how your group would like to rearrange the classroom.
   • Place or affix your flag on any piece of furniture in the classroom that your group would like to "claim" as yours in the new arrangement. After you do so, say, "I claim this piece of furniture in the name of (your group's name)." When we rearrange the class, all furniture with your group's flag on it can be placed where your group desires.

   The sequence of the steps are different on the two handouts so that one of the groups— the one with **Student Handout 3.1A**—will begin to claim furniture before the others, which will likely trigger a panic or race for the furniture. *Do not let groups know they are receiving different handouts.*

4. Tell groups to follow the directions precisely. Do not provide any other information. Before groups begin, provide them with several index cards and tape (or adhesive note pads).

5. Expect that groups with **Student Handout 3.1A**—which directs students to claim furniture before creating a new classroom map—will begin claiming furniture first, like Belgium, England, and France did with territory in Africa in the 1870s. Make sure they proclaim, "I claim this piece of furniture in the name of (group's name)," which should inspire competition among the groups. As the other groups notice this, they may immediately begin the race to claim some of the furniture, like Germany, Spain, Portugal, and Italy did with other parts of African territory.

6. Allow the "scramble" to go on until either most of the furniture has been claimed or groups get too unruly in their desire to make their territorial claims. Expect that some students may attempt to stake a second claim on a piece of furniture. Once groups have settled down, ask each group to point out its claims. Usually, one or two of the groups will have significantly greater claims than the others.

Connecting the Experience with History

1. Hold a class discussion to help students connect the experience with history. Center the discussion on these questions:

   - **How did you feel during this activity?**
   - **Why did you compete with the other groups to claim the furniture?**
   - **Do you think this was a fair way to claim the furniture? What might have been a better way?**
   - **If unclaimed furniture remains, who should get it?**

2. As students discuss these questions, the students in the group that had **Student Handout 3.1A** will likely argue that the process was fair and that the desks are rightfully theirs because they claimed them first. Conversely, the other groups will likely suspect that the "winning" groups cheated or had an unfair advantage. Students may suggest that the furniture be divided up evenly, or that at least the remaining furniture be granted to those groups with few or no claims.

3. Once the class has concluded its discussion about the fairness and validity of each group's claims, tell students that this activity was an exercise designed to help them understand European imperialists' scramble for territory in Africa in the late nineteenth century. Project Transparency 3.1A, which shows a map of European territorial claims in Africa in 1850. Then project Transparency 3.1B, which shows a map of European territorial claims in Africa in 1914. Ask students: **In what ways are these maps different? Based on your experience in this activity, what do you think occurred among European countries in Africa from 1850 to 1914?**

4. As students examine the transparencies, use the following information to help make connections between the activity and the scramble for Africa:

- The students (European colonial powers) become caught up in a competitive race to claim pieces of furniture (African territory) in the other side of the room (Africa).

- The students (colonial powers) used flags (national flags) to stake their claim.

- The students (colonial powers) claimed furniture (colonies) without knowing exactly how it would benefit them (territories were unknown and few colonies reaped any benefit for the colonial powers at the time).

- One group of students (Britain) had directions that told the group to start sooner (Britain had a head start in acquiring colonies) and other students (other colonial powers) resented this unfair privilege and scrambled to try and catch up.

- The students (colonial powers) discussed the fairness of the scramble and who should keep what furniture (the Berlin conference of 1884–1885, in which the Europeans divided African territory amongst themselves and agreed on a colonial map of Africa).

> **R** | **Idea for Class Notes:** Have students draw a picture of two students trying to claim a desk on the right side of their notebooks. Have them take notes on the European scramble for African territory by labeling the drawing according to the information above.

> **L** | **Idea for Student Response:** On the left side of their notebooks, have students complete this response: *The scramble for African territory among European powers was like...* Have students choose one of the following analogies or create one of their own: prospectors racing to stake a claim in the gold country, concert goers clamoring for the best seats, sharks in a feeding frenzy. Below their response, have them make a simple drawing of the analogy and label the historical comparisons. For example, a student might draw a prospector (labeled "Britain") staking his claim (labeled "African colony") in the gold country (labeled "Africa") while other prospectors (labeled "European countries") are seen approaching in the distance.

Planning a New Classroom Arrangement

Directions: Carefully follow the steps below to plan a new classroom arrangement.

1. Decide on a name for your group. (Take no more than a minute to decide.)

2. Create a simple flag to represent your group. Draw it on your index cards. (Take no more than a few minutes to do this.)

3. Place your flag on any piece of furniture in the classroom that your group would like to "claim" as yours in the new arrangement. After you do so, say, "I claim this piece of furniture in the name of (your group's name)." When we rearrange the class, all furniture with your group's flag on it can be placed where your group desires.

4. Create a map that shows how your group would like to rearrange the classroom.

Planning a New Classroom Arrangement

Directions: Follow the steps below to plan a new classroom arrangement. The steps must be completed in the exact sequence outlined.

1. Decide on a name for your group.

2. Create a simple flag to represent your group. Draw it on your index cards.

3. Create a map that shows how your group would like to rearrange the classroom.

4. Place your flag on any piece of furniture in the classroom that your group would like to "claim" as yours in the new arrangement. After you do so, say, "I claim this piece of furniture in the name of (your group's name)." When we rearrange the class, all furniture with your group's flag on it can be placed where your group desires.

Debating Mainstream and Counterculture Views in the 1960s

Writing for Understanding

Overview

In this **Writing for Understanding** activity students explore and write an editorial about the cultural rift between the American mainstream and the counterculture during the 1960s. First, working in pairs, students read information about mainstream culture and the counterculture. Then, the class discusses the historical influences and values of the mainstream and counterculture, and students complete a T-chart. Next, students assume the roles of representatives from the mainstream or the counterculture and respond to a series of prompts to debate six topics: fashion, communal living, political activism, sexuality, music, and drugs. The teacher then holds a class discussion on the cultural rift between the mainstream and the counterculture during the 1960s. Finally, students write an editorial about whether the effects of the counterculture on American society were positive or negative.

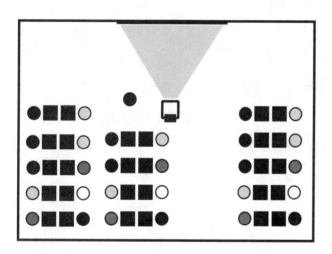

Procedures at a Glance

Place students in mixed-ability pairs and tell them they will learn about the cultural rift between the American mainstream and the counterculture during the 1960s. Pass out **Student Handout 3.3A,** and have pairs read the information. Then pass out **Student Handout 3.3B** and have the class complete the T-chart. Pass out **Student Handout 3.3C** and have students put on costumes. Next, project Transparency 3.3A, project **Transparency Master 3.3D,** and have students debate the first topic by responding to prompts. Using Transparencies 3.3B through 3.3F, repeat this process for the other topics. Finally, project **Transparency Master 3.3E,** and have students write an editorial about the effects of the counterculture on American society.

Procedures in Detail

1. Before class, place students in mixed-ability pairs. Prepare an overhead transparency that shows students who their partners are and where to sit. Project the transparency, and ask students to move into their correct places.

> **L** **Idea for Student Response:** To preview this activity, have students respond to these questions on the left side of their notebooks: *What are the key differences between your generation and your parents' generation? Do the differences help create harmony or conflict? Explain.* Afterward, have students share their answers. Lead a discussion to help students make connections between their own experience and the "generation gap" of the 1960s.

2. Tell students that in this activity they will explore and write an editorial about the cultural rift between the American mainstream and the counterculture during the 1960s. Use the following information to introduce students to the discord of the 1960s:

The 1960s was a decade characterized by political, social, and cultural discord. Demonstrations against the Vietnam War led to violent confrontations between rock-throwing protesters and riot police armed with canisters of tear gas. Riots exploded in American cities as African Americans agitated for their civil rights and a fair share of American prosperity. The assassinations of John F. Kennedy, his brother, presidential candidate Robert Kennedy, and Martin Luther King Jr. shocked the nation. Everything that seemed certain to the mainstream population—family, home, God, and country—was under attack. Emerging from the conservative and stolid 1950s, many Americans became disoriented. Folk singer Bob Dylan wrote a song that claimed that the answers were "blowing in the wind." With instability across the country, he might have sung "America is blowing in the wind."

Young people led the siege on American traditions. Some burned presidential dummies in effigy, others torched their draft cards or occupied public buildings. Much of the unrest of the era can be attributed to the Vietnam War. However, deeper cultural changes were occurring. Younger Americans established a counterculture that stood in stark contrast to the mainstream of American society. The counterculture challenged every line of traditional thinking—from sexual mores, to religious beliefs, patriotism, music, fashion, and drug use. Many envisioned a world based on individual expression, freedom from tradition, love, community, sex, drugs, and rock and roll. Others spoke out against the Vietnam War and demanded dramatic political changes. Many of their parents were appalled. While the cultural gap between the generations had seemed narrow in the 1950s, the gulf between the youth in the counterculture and their mainstream parents during the 1960s was enormous.

Some look back at the emergence of the counterculture with nostalgia. In their view, those were the days when money, jobs, and responsibility were less important than the spirit of love, togetherness, and harmony with nature. They argue that the political activism of the 1960s led to important societal changes. Others argue that the counterculture had a negative influence on American society. They say that the movement opened the floodgates to a permissiveness in society where drug use and sexual disease is rampant, and where belief in traditional values is scorned. At the end of the twentieth century, Americans still could not agree on an assessment of the tumultuous 1960s.

3. Once students have been introduced to the discord of the 1960s, pass out **Student Handout 3.3A:** Information on Mainstream Culture and the Counterculture to each student. Have pairs carefully read the information on the handout and discuss the "Stop Here and Discuss" questions.

4. When students have read and discussed the background information, pass out **Student Handout 3.3B:** T-Chart of the Mainstream and the Counterculture. Draw the T-chart on an overhead transparency. Ask students to list the historical influences and values of the two groups. During the discussion, record notes on the transparency, and have students complete the T-chart on the handout.

5. After students have completed the T-chart, tell them they will now assume the roles of representatives from the mainstream and the counterculture to debate six topics: fashion, communal living, political activism, sexuality, music, and drugs. For each pair, assign one partner to represent the mainstream culture and one to represent the counterculture. To help students get into their roles, pass out the appropriate page of **Student Handout 3.3C:** [group] Costume to each student. Have students cut out the costumes and affix them to their clothing or hair. (**Option:** You may want to have students color their costumes or prepare appropriate costumes ahead of time and wear them to class for the debate.)

6. Once students have assumed their roles, project Transparency 3.3A, which shows a row of women and a couple embracing. Once students have carefully examined the transparency, ask them to identify the mainstream and counterculture image, using details from **Student Handout 3.3A** and the transparency to support their answers. Use the **Teacher's Guide** to provide additional information about the transparencies. Then project **Transparency Master 3.3D:** Prompts for Debating Mainstream and Counterculture Views. Cover the transparency so that only the first prompt is showing. Read the first prompt aloud, and have the student from each pair representing the mainstream repeat it and complete the sentence to begin a discussion with the opposing student. Have pairs discuss the prompt for 1 to 2 minutes. Signal students to stop talking by flicking the lights or clapping your hands. Repeat this process with the next prompt,

this time having the students representing the counterculture read the prompt to begin the discussion. Using Transparencies 3.3B through 3.3F, repeat this process for the remaining five topics. (**Option:** Depending on the level of student interaction, you may want to increase or decrease the amount of time students have to respond to the prompts. This helps keep students on task and allows the exchange of dialogue to flow more naturally.)

Wrap Up

1. After students have discussed all the prompts, have students return their desks to the normal classroom setup. Hold a class discussion about the cultural rift between the American mainstream and the counterculture during the 1960s. Center the discussion on these questions:

    -   **What were the major differences between the mainstream and the counterculture?**
    -   **Why was there such a huge cultural rift during the 1960s?**
    -   **With which group do you most identify? Why?**
    -   **If you modeled your life after mainstream values, what would it be like?**
    -   **If you modeled your life after the counterculture, what would it be like?**
    -   **Which result best fits who you want to be in the future?**
    -   **In your opinion, was the counterculture's agenda a positive one?**
    -   **Do you think the effects of the counterculture on American society were positive or negative? Explain.**

2. After students have discussed the cultural rift between the American mainstream and the counterculture during the 1960s, they are ready to write editorials. Tell students they will assume the roles of journalists to write an editorial in the *New York Times* that comments on whether the effects of the counterculture on American society were positive or negative. Explain what an editorial is. (**Note:** You may want to provide students with examples of newspaper editorials.) Project **Transparency Master 3.3E:** Guidelines for Writing an Editorial on the Counterculture, and review the guidelines. You may want to provide sample topic sentences for each section of the editorial. Once students understand the guidelines, have them begin working. Encourage them to incorporate authentic quotes from adults who lived through the 1960s and to support their points of view with as much historical evidence as possible.

3. Give students adequate time to write their rough drafts, incorporate your feedback, and complete their final drafts. (**Option:** After students have completed their final drafts, you may want to allow pairs of students to read their editorials for the class.)

Teacher's Guide

- In **Transparency 3.3A** we see, at top, a row of contestants for the title of National College Queen wearing conservative fashions in New York in 1961. At bottom, we see hippies wearing attention-getting fashions in 1968 as a young hippie couple marries outdoors in Los Angeles.

- In **Transparency 3.3B** we see, at top, a mother and father barbecuing for their two children in 1968. At bottom, we see women cooking in the kitchen of a New York commune called the Hog Farm in the 1960s.

- In **Transparency 3.3C** we see, at top, residents of Chicago's West Side celebrating the Fourth of July with a display of American flags in 1961. At bottom, we see demonstrators at a draft induction center in Los Angeles in 1970 carrying an American flag decorated with a peace symbol.

- In **Transparency 3.3D** we see, at left, a couple kissing modestly at the altar during their wedding in a New York church in 1965. At right, we see a couple kissing passionately on a street in 1975.

- In **Transparency 3.3E** we see, at left, Lawrence Welk dancing with Janet Lennon on the *Lawrence Welk Show* in 1965. At right, we see Steve Marriott, lead guitarist for the rock group Humble Pie, performing in Long Beach, California, in 1974.

- In **Transparency 3.3F** we see, at left, a party hosted by millionaire Paul Getty in 1961, at which guests are drinking cocktails and smoking cigarettes. At right, we see a hippie girl smoking marijuana with a pipe in 1967.

Information on Mainstream Culture and the Counterculture

The Mainstream Culture

For millions of Americans, the post–World War II period of 1945 to 1960 brought an unforeseen era of economic growth and affluence. These Americans—adult, mostly white, middle- and upper-class people—were the mainstream of the population. Mainstream men and women had survived the Great Depression and learned the value of frugality, how to make the smallest amount of money—or food—go the furthest. This was also the generation that fought and sacrificed during World War II. After coming together as a nation to defeat an evil enemy, this generation displayed a sense of patriotism not shown since the American Revolution. Mainstream Americans welcomed the hard-earned peace and economic stability of the postwar era. They bought homes in the suburbs, found good jobs, and settled down to raise families with the assumption that their children would go to college.

Mainstream Americans believed that their shared beliefs in traditional American values were the foundation of a better life. First, they were typically very patriotic, as evidenced by a popular bumper sticker that appeared during the mid to late 1960s: "America: Love It or Leave It." Second, men and women who said they were in love got married—and stayed married. For unmarried couples to consider living together was not only unacceptable, but almost unheard of. Third, the mainstream generally believed that the "American dream"—a good education, a good job, and a good home—could come true for anyone who worked hard, was dedicated and honest, and believed in the United States. Anyone who challenged this kind of thinking was accused of being "un-American." Fourth, mainstream Americans believed people should conform to traditional values in everything from personal behavior to fashion and grooming. For example, many people expected men to have short hair, be clean shaven, and wear suits. Women were expected to wear tasteful amounts of makeup, have their hair done, and mostly wear dresses, even while relaxing at home.

- **What key events shaped the outlook of mainstream Americans?**
- **What were the four shared beliefs of mainstream Americans?**

The Counterculture

In the 1960s, a group of mostly young, white Americans born just before or just after the war began to challenge the established values of the older mainstream culture. This group soon came to be called the *counterculture*. The counterculture movement encouraged the pursuit of personal freedom and alternative lifestyles, rebellion against rigid conformity and materialism (the desire to accumulate wealth), and political activism to stop racism, war, and poverty. *Counterculture* is a broad term used to describe many different movements and lifestyles explored by young people in the 1960s. What follows are six common characteristics.

Communal Living   Many counterculture youth settled in urban neighborhoods, such as Haight-Ashbury in San Francisco and New York's East Village. However, another segment

Sample 7

left city life altogether and set up communes in isolated places such as the mountains of California and the wide-open spaces of New Mexico. These communes rejected the competitive mainstream lifestyle and tried to construct a totally self-sufficient environment. They attempted to base their lives on cooperation and love, and to live in harmony with nature rather than to conquer it. Many communes were established on farms, where people grew their own food, baked their own bread, and set up their own schools. Some also shared drugs and engaged in "free love," or casual sex, defying traditional concepts of marriage and the family. While many women who joined communes were able to live more independently and self-sufficiently, they were also dismayed to learn that, just as in mainstream American society, male supremacy was an integral part of the structure of most communes.

Drugs   For many counterculture youth, drugs were an important part of rebellion and personal freedom. The most popular drug was marijuana. Timothy Leary, a former Harvard University psychology instructor, advocated a new mind-altering drug called LSD. He urged people to "turn on, tune in, and drop out," a phrase that became the motto for many drug users. LSD was a strong hallucinogenic drug that sent users on dreamlike "acid trips," which could be exciting—and sometimes deadly. While drug use had long been part of life for some Americans, the counterculture brought drug use to new heights. By the late 1960s, it was impossible to attend a rock concert without smelling marijuana or seeing concertgoers "tripping out." Newspapers frequently published stories of young people who had died from drug overdoses. In the face of intense criticism from the mainstream, counterculture youth pointed out that alcohol was the mainstream drug of choice. They also said that their actions did not hurt anyone besides themselves and so should be left to their own discretion.

 • **How was the counterculture different from mainstream culture?**
 • **Why were young people attracted to drugs and communal living?**

Fashion   Counterculture youth called themselves hippies, from the slang expression "hip," which meant knowledgeable or "with it." Hippies dressed in outrageous, colorful, controversial, and sometimes ridiculous clothes that shocked the mainstream. They wore beads around their necks, and shirts tie-dyed in crazy colors or covered with odd designs, even replicas of the American flag. Young men wore fringe jackets and army surplus clothes. Young women often went braless and wore blouses that left their midriffs exposed. Some women wore the mini, a skintight skirt that rose a full three inches above the knee. While short skirts were in, short hair was out—especially for men. Not since the colonial days had so many American males worn their hair in pony tails. Others let it grow halfway down their backs. Many adults claimed it was difficult to tell the boys from the girls. The hippies' final fashion statement was flowers in their hair, a sign of "peace and love." This trend earned the counterculture youth the nickname "flower children."

Political Activism   In the minds of many Americans—particularly the mainstream—the counterculture and the antiwar protest movement of the 1960s were inseparable. By the late 1960s, the media showed images nearly every week of long-haired protesters marching against the Vietnam War. Despite what many Americans thought, these protesters never fit into one easily categorized group. Some protesters were confrontational, burning the U.S. flag and screaming "Stop the war," as they cursed and goaded the police or National Guard troops who were on duty to protect government property. Other protesters were more interested in making a gentle "statement for peace." They often marched in silence, carrying peace signs, and frequently placing flowers in the gun barrels of government troops to show their nonviolent nature. This "dual nature" of the protest movement was often lost on mainstream Americans. They saw all student protesters as "long-haired, filthy, drug-crazed," disloyal Americans who were betraying their country.

• **What values were represented in counterculture fashion?**
• **What event motivated counterculture political activism?**

Music The folk, pop, and rock music of the 1960s challenged mainstream values. Bob Dylan's folk-rock ballads became counterculture anthems. In "The Times They Are A-Changin'," he told parents that their children were "beyond [their] command" and not to "criticize what [they] can't understand." The Beatles wrote songs like "Revolution" and "Why Don't We Do It in the Road," inspiring young people to chart a new course. Joni Mitchell advocated respect for nature, singing "They paved paradise and put up a parking lot." During the late 1960s, "psychedelic" rock became a major musical genre. Groups such as Jefferson Airplane and the Doors, and artists like Jimi Hendrix, combined a heavy guitar and drums-based rock sound with lyrics that often glorified the drug experience. In 1969, all these elements came together at a famous musical event: Woodstock. More than 500,000 young people spent a weekend camping out, getting high on drugs, engaging in "free" love—and listening to a continuous stream of rock and roll.

Sexuality There was a sexual revolution during the 1960s, and the counterculture was largely responsible for it. Counterculture youth saw themselves as sexually liberated. They scoffed at sexual inhibitions of their parents' generation, and replaced them with casual sex, or "free love." Medical advances such as the birth control pill made it easier for young women and their partners to become sexually active and not be concerned about unwanted pregnancies. Thousands of unmarried young people engaged in one sexual relationship after another, many of them never lasting more than one night. At rock festivals, on communes, on the beaches, in parks—everywhere it seemed—the youth of America was flaunting their open attitude about sexual conduct. Soon, the entire country underwent a change in attitude about sex. Women went braless, or burned their bras. Movies showed men and women in graphic lovemaking scenes. Music references to sex—almost unheard of a decade before—became common. The counterculture's rejections of mainstream American sexual values was widely criticized and condemned. However, the counterculture continued, unperturbed, saying: "Make love, not war."

• **What values were represented in counterculture music?**
• **How did counterculture views of sexuality differ from the mainstream?**

T-Chart of the Mainstream and the Counterculture

Directions: During the class discussion, record the historical influences that affected the counterculture and the mainstream, and the values each promoted, on the T-chart below.

The Mainstream 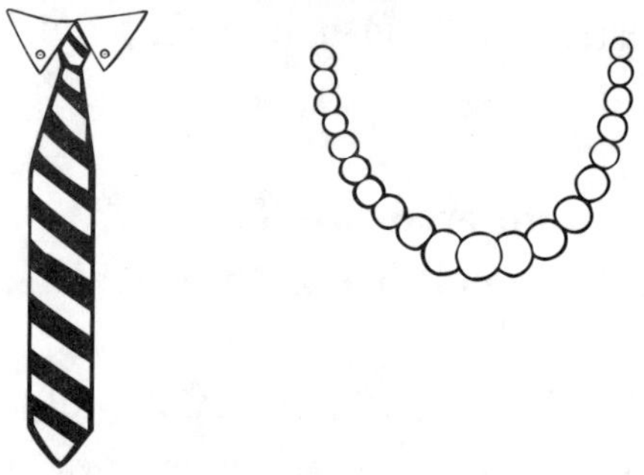	The Counterculture 

Mainstream Woman's Costume

Directions: Cut out your costume. Assume the role as a representative of the mainstream by putting tape on back of the costume and affixing it to your shirt.

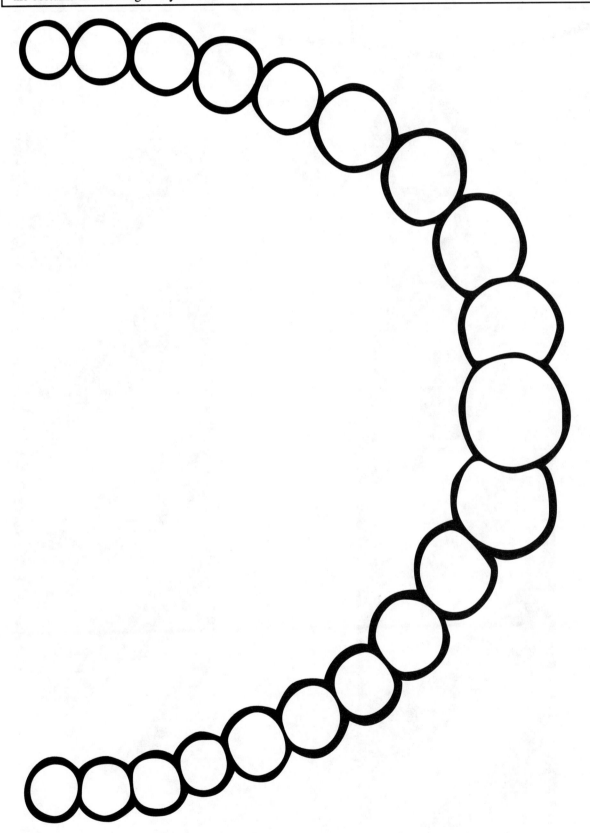

Mainstream Man's Costume

Directions: Cut out your costume. Assume the role as a representative of the mainstream by putting tape on back of the costume and affixing it to your shirt.

Counterculture Costume

Directions: Cut out your costume, and tape the strips together to create a headband. Assume the role of a representative of the counterculture by placing the headband on your head.

Prompts for Debating Mainstream and Counterculture Views

Fashion

Mainstream: You will never get anywhere in life dressed like that.

Counterculture: Why don't you loosen up? You dress like everyone else. Be an individual.

Communal Living

Mainstream: How can you live in all that dirt with so many people? Don't you miss your privacy?

Counterculture: Why do you feel the need to fence yourself off from everybody else? Don't you feel isolated?

Political Activism

Mainstream: You should either love America or leave it.

Counterculture: How can you just blindly swear allegiance to the American government?

Sexuality

Mainstream: Your sexual conduct is not only immoral but dangerous.

Counterculture: Why can't you respect my choices?

Music

Mainstream: You call this music? How can you listen to it?

Counterculture: Your music is boring and unimaginative. Why don't you get with it?

Drugs

Mainstream: Drugs are against the law and will take you nowhere.

Counterculture: I'm not hurting anyone. Why don't you just lay off?

Guidelines for Writing an Editorial on the Counterculture

Imagine that you are a journalist who wants to write an editorial for the *New York Times* that comments on whether the effects of the 1960s counterculture on American society were positive or negative. Use the ideas you recorded on **Student Handout 3.3B** to help you write your editorial. Your editorial should be written to the American public. Follow these guidelines:

1. Ask at least three adults who lived through the 1960s whether they believe the effects of the counterculture on American society were positive or negative. Record their responses on an audiotape or in writing.

2. Write a headline for your editorial that reflects your point of view about the effects of the counterculture on American society.

3. Structure your editorial in this way:

   Introduction: Provide a brief introduction to the counterculture during the 1960s. State whether you think the overall effects of the counterculture on American individuals and society are/were mostly positive, mostly negative, or mixed.

   Positive or negative effects: Include one to two paragraphs that explain the positive or negative effects of the counterculture on individuals and/or society.

   Rationale: Include one to two paragraphs that explain why you think the effects of the counterculture on American individuals and society are/were mostly positive, mostly negative, or mixed. Include quotes from the adults you interviewed to help support your point of view.

4. Include vivid and accurate references to at least four of these topics: fashion, communal living, political activism, sexuality, music, and drugs

5. Include a drawing, graph, quote, or cartoon that illustrates at least one of the main ideas of the editorial.

6. Make your editorial at least two pages in length. Have your teacher review your rough draft. Type or write your final draft neatly in ink.

Sample 7

References

Armbruster, Bonnie B. 1984. The problem of "inconsiderate text." In G. G. Duffy, L. R. Roehler, and J. Mason (Eds.), *Comprehension Instruction: Perspectives and Suggestions*. New York: Longman.

Berger, Joseph, Susan Rosenholtz, and Morris Zelditch, Jr. 1980. Status organizing processes. *Annual Review of Sociology* 6: 479–508.

Billmeyer, Rachel. 1996. *Teaching Reading in the Content Area: If Not Me, Then Who?* Aurora, CO: Mid-Continental Regional Educational Laboratory.

Bruner, Jerome. 1960. *The Process of Education*. Cambridge, MA: Harvard University Press.

Cohen, Elizabeth. 1986. *Designing Groupwork: Strategies for the Heterogeneous Classroom*. New York: Columbia University Teachers College.

Gardner, Howard. 1993. *Frames of Mind: The Theory of Multiple Intelligences*. 10th anniversary edition. New York: Basic Books.

Harvey, Stephanie. 1998. *Nonfiction Matters: Reading, Writing, and Research in Grades 3–8*. Portland, ME: Stenhouse.

Hughes, Robert. 1993. *Culture of Complaint: The Fraying of America*. Oxford, UK: Oxford University Press.

Keene, Ellen O. and Susan Zimmermann. 1997. *Mosaic of Thought: Teaching Comprehension in a Reader's Workshop*. Portsmouth, NH: Heinemann.

Kinsella, Kate. 2001. Using expository text with fifth graders. In *History Alive! America's Past: User's Guide*. Palo Alto, CA: Teachers' Curriculum Institute.

National Association of Colleges and Employees. 2002. "Job Outlook 2003 Survey of Employers." Bethlehem, PA: author.

Newmann, Fred M., Joseph Onosko, and Robert B. Stevenson. 1990. Staff development for higher-order thinking: A synthesis of practical wisdom. *Journal of Staff Development* 11(3): 48–55.

Ogle, Donna. 1986. K-W-L: A teaching model that develops active reading of expository text. *The Reading Teacher* 39: 564–570.

Shulman, Judith H., Rachel A. Lotan, and Jennifer A. Whitcomb (Eds.). 1998. *Groupwork in Diverse Classrooms: A Casebook for Educators*. New York: Teachers College Press.

Teachers' Curriculum Institute. 2002. *The TCI Approach to Learning for Middle and High School*. Rancho Cordova, CA: author.

Tierney, R. J., J. E. Readance, and E. K. Dishner. 1995. *Reading Strategies and Practices: A Compendium*. 4th ed. Needham Heights, MA: Allyn and Bacon.

Credits

17, Library of Congress; 18, PictureQuest; 20, Comstock; 23, TCI photo; 26, Library of Congress; 27, *Puck,* April 5, 1905; 29 (upper), U.S. Army Historical Collection; 29 (lower), U.S. Army Historical Collection; 31, Library of Congress; 32, Library of Congress; 35, Library of Congress; 36, Library of Congress; 37, Military Archives; 67, Library of Congress; 68, "Tenting On the Old Camp Ground," words/music by Walter Kittredge, published by Oliver Ditson, Boston:1864. Historic American Sheet Music Project, Music A-4825, Duke University Rare Book, Manuscript, and Special Collections Library, URL: http://scriptorium.lib.duke.edu/sheetmusic/; 70, National Archives; 71, M & E Bernheim/Woodfin Camp & Associates; 129 (upper), Library of Congress; 129 (lower), Library of Congress; 195, Library of Congress; 230 (upper), Library of Congress; 230 (upper middle), Military Archives, 230 (lower middle), Library of Congress; 230 (lower), Library of Congress; 233, Library of Congress

Sample Lessons

Sample 1: 256, © Trustees of the British Museum, London; 274, © Gianni Dagli Orti/Corbis; 275, Iraq Museum, Baghdad, Iraq; © Scala/Art Resource, NY; 276, © The Oriental Institute Museum of The University of Chicago; 277, © Trustees of the British Museum, London; 278, Iraq Museum, Baghdad, Iraq; © Scala/Art Resource, NY; 279, © Boltin Picture Library; 280, Iraq Museum, Baghdad, Iraq; © Scala/Art Resource, NY; 281, © Boltin Picture Library; 282, © Trustees of the British Museum, London; 283, Doug Roy; 284 (right), British Musem, London; © Winfield Parks/National Geographic Image Collection; 285, © Roger Wood/Corbis; 286, © Nik Wheeler/Corbis; 287, North Wind Picture Archives; 288, Robert Harding; 289, © Trustees of the British Museum, London; 290, © Erich Lessing/Art Resource, NY; 291, © Trustees of the British Museum, London

Sample 2: 318, © Massimo Listri/Corbis; 319, Len Ebert; 320, Len Ebert; 321, © Gianni Dagli Orti/Corbis; 322, © Réunion des Musées Nationaux, Paris/Art Resource, NY; 323, British Museum, London; Werner Forman/Art Resource, NY; 324, © Bettmann/Corbis; 325, © Gianni Dagli Orti/Corbis; 326, © Scala/Art Resource/NY; 327, © Gianni Dagli Orti/Corbis; 328, © Erich Lessing/Art Resource, NY; 329, © Erich Lessing/Art Resource, NY; 330, © Archivo Iconografico, S.A./Corbis; 331, © Erich Lessing/Art Resource, NY

Sample 3: 341 (upper), Library of Congress; 341 (lower), Library of Congress; 360, The Granger Collection, New York; 362, Library of Congress; 363, George Lepp/Corbis; 364 (upper), Library of Congress; 364 (lower), The New-York Historical Society; 365, The Granger Collection, New York; 367, Library of Congress; 368, Library of Congress; 369, The Granger Collection, New York; 371, Library of Congress

Sample 4: 385, Library of Congress; 394, Library of Congress; 396, The Granger Collection, New York; 397, Corbis; 398, The Granger Collection, New York; 399, The Granger Collection, New York; 400, State Archives of Michigan; 401, Library of Congress; 402, *Pic Nick Camden Maine* by Jerome B. Thompson/Museum of Fine Arts, Boston. Gift of Maxim Karolik for the M and M Karolik Collection of American Paintings, 1815–1865; 403, Bettmann/Corbis; 404 (upper), Corbis; 404 (lower), The Schlesinger Library/Radcliffe Institute; 405, AP/Wide World Photos; 405 (inset), AP/Wide World Photos

Overhead Transparencies: 471, © Trustees of the British Museum, London; 473, British Museum, London; Werner Forman/Art Resource, NY; 474, © Gianni Dagli Orti/Corbis; 475, © Scala/Art Resource, NY; 476, © Erich Lessing/Art Resource, NY; 477, © Erich Lessing/Art Resource, NY; 478, The Granger Collection, New York; 479, Library of Congress; 480, Library of Congress; 481 (upper), George Lepp/Corbis; 481 (lower left), Library of Congress; 481 (lower right), The New-York Historical Society; 482, The Granger Collection, New York; 484, Library of Congress; 485, The Granger Collection, New York; 486, Library of Congress; 487 (upper), UPI/Corbis Bettmann; 487 (lower), Henry Diltz/Corbis; 488 (upper), Charles Moore/Black Star; 488 (lower), Henry Diltz/Corbis; 489 (upper), UPI/Corbis Bettmann; 489 (lower), UPI/Corbis Bettmann; 490 (left), UPI/Corbis Bettmann; 490 (right), Owen Franken/Corbis; 491 (left), UPI/Corbis Bettmann; 491 (right), Neal Preston/Corbis; 492 (left), AP/World Wide Photos; 492 (right), Henry Diltz/Corbis